The Vicar's Pe

George Manville Fenn

Alpha Editions

This edition published in 2024

ISBN : 9789362924933

Design and Setting By
Alpha Editions
www.alphaedis.com
Email - info@alphaedis.com

As per information held with us this book is in Public Domain.
This book is a reproduction of an important historical work. Alpha Editions uses the best technology to reproduce historical work in the same manner it was first published to preserve its original nature. Any marks or number seen are left intentionally to preserve its true form.

Contents

Chapter One. .... - 1 -
Chapter Two. .... - 9 -
Chapter Three. .... - 14 -
Chapter Four. .... - 19 -
Chapter Five. .... - 26 -
Chapter Six. .... - 33 -
Chapter Seven. .... - 39 -
Chapter Eight. .... - 44 -
Chapter Nine. .... - 47 -
Chapter Ten. .... - 55 -
Chapter Eleven. .... - 58 -
Chapter Twelve. .... - 65 -
Chapter Thirteen. .... - 69 -
Chapter Fourteen. .... - 80 -
Chapter Fifteen. .... - 86 -
Chapter Sixteen. .... - 93 -
Chapter Seventeen. .... - 101 -
Chapter Eighteen. .... - 109 -
Chapter Nineteen. .... - 114 -
Chapter Twenty. .... - 121 -
Chapter Twenty One. .... - 128 -
Chapter Twenty Two. .... - 134 -
Chapter Twenty Three. .... - 141 -
Chapter Twenty Four. .... - 145 -
Chapter Twenty Five. .... - 152 -
Chapter Twenty Six. .... - 155 -

Chapter Twenty Seven.	- 162 -
Chapter Twenty Eight.	- 167 -
Chapter Twenty Nine.	- 172 -
Chapter Thirty.	- 179 -
Chapter Thirty One.	- 191 -
Chapter Thirty Two.	- 197 -
Chapter Thirty Three.	- 202 -
Chapter Thirty Four.	- 205 -
Chapter Thirty Five.	- 209 -
Chapter Thirty Six.	- 213 -
Chapter Thirty Seven.	- 219 -
Chapter Thirty Eight.	- 226 -
Chapter Thirty Nine.	- 234 -
Chapter Forty.	- 239 -
Chapter Forty One.	- 245 -
Chapter Forty Two.	- 250 -
Chapter Forty Three.	- 259 -
Chapter Forty Four.	- 265 -
Chapter Forty Five.	- 272 -
Chapter Forty Six.	- 282 -
Chapter Forty Seven.	- 291 -
Chapter Forty Eight.	- 298 -
Chapter Forty Nine.	- 304 -
Chapter Fifty.	- 313 -
Chapter Fifty One.	- 320 -
Chapter Fifty Two.	- 324 -
Chapter Fifty Three.	- 331 -
Chapter Fifty Four.	- 337 -

Chapter Fifty Five. ....- 340 -
Chapter Fifty Six. ....- 345 -
Chapter Fifty Seven. ....- 349 -
Chapter Fifty Eight. ....- 355 -
Chapter Fifty Nine. ....- 358 -
Chapter Sixty. ....- 361 -
Chapter Sixty One. ....- 366 -
Chapter Sixty Two. ....- 371 -

Chapter One.

Penwynn, Banker.

"H'm! ah! yes! of course! 'Clever young engineer—thoroughly scientific—may be worth your while.' Geoffrey Trethick! Cornishman by descent, of course."

"It sounds like a Cornishman, papa."

"Yes, my dear, Rundell and Sharp say they have sent me a paragon. Only another adventurer."

"Poor fellow?" said Rhoda Penwynn, in a low whisper.

"What's that?" said the first speaker, looking up sharply from his letters to where his daughter sat at the head of his handsomely-furnished breakfast-table.

"I only said, 'Poor fellow!' papa," and the girl flushed slightly as she met the quick, stern look directed at her.

"And why, pray?"

"Because it seems so sad for a young man to come down here from London, full of hopefulness and ambition, eager to succeed, and then to find his hopes wrecked in these wretched mining speculations—just as our unhappy fishing-boats, and the great ships, are dashed to pieces on our rocky shore."

Mr Lionel Penwynn, banker of Carnac, took the gold-rimmed double eye-glass off the bridge of his handsome aquiline nose, leaned back in his chair, drew himself up, and stared at his daughter.

She was worth it, for it would have been hard to find a brighter or more animated face in West Cornwall. Her father's handsome features, high forehead, dark eyes, and well-cut mouth and chin were all there, but softened, so that where there was eagerness and vigour in the one, the other was all delicacy and grace, and as Rhoda gazed at the gathering cloud in her father's face the colour in her cheeks deepened.

"Wretched mining speculations—unhappy boats! They find you this handsomely-furnished house, carriages and servants, and horses," said Mr Penwynn, sharply.

"Oh, yes, papa," said the girl; "but sometimes when I know the troubles of the people here I feel as if I would rather—"

"Live in a cottage, and be poor, and play the fool," exclaimed Mr Penwynn, angrily. "Yes, of course. Very sweet, and sentimental, and nice, to talk about, but it won't do in practice. There, don't look like that," he continued, forcing a smile to hide his annoyance. "Give me another cup of coffee, my dear."

Rhoda took and filled his cup, and then carried it to him herself, passing her hand over his forehead, and bending down to kiss it afterwards, when he caught her in his arms, and kissed her very affectionately.

"That's better," he said, as his child resumed her seat, "but you make me angry when you are so foolish, my dear. You don't know the value of money and position. Position is a great thing, Rhoda, though you don't appreciate it. You don't understand what it is for a man to have been twice mayor of the borough, even if it is small."

"Oh, yes, I do, papa; and it is very nice to be able to help others," said Rhoda, sadly.

"Yes, yes, of course, my dear; but you give away too much. I would rather see you fonder of dress and jewellery. People should help themselves."

"But some are so unfortunate, papa, and—"

"They blame me for it, of course. Now, once for all, Rhoda, you must not listen to this idle chatter. They come to me and borrow money on their boats, or nets, or fish, or their expectations. I tell them, and Mr Tregenna, who draws up the agreements, fully explains to them, the terms upon which they have the money, which they need not take unless they like, and then when they fail to pay, the boat or fish, or whatever it may be, has to be sold. I never took advantage of any of them in my life. On the contrary," he continued, assuming an ill-used, martyred air, "I have been a great benefactor to the place, and the good opinion of the people is really important to a man in my position."

Rhoda looked across at him with rather a piteous face as he went on.

"They would often be unable to make a start if it were not for me; and I always charge them a very moderate rate of interest. You must not do it; Rhoda; you must not indeed. I thought you a girl of too strong sense to listen to all this wretched calumny. You mix too much with the people, and are too ready to believe ill of me."

"Oh, no, no, papa!" cried the girl, with tears in her eyes, and she rose once more to go to his side, but he motioned her away.

"There, there: that will do, my dear," he said, forcing a laugh. "You spoil my breakfast. Give me one of those fried soles. There, of course, half cold with our talking. Dear me, dear me, what a lot of grit and sand we foolish people do throw into our daily life."

He smiled across the table, and poor Rhoda smiled back; then her eyes dropped, and she saw her face so grotesquely reproduced in the highly-polished silver coffee-pot that she felt ready to burst into a hysterical fit of laughing; which she checked, however, as her father chatted on, and read scraps from his other letters, talking pleasantly and well, as his handsome face brightened, and the sun that shone in upon the silver and china upon the fine white damask gave a sparkle to his short, crisp grey hair, though, at the same time, it made plain the powder upon his cleanly-shaven face.

He had so many pleasant things to say on that sunny, spring morning that the breakfast-table was soon as bright as the dappled opalescent sea that sparkled and flashed as it played round the rocky promontory upon which stood the ruins of Wheal Carnac Mine, or lifted the dark hulls of the fishing-luggers moored to the buoys, some of which had their dark cinnamon-hued sails hung out to dry, forming, through the heavily-curtained window, with its boxes of ferns, a charming bit of sea, like some carefully-selected specimen of the painter's art.

Rhoda had forgotten the little cloud in the present sunshine, when, after a preparation of pleasant words, Mr Penwynn suddenly said,—

"Oh! by the way, I did not tell you about Tregenna."

"About Tregenna, papa?" said Rhoda, whose face suddenly lowered.

"Yes, my dear," said Mr Penwynn, putting on his glasses and taking up the paper, as he shifted his chair sidewise to the table, "he's coming here this morning. By the way, Rhoda, you are twenty-one, are you not?"

"Yes, papa, of course, but—"

"I told Tregenna you were," he said, quietly, and with an averted face. "He's thirty-three."

"I don't understand you, papa," said Rhoda, quietly.

"Has Tregenna been attentive to you lately?"

"Oh, yes, papa," said Rhoda, impatiently; "but what do you mean?"

"Of course he would be," said Mr Penwynn, as if to himself. "What's this alarming earthquake in Peru? Ah! they're always having earthquakes in Peru; but it's a fine mining country."

"Papa, you are not paying any attention to what I say," cried Rhoda. "What do you mean about Mr Tregenna?"

"Oh, nothing, nothing, my dear," said Mr Penwynn, re-adjusting the gold-rimmed glasses upon his nose. "Some nonsense of his. He declares that he is terribly smitten with you."

"Papa!"

"And that he can never be happy without you."

"Papa!"

"And I told him he had better come and talk to you himself."

"You told him that, papa?" said Rhoda, pushing back her chair.

"To be sure, my dear," said Mr Penwynn, rustling the newspaper in the most unruffled way. "Of course it is all nonsense."

"Nonsense, papa? You know Mr Tregenna is not a man who talks nonsense."

"Well, perhaps not, my dear. He certainly is a very clever, sensible fellow."

"Oh!" ejaculated Rhoda, beneath her breath, as she gazed at the handsome profile before her.

"You might do worse, my dear," continued Mr Penwynn, skimming the paper.

"Do I understand you, papa, that you sanction Mr Tregenna's proposal?"

"Sanction?" he said, looking up from the paper for a moment to glance over his glasses at his child. "Oh, yes, my dear: of course."

"I can not—I will not, see Mr Tregenna," said Rhoda, firmly, and one of her little feet began to beat the thick Turkey carpet.

"Don't be foolish, my dear. He is desperately taken with you, and will make you a capital husband."

"Husband?" cried the girl, passionately. "Oh, papa, you cannot mean this. Mr Tregenna is—"

"A gentleman, my dear, a great friend of mine—of ours, I should say—of great assistance to me in my business arrangements, and I think the match most suitable—that is, if he is in earnest."

"In earnest? Oh, papa?" cried Rhoda, piteously, "have you thought—have you considered Mr Tregenna's character?"

"Character?" said Mr Penwynn, turning his head in astonishment.

"Yes, papa. People—Miss Pavey, Mr Paul, Dr Rumsey—all say—"

"Bah! rubbish! stuff! you silly goose! All sorts of things, of course, as they do about every handsome, well-to-do young bachelor. They are a set of whist-playing, gossiping, mischief-making old women, the lot of them, and if Rumsey don't mind what he's about he'll lose what little practice he has. He don't come here again."

"No, papa, you will not visit my hasty words on poor Dr Rumsey," said Rhoda, with spirit.

"And as for old Paul," continued Mr Penwynn, from behind the paper, "he's a bilious, chronic, ill-tempered, liverless old capsicum, who would rob his own mother of her good name—if she had one."

"I believe he is a true gentleman at heart," said Rhoda, quickly.

"Then I'd rather not be a gentleman," said Mr Penwynn, laughing, "or a lady either like Miss Pavey. Poor little red-nosed thing. Pity she wasn't married twenty years ago. I see: I see: that's it," he said, laughing heartily, and taking off and wiping his glasses. "Poor little Martha Pavey, of course! She fell desperately in love with Tregenna, and—and—ha! ha! ha! ha!—he—he did not return the passion. Heavens! what a wicked wretch."

Rhoda had risen, and stood with her hand upon the back of her chair, looking very much agitated, but cold and stern, as she watched her father, and waited till his assumed gaiety was at an end.

"Papa," she said, at length, in a tone that taught him that he was on the wrong tack, and that he must speak to his daughter upon this important point as if she were a woman, and not as a silly, weak girl, "I do not base my objections to Mr Tregenna upon what people say alone."

"Then on what, pray?" he exclaimed, with his glass now falling inside his open vest. "What has he done? Did he once upon a time kiss some pretty fisher-girl, with bare legs? or a nice-looking miner's daughter? If so, it was very bad taste, but very natural."

"Mr Tregenna is a gentleman I could never like," retorted Rhoda, without condescending to answer this banter, "and I believe he is already engaged to Margaret Mullion."

"Engaged? Madge Mullion? Now, my dear Rhoda, what nonsense. Is it likely that if Tregenna were engaged to Madge he would talk as he has several times talked to me? How can you be so absurd?"

"But he must be, papa," said Rhoda, quickly.

"Nonsense! Absurd!"

"I have myself met them on the cliffs and up An Lowan."

"Well, and if you did, it was only a bit of silly flirtation with a very handsome girl. Tregenna could not care for her. Besides, she is a notorious flirt."

"I have nothing to say to that, papa," replied Rhoda, quietly.

"But I have," he said, now angrily, "and I really am surprised at you—a girl of so much sense—bringing up some silly flirtation against a man who proposes for your hand. What do you want to marry—an archangel?"

"No, papa," said Rhoda, coldly.

"Now look here, Rhoda," exclaimed Mr Penwynn, growing angry at the opposition he was encountering, "you have some reason for this."

"I have given you my reasons, papa. I do not, and never like Mr Tregenna."

"Then," he cried, passionately striking the table with his fist, "there is some one in the way. Who is it?"

"Who is it, papa?"

"Yes; I insist upon knowing who it is. And look here, if you have been entering into an engagement with some beggarly up start, who—"

"Papa," said Rhoda, looking him full in the face, "why do you speak to me like that? You would not if you were not in a passion. You know perfectly well that I keep nothing from you."

This was a heavy blow for Mr Penwynn, and it made him wince. It cooled him, and he shook his head, muttered, and ended by exclaiming,—

"Sit down, Rhoda. What is the use of your being so obstinate and putting me out? You make me say these things. Come, be reasonable. See Mr Tregenna, and let him speak to you."

"I would far rather not, papa," said Rhoda, firmly.

"But you must. I insist; I beg of you. It is not courteous to him. Come; see him, and hear what he has to say. There, there, I knew you would. Look here, Rhoda, tell me this. I ask it of you as your father. Had your sweet mother been alive, it would have come from her; I would not intrude upon the secrets of your heart. Have you cared, do you care, for any one else?"

Rhoda smiled sadly.

"I have no secrets in my heart, papa," she said, quietly, "and I feel urged to say that I will not answer your question; but I will answer it," she continued with her dark, clear eyes fixed on his. "No, papa, I never have cared for any one else, neither do I. I might almost say that I never thought of such a thing as marriage."

Mr Penwynn uttered a sigh of relief.

"And you will see Tregenna when he calls. I beg, I implore you to, Rhoda."

"I will see him then, papa; but—"

"No, no. Let me have no hasty declarations, my dear," he said, rising, and taking her hand. "Marriages are a mystery. See Mr Tregenna, and take time. Hear what he has to say; give him time too, as well—months, years if you like—and, meanwhile, shut your ears against all paltry scandal."

"I will, papa."

"And, my darling, if it should come off, you will have won a good husband for yourself, and a valuable friend and counsellor for me."

"But—"

"No more new, my dear; no more now. We have said enough. Take time, and get cool. Then we shall see."

Evidently with the idea of himself getting cool he began to walk slowly and thoughtfully up and down the room, his hands behind him, his feet carefully placed one before the other, heel to toe, as if he were measuring off the carpet,—rather a ridiculous proceeding to a stranger, but his daughter was accustomed to the eccentricity, and now saw nothing absurd in his struggles to retain his balance.

"Yes," he said suddenly, after pacing up and down the carpet a few times, "take time, and get cool."

As he spoke he left the room, and Rhoda Penwynn seated herself in the window, with her eyes apparently fixed upon the dancing boats at sea, though they saw nothing but the dark, handsome face of John Tregenna, with the slight puckering beneath his eyes, and the thin, close red line of his lips, as he appeared to her last when he took her hand to raise it respectfully to the said thin lips; and, as she, seemed to meet his eyes, she shuddered, and wished that she could change places with the poorest girl upon the cliff.

"Miss Pavey, ma'am," said a footman, and she started, for she had not heard him enter; "in the drawing-room, ma'am."

Rhoda rose hastily, and tried to smooth away the lines of care, as she hurried into the room to meet her visitor.

Chapter Two.

The Adventurer.

"How much farther is it, coachman?"

"Carnac, sir? Just four miles. There it lies! Yonder white houses, by the cove, with the high rocks o' both sides."

"Four miles? Why, it does not seem two."

"It's all four, sir," said the driver, giving his long whip a *whish* through the air, making the leaders of the four-horse coach shake their heads and increase their speed, as he deftly caught the end of the lash, and twisted the thong around the whip-shaft by a turn of his wrist.

"Ah!" said the first speaker, a young man of about thirty, "the air is so fine and clear. I presume that you are going on to Felsport?"

"No, no," said the gentleman addressed, in a hesitating tone of voice; "I am going to stop at Carnac."

His long black coat, broad-brimmed round-topped hat and tassel, suggested that he was a clergyman of advanced—or retrogressive—views, and he paused wearily, as if annoyed at being interrupted, as he spoke—

"How strange! Do you know the place?"

"N-no; I have never seen it."

The clergyman lowered his eyes, and began once more reading a little book, with very small type, while the first speaker raised his eyes in wonder that a stranger could read while passing through the wild beauties of the grand Cornish region spread around. He then leaned forward once more to speak to the coachman, who was ready enough to answer questions about that mine, in full work, where a tall granite building, like a clumsily-formed church tower, stood up on the bleakest point of wind-swept barren hill, with what seemed like a long arm thrust out on one side, the said arm being apparently engaged in telegraphing to them mysterious signs as it slowly rose up and stopped, then went half-way down and stopped before descending to the earth, and finally rose, but all in the most peculiar and deliberate manner.

"That's Wheal Porley, sir. Bringing a good bit of copper to grass there just now."

"And what mine's that on the next hill?"

"Oh! that's tin, sir. Old Friendship they call it; but there's little doing now. Tin's very low. I hear they bring over such a lot from Peru, and 'Stralia, and Banky, and them other gashly outlandish places."

"Peru, eh? I did not know that was a tin country."

"Perhaps it wasn't Peru, sir. I arn't sure. That's a rare old place yonder," the driver continued, pointing with his whip to a large granite engine-house, with towering chimney, standing on a point running out into the sea.

"But it isn't working. It seems to be in ruins."

"Ruins, sir? Ah! and it's put lots o' people in ruins too. There's a heap o' money gone down that mine."

"Yes, there are failures, I suppose; but is it a tin-mine?"

"Yes, sir,—tin. That's what it is, or what it was meant to be by the adventurers; but they never got any thing out that would pay. They're a bad lot, those adventurers."

"Are they?" said the young man dryly, and he smiled as he let his eyes wander over the country, with its deeply-scored ravines, into which the whole of the fertile soil of the high ground seemed to have been washed, for they were as rich in ferns and lush foliage as the granite heights were bare.

To his left swept away the soft blue sea, dotted with the warm brown sails of the fishing-luggers, and with here and there the white canvas of a yacht or passing ship.

The young man drew back, and seemed to inflate his chest with the fresh, pure air. His dark eyes brightened, and a pleasant smile began to play about his lips, but it was half hidden by his crisp, short beard. As they went on he glanced sharply from place to place, eager to take in the surroundings of a land that was to be his future home; and the result seemed to be satisfactory, for he took off his hat, let the sea-breeze blow through his short curly hair, and once more turned to his reading companion.

They formed a striking contrast, the one sitting hatless, dark, eager, and apparently full of repressed vitality, his muscles standing out from arm and leg, and his whole aspect bespeaking the informal and natural; while the other was a pale, delicate, handsomely-featured, fair man, apparently of the same age, with his face smoothly shaven, his hair very closely cut, the hand that held the book tightly gloved in black, the other that turned down a leaf that seemed disposed to dally with the wind, delicate, long-fingered, white, and with nails most carefully trimmed. Formality, culture, and refinement were visible at every turn, and as he became aware that his travelling-companion was watching him, he looked up with a half-haughty, half-annoyed air, and met the sharp, keen glance.

"Book interesting?" said the other, in a quick, imperative way.

"I always find my studies interesting," said the young clergyman coldly, and speaking as if compelled to answer in spite of himself. He then lowered his eyes, and was about to continue his reading.

"What is it?" said the other. "Ah! I see, 'Early Fathers,' and the rest of it. My word! what a lot of time I did waste over that sort of thing!"

"Waste?" said the clergyman, indignantly.

"Yes: I call it waste. You don't."

"I never knew that study could be considered a waste of time, sir."

"No, of course not, when it is to do yourself or somebody else good."

A hot, indignant retort was on the young cleric's lips, but he checked it, and was taking refuge in reserve, when the other went on,—

"Don't think me rude: it's my way. I saw you were an Oxford man; that's why I spoke. Is old Rexton still at Maudlin?"

"The Dean, if you mean him, is still at Magdalen College, sir," said the clergyman, frigidly.

"Rum old fellow. How he used to sit upon me. Not a Maudlin man, I suppose?"

"I had the honour of being at that college, sir, when at Oxford."

"Indeed! then it couldn't have been very far from the time when I was there."

"You—were you an Oxford man?" said the clergyman, staring blankly at his companion, who smiled at his astonishment.

"To be sure I was. You'll find my name there—Geoffrey Trethick."

"I—I have heard the name."

"And I am addressing—"

For answer, after a little hesitation, the clergyman drew out a small pocket-book, with red edges to the diary, and carefully extracted a card, on which the other read aloud,—

"'Reverend Edward Lee, Carnac.' Humph! that's odd," he said. "I'm going to live at Carnac. Do you know a Mr Penwynn there?"

"Penwynn, the banker, sir?" said the coachman, turning his head sharply, and pointing to a grey house just above the town, sheltered amongst some trees at the head of the little bay. "That's his house, sir—An Morlock."

"Thanks, coachman. Did you say you knew him, Mr Lee?"

"Not at present," said the clergyman, still keeping up his reserve, but all the time feeling, in spite of himself, drawn towards his travelling-companion. "I am a stranger here."

"I hope we shall be strangers no longer. Beautiful country, is it not?"

"Ye-es. Very picturesque," said the clergyman, gazing vacantly around, the other watching him in an amused way, as, after letting his eyes rest for a few moments on the beautiful expanse of rocky hill, shady ravine, and glistening sea, he once more raised his book and went on reading.

"Books always, and not men's minds," muttered Geoffrey Trethick. Then, bending forwards, he once more engaged the coachman in conversation, to the clergyman's great relief; and, putting a set of leading questions, he drew from the driver all the information he could about the neighbourhood and its people, the man finishing with,—

"Ah, sir, it's as fine and good a country as any in England, if it wasn't for the adventurers, and they about ruin it."

"Indeed!" said the young man, with the air of being once more very much amused; and then the coach drew up at the door of the principal inn. There was a little bustle, and the occupants of the various seats climbed down, luggage was handed out of the boots, and the two travellers stood together on the rough paving-stones.

"Take my portmanteau in, boots," said Trethick, sharply. "Do you breakfast here at the hotel, Mr Lee?"

"Sir," said the clergyman, distantly, "I have not yet made my plans."

"Oh! all right; no offence. I was going to say, let us breakfast together for company. I'm off to present my letters of introduction. Good-day; I dare say we shall meet again."

"I hope not," thought the Reverend Edward Lee, upon whom his travelling-companion seemed to act like a strong blast, bending him bodily and mentally as well, and he turned into the hotel, hearing, as he did so, the voice of one of the hangers-on exclaiming, in a sing-song tone,—

"Mr Penwynn's, An Morlock, sir? Right up street, and out by the hill I'll show you the way."

"Thanks; no, my lad, I shall find it. Catch!" There was the ring of a small piece of silver falling upon the pavement, and the young clergyman sighed with relief to think his travelling-companion had gone.

Chapter Three.

The Carnac Gazette.

Rhoda Penwynn's visitor was in the drawing-room at An Morlock, making the most use possible of her eyes while she was alone. She had seen who had called and left cards, and what book Rhoda was reading. She had also mentally taken the pattern of the new design of embroidery, and meant to work a piece exactly the same; and now she was filling up the time before Rhoda entered by gazing at herself in one of the large mirrors.

It was not a bad reflection—to wit, that of a refined, fair face, that must have been very pretty fifteen or twenty years before; but now there was an eager sharpness in the features, as if caused by expectancy never gratified; the fair white skin had a slight ivory—old ivory—tinge, and the pretty bloom that once hid beneath the down of her cheeks had coalesced and slightly tinted the lady's nose. It was but slight, but it was unmistakable.

Miss Pavey was well and fairly, even fashionably, dressed, and generally she wore the aspect of what she was—a maiden lady who loved colour, and had, after sundry matrimonial disappointments, retired to a far-off west-country, sea-side place, where her moderate independency would be of so much more value than in a large town.

She sighed as she contemplated herself in the glass, and then held her handkerchief to her face and bent her eyes upon a book as she heard the rustle of a dress, and the door opened, when she rose to meet Rhoda with effusion, and an eager kiss.

"My dearest Rhoda, how well you do look!" she exclaimed. "What a becoming dress!"

"Do you think so, Miss Pavey," said Rhoda, quietly. "Miss Pavey again! Why will you keep up this terrible distance? My dear Rhoda, is it never to be Martha?"

"Well then, Martha," said Rhoda, smiling. "I did not expect to see you so early."

"It is early for visitors, my dear; but I thought you would like to know the news. We have so little here in Carnac."

"Really, I trouble very little about the news, Miss Martha," said Rhoda, smiling. "But what is the matter?" she added, as her visitor once more held her handkerchief to her face.

"That dreadful toothache again," sighed Miss Pavey. "I really am a martyr to these nervous pains."

"Why not boldly go to Mr Rumsey and have it out?"

"Oh, no! oh, dear no!" cried Miss Pavey, with a look of horror, "I could not bear for a man to touch my mouth like that. Don't mind me, dear, it will be better soon;" and it seemed to be, for it was a pleasant little fiction kept up by Miss Pavey—that toothache, to add truthfulness to the complete set she wore, and whose extraction she carefully attended to herself.

"Of course you don't care for news, my dear," continued the lady; "I used not when I was your age. But when one comes to be thirty-two one's ideas change so. One becomes more human, and takes more interest in humanity at large than in one's self. You are such a happy contented girl, too; nothing seems to trouble you."

"But your news," said Rhoda, to change the conversation, as Miss Pavey smoothed down her blue silk dress.

"To be sure, yes, my dear. I saw the coach come over from the station—what a shame it is that we don't have a branch railway!—and what do you think?"

"Think?" said Rhoda, looking amused, "I really don't know what to think."

"Pylades and Orestes!"

"I don't understand you."

"They've come, my dear,—they've come!"

"Pylades and Orestes?"

"Well, of course, that's only my nonsense; but, as I told you, I saw the coach come in, and two gentlemen got down, both young and handsome—one fair, the other dark; and one is evidently our new vicar, and the other must be his friend. I am so glad, my dear, for I have been exceedingly anxious about the kind of person we were to have for our new clergyman."

"Indeed!" said Rhoda, looking amused. "Why, I thought you went now to the Wesleyan chapel?"

"What a dear satirical girl you are, Rhoda. You know I only went there on account of Mr Chynoweth, and because Mr Owen stared at me so dreadfully, and was so persistent in preaching about dress."

"But surely that was only at the mining and fishing women, who have been growing dreadfully gay in their attire."

"Oh dear, no, my dear! oh dear no!" said Miss Pavey, shaking her head. "I have the best of reasons for believing it was all directed at me. You remember his text the last Sunday I was at church?"

"I am sorry to say I do not."

"Dear me, I wonder at that. It was so very pointed. It was—'Who is this that cometh with dyed garments from Bozrah?' and he looked at me as he spoke. I think it was disgraceful."

"But, my dear Martha, I think you are too sensitive."

"Perhaps I am, my dear; perhaps I am. I have had my troubles; but that Mr Owen was dreadful. You know, my dear, he had—perhaps I ought not to say it, but I will—he evidently wanted to make an impression upon me, but I never could like him. He was so coarse, and abrupt, and short-sighted. He used to smoke pipes too. Mrs Mullion has told me, over and over again, that he would sit for hours of a night smoking pipes, and drinking gin and water, with that dreadfully wicked old man, Mr Paul. Really, my dear, I think some one ought to warn our new clergyman not to go and lodge at Mrs Mullion's. You see there is hardly any choice for a gentleman, and for one who looks so refined to go and stay at Mrs Mullion's would be dreadful."

"Mrs Mullion is very good and amiable," said Rhoda.

"Yes, my dear, she is; but Mr Paul is not a nice person; and then there is that Madge—dreadful girl!"

Rhoda's heart gave a higher-pressure throb at this last name, and Miss Pavey ran on, as she could if she only obtained a good listener,—

"I do think that girl ought to be sent away from Carnac; I do, indeed. Really, my dear, if I had felt disposed to accept any advances on the part of Mr Tregenna, his conduct with that flighty creature would have set me against him."

Rhoda's heart beat faster still, and the colour went and came in her face as she listened. She blamed herself for hearkening to such petty gossip, but her visitor was determined to go on, and added confidence to confidence, for, as it may be gathered, Miss Martha Pavey's peculiar idiosyncrasy was a belief that was terribly persecuted by the male sex, who eagerly sought her hand in marriage, though at the present time a gossip of Carnac had told another gossip that Miss Pavey was "setting her gashly old cap now at Methody Parson."

"Don't you think, my dear," continued the visitor, "that your papa ought to interfere?"

"Interfere? About what?" exclaimed Rhoda, whose thoughts had run off to her conversation with her father that morning.

"Why, what are you thinking about, Rhoda?" cried Miss Pavey. "Oh, you naughty, naughty girl, you! You were thinking about our handsome young clergyman and his young friend. Oh, for shame, for shame?"

"Indeed, I was not!" exclaimed Rhoda, half amused, half indignant at her visitor's folly.

"Oh, don't tell me, dear," said Miss Pavey, shaking her head. "It's very shocking of you, but I don't wonder. See how few marriageable gentlemen there are about here."

"Miss Pavey, pray don't be so absurd," exclaimed Rhoda.

"Oh, no, my dear, I will not," said the visitor, blushing, and then indulging in a peculiar giggle; "but after all, there is a something in wedlock, my dear Rhoda."

"A something in wedlock?"

"Yes, dear, there is, you know, speaking to one another as confidantes—there is a something in wedlock after all, as you must own."

"I never think of such a thing," said Rhoda, laughing, for Miss Pavey's evident leanings towards the subject under discussion were very droll.

"Of course not, my dear," said Miss Pavey, seriously. "We none of us ever do; but still there are times when the matter is forced upon us, as in this case; and who knows, my dear, what may happen? You did not see them, I suppose?"

"See? whom?"

"My dear child, how dense you are this morning! The two new-comers, of course. And don't you think that something ought to be done to warn them about where they are to take apartments?"

"Certainly not," said Rhoda. "It would be the height of impertinence."

"Oh, really, I cannot agree with you there, my dear Rhoda. I think it would be grievous to let this young clergyman go to Mullion's, and really there is not another place in Carnac where a gentleman could lodge. In fact, I would sooner make the offer that he should board at my little home."

"Board—take apartments at Dinas Vale?"

"Certainly, my dear. He is a clergyman, and we ought to extend some kind of hospitality to him. I regret that my limited income does not permit me to say to him, 'Take up your home here for the present as a guest.' Of course I would not open my doors to any one but a clergyman."

"Of course not," said Rhoda, absently; and soon after Miss Pavey took her leave, Rhoda going with her to the door, and on re-crossing the hall noticing a card lying upon the serpentine marble table, against whose dark, ruddy surface it stood out clear and white.

At another time it would not have attracted her attention, but now, as if moved by some impulse beyond her control, she went up close and read upon it the name,—

"Geoffrey Trethick."

Nothing more—no "Mr" and no address.

Chapter Four.

The Wrong Place for the Right Man.

"Well, Chynoweth," said Mr Penwynn, entering his office which was used as a branch of the Felsport bank, "any thing fresh?"

Mr Chynoweth, the banker's manager, generally known as "The Jack of Clubs," was a little man, dark, and spare, and dry. He was probably fifty, but well preserved, having apparently been bound by nature in vellum, which gave him quite, a legal look, while it made him thick-skinned enough to bear a good many unpleasantries in his daily life. He was rather bald, but very shiny on the crown. His face was cleanly shaved, and he had a habit of bending down his head, and gazing through his shaggy eyebrows at whosoever spoke, and also when he took up his parable himself.

Mr Chynoweth had been busy inside his desk when he heard his principal's step, and there was plenty of room beneath the broad mahogany flap for him to do what he pleased unseen.

What Mr Chynoweth pleased that morning was to play over again a hand of whist, as near as he could remember—one that had been played at Dr Rumsey's house the night before, when one of the guests, Mr Paul, had, to use his own words, "picked the game out of the fire," Mr Chynoweth being, in consequence, five shillings out of pocket.

He kept a pack of cards and a whist guide in this desk, and it was frequently his habit to shuffle, cut, and deal four hands, spread them below the flap, and play them out by himself for practice, the consequence being that he was an adversary to be feared, a partner to be desired, at the snug little parties held at two or three houses in Carnac.

On this particular morning he had just arrived at the point where he felt that he had gone astray, when Mr Penwynn's step was heard, the mahogany flap was closed, and "The Jack of Clubs" was ready for business.

"Fresh? Well, no. Permewan's time's up, and he wants more. Will you give it?"

"No: he has made no effort to pay his interest. Tell Tregenna to foreclose and sell."

Mr Chynoweth rapidly made an entry upon an ordinary school slate on one side, and then crossed off an entry upon the other, refreshing his memory from it at the same time.

"Dr Rumsey wants an advance of a hundred pounds," he said next, gazing through his shaggy eyebrows.

"Hang Dr Rumsey! He's always wanting an advance. What does he say?"

"Pilchard fishery such a failure. Tin so low that he can't get in his accounts."

"Humph! What security does he offer?"

"Note of hand."

"Stuff! What's the use of his note of hand? Has he nothing else?"

"No," said Mr Chynoweth. "He says you hold every thing he has."

"Humph! Yes, suppose I do."

"Without you'd consider half-a-dozen children good security?"

"Chynoweth, I hate joking over business-matters."

"Not joking," said Mr Chynoweth, stolidly. "That's what he said."

"Rubbish! Can't he get some one else to lend his name?"

"Said he had asked every one he could, and it was no use."

"Confound the fellow! Tut-tut-tut! What's to be done, Chynoweth?"

"Lend him the money."

"No, no. There, I'll let him have fifty."

"Not half enough. Better let him have it. You'll be ill, or I shall, one of these days, and if you don't let him have the money, he might give it us rather strongly."

"Absurd. He dare not."

"Well, I don't know," said Chynoweth. "When one's on one's back one is in the doctor's hands, you know."

"There: let him have the money, but it must be at higher interest. But stop a moment," continued Mr Penwynn, as his managing man's pencil gave its first grate on the slate. "You're a great friend of Rumsey: why not lend him your name to the note?"

Mr Chynoweth had no buttons to his trousers pockets, but he went through the process of buttoning them, and looked straight now at his employer.

"How long would you keep me here if you found me weak enough to do such a thing as that, Mr Penwynn? No, no," he said, lowering his head once more, and looking through his eyebrows, "I never lend, and I never become security for any man. I shall put it down that he can have the money."

Mr Penwynn nodded, and his manager wrote down on one side and marked off on the other.

"Any thing else?"

"Wheal Carnac's for sale."

"Well, so it has been for a long time."

"Yes, but they mean to sell now, I hear; and they say it would be worth any one's while to buy it."

"Yes, so I suppose," said Mr Penwynn, smiling; "but we do not invest in mines, Chynoweth. We shall be happy to keep the account of the company, though, who start. How many have failed there?"

"Three," said Chynoweth. "There has been a deal of money thrown down that place."

Mr Penwynn nodded and entered his private room, when Chynoweth gave one ear a rub, stood his slate upon the desk, raised the flap and let it rest on his head, and then proceeded to finish his hand at whist, evidently with satisfactory results, for he smiled and rubbed his hands, placed the cards in a corner, and next proceeded to write two or three letters, one of which, concluded in affectionate terms, he afterwards tore up.

Some hours passed, when a clerk brought in a card.

"For Mr Penwynn, sir."

"Geoffrey Trethick," said Mr Chynoweth, reading. "Take it in."

The clerk obeyed, and a few minutes later he ushered the new visitor to Carnac into Mr Penwynn's private room, where the banker and the stranger looked hard at each other for a few moments before the former pointed to a chair, his visitor being quite a different man from what he had pictured.

"Glad to see you, Mr Trethick," he said. "I have read the letters you left for me, and shall be happy to oblige my correspondent if I can; but they seem to be quite under a misapprehension as to my powers. In the first place, though, what can I do for you?"

"Do for me?" said Geoffrey, smiling. "Well, this much. I come to you, a leading man in this great mining centre."

Mr Penwynn made a deprecatory motion with his hand.

"Oh, I am no flatterer, Mr Penwynn," said the visitor, bluffly. "I merely repeat what your correspondents told me, and what find endorsed here in this place."

"Well, well," said Mr Penwynn, as if owning reluctantly to the soft impeachment, "Penwynn and Company are a little mixed up in mines—and the fisheries."

"Fisheries? Ah, that's not in my line, Mr Penwynn. But to be frank with you, sir, I want work. I am a poor younger son who decided not to take to church, law, or physic, but to try to be a mining engineer. I am a bit of a chemist, too, and have studied metallurgy as far as I could. My education has taken nearly all my little fortune, which I have, so to speak, sunk in brain-work. That brain-work I now want to sell."

"But, my dear sir," said Mr Penwynn, "I am a banker."

"Exactly. To several mining companies. Now, sir, I honestly believe that I am worth a good salary to any enterprising company," said Geoffrey, growing animated, and flushing slightly as he energetically laid his case before the smooth, polished, well-dressed man, whose carefully-cut nails gently tapped the morocco-covered table which separated him from his visitor.

"May I ask in what way?" said Mr Penwynn, smiling. "Labour is plentiful."

"Certainly," said Geoffrey. "I have, as I tell you, carefully studied metallurgy, and the various processes for obtaining ore, especially tin, and I am convinced that I could save enormously by the plans I should put in force; and, what is more, I know I could save almost half the expense in some of the processes of smelting."

"Indeed!" said Mr Penwynn, coolly.

"Yes; and also contrive a good many improvements in the sinking and pumping out of mines."

"Then you have come to the right place, Mr—Mr—Mr Geoffrey Trethick," said the banker, raising his gold-rimmed passes to glance at the visiting-card before him.

"I hope so," said Geoffrey, with animation. "Ours is an old Cornish family, and I ought to be at home here."

"Exactly," said Mr Penwynn, sarcastically, "and you have come at the right time."

"Indeed?" said Geoffrey, eagerly.

"Most opportunely; for most of our great milking companies are in a state of bankruptcy."

"Yes, so I have heard. Well then, Mr Penwynn, if you will give me a letter or two of introduction, I should think there ought to be no difficulty in the way."

"My dear sir," said Mr Penwynn, smiling, "I'm afraid you are very sanguine."

"Well—perhaps a little, sir, but—"

"Hear me out, Mr Trethick. It seems to me you have come to the worst place in the world."

"The worst! Why so?"

"Because every one here will look upon your schemes as visionary. If you had a vast capital, and liked to spend it in experiments, well and good. People would laugh at your failures, and applaud your successes—if you made any."

"If?" said Geoffrey, smiling. "Then, sir, you are not sanguine?"

"Not at all," said the banker. "You see, Mr Trethick, you will not find any one in this neighbourhood who will let you run risks with his capital and machinery, or tamper with the very inadequate returns that people are now getting from their mines. If you wanted a simple post as manager—"

"That's what I do want," said Geoffrey, interrupting. "The other would follow."

"I say, if you wanted a simple post as manager," continued the banker, as calmly as if he had not been interrupted, "you would not get it unless you could lay before a company of proprietors ample testimonials showing your experience in mining matters. Believe me, Mr Trethick, you, a gentleman, have come to the wrong place."

"Let us sink the word *gentleman* in its ordinary acceptation, Mr Penwynn," said Geoffrey, warmly. "I hope I shall always be a gentleman, but I come to you, sir, as a working man—one who has to win his income by his brain-directed hands."

"You should have gone out to some speculative mining place, Mr Trethick," said the banker, taking one leg across his knee and caressing it. "Nevada or Peru—Australia if you like. You would make a fortune there. Here you will starve."

"Starve! Not if I have to help the fishermen with their nets, Mr Penwynn. I can row well, sir," he said, laughing, "and I have muscle enough to let me pull strongly at a rope. Starve? I've no fear of that."

"No, no; of course not. I mean metaphorically. But why not try the colonies or the States?"

"Because I have a mother who impoverished herself to complete my expensive university education, Mr Penwynn; and it would almost break her heart if I left England."

"Exactly," said the banker, with a slight sneer; "but you have come as far from civilisation as you could get in visiting Carnac. Now then, take my advice. Come up to An Morlock, and dine with me this evening—seven sharp. I can give you a bed for a night or two. Then have a run round the district, see a few of the mines, and spy out the nakedness of the land. You will soon get an indorsement of what I say. You can then go back to London with my best respects to Rundell and Sharp—most worthy people, by the way, whom I would gladly engage—and tell them you have returned a sadder but a wiser man."

He rose as he spoke to indicate that the interview was at an end, holding out his hand, one which Geoffrey gripped heartily, as he sprang, full of energy, to his feet.

"Thank you, Mr Penwynn. I'll come and dine with you this evening. Most happy. As to the bed—thanks, no. I am going to hunt out lodgings somewhere, for I cannot take your advice. You don't know me, sir," he said, looking the banker full in the eyes. "I've come down here to work, and, somehow or other, work I will. I have enough of the sturdy Englishman in me not to know when I am beaten. No, sir, I am not going to turn back from the first hill I meet with in my journey."

"As you will," said Mr Penwynn, smiling. "Till seven o'clock then. We don't dress."

"Thanks; I will be there," said Geoffrey, and the door closed as he left the room.

"He has stuff in him, certainly," said the banker, gazing at the door through which his visitor had passed. "Such a man at the head of a mine might make a good deal of money—or lose a good deal," he added, after a pause. "He'll find out his mistake before he is much older."

With a careless motion of his hand the banker threw his visitor's card into the waste-paper basket, and, at the same time, seemed to cast the young man out of his thoughts.

Chapter Five.

A Look Round Carnac.

"Tell'ee what, Tom Jennen, you fishermen are more nice than wise."

"And I tell'ee, Amos Pengelly, as you miner lads are more nasty than nice. Think of a man as calls hisself a Christian, and preaches to his fellows, buying a gashly chunk of twissening snake of a conger eel, and taking it home to eat."

"And a good thing too, lad. Why, it's fish, ar'n't it?"

"Fish? Pah! I don't call them fish."

"Why, it's as good as your hake, man?"

"What, good as hake? Why, ye'll say next it's good as mack'rel or pilchar'. I never see the like o' you miner lads. Why, I see Joe Helston buy a skate one day."

"Ay, and a good thing too. But look yonder on Pen Point! There's some one got hold of the bushes. I say, Tom Jennen, who's yonder big, good-looking chap?"

"I d'no'. Got on his Sunday clothes, whoever he be. Don't call him good-looking, though. Big awk'ard chap in a boot. He'd always be in the way. He's a 'venturer, that's what he is. Whose money's he going to chuck down a mine?"

"What a chap you are, Tom Jennen! What should we mining folk do if it wasn't for the 'venturers? We must have metal got up, and somebody's obliged to speck'late in mines."

"Speck'late in mines, indeed," said the other, contemptuously. "Why don't they put their money in boots or nets, so as to make money out of mack'rel or pilchar'?"

"Ah, for the boots to go down and drown the poor lads in the first storm, and the nets to be cut and swept away."

"Well, that's better than chucking the money down a hole in the ground."

"Hey, Tom, you don't know what's good for others, so don't set up as a judge," and the speaker, a short, lame, very thick-set man, in a rough canvas suit, stained all over of a deep red, showed his white teeth in a pleasant smile, which seemed like sunshine on his rough, repellent face.

"Maybe I do; maybe I don't. I say I don't call him a good-looking chap."

"Just as if you could tell whether a man's good-looking or not, Tom Jennen. That's for the women to do."

"Ha—ha—ha! yes. Bess Prawle says you're the plainest man she ever see."

The miner flushed scarlet, and an angry light flashed from his eyes, but he seemed to master the annoyance, and said cheerfully,—

"I dare say she's right, Tom. I never set up for a handsome man."

"Like yonder 'venturer chap. He's the sort as would please old smuggler Prawle's lass."

The angry flush came into the miner's face again, but he mastered his annoyance, and said, rather hoarsely,—

"Hold your tongue, lad; the gentleman will hear what you say."

"What's that man doing up on the cliff?" said Geoffrey Trethick, who had walked down by the harbour in making a tour of his new home. "The one waving those things in his hands."

"Sighting a school," said Tom Jennen, in a sing-song tone, as, after the manner of sea-side men, he leaned his back against the stout rail which guarded the edge of the cliff.

"Sighting a school, eh? Of fish, of course?"

"Mack'," said Tom Jennen, so curtly that he cut the word in half, and then proceeded to add to the brown stains at the corners of his mouth by hacking off a piece of tobacco with his big knife.

"They do it in partnership like, sir," said the miner, eagerly, as he gazed in the new-comer's face, as if attracted by the sound of the word "adventurer."

"One of them goes up on the highest part of the cliff yonder, Pen Dwavas that is, and he watches till he sees a school coming."

"How can he see a school of fish coming?"

"Colour," growled Tom Jennen, who had now turned round, and was trying to spit upon a particular boulder on the shore below.

"Yes, by the colour, sir," said the miner, Amos, or more commonly Preaching Pengelly—"colour of the water; and then he signals to his mates. That's them gone off in yon boat."

"I see."

"They have their boot ready with the seine in—long net, you know—and rows out, just as you see them now."

"Yes; but what's the use of his waving those things now?"

"Them's bushes, sir," continued the miner, who was talking, and reading the new-comer at the same time. "Don't you see, them in the boot being low down, couldn't see which way to go, so he waves them on with the bushes."

"To be sure, yes," said Geoffrey. "I see now. They are throwing something over—yes, of course, the net. So that dark, ripply patch, then, is where the fish lie?"

"Yes, sir, that's them," said the miner, who seemed strangely attracted; "but you've got good eyes."

"Think so?" said Geoffrey, smiling. Then, nodding his thanks, he walked farther along the cliff to watch what was a novelty to him—the taking of the shoal of mackerel.

"Ha, ha, ha?" laughed Tom Jennen. "On'y to think o' the ignorance o' these foreigners! Here's a big, awkward chap of a good thirty year of age, and knowed nothing about bushes and a seine boat. If it had been you, Amos Pengelly, as is always grubbing down under the earth, like a long lug-worm, I shouldn't have wondered; but a man as dresses up fine, and calls hisself a gentleman. Lor', such gashly ignorance do cap me."

"Well, I don't know," said Amos, staring down at his section of conger eel, which he was carrying by a string. "Some folks seem to know a deal too much, Tom;" and, with a good-humoured nod, he followed the new-comer as if eager to see more of one who might be an adventurer, and the opener out of some great vein of tin or copper, till he saw him stop.

Geoffrey Trethick found that he was not the only one interested in the seine boat, for silvery mackerel meant silver coin to the fisher-folk of Carnac. The news had spread, and group after group began to assemble, and to note the progress of those shooting the net.

For, after rowing in various directions, as guided by the waving bushes on the point, the men in the boat had begun to pass their dark brown net rapidly over the stern, while those in the bows rowed steadily on, forming the arc of a circle, which was to enclose the fish; while these latter, having swum closer in, could now be seen to make the bright waters of the bay all a ripple of blue and silver sheen, with here and there a dash of pink and gold, as if the fish had left upon the surface the impress of their glowing sides.

It was an interesting sight to a stranger from town, and as Geoffrey Trethick watched he could hear the remarks of old hands around him canvassing the probability of the fish escaping, or the nets getting entangled among the rocks.

But the boat went steadily on, the men cautiously dipping their oars so as not to alarm the mackerel, and fathom after fathom of the piled-up brown stack of net glided into the sea, being passed out so skilfully that as the corks dotted the water the meshes stretched and fell softly down lower and lower till they formed a frail fence of umber thread in the bright waters of the calm bay, every fathom increasing the wall that was soon to encircle the shoal.

One dart of a frightened fish towards the unenclosed part, and away would have gone the whole school; but the mackerel seemed to be intent on playing near the surface, and the seine boat went on shaking out fathom after fathom of the net till seaward there was a half-circle of brown corks, ever increasing to three-quarters.

And now Geoffrey Trethick, who had become deeply interested, unaware of the fact that he was the chief object of attraction to the people on the cliff, saw for the first time that a small boat, managed by a couple of men, remained by the other end of the net, and that as the first boat came nearer towards making a circle, the lesser boat was put in motion.

These were the most anxious moments, and the little crowd upon the cliff seemed to hold its breath. Then as the dark dots that represented the corks were seen to have nearly joined, the two boats being in the open space, there was a bit of a cheer.

"Tchah! Fools!" said a harsh voice close to Trethick's ear. "They have not caught them yet!"

Geoffrey turned, and found that the words proceeded from a little, withered, yellow-faced man, in a very old-fashioned dress. He was well-to-do, evidently, for a bunch of heavy gold seals hung from a black watch-ribbon, his Panama hat was of the finest quality, and there was something dapper and suggestive of the William the Fourth gentleman, in the blue coat, with gilt buttons, and neat drab trousers.

"I said, Tchah! Fools!" repeated the little man, on noticing Geoffrey's inquiring gaze. "They have not got them yet!"

"Many a slip betwixt cup and lip, eh?" said Geoffrey, quietly. "Yes: one pull of the net over a rock—one blunder, and away goes the school; and that's life?"

"You mean that's your idea of life," said Geoffrey. "No, I don't, boy. I mean that's life!"

"According to your view," said Geoffrey, smiling.

"According to what it is," said the old man, testily. "What the devil do you know of life, at your age?"

"Ah! that would take some telling," replied Geoffrey. "You and I would have to argue that matter out."

"Argue? Bah! Do I look a man with time to waste in argument?"

"Well, no; nor yet in getting out of temper, and calling people fools," said Geoffrey, with a smile.

The old man thumped his thick malacca cane upon the stones, and stared aghast at the stranger who dared to speak to him in so free and contradictory a manner in a place where, after a fashion, he had been a kind of king.

"Here, you: Rumsey!" he cried, panting with anger and pointing at Geoffrey with his cane, as a fair, fresh-coloured man in grey tweed came slowly up; "who the devil is this fellow?"

"Don't be cross, old gentleman," said Geoffrey, laughing. "I will tell you my name if you like."

"Confound your name, sir! What the deuce are you—a bagman?"

"No," said Geoffrey; "but look," he added quickly, as he pointed to the circle of nets. "What does that mean?"

"Ha, ha, ha! I told you so," chuckled the old man, whose face underwent a complete change. "They've got on a rock, and the whole school has gone."

"Poor fellows! What a disappointment," said Geoffrey.

"Bah! A man must expect disappointments here. Rumsey, I'm horribly bilious this morning," he continued, turning to the fresh-coloured man.

"Yes, so you seem," was the reply; and Geoffrey smiled at the frank confession. "Exceeded your dose last night."

"Dose?" said the old gentleman. "Hang it, man, don't call a glass of spirits and water by the same name as your filthy drugs. Good-morning, boy! and don't you laugh at me."

Hooking the fresh-coloured man by the arm, he was moving off.

"Good-morning," said Geoffrey, smiling. "But stop a moment. Perhaps you gentlemen can help me."

"Come away, Rumsey!" cried the old fellow, with mock horror in his thin face. "He's a book canvasser, or a collector for some confounded charity. Who the devil are you, sir; and what do you want?"

"Why, what a jolly old pepperbox you are!" cried Geoffrey, merrily. "Have you been out in India?"

"Yes, sir—I have been out in India," cried the old man, turning yellow with anger once more. "Confounded puppy!" he muttered, thumping down his stick.

"I thought so," replied Geoffrey, coolly; "I had an uncle just like you."

"Confound your uncle, sir!" cried the choleric old man. "Hang it all, Rumsey, don't you hear the fellow insulting me? Why don't you knock him down, or poison him?"

"Have I the pleasure of addressing Dr Rumsey?" said Geoffrey.

"That is my name," said the fresh-coloured man, looking suspiciously at the speaker as one who seemed too lusty and well to be in his way.

"I am coming to live here, doctor," said Geoffrey, in a free, frank way that seemed to set him at ease with those whom he had addressed. "I only came in by the coach this morning. Where can I get comfortable, inexpensive apartments—just a bed and sitting-room, you know? I have been asking everywhere, but there seems to be no such thing to be had."

The doctor glanced at the old gentleman, and the old gentleman returned the look, following it up by poking Geoffrey in the side with his cane.

"Here, young fellow—you, sir! Who are your—what are you?" he exclaimed.

"Who am I, my unceremonious old friend, and what am I? Well, my name is Trethick, and I'm a mining engineer."

"But are you respectable?"

"No," said Geoffrey, solemnly. "I am very poor; so I don't think I am."

"Confound you, sir!" cried the old gentleman. "Your eyes are twinkling. You're laughing at me."

"True, oh, king," said Geoffrey.

"But can you pay regularly for your lodgings?"

"I hope so," replied Geoffrey, whom the choleric old fellow thoroughly amused.

"Come here," cried the latter, dropping the doctor and hooking Geoffrey by the arm, as if taking him into custody. "You're good for the bile! Rumsey, I'll take him up to Mrs Mullion's, or she'll be letting her rooms to the new parson out of spite."

Chapter Six.

Apartments to Let.

Geoffrey looked in astonishment at the old gentleman, and then glanced at the doctor.

"You can't do better, Mr Trethick," said that individual, "for those are the only decent apartments you are likely to get here."

"Of course," said the old gentleman. "Come along, boy;" and thumping the ferrule of his cane down upon the granite paving-stones, which in rough irregular masses formed the path, he led the way along the cliff, and then turned off up a very steep zigzag path, which led up higher and higher, the old fellow pausing at every turn to get breath, as he pointed with his stick at the glorious prospects of sea and land which kept opening out.

"Lovely place, boy," he panted. "Come along. Takes my breath away, but it's better for the bile than old Rumsey's drugs. Suppose you could run up here?"

"I dare say I could," said Geoffrey; "or carry you up if I tried."

"Confound your ugly great muscles! I dare say you could. But look yonder—that's some of your work."

"My work?" cried Geoffrey, as the old man pointed to the great granite engine-house on the promontory already known to the new arrival as Wheal Carnac.

"Well, the work of you engineering mining fellows. Thousands of pounds have gone down that hole."

"Yes, I suppose so," replied Geoffrey, as they still ascended, until the old gentleman stopped short before a pretty granite-built house in a nook of the huge cliff that sloped down to the sea. It was well sheltered from the north and east, and its broad terrace-like garden was blushing with bright-hued flowers. In one corner was a well-built summer-house, which served as a look-out over the shimmering sea, and from which the putting out of the fishing-fleet, or the sailing to and fro of the great vessels in the Channel, could be plainly seen.

"Ah! this looks homely and snug," said Geoffrey, as he noticed the clean windows, white curtains, and pleasant aspect of the place.

"Yes, it's pretty well," said the old gentleman, who was always furtively watching his companion, and as he spoke he laid his hand upon the green gate at the foot of a rough granite flight of steps. "This is the way up from the cliff; there's a road from Carnac town on the other side. Will it do?"

"Depends on terms and accommodation," said Geoffrey, sharply, as he followed his guide up to the pleasant green terrace lawn.

"Humph! Go and see Mrs Mullion, then, and say Mr Paul sent you. I am going in here to smoke a cheroot," and he pointed to the summer-house.

"Do you live here, then?" said Geoffrey, for the old man seemed quite at home.

"Live here?" said the choleric old fellow, sharply. "Of course I do. Didn't see a shell on my back, did you? Where the deuce do you suppose I lived?"

As he spoke he drew out a handsome silver cigar-case, and selecting a very long, black cheroot, held it out to his companion.

"Here," he said, "can you smoke one of these?"

"To be sure I can," said Geoffrey. "Try one of mine."

"It's strong. Mind it don't make you sick, boy," said the old fellow grimly, as Geoffrey took the black cheroot, and then opened his own case—an effeminate silk-worked affair—which he handed to his companion.

The old man turned it about with the yellow corners of his lips curled down in disgust.

"Girl work that for you?" he said, with quite a snarl.

"No! Mother," said Geoffrey, abruptly.

"Ho!" said the old gentleman, picking and turning over one cigar after another, and then replacing it. "There, take your case, boy; I can't smoke your town-made trash."

"Town-made trash, eh?" said Geoffrey, laughing. "Why, they're as good as your Trichinopolies."

"Rubbish!" said the old fellow.

"Real Havanas, given me by old Sir Harry. Dunton."

"Not Harry Dunton, Governor of Ginjaica?"

"Yes! Do you know him?"

"Did once," said the old fellow, with asperity. "Here, boy, I'll have one. Now go and see about your lodgings; and come back to me," he added imperatively.

Geoffrey stood smiling at him for a few moments.

"I say, old gentleman," he said, "how many coolies used you to have under you in the East?"

"Over a thousand, sir," said the old gentleman, irascibly.

"I thought so," said Geoffrey, and he turned on his heels, and walked up to the clematis-covered porch that shaded the open door.

"I'd give some thousands to be as young and strong, and—and yes, confound him!—as impudent as that fellow. Hang him! he hasn't a bit of veneration in him," muttered the old gentleman, entering the summer-house, and striking a match for his cheroot. "He'll just be right for them, as they've lost the parson. Hang 'em, how I do hate parsons!"

He took a few pulls at his cheroot, and emitted cloud after cloud of smoke, as he stood in the shade of the summer-house, looking at Geoffrey's back.

"He's a good-looking fellow, too, and—phew!" he added, with a long-drawn whistle, "what a fool I am. There's Madge, of course, and at the door first thing."

"If I am any thing of a judge, you are a very pretty girl," said Geoffrey to himself, as his summons was answered by a merry-looking brunette, in a very simple morning dress and print apron, a book in one hand, a feather dusting-brush in the other. Her rather wilful hair, of a crisp, dark brown, had evidently been touched by the sea-breeze, for a waving strand was brushed hastily back as the girl saw the visitor; and the same, or other breezes, had given a rich tone to her complexion, which was heightened by the flush which came to her cheeks, as she hastily threw brush and book on to a chair, and gave a tug at the string of her apron, which absolutely refused to come off.

"Can I speak to Mrs Mullion?" said Geoffrey, unable to repress a smile at the girl's vanity and confusion.

"Oh! yes. Please will you step in?"

"Who's that, Madge?" cried a voice from somewhere at the back. "If it's Aunt Borlase, we don't want any fish to-day, and tell her—"

"Hush, mamma!" exclaimed the girl, turning sharply, but without checking the voice, whose owner—a very round, pleasant-looking little matron—came forward, with a piece of black silk in one hand, a sponge in the other, and bringing with her a peculiar smell of hot irons lately applied to the material she held.

"Well, my dear," she said, volubly, "how was I to know that it was company? Oh! good-morning, sir."

"Good-morning," said Geoffrey, who was pleasantly impressed by the mother and daughter, who now led the way into a comfortable old-fashioned parlour, whose window looked direct upon the foam-fringed promontory on which stood the ruined mine. "A Mr Paul, whom I have just left, advised me to see you about your apartments."

"Oh! yes," said the elder lady, smoothing herself down in front, as if trying to free herself from a little exuberance—the younger lady having now got rid of brush, book, and apron, and given a furtive touch to her pretty hair. "You are Mr Lee, our new clergyman," she continued volubly, "and—"

"Indeed I am not!" said Geoffrey, laughing, and glancing at the younger lady, who blushed, and gave her head a conscious toss.

"But I sent word to the hotel that I should be glad to take him in," said the elder lady; "and now that's just the way with that Aunt Borlase. Madge, dear, they never got the message."

"Is this one of the rooms?" said Geoffrey, to stem the flood of eloquence.

"Yes, sir; and Mr Paul, who is my late husband's half-brother, has the other front parlour, which we sometimes share with him when he is in a good temper. When he isn't, my daughter and I—this is my daughter, sir—sit in the—"

"Oh, mamma, hush!" exclaimed the younger lady, acknowledging Geoffrey's bow.

"Well, my dear, it's the simple truth," said mamma. "I hope you don't object to the smell of black silk being ironed, sir?"

"Oh, dear, no," said Geoffrey, smiling.

"It's the being sponged over with beer first," continued the little woman. "It makes it so stiff, and when it's done it looks almost as good as new."

"But, mamma," remonstrated the younger lady.

"It's nothing to be ashamed of, my dear. Quite superior people turn their black silks, and have them re-made over and over again. There really is no cheaper wear than a good black silk."

"But about the apartments," said Geoffrey, to the younger lady's great relief.

"Oh! yes; of course. To be sure," continued the little lady. "I let the bedchambers over the rooms, sir. One to each."

"Exactly," said Geoffrey, who was much amused at the simplicity of the elder lady, and the assumption of gentility on the part of the younger; "but do I understand you to say that the apartments are engaged?"

"Well, sir, I feel as if I ought to wait and see if Mr Lee, our new clergyman, wants the rooms, especially as there are no other apartments fit for a gentleman to be had in Carnac, and where he could get proper attention. Not that I make a profession of letting lodgings, sir. Oh, dear, no! Mr Paul is a relative, and he occupies—"

"Mamma, dear," said the younger lady, "I don't think this gentleman will care to hear that."

"But how can he understand my position, Margaret, if I do not explain it?" remonstrated the elder.

"You hold out very pleasant prospects," interposed Geoffrey, hastily. "No other apartments to be had. But suppose Mr Lee does not take them?"

"Who the deuce is Mr Lee?" said a sharp voice at the open window. "Come: what is it—terms? Haven't you settled yet?"

"Mr Lee is the new clergyman, brother Thomas," said the plump little lady, giving herself another smooth down, "and if he wants the rooms that Mr Owen had, dear, why of course—"

"He'll have to want them," said the old gentleman, sharply, as he sent a puff of smoke into the room. "I won't have another parson in the house while I stay. If you mean to have him here, I go."

"Oh, pray don't talk like that, brother Thomas!" cried Mrs Mullion, hastily, her aspect showing plainly enough that she was greatly in awe of the old man. "Of course you know, dear, that I will do precisely as you wish."

"What I wish? Do what I wish?" snapped out the old gentleman. "Do what you like. But you told me distinctly that you were very eager to let these two rooms, and I take the trouble to put myself out, and go out of my way when I had a pressing engagement with Dr Rumsey, to bring up a—a—somebody who wants them. What more would you have? You, Madge," he added fiercely, "don't make eyes at strangers like that: it's rude."

"Oh, uncle?" cried the girl, indignantly, and her face was scarlet.

"So you were. Give me that letter off the chimney-piece."

The girl obeyed, fetching a large blue missive ready directed for the post, and stood holding it while the old gentleman, smoking away the while, took some stamps from his pocket-book, and tore one off.

"Now then," he continued, sharply, and to Geoffrey Trethick's great astonishment, "put out your tongue."

"I'm—I'm quite well, uncle," stammered the girl.

"Put out your tongue, miss!" cried the old fellow, sharply. "I don't care how you are: I want to wet this stamp."

"Oh, uncle!" cried the girl, in confusion, and she rushed out of the room, leaving the old man chuckling with satisfaction.

"Ah, well; I must lick it myself," he said. "I hate licking stamps. Here, Jane, you put it on," he continued, handing letter and stamp to the little woman, who proceeded to obey his command. "Well, now then, are you going to let the rooms, or are you not? This gentleman can't stop shilly-shallying all day."

"I shall be very happy to let them, I'm sure," stammered the poor woman; and, after the settlement of a few preliminaries, it was arranged that the new-comer's luggage should be fetched from the hotel, and he took possession at once, after the old gentleman had suggested that a month in advance should be paid for, which was done.

Chapter Seven.

Uncle Paul Utters Warnings.

"You see, you are quite a stranger," said the old gentleman, in a kind of gruff apology; "and I'm obliged to look after that poor woman's interests. Now, then," he continued, leading the way into the garden, "light up and come into the look-out, boy; I want to talk to you."

Geoffrey followed him, and as soon as they were seated they smoked and stared at each other in silence for a time, the young man rather enjoying his elder's keen scrutiny.

"Pleasant woman, my sister-in-law," said Mr Paul, at last.

"Yes; she seems homely and nice. Takes pride in her house."

"Humph! Yes."

"Widow, of course?"

"Yes: didn't you see she was?"

"Yes."

"Then why did you ask?"

"For confirmation. Is yours a bad cigar?"

"No. Why?"

"Because it don't seem to act as a sedative. A good one always makes me calm and agreeable."

"Then you think I am disagreeable?" said the old man, sharply.

"Not to put too fine a point upon it—yes; very."

"I always am," said the old gentleman, with a harsh laugh. "What do you think of my niece?"

"Very pretty," said Geoffrey, quietly.

"Oh! You think so?"

"Yes. Don't you?"

"Humph! Yes. But, look here, young man, you are from London, are you not?"

"Yes."

"Then none of your town manners, please. No putting silly notions in that girl's head. It's full enough already."

"Who? I? Put silly notions in her head?" said Geoffrey, showing his white teeth as he removed his cigar from his lips and exhaled a great cloud of smoke. "Don't be afraid, old gentleman. I'm a man without a heart. Besides which, I'm engaged."

"More fool you. Bah! Look at me."

"I have looked at you," said Geoffrey, coolly; "I know you by heart already."

"Bah!" ejaculated the old gentleman, testily. "Engaged—married—insanity! A young man madly makes up his mind to keep a woman and a lot of children in bread and butter, like poor Rumsey, our doctor. Thinks it is going to be a pleasant burthen, and dreams on till he wakes—poor devil!"

"You don't approve, then, of matrimony?"

"Approve? No, I don't. I have seen too much of it in others. Young half-brother of mine marries that woman there; keeps poor in consequence; dies poor, leaving her and her child poor—paupers both of 'em."

"Hah! yes," said Geoffrey; "there are more poor than rich in the world."

"Their own fault. Don't you make a poor man of yourself."

"Don't mean to," said Geoffrey, quietly. "My mistress—my wife, if you like—is Science. Do you like bad smells?"

"Do I like *what*?"

"Bad smells. Because my chemicals will be down in a few days. I try experiments, and sometimes strong odours arise."

"Humph!" growled Uncle Paul. "Open the window, then. So your wife's Science, is she?"

"Bless her: yes," cried Geoffrey, emphatically. "She's a tricksy coquette, though."

"So's Madge, there," said the old man.

"Is she?" said Geoffrey, looking at him, curiously. "I say, old gentleman, you are not very complimentary to your relatives; but I understand your hints: so look here. I'm not a lady's man, and your niece will be free from any pursuit of mine; and if she gets—what do you call it?—setting her cap at me, she'll give me up in four-and-twenty hours in disgust."

"On account of Miss Science, eh?" said the old gentleman, grimly. "But I thought you said you were an engineer?"

"I am."

"Then—then, why are you here? got an appointment?"

"Look here, Mr Paul," said Geoffrey, laughing, "as we are to be such near neighbours, and you evidently would like me to make a clean breast of it, here it all is:—I am a mining engineer; a bit of a chemist; I have no appointment; and I have come down to get one."

"Then you've come to the wrong place, young man."

"So Mr Penwynn told me."

"Oh, you've been there, have you?"

"Yes."

"Seen his daughter?"

"No, nor do I want to see her," said Geoffrey, throwing the end of his cheroot out of the window. "I'll take another of those cheroots, sir. They're strong and full-flavoured; I like them. So you think I've come to the wrong place, do you?"

"Yes," said Uncle Paul, passing the blackest and strongest cheroot in his case. "Of course I do. The mining is all going to the dogs. The companies are one-half of them bankrupt, and the other half pay no dividends. The only people who make money are a set of scoundrelly adventurers who prospect for tin, and when they have found what they call a likely spot—"

Here there was a pause, while the old gentleman also lit a fresh cheroot.

"—They get up a company; play games with the shares, and get fools to take them, whose money goes down a big hole in the earth."

"And never comes up again, eh?"

"Never?" said the old man, emphatically.

"Ever been bitten that way?" said Geoffrey, smiling.

"Yes: once," snarled the other. "They got a hundred pounds out of me over a promising-looking affair—that mine down yonder on the point—Wheal Carnac. Smooth-tongued scoundrel talked me over. Just such a fellow as you."

"Indeed!" said Geoffrey, smiling.

"Been a lesson to me, though, that I've never forgotten."

"And yet there is money to be made out of mines," said Geoffrey, quietly. "With proper care, judgment, and good management there are plenty of lapsed undertakings that could be revived, and would pay their shareholders well."

"Make Wheal Carnac pay, then, and my hundred pounds something better than waste paper."

"I do not see why not," said Geoffrey, earnestly.

Old Mr Paul pushed back his chair and made it scroop loudly on the summer-house floor, as he bared his yellow teeth in a grin.

"I thought so," he exclaimed, with a harsh chuckle. "There, out with it, man! What's the mine? Is it Wheal Ruby, or Bottom Friendship, or Evening Star, or what? How many shares are you going to stick into some noodle or another?"

"I sell shares? Ha, ha, ha!" laughed Geoffrey. "I never held or sold one in my life. No, sir, I am no share-jobber. I have come down here to carve my way in quite different fashion."

"In granite?" sneered the old man.

"In the world, Mr Paul," said Geoffrey, rising. "And now I must be off. I want to have a good look round. I see that you and I will get on capitally together. Whenever you are in the humour throw open your door, and I'll open mine, and we'll quarrel. I enjoy a good row."

He nodded shortly, and strode off, his stout boots rattling the shingle stones of the path, and the gate giving a loud bang behind him, while directly after the echo of his steps could be heard as he clattered down over the rough granite paving towards the shore.

"Curse him!" cried the old man, getting up and craning his neck out of the summer-house window to stare after his late companion. "He's a great ugly, overgrown puppy: that's what he is, and I was an old idiot to bring him up here. Insulted me. Laughed in my face. As good as told me that I was an old fool. Never mind: I'll bring him down, big as he is, and he'll do to keep out the parson. Here! hi! somebody, Madge, Madge," he shouted, reseating himself, and banging the floor with his cane.

There was no reply.

"Madge!" roared the old man again, beating the table for a change.

"Madge has gone out, dear," said plump Mrs Mullion, hurrying out to the summer-house.

"Where's my newspaper?" cried the old man, angrily. "I never get my newspaper to the time. Do you hear, I want my newspaper. If you can't have me properly attended to by that cat of a girl, I declare I'll go. Do you hear? I'll go. I'm looking out now for a plot of land to build a house where I can be in peace and properly attended to. Do you hear? I want my newspaper—'The Times.'"

"There it is, dear," said Mrs Mullion, upon whom this storm did not seem to have the slightest effect, "you are sitting upon it."

"Then why, in the name of Buddha, was the paper put in my chair? A table's the place for a paper. Where's Madge?"

"Gone out for a walk, dear."

"She's always gone for a walk. I wish to good—"

Rustle—rustle—rustle of the paper.

"—To goodness I had nev—"

Rustle—rustle—rustle—

"—Had never come to this con—"

Rustle—rustle—rustle. Bang in the middle and double up.

"—Come to this confounded place. Hang Madge! She'll get into disgrace one of these—and—eh—um—oh. Hah! at last! um—um—um. 'North-west provinces. This important question came on last night,' um—um—um."

The old man's irritable voice toned down into a hum like that of a gigantic bee, for Uncle Paul was safe now to be in peace and good temper for a couple of hours at least over the debates in his newspaper, and Mrs Mullion, as unruffled as ever, was already back indoors, thinking over her half-brother's words, and wondering whether they would ever prove true.

Chapter Eight.

Geoffrey Makes a Discovery.

There were plenty of heads thrust out of the granite cottages on either side of the steep way as Geoffrey strode on, ready to give back frank, open look for curious gaze, and to take notice that the people were dark and swarthy; that there were plenty of brown fishing-nets, and blackened corks, and swollen bladders, hanging from the walls, in company with a pair or two of sculls, a hitcher and a mast from some small boat, with now and then what seemed to be a human being split and hung up to dry after the fashion of a haddock, but which proved to be only an oilskin fishing-suit.

At one cottage door a huge pair of fisher's boots stood out in the sun, as if they were being worn by some invisible prince or Cornish giant. At another door sat a woman cleaning a long, snaky-looking hake, opposite to a neighbour who was busily counting pilchards, which had evidently been brought up from one of the boats by a big, brown, bluff-looking man, who, from top to toe, seemed as if he had some idea of going into the harlequin profession, so spangled was he with silver scales.

"Can I get down to the beach this way?" Geoffrey asked of the latter.

"Can 'ee get down to ba-ach this way! Iss my son," said the man, in a sing-song tone; and, after a very steep descent, Geoffrey found himself where he desired to go.

Not upon a soft, sandy, or pleasant shingly beach, but upon one literally paved with great masses of rock—black shale, granite, and gneiss—over which the huge Atlantic waves came foaming in stormy weather, rolling and polishing the surface with the rounded boulders, which seemed to average the size of a goodly cheese. Even now the rocky promontory that ran out and sheltered the little place and its tiny harbour was fringed with foaming water as the blue waves came slowly rolling in, to break on the black rocks, run up and fall back in silvery cascades to the heaving sea.

Geoffrey's keen eyes scanned the rocks, with their great white veins of milky quartz; running through the beautiful sea-scape on his left, the piled-up rocks upon his right, and then they rested on the grey engine-house upon the promontory—the mark of the great disused unsuccessful mine that had been pointed out to him as Wheal Carnac.

This place had a sort of fascination for him, and, clambering up, as he drew nearer he noticed every thing—the roughly blasted-out road, the furnace-house, so arranged that its chimney trailed over the ground like a huge serpent along the slope of the cliff, and higher and higher, till, quite a hundred and fifty yards away, it ended in a masonry shaft, towering up on the very summit of the cliff.

"What a blast they could get up here!" muttered Geoffrey, as he leaped from rock to rock, till, quite breathless, he reached the great tongue of land, and found that by clambering laboriously up a rough path he could stand on the chine of the promontory and look down upon the deep blue sea upon the other side, quite a mile away, and where the rugged shore was one mass of foam.

But though the sight was grand it was not practical, and, soon descending, he made his way towards the great engine-house, to find everywhere traces of wasted enterprise, followed by ruin and neglect. A deep mine shaft had been sunk close to the edge that sloped down to the shore, and from a platform of rock where he stood he could see quite a vast embankment of the *débris* that had been toilsomely dug out and allowed to run down into the sea.

There were granite buildings, but they were windowless, and a glance showed that the machinery had been torn out, to leave the place a ruin.

"I wonder how many thousands were sunk here," said Geoffrey, half aloud, "before the heart-sick proprietors gave it up, perhaps just on the eve of a great discovery. What a chance now, if there are good tin-bearing strata, for a fresh set of proprietors to take up the others' work and carry it on to success."

"It looks tempting!" he muttered, as he went on from place to place, picking up specimens of the rock that had been chipped out and thrown from the shaft, and examining each piece attentively with a pocket-lens. "That's antimony; yes, that's tin," he continued, as he examined a piece of reddish quartz, on one side of which sparkled some black grains, looking as unlike tin as can be imagined.

"Dash of copper there," he said, after a time, as he went on and on, till he stopped at the edge of the profound square shaft, which went down into darkness, right below where the waves beat upon the shore.

"How deep, I wonder?" he said, as he gazed down into the pitchy blackness, and then threw in one of the fragments of rock which he held in his hand, listening attentively for some considerable time till there came up a weirdly strange, hollow, echoing plash, full of strange whisperings, each telling of the terrible depth down to where the water lay, filling up the profundities of the awe-inspiring place.

"Thousands upon thousands of pounds must have gone down that hole?" mused Geoffrey, seating himself on the very edge, with his legs hanging down into the shaft, into which he gazed as if it fascinated him and something was drawing him downward to his death.

"What a pit for a fellow to fall into!" he said, with a shudder. "He might slip or jump in, or throw in his enemy or any one he wanted to get rid of, and not a soul would be the wiser. It's a regular gateway into the other world.

"What stuff!" he said directly after, with a half-laugh. "Why, I'm turning morbid. It's a gateway to the golden land of success, and if I had a chance I'd make it pay."

He rose directly after, and with each wave as it broke below making his steps inaudible even to himself, he went on, peering first into one building and then into another, all seeming to be built on a goodly, if not extravagant, scale, which he noted at once for future purposes.

He crossed a patch of heathery turf next, and had nearly reached the doorway of a low shed-like place, probably the stables for the horses that had been used in connection with the mine, when he stopped short, for mingled with the low roar of the sea he seemed to hear voices.

He stopped short and listened, but heard nothing more.

"Ghosts of dead and gone disappointed shareholders, or the noises of the Kobolds of the mine," he said laughingly, and stepping forward he entered the doorway to find that to him, coming out of the full blaze of the sun, the place was very dark. He stretched out his hands to avoid running against any thing, and hardly knowing why, only that he seemed to be drawn on to investigate the place, he went forward, with the darkness growing lighter, when he stopped short again.

This time there was no mistake, for he heard a sob, and before he could make up his mind what to do, he heard a woman's voice speaking in tones of appeal.

Chapter Nine.

More of the Vicar's People.

"I really cannot come again!" exclaimed somebody, piteously, as Geoffrey stood there half-paralysed by surprise.

"What nonsense!" said a man's voice. "You can if—"

Geoffrey heard no more, for he beat a rapid retreat back into the sunshine, and hurried away, with a comical expression of vexation upon his countenance.

"Lovers, by all that's wonderful!" he exclaimed. "Hang 'em, they're everywhere! Fancy finding them in this out-of-the-way, forsaken place of all others in the world. Why, hang me! if I don't believe that's why some women go up Mont Blanc—they go up to court."

He strode away, whistling a merry air, little thinking what an influence all this would have upon his future life; and, thrusting his hands down into his pockets, he went on, leaping from rock to rock, making for the other side of the promontory, evidently intending to see as much of the country as he could before returning to dinner.

"Why, hallo!" he suddenly exclaimed, stopping short. "Surely I've heard one of those voices before? No: impossible!" he said, "I don't know any ladies down here."

Going on again, he soon crossed a sort of heathery down, dotted with masses of rock, which cropped up here and there; sent several couples of agile sheep bounding away, and noted that they were linked together at the neck; drew long, bracing breaths of the fresh, pure air; and, after skirting along the edge on the far side of the promontory, he went on inland, comparing the glorious sea to violet and gold, as it gleamed in the sunshine and reflected the brighter tints of the cliffs.

He soon hit upon a foot-track, which evidently led towards Carnac if he turned to the right, while on the left it led—

"Let's see where!" said Geoffrey.

Half an hour's walking showed that it led onward to a farther point on the sea, and he hesitated as to whether he should go on. A glance at his watch told him that he had ample time, and as there was another ruined engine-house evidently by the track, he walked on, finding that the path led direct to the side of another mining venture, but evidently of much older date, and he quite started as he found how near the path went by a yawning shaft.

It had probably once been protected by a wall of loosely piled-up stones, but these lay scattered here and there, while the great engine-house had half fallen, the chimney only being intact.

"How dangerous," thought Geoffrey, as he gazed down into the shaft, and noted how the grass and heath had grown over the embankment of *débris* which ran down in a slope landward, joining a precipitous descent from the engine-house, which stood upon a ridge quite a hundred and fifty feet above the sea, which ran in diamond sparkling cascades over the rocks that fringed the shore nearly a quarter of a mile away.

"They seem to have always perched these places on a ridge," he mused, as he looked into the ruined engine-house, and laughingly wondered whether there would be any lovers there.

"Quite a wonder!" he exclaimed, as he glanced round the ruin, and, finding nothing to excite his interest, he returned to the well-worn edge of the shaft.

He could not look straight down, for the top had crumbled in, making a sharp slope all round the edge; so, laughing at himself, he picked up one of the great lichen-covered pieces of granite that had formed the protecting wall, hurled it from him, and listened till with a roar came up the sound of a tremendous plash.

"That's about a hundred and fifty feet down to the water," he said aloud. "I believe it comes natural to a fellow to want to throw stones down every hole he sees. I'll be bound to say that Cain and Abel used to do just the same. Adam never was a boy."

He stood thinking for a few minutes, these old mine shafts attracting him greatly.

"I wonder whether any one was ever thrown down that shaft?" he said aloud. "She would never come out alive."

He found himself wondering again why his thoughts had taken such a turn, and why he should have said "she."

"What nonsense!" he exclaimed. "I shall be writing a romance of a ruined mine directly," and going on to the slope of *débris* he began kicking out and examining the old fragments that had been dug from the bowels of the earth, taking out his pocket-lens, and minutely inspecting each piece for traces of metallic ore, but finding little to reward his pains.

"There was a lot of money wasted here, I'll be bound," he exclaimed, as he turned off and once more began to follow the track.

"It's a grand coast-line," he thought, as he walked on past and under the huge masses of grey granite, dotted with green fern and pink stonecrop, till he found the path begin to descend rapidly into a ravine, full of ferny nooks and spots made musical by the dripping water of the springs. The place had very precipitous sides, with a bright rushing stream foaming on towards the sea, where it spread its waters over the pure sands of a tiny cove.

There were a couple of boats drawn up below a large straggling granite cottage, built evidently a portion at a time upon a shelf of rock well out of the reach of the waves; and upon a platform in front of the unlovely place, hedged in with stones, was some attempt at a garden.

So steep was the track down as he approached the place, Geoffrey could easily have leaped from this slope on to the cottage roof, which was as rugged as the walls, and altogether the dwelling had a wild, uncouth aspect, in no wise improved by some old ship wood and lumber lying about.

But this was all redeemed by the beauty of the little cove, with the breaking waves which seemed to sweep up the waters of the little stream after its gurgling course, amidst lichenous stones from where it had sprung high up the ravine out of a bower of many-tinted greens.

"Just the spot for a smuggler or a wrecker, or a fellow to build a house to boat and fish, and live away from the world. I should like to lodge here," he continued, as his eyes wandered over the scene. "Wish I could paint, and—ah! you would come in capitally. Hallo! she's coming to me. No, my lass," he said, as if speaking to her, though she was too distant to hear, "it's labour in vain. I don't want a guide to any caves or dripping wells, or to buy specimens of ore, spar, or the like. By Jove, though, she's very handsome. Why, she must be a gypsy."

This was said as a young woman came into sight from the cottage below, looked up, and on catching sight of the visitor seemed to speak to some one within, and then hurried up to meet him.

As Geoffrey remarked, she was very handsome, but it was a wild, rugged, half-savage kind of beauty. Dark-eyed, brown-skinned, with a ruddy flush which showed how little she sheltered from the weather, while her abundant black hair was carelessly twisted up, and hung down in a massive knot between her shoulders. Her dress was of the commonest cotton, and slovenly made, a short print gown being tied round her waist, over a bright-coloured serge petticoat, while in one hand she held a print hood. But, in spite of her ungraceful clothing, Geoffrey could see that she was lithe, strong, and active, and there was no little natural grace in the undulations of her unfettered form, as she hurried up to meet him.

"Come here and buy some sweets," she said, in a voice as full of command as entreaty, and as she looked him boldly yet curiously in the face, he saw that her lips were red and full, over large but beautifully white teeth.

"Sweets? Nonsense, my lass. I don't eat sweets. What cove is this?"

"Gwennas," said the girl. "Come down and buy some sweets. Here's the money."

Geoffrey stared, as the girl held out a penny in her large, well-shaped hand.

"Poor lass! A love case for a sovereign. She's crazy," said Geoffrey to himself, and, changing his manner, he took the coin from the girl's hand, receiving, at the same time, a smile for reward. "What's your name, my lass?" he said aloud.

"Bessie—Elizabeth Prawle," said the girl, shortly. "You're a stranger."

"Yes," he said, looking at her sidewise. "Do they sell sweets here?"

"Yes," said the girl, sharply.

"And you are very fond of them, eh?"

They were going side by side towards the cottage, when the girl faced round, looked at him in a puzzled way for a moment, and then laughed merrily.

"They are not for me," she said, sharply, as they reached the rough rocky platform in front of the cottage. "Here, father, this gentleman is going to buy some sweets."

"Is he? Oh!"

This was uttered in a low, hoarse growl, by a strongly-built, rugged fisher-looking man, in a blue Jersey, and very thick flannel trousers, braced up right over his chest. He wore no hat, but a shaggy crop of grizzled hair shaded his weather-beaten, inflamed face, as he sat on a block of granite, as rugged as himself, overhauling a long fishing-line, whose hooks he was sticking in pieces of blackened cork.

He looked up for a moment frowningly at the visitor, with a pair of dark piercing eyes, drew a great gnarled hand across his mouth to wipe away the tobacco-juice, lowered his eyes, got up, stooped, and displayed an enormous patch upon his trousers, reseated himself, and went on with his work.

"Come in," said the girl, quickly, and she led the way into a large low room, roughly but well furnished, and scrupulously clean. It was a compound of rustic farmhouse kitchen with a flavour of parlour and ship's chandlery or boating store. For along the massive beams, and wherever a great peg could be driven in, hung nets, lines, and other fishing gear. A ship's lantern hung here; there was a binnacle there. Odds and ends of cabin furniture were mingled with well-polished Windsor chairs, and brass decorated chests of drawers. There was plenty of ornamentation too. Shells, a sword-fish, dried marine animals, sponges and seaweeds, masses of coral, fragments of bright spar, and some gay pieces of china, lay upon chimney-piece and shelves; in addition to which there was the model of a full-rigged ship in full sail, fitted up in a great glass case.

"Quite an old curiosity shop," thought Geoffrey, as he saw all this at a glance, and noted that the well-cleaned floor was sprinkled with sand, save where a great home-made shred rug lay in front of the bright black fireplace, on whose hob a great copper kettle shone from its dark corner like a misted sun.

The light came through the open door, and formed quite a Rembrandtish picture in the low, darkened room, falling as it did in mote-sparkling rays, like a band of sunbeams, right across a bent figure in an old well-washed chintz-covered armchair.

The first thing that struck Geoffrey was the figure's occupation. The day was warm, but she was seated very close to the fire, airing a garment carefully spread over her knees, and from which came a most unmistakable odour of scorching, reminding the visitor very strongly of his late visit to Mrs Mullion's on the cliff. A pair of very thin white hands were busy adding mesh after mesh to a herring net, while as they entered, the bent down head was eagerly raised, and Geoffrey saw a face whose white hair and pallid, piteous look, told its own tale, as the weary-looking eyes scanned his face.

"Another customer, mother," said the girl, quickly. "Oh, why don't you be more careful? you'll burn yourself to death."

"It's cold, Bessie; it's cold, dear, but that's well—that's well," said the invalid, whose hands began to tremble, so that she missed a stitch or two in her net. "Be quick, dear, be quick."

"Yes, mother. Did you say a pen'orth, sir?"

"No, I want sixpen'orth, my lass," said Geoffrey.

The girl darted a grateful look at him as she took a covered glass jar from the window-sill, and as she rattled the coloured sticks of candy which were its contents, Geoffrey heard a sigh of satisfaction from the invalid, a glance showing him that the head was once more bent down over the net.

"Fine weather, Mrs Prawle," said Geoffrey, hazarding a shot, as the girl busily rustled a paper bag.

"Yes, yes," said the invalid, looking up at him, "I suppose it is, sir. I hope you will come again."

The girl darted a quick look at him.

"Oh, yes! of course," replied Geoffrey, whose eyes wandered over the pitiable picture before him. "I shall come again."

"I'm so anxious to get up a connection, sir," continued the invalid, "and Gwennas Cove is rather out of the way."

"I should think it is—rather!" said Geoffrey to himself, and he could hardly refrain from smiling at the poor woman's idea of getting up a connection in that wild spot.

"Yes, Bess, take the money. Thank you kindly, sir. Good-day, sir; good-day;" and the invalid began to carefully turn the airing garment upon her knees, though there was no more dampness in it than in one of the red-hot pieces of wood over which she hung.

Geoffrey felt disposed to stay, but his time was short, and, after a cheery "good-day," he strode out, followed by the girl, to find that the rugged-looking old man was gone, patch and all; but the girl hurried on before him for a few yards, as if to be out of hearing at the cottage, and then held out her hand.

"What? Good-by!" said Geoffrey, smiling, and he held out his own.

"No, no, nonsense," said the girl, flushing. "Give me the sweeties, and take your money back."

"Then you carry that on to please the old lady, eh?" said Geoffrey.

"Yes, of course," replied the girl, sharply. "Didn't you know?"

"Not I; but I guessed as much."

"Mother's been ill these twenty years, and has to be carried to her bed. She thinks she's a burthen, so we do it to humour her."

"I thought as much."

"Then why don't you take your money?" said a hoarse, rough voice, that chased away all the sentiment of the affair, and Geoffrey started round to see that the fierce-looking old man was leaning over a block of granite, his arms crossed, and his chin resting upon them. "Take your money and go."

"No," said Geoffrey, in his off-hand way. "No: thanks. I want the sweets for the children."

"Yours?" said the old fellow, roughly.

"Mine? Hang it, man; no."

Geoffrey turned to the girl, and looked at her, laughing merrily; but this seemed to irritate the old man, who came fiercely from behind the granite block, thrusting his hands far down into his pockets, and scowling angrily.

"Look here, young man," he said, hoarsely, "you're a stranger here, and don't know us."

"Not yet," said Geoffrey, "but I dare say I soon shall."

"Take your money, and don't come again," said the old man, hoarsely.

"You are a nice, pleasant-spoken old gentleman," said Geoffrey, nonchalantly, as he coolly opened the paper bag, and took out one of the sticks of candy. "Have a sweet?"

The man uttered a fierce growl that sounded like an oath, and took a step forward in a menacing way, but the girl sprang forward, and threw her arm across his chest.

"D'yer want me to hurl you off the rocks?" he said savagely.

"Be quiet, father," cried the girl. "The gentleman means no harm."

"Go in, Bess," he shouted, and, shaking her off, he went close up to Geoffrey, who did not give way an inch, but looked full in the fierce, repulsive face thrust close to his, till the old man lowered his eyes, and stepped on one side, muttering angrily.

"Do you always treat strangers like this, Master Prawle?" said Geoffrey, smiling.

"Go away, I tell ye," said the old man, fiercely. "We want no dealings with the people."

"Don't anger father, sir," said the girl, who, however, seemed to be in no wise put out by the old man's savage resentment.

"Not I, my girl," replied Geoffrey; "but what is the matter with your mother?"

"She fell off the cliff one night," said the girl, quickly.

"Tell him to go, Bess," growled her father. "We don't want him here."

"I asked the gentleman to come, father," said the girl. Then, turning to Geoffrey, "Thank you kindly, sir. It pleases mother."

"Don't name it, my lass," replied Geoffrey, smiling, and the girl looked at him very fixedly, as she watched every turn in his frank, open face. "Good-day," he continued. "Good-day, Master Prawle."

The old man scowled at him by way of reply, and then stood watching him till he had climbed back to the edge of the ravine, where, turning to glance down, Geoffrey saw father and daughter below, the latter returning his salute, as he waved his hand before passing out of their sight.

"Old boy thought I was a hawk after his pigeon," said Geoffrey, lightly. "What an ill-conditioned old ogre! But there must be some good under his rough bark. Prawle, eh? Elizabeth, otherwise Bess. And the old woman! What a piteous face! Twenty years an invalid! Ah, well! I don't think Mr Prawle, of the hoarse voice and fierce tone, need be afraid; but I'd rather not offend him, say about the fair Elizabeth, and then meet him—angry—say beside the shaft of one of those old mines."

He glanced then at his watch, and hastened his steps, for the time of his engagement at An Morlock was drawing near.

Chapter Ten.

Geoffrey Makes a Discovery.

"You are an extremely handsome young woman, and I like the bright, intelligent look in your eyes," said Geoffrey Trethick to himself; "but I'll swear you have got a temper."

"You are a nice, frank, manly fellow," said Rhoda Penwynn to herself; "and I wonder whether you are as sensible and not so stubborn as you look."

Introductions were just over in Mr Penwynn's drawing-room, and Geoffrey, who was in no wise taken aback by the splendour of his host's surroundings, walked across to where, cold and stiff and quiet, his travelling-companion stood, with one arm upon the mantelpiece, looking uneasily on.

"It seems as if we are to be thrown together," said Geoffrey, offering the young clergyman his hand, which the latter took as if under protest, and then glanced from Mr Penwynn to his daughter, as if in apology for allowing himself to be claimed as an acquaintance by his bluff travelling-companion.

"You have met Mr Lee, then?" said the host stiffly.

"Yes—yes," said the new vicar; "Mr Trethick is an old Oxford man."

"And you don't like him," said Rhoda to herself, as she observed every thing; "and I don't like you."

"We were fellow-passengers by the coach this morning," said Geoffrey, and as he spoke he glanced by Mr Penwynn at where Rhoda was re-arranging some flowers, and found that the Reverend Edward Lee had brought his spectacles to bear in the same direction. Then, looking back at his host, he fancied that this gentleman had not been unobservant of the glances of his guests.

Mr Penwynn smiled to himself directly after as Geoffrey moved towards Rhoda, and began talking to her about the view from the drawing-room window and his walk along the coast; but the young clergyman looked at his host as if in remonstrance at his allowing this stranger to make so free, when the door opened, and the servant announced,—

"Mr Tregenna!"

"Ah, Tregenna! You are late. Glad to see you."

"Business, my dear sir. The old story—business. My dear Miss Penwynn, you must forgive me," he continued, speaking in a low voice full of deference, but with lips that did not seem to move as he spoke, as Rhoda turned from Geoffrey, and took a couple of steps towards the fresh comer—a tall, handsome man of *distingué* appearance, but with a rather sallow complexion, made deeper by his jet black hair and whiskers.

Geoffrey started slightly, and then gazed keenly at this man, who bent down over Rhoda Penwynn's hand as he took it, and retained it just a moment longer than custom dictates, and smiled in her face directly after as, in a quiet, self-possessed way, she said that they had not been waiting.

"Waiting? No!" said Mr Penwynn smiling; "but I should have thought you would have been first."

"I hurried all I could," said Tregenna, as a slight flush came over Rhoda's cheek; "but one cannot always command one's time, even to devote it to one's aims."

Geoffrey Trethick half-closed his eyes, as he looked on trying to think out something which had puzzled him, but without avail, and for the moment he gave it up, and began to turn over the leaves of an album, but taking ample notice the while of what was going on.

"If I were interested in mine host's daughter," mused Geoffrey, "I should feel uncomfortable about that dark, smoothly-shaven gentleman. I don't like the look of his mouth, and I don't like his eyes, and—Most happy!"

This last in answer to his host's introduction to the last comer, who smiled upon him in the most friendly of ways, asked him what he thought of Carnac, seemed to be particularly refined, and then turned to go through a little preliminary chat with the new clergyman, who was more bland and agreeable than he had been to his travelling-companion.

"Ah! the parson gets on better with you, my fine fellow," said Geoffrey. "You haven't so many corners as I have. Humph! I don't like you, though. You seem to be the man in possession, though, here, and certainly she is a very charming girl."

He met Rhoda's eyes as these thoughts passed through his mind, and she encountered his gaze with a frank, open look, though he fancied that she seemed a shade paler than when he was talking to her a few minutes before.

Just then dinner was announced, and Mr Penwynn turned to speak to Geoffrey, but bit his lip and glanced at Tregenna, who, however, only smiled back and nodded, as if amused; for Rhoda, acting the part of mistress of the house, extended her gloved hand so unmistakably that Geoffrey stepped forward, the hand was laid upon his arm, and, passing the others, he led her across the hall to the handsome dining-room, thinking to himself that by rights the Reverend Edward Lee ought to have occupied his place.

The dinner was good and well served, every thing making it evident that Mr Penwynn was a wealthy man, and one who liked to show it; but the ostentation was a good deal toned down by his child's refined taste, and was not obtrusive. The conversation kept up was such as would be heard at any gentleman's table, and it soon became evident that the West-country banker and his daughter were well-informed, and loved and cultivated refinement.

Geoffrey particularly noted how clever and gentlemanly Mr Tregenna could be. By degrees it dawned upon him that he was the principal solicitor of the place, and without its troubling him in the slightest degree, he made out that Tregenna was evidently a suitor for Rhoda Penwynn's hand. Both father and lover showed this, the former being plainly in favour of the match; while, in spite of her efforts to the contrary, Rhoda Penwynn displayed her consciousness of Tregenna's expressive looks by redoubling her attention to Geoffrey and the new vicar—Geoffrey chatting freely, and in the most unembarrassed way, so different to any young man she had met before, and questioning her largely about the place and people.

"A glass of wine with you, Mr Trethick," said the host, who, in spite of advances, adhered somewhat to old customs. "Tregenna, will you join us?"

"With pleasure," said the latter, looking up and smiling, and as he did so the thought that had been puzzling Geoffrey all through the dinner met with a solution.

He had been wondering—his wonder running like a vein through the whole of the conversation—where he had met Tregenna before; but now it came to him that for certain they had never met, but that it was that smooth, deep, mellow voice that he had heard, but where?

"I have it," he mentally exclaimed, as, raising his glass, he looked full in John Tregenna's eyes. "You were the fellow I heard talking to that girl by the ruined mine?"

Chapter Eleven.

An Opinion of Tregenna.

"You're a nice, smooth scoundrel," said Geoffrey to himself, as he set down his glass, "and I have been drinking with you when I ought to have thrown the wine in your face, and told you that you were a blackguard.—But we don't do this sort of thing in society. As long as there is a good thick coat of whitewash over the sepulchre, society does not mind, but smiles on ladies with no reputation if they are rich, and never opens its ears to the acts, deeds, and exploits of our nice young men. I wonder whether mine host knows your character, and what my fair young hostess feels? Don't seem very sentimental about him, anyhow; and here's my reverend friend quite cottoning to black whiskers, and enjoying his small talk. Ah! it's a strange world."

A brisk little conversation was just now going off between Rhoda Penwynn and the new vicar, Tregenna throwing in a word here and there, Mr Penwynn smiling approval as he listened, while Geoffrey went on eating heartily, and following his thought.

"I may be wrong," he went on, "but I feel pretty sure I could say something that would make you change colour, my smooth, cleanly-shaven gentleman, and if I did I should make you my enemy for life. Well, perhaps I could bear that, but I don't want enemies, I want friends. If I'm right, though, I don't think you ought to win ma'mselle unless you reform, probationise, and she condones. There, what a string! As the old women say—'tain't no business of mine."

He glanced across at Tregenna just then, and that gentleman met his eye, smiled, and the discussion being over, asked him how long he meant to stay in the west.

"Stay?" said Geoffrey sharply. "Altogether."

Tregenna raised his eyebrows a little, and just then the young vicar, in reply to a question from Mr Penwynn, began speaking, in slow measured accents, about the vicarage to be built, and the alterations he meant to make at the church. A bright colour suffused his smooth pale face, as he found that Rhoda was listening to him, and that he was now monopolising the attention of the rest. However, he seemed to master his nervousness, and spoke out firmly and well to the end.

"You may try," said Mr Penwynn, smiling, "but I am afraid, my dear sir, that your ideas are as Utopian as those of Mr Trethick there. However, experience teaches, as the Latin proverb goes; but, as an old inhabitant, I venture to say that before many weeks are over, both of you gentlemen will confess that you have undertaken a Herculean task. Religiously, the people of the lower orders are as wedded to Wesleyanism as in their mining tactics they are to their old-fashioned ways. Our rough Cornish folk, gentlemen, are as hard to move as our own granite."

"Perhaps so, papa," said Rhoda; "but we have not had many efforts made here to move them."

"Thank you, Miss Penwynn," said Geoffrey, flushing, and speaking with animation. "Those are the first encouraging words I have heard. Your daughter has touched the very point, Mr Penwynn. I don't want to talk like an egotist, but, speaking as an engineer, if you will show me one of your biggest pieces of Cornish granite, I'll find a means of giving it a start; and I'll be bound to say that if Mr Lee here is as determined as I, he will find a way of moving the hardest of your Cornish hearts. Sir, I believe in that little word 'Try!'"

The Reverend Edward Lee coloured slightly, and turned his glasses with more of interest upon the speaker, but he did not interpose.

"I wish you both every success," said Tregenna, smiling first on one and then on the other, and Mr Penwynn nodded his head, and laughed, saying,—

"Youth is sanguine, Mr Trethick. *Try!*"

"I will, Mr Penwynn," said Geoffrey, in a voice that, though quiet, was so full of the spirit expressed by those two determined words that Tregenna glanced sharply at him, and then at Rhoda, to see what effect they had had upon her.

She was bending a little forward, her lips parted, and a curious look in her face, as she gazed in the guest's countenance, till, instinctively becoming aware that Tregenna's eyes were fixed upon her, she let her own fall, but only to raise them directly after with a half-offended look of inquiry, as if asking why she was watched, and soon after she left the table.

The gentlemen stayed but a short time over their wine, for Tregenna, after exchanging glances with Mr Penwynn, rose and made for the drawing-room, while Mr Penwynn suggested a cigar in the garden.

"Yes, I should enjoy a smoke," said Geoffrey, who suspected that this was a manoeuvre to give Tregenna an opportunity for a *tête-à-tête*, but the vicar declined.

"I have not smoked now for many years," he said, and he glanced to the door as if to escape to the drawing-room in Tregenna's wake, but Mr Penwynn proceeded to endorse Geoffrey's suspicions.

"Then I will not smoke either," he said, passing his arm through that of his guest. "We'll have a look round at the ferns and flowers till Mr Trethick has finished his cigar. They'll bring us coffee directly, and then we will join them in the drawing-room."

There was no escape, so the young clergyman was marched off to inspect the peculiarities of his host's choice ferns, with the beauties of the various sub-tropical plants that the banker had collected in his well-kept, rock-sheltered terrace. These being ended, the various points of interest in the distance about the bay were pointed put, evidently to gain time.

Meanwhile Geoffrey, who felt somewhat amused, sat upon a rock, smoked an excellent cigar, and thought a good deal as he gazed out to sea.

"Parson's bored," he said to himself. "He wants to get off to the drawing-room, and beam through his glasses on Miss Penwynn, who is unmistakably being courted by the smooth, dark gentleman. Most likely he is just now, with papa's consent, popping the question. If she accepts him I should think it's a pity, for somehow Mr Tregenna is not my *beau-ideal* of a gentleman, while she is a bright, clever girl. However, it is no business of mine."

He paused to knock the very long, carefully-preserved ash off the end of his cigar, which process seemed to be looked upon as one of very great importance, the cigar being petted and carefully smoothed down at the moist end where a little of the leaf was loose, lest this opening should at all interfere with the drawing; after which he tenderly replaced the roll of weed in his lips, uttered a sigh of satisfaction, such as might be given by any young man whose digestion was in perfect order, and exhaled a soft blue cloud of smoke.

"Curious thing this love," he continued to himself. "Every one seems to go in for it, to the ruffling of a calm, smooth life, and gets into trouble. What a blessing it is that I have no inclinations in that direction! Humph! I wonder what the lady has said? Bah! stuff! nonsense! what is it to me? I'm not going to set up as head moralist, and meddle with these affairs. Her father must know best."

He rose, and strolled down to the end of the terrace, to lean over a rugged mass of granite, and he was still there, enjoying the delicious calm of the evening, and marvelling at the beauty of the shadowy, phosphorescent sea, when he heard his host's voice, and throwing aside the fragment of the cigar whose aroma was beginning to be marred by touches of burnt moustache, he turned to meet him.

"Tea is ready, Mr Trethick," he said. "Really I ought to apologise for my neglect."

"Neglect, eh?" said Geoffrey, laughing. "Why, I could bear to be neglected like this every night. You gave me one of the best cigars I ever lit, and let me lounge here and smoke it in peace. Don't apologise, Mr Penwynn; I am quite satisfied."

In spite of his indifference, however, Geoffrey could not refrain from looking curiously at Rhoda and Tregenna as he entered the drawing-room, but their unruffled features told no tales.

Rhoda was seated near the window, and Tregenna on the opposite side, looking more gentlemanly and polished than ever; while Rhoda at once rose, and began talking to the new vicar, leaving Geoffrey to chat over the handed-round tea to Tregenna about mines, their few successes, and their many failures.

"Parson's happy now, I hope," thought Geoffrey, as Mr Penwynn came and carried off Tregenna, after a word of apology about business; and then, as they stood talking at the other end of the room, Mr Penwynn's face was so fully in the light, that Geoffrey could not help noticing that he changed countenance.

"Master Tregenna's saying something unpleasant about business," thought Geoffrey. "The glorious uncertainty of the law is, perhaps, having mine host upon the hip."

"Do you like music, Mr Trethick?" said a voice at his side, and he found that Rhoda Penwynn had left the vicar and approached unobserved.

"You wicked young puss," he said to himself. "You've come to make a buffer of me. That's it, is it? Papa is turning angry about you, eh? and you fear a collision? Well, you shall find me full of spring." Then, smiling—"Yes, I love music," he said aloud. "I am a worshipper at a distance—rather a mild one, I should say. You will sing something, I hope?"

Rhoda crossed readily to the piano, and sang a couple of ballads very sweetly, her voice being rich and resonant, and then it seemed to Geoffrey, who was turning over the music for her, that, in spite of a very brave effort to appear unconcerned, she was growing extremely nervous, for, instead of leaving the piano, she began to pick up piece after piece of music, glancing sharply from her father to Tregenna, and then at the vicar, who was placidly examining an album of scraps.

"I wish you sang, Mr Trethick," she said at last.

"Do you?" he said, looking down at her troubled face.

"Yes. Do you? Will you?"

"Nature has not been very generous to me in the matter of voice. At least she has given me plenty, but the quality is coarse. I'll try something though—with you."

"A duet? Oh, yes!" she said eagerly. "What have we? Could you—do you like Italian?"

"Yes," he said quietly, as he noticed how agitated she was growing, and how bravely she fought to keep it down, and preserve her composure towards her father's guests. "Shall we try that *Trovatore* piece that you just turned over—*Ai nostri monti*."

"Oh, yes!" she exclaimed, and there was a silence in the room as the rich harmony of the well-blended voices floated out upon the night air. For, in spite of his modest declaration, Geoffrey Trethick possessed a full deep voice, and, being a good musician, he thoroughly enjoyed his task.

"Rather hard on a baritone to set him to sing tenor, Miss Penwynn," he said, laughing. "But I say, what a delicious voice you have!"

Rhoda glanced at him sharply, but the expression of admiration she could see was perfectly sincere, and she knew at once that he was not a man likely to flatter.

That duet gave Rhoda Penwynn time to recover herself, and she was perfectly calm by the end—a calm she managed to maintain until the guests were about to depart.

"By the way, Mr Lee," said the banker, "have you obtained apartments? It is a disgrace to our place that the vicarage is not rebuilt."

"Oh, yes!" said the vicar, mildly, "I have obtained rooms."

"At Mrs Mullion's, I presume?"

"No," said the vicar, turning his glasses for a moment on Geoffrey. "Mr Trethick has taken those."

"Indeed! Then you are at the hotel?"

"No; I have made arrangements to board with a Miss Pavey, at a very pleasant cottage—Dinas Vale. Good-night!"

"I'll walk as far as your rooms with you, Mr Trethick," said Tregenna, as they stepped out into the road. "Have a cigar?"

They lit up, and strolled along the up-and-down ill-paved way, Tregenna evidently laying himself out to make friends with the new arrival, who made himself frank and pleasant, but, somehow, not cordial.

"Drop in and have a chat with me, Mr Trethick," said Tregenna, at parting. "I may be able to further your views. Any one will show you my place."

"Know it," said Geoffrey. "Saw the brass plate on the gate."

"Yes," laughed Tregenna, "one has to put out a sign. But come and see me; perhaps I can help you."

"I don't like after-dinner promises," laughed Geoffrey. "They are rash. I may put you to the test."

"Rash? Oh, no! We are not like that in the west. I shall be only too glad to help you to the best of my power. Good-night!"

"Good-night!"

Geoffrey remained at the garden gate thinking that his companion had spoken a great deal more loudly than was necessary. Then, as he had not finished his cigar, he resolved to smoke it out, and enjoy for a few minutes the cool night air.

"I don't like to be hasty," he thought, "but I scarcely think that I shall trust you, Mr Tregenna, beyond the reach of my hand. If I am not very much mistaken your civility has a meaning, and you are a confounded scoundrel. If not, I beg your pardon."

"Yes," he said, half aloud, after smoking on for a few minutes and thinking deeply, "it was your voice that I heard down in that old building. Now I wonder who was the girl?"

As the thought crossed his mind, the faint sound of a closing casement smote his ear, when, like a flash, the light came.

"By George! of course," he said. "The other voice was familiar, too. It was our pretty little maiden here. Hang it all! I've tumbled into the thick of a mystery, and if I don't take care I shall be in the middle of the mess."

"Hah?" he exclaimed, as he tapped at the door, "As I said before, it's no business of mine, and her father knows best; but this love-making is the greatest nuisance under the sun, or I ought to say the moon."

Chapter Twelve.

Cold Water.

Mr John Tregenna had lost no time upon leaving the dining-room, but joined Rhoda, who sat looking rather pale, but prepared for the attack.

She knew that it must come, and, in spite of a feeling of dread, she felt almost glad, when, seating himself beside her, he began, with plenty of calm, quiet assurance, to plead his cause, she listening patiently the while to all he had to say.

Every word he uttered was to Rhoda as so much trouble over, and she would not look nor speak until he had finished, being determined to hear all he had to say, and to let him say it without hinderance, so that the matter should be ended once and for all.

He was too cunning a man—too well versed in human nature—to attempt heroics with such a girl as Rhoda, and there was no enraptured catching of hands, no falling upon one knee, no passionate adjuration. Tregenna began by telling her that he had her father's consent, and that he only wanted hers. That for years past he had loved her with a patient, growing love, which now permeated—he said permeated—his very being, and that it was his only desire that she should become his wife.

As he spoke he held ready in one hand a very handsome diamond hoop ring, which was to be the token of their betrothal, for he felt no doubt upon the subject. Rhoda might make a little demur, and be a bit distant and coquettish, but he felt sure that she had been well schooled by her father, and she was just the woman to become his wife. She attracted him with her handsome face and fine *svelte* figure; she would look well at the head of his table; she would give him position; and, what was more, her father was very wealthy, and that wealth must finally come to him.

Rhoda caught a glimpse of the ring in his hand, for as he fidgeted it about a ray flashed from it betraying its presence, and she knew what it was, for her lips tightened, and a hard look came into her eyes.

At last he was silent, and waiting her reply.

It was a hard task, but she was now well strung up, and turning to him quietly, she said,—

"Don't you think, Mr Tregenna, that it is necessary in such a case for there to exist a mutual feeling of attachment?"

There was something so terribly cold and matter-of-fact in this—something, so to speak, so ungirlish—that it came upon Tregenna like a thunder-clap; but he was equal to the emergency.

"No," he said eagerly; "certainly not, if the lady has no prior attachment, which you, dear Rhoda, I am sure, have not."

"No, Mr Tregenna, I certainly have not," she replied, quietly.

"It is only necessary," he exclaimed, "that the man should love. The love of the woman will grow."

"I do not agree with you, Mr Tregenna," she replied, quietly.

"But, my dearest Rhoda—"

"Mr Tregenna," she said firmly, "let us understand one another at once. From a feeling of respect for my father's friend I have heard you to the end, and my respect for you has grown as I have noticed the gentlemanly manner in which you have made known to me your unfortunate attachment."

"Unfortunate?" he exclaimed, looking at her almost stunned.

"Yes, unfortunate; because I must tell you frankly, Mr Tregenna, that I cannot give you the slightest hope."

"My dear Rhoda," he exclaimed, "you mistake me. I do not ask you to be my wife now, but by-and-by. I only ask for time."

"Time can make no difference, Mr Tregenna," said Rhoda, firmly; "and I have to ask you now, as a gentleman, to accept my refusal of your suit. Once, Mr Tregenna, for all, I can never become your wife."

"Then you do love some one else," he cried, his rage for the moment mastering him.

"Mr Tregenna," said Rhoda, coldly, "this is a matter I am not bound to confess to you, but you will please recollect that I told you I had no prior attachment."

"Yes, yes," he exclaimed hastily. "I had forgotten. I was mad. Pray forgive me, Rhoda. But listen, pray listen. You cannot think how cruelly this cuts me to the heart."

"I grieve to cause you pain, Mr Tregenna," said Rhoda, "but you must give me credit for the fact that this has been none of my seeking. I must ask you now to let me bring what has been a most painful interview to an end."

"Painful?" he cried passionately. "It is death to all my hopes. But I cannot accept this as final. Time will work a change."

"Time will work no change, Mr Tregenna," said Rhoda, firmly. "As my father's friend I have heard you out, and I have tried to reply as kindly as I could."

Tregenna saw that he would be only injuring his cause by pressing his suit, and he desisted; but there was a curious look in his eye, which made Rhoda shiver, as he exclaimed,—

"But the future, Rhoda—Miss Penwynn—dear Miss Penwynn? I am not to take this as a complete dismissal from your presence."

"Mr Tregenna," replied Rhoda, "I have told you plainly that I can never become your wife. If I have been too blunt, or seemed unmaidenly, you must forgive it, and recollect that I have never known a mother's care, but from a child had to assume a woman's duties as the mistress of this house. As to the future—you are my father's friend."

"And yours," he cried eagerly.

"My father's friends are my friends," said Rhoda, rather coldly. "We will then henceforth consider the words which you have addressed to me to-night as having never been spoken."

"As you will," he said hoarsely; "but so long as this heart continues to beat I shall—"

"Mr Tregenna," exclaimed Rhoda, rising, and speaking with dignity, "you are hurt and grieved, but I must ask your forbearance in this."

"Forgive me," he said humbly, as he bent down his head, and hid the strange look that crossed his face, "it shall be as you wish. We are friends, then. What shall we talk about now," he added, with an almost imperceptible sneer, "books or flowers?"

"I was about to ask you what you think of our guests," said Rhoda, trying to be calm and unconcerned, for Tregenna made no effort to leave her.

"Indeed!" he said listlessly, sinking back in his seat as Rhoda took a chair at a short distance. "Do you wish to know?"

"Yes, I should be glad to hear."

"Well," he said cynically, "my honest conviction about our new vicar is that he is a conceited, self-sufficient University prig, stuffed full of classics, and no more suited to manage the people of these parts than that rather obtrusive, stubborn-looking gentleman, Trethick, is to make his way amongst our miners. They will both come to grief."

"Do you think so?"

"Undoubtedly. One will stay three months, and then exchange; the other three weeks, and then probably go abroad."

"Am I to take that as a prophecy?" said Rhoda, smiling.

"Yes; and mark its fulfilment," he replied, trying to speak lightly.

"I think differently," said Rhoda. "As to Mr Lee, I will hazard no conjecture; but Mr Trethick seems to me the kind of man who will force his way by sheer energy."

Tregenna's eyes glistened as he watched the face before him with jealous suspicion, but it was as placid and emotionless as could be.

"Do you think so?"

"I do indeed," replied Rhoda.

"Perhaps you are right," he said. "He is an interesting-looking youth."

He felt ready to bite off his own tongue as he uttered this sneer, which escaped him in the bitterness of his spirit, and he awoke to the falseness of the step he had taken by the look of surprise and resentment that appeared in Rhoda's face.

"Then we are to be friends," he hastened to say eagerly; "always to be the best of friends?"

"Yes, Mr Tregenna," replied Rhoda, coldly; and their *tête-à-tête* was ended by the entry of the party from the garden.

Chapter Thirteen.

A Visit Underground.

"Well, boy!"

"Well, old gentleman!"

The old gentleman, to wit, Uncle Paul, very yellow, very clean-shaven, and carefully got up, seemed disposed to resent this bluff manner of address; but he swallowed his annoyance with a gulp, thumped his cane on the gravel, and went on,—

"Up early, then. The early bird gets the first pick of the worms."

"Yes, and stands the best chance of being caught by a prowling cat," said Geoffrey.

"Never mind; get up early and work. Be industrious, and save your money. That's the way to get on. Take care of the pennies; the pounds will take care of themselves."

"Nonsense!" replied Geoffrey. "While you are scraping for pennies, you are missing your pounds."

"Rubbish!" said the old man, sharply. "Get up early, sir, and work. Early to bed, and early to rise, makes a man healthy, and wealthy, and wise."

"Which is duly proved, as *Punch* says," laughed Geoffrey, "by the enormous fortunes accumulated, the health enjoyed, and the wisdom displayed by chimney-sweeps, and other people who rise before the lark."

"Why, you're a sceptic, sir," said the old man, showing his yellow teeth. "Do you know that's a time-honoured proverb?"

"Yes; but I don't believe in time-honoured proverbs," replied Geoffrey. "Early to bed, and early to rise, makes a man healthy, and wealthy, and wise, indeed!"

"And you are neither of the two last," chuckled Uncle Paul, "even if you are the first."

"Quite right, old gentleman," said Geoffrey, good-humouredly; "but I get up early on principle."

"Well, then, you didn't have too much wine last night?"

"No."

"Dine with Penwynn?"

"I did."

"Any one else there?"

"Yes."

"Who?"

"A Mr Tregenna. Like to know what we had for dinner?"

"No?" roared Uncle Paul. "Hang the dinner, sir. Any one else there?"

"The new vicar."

"Hang the new vicar. The other fellow had some sense. He never asked me why I didn't go to church."

"Don't you go?"

"I? no. It's very odd," said the old man, grimly; "but I always have a fit of bile coming on about Saturday night, and it lasts all Sunday. So you saw Tregenna?"

"Yes, I saw Mr Tregenna."

"Slimy serpent. Hang him."

"By all means, if you like," said Geoffrey, laughing, for the choleric ways and speeches of the old man amused him.

"What did you think of the daughter, eh?" said the old fellow, with a croak that was evidently intended to do duty for a chuckle.

"Very nice, sensible girl."

"Oh! you think so, do you?"

"I do certainly."

"Marry her," said Uncle Paul, giving him a poke with his cane. "Plenty of money. Couldn't do better."

"But she could," replied Geoffrey, laughing. "No, old gentleman, I'm not a marrying man."

"Or look here," chuckled the old man, "I can find you a wife. No need though, she'll fall in love with you herself without asking. Lovely woman, sir. Martha—Martha Pavey. Patty you know, but she's not plump. He! he! he! Well matured and has a little income of her own. She isn't above forty-four. Good-looking once. Nice shaped mouth till she set up in it a couple of rows of enamelled tombstones to the memory of so many departed teeth. Looks hard and unkissable now. I laughed at 'em when I saw 'em first. Never forgiven me since, and she always looks at me as if she would bite. Poor thing! Thinks I didn't detect 'em, and goes about complaining of toothache."

"Poor woman," said Geoffrey.

"Poor fool!" snarled the other. "She thinks of nothing else but men."

"Woman's nature," said Geoffrey, "but I suppose it is the privilege of the old to be severe. You are old, you know."

"Devilish," said the other. "Ah, boy, when you lean your face on your hand, and can feel your skull easily through your skin, you may take it for granted that you are pretty old."

"Suppose so," said Geoffrey. "Going my way? No, I suppose not."

"How the devil d'you know where I'm going?" cried the old fellow, fiercely. "I am going your way, sir; I am."

"Come along, then," said Geoffrey, coolly.

"Where?" said Uncle Paul, who was thrown off his guard.

"I'm going underground."

"Bah! That's very clever, I suppose you think. That's modern sharp, fast wit, is it? I'm going underground when my time comes, sir, like a man, and perhaps that won't be till after you, sir."

The old man wiped his face upon his orange bandanna here, and looked fiercer than ever.

"Why, what a jolly old pepperbox you are!" cried Geoffrey, laughing outright. "You are all cayenne and gunpowder. Wit be hanged! I said I was going underground, and so I am. I'm going down Horton Friendship mine. Mr Tregenna gave me his card for the manager."

"Ho!" ejaculated the old gentleman, calming down. "Nice man, Tregenna. Smooth and polished. Make a great friend of him; I would if I were you. He'll show you how to go to the devil faster than any man I know."

"I'm afraid I want no teaching, Mr Paul," said Geoffrey, gravely. "I say, by the way, whose cottage is that down in the cove about a couple of miles along the cliff?"

"Oh! you've been there, have you," said the old man, chuckling. "You are making some nice acquaintances, boy! Did you see pretty Bess?"

"I saw a fine, handsome-looking lass."

"That's she. Did she ill-wish you?"

"Not that I know of. Does she do that sort of thing?" said Geoffrey, smiling.

"Oh, yes!" sneered the old gentleman. "They say she's a witch, and her father's as scoundrelly an old wrecker and smuggler as ever breathed. He's one of your kidney, too. Been a miner."

"A nice character to give a neighbour," said Geoffrey.

"Confound him! He's no neighbour of mine, sir. You'd better get your new friend to go down Horton mine with you."

"What—Tregenna?"

"No, no; Smuggler Prawle. He knows more about the mines than any one here."

"Does he?" said Geoffrey, eagerly. "Well, perhaps I may ask him some day."

They were standing just in front of the cottage, and as he spoke Geoffrey glanced upward, to see that Madge Mullion was at the upper window, standing back, but evidently gazing intently down upon him, ready to dart back, though, the moment he raised his eyes; and he went away thinking of his little adventure at Wheal Carnac the previous day, and of how strangely he had become possessed of a secret that might, if it were known, raise him up one, two, if not three, bitter enemies during his stay.

It was a great nuisance, he thought, this bit of knowledge, for his conscience pricked him, and he asked himself whether he ought not to make some communication to Uncle Paul or Mrs Mullion.

"And be called a meddlesome fool for my pains!" he exclaimed angrily. "No; I will not interfere with other people's business. I have my hands full enough as it is."

His way out of the little town was over a rough granite-strewn hill, where the wind blew briskly, and the grass and heather seemed to be kept cut down close by the sharp Atlantic gales. His goal was a gaunt-looking building, perched on the highest point of the eminence, and of the customary Cornish mining type—a square, granite engine-house, with tall chimney, and a great beam projecting from the side, rising and falling at slow intervals as it pumped the water from the depths below, to send it flowing in a dirty stream towards the sea.

Geoffrey went swinging along as if he had all the work in the world upon his shoulders, till he became aware of a figure coming in his direction by another track—one which evidently joined his a little on ahead—and he noted that the figure carried a fly-rod over his shoulder.

"Why, it's the doctor off fishing!" said Geoffrey to himself, as he recognised the fresh-coloured face surmounting the light tweeds. "What a horribly healthy place this must be. Morning, doctor!"

"Good-morning. Did you get your lodgings all right?" said the newcomer, scanning Geoffrey's face as if in search of the seeds of disease, and looking disappointed.

"Yes, thanks."

"Well, don't fall in love with Madge Mullion, or old Mr Paul will be setting me to work to poison you."

"Confound it all!" cried Geoffrey, facing round as he stopped short. "Do you people here think of nothing else but falling in love?"

"Well, I don't know," said the doctor, dreamily, as he pushed his soft hat on one side, and gave his head a rub. "Fortunately for me they do think a great deal of that sort of thing."

"So it seems. I've heard enough of it during the past four-and-twenty hours to make it seem as if your people thought young women were gunpowder, and I was a match."

"Ah, yes!" said the doctor, sadly. "It's the old story, you know—marrying and giving in marriage. What should we do for our population without?"

"Population don't seem to keep you very busy, doctor."

"Pretty well," he said quietly: "pretty well; people have very large families about here, but they emigrate."

"Do they?" said Geoffrey.

"Yes, the mining trade has been bad. But people have very large families about here," said the doctor, with a sigh. "I've got ten of them."

"Fruitful vine and olive branches round the table, eh?" said Geoffrey.

"Ye-es," said the doctor, making an imaginary cast with his fly-rod over the heather; "but when the vine is too fruitful it rather shades the table, you know."

"So I should suppose," replied Geoffrey, with a slight grimace. "Have you good fishing here?"

"No—oh no! Nothing but small trout in the little streams, and they are getting poisoned by the mining refuse."

"I'll try them some day," said Geoffrey.

"I wouldn't if I were you," said the doctor, nervously. "It isn't worth your while, and it's very hard work to get a dish now-a-days," and he glanced with anxious eyes at his companion. For, on non-busy mornings, Mr James Rumsey, MRCSE—the "doctor" being a local degree—found it useful to take his rod and capture a dish of trout for the home dinner, if he did not go out in the bay, in a borrowed boat, in search of something more substantial.

"Ah well, we'll see," said Geoffrey. "Yonder's Horton Friendship, is it not?"

"Yes, that's it," said the doctor, who seemed relieved. "That's the manager's office close by. They've got a manager there."

"Oh! have they?" said Geoffrey, who was amused by the doctor's subdued, weary way. "All right; I'm going to see it, though. Good-morning."

"Good-morning," said the doctor, and making dreamy casts with his rod, he went on over the heather.

"Looks dull, and as if he had lived too much in the shade—of the vine and olive branches," said Geoffrey, as he strode along. "Well, ten branches would keep off a good deal of the sun of a man's life. What a row those stamps make!"

The rattling noise was caused by a row of iron-faced piles, which were being raised and let fall by a great cogged barrel upon a quantity of pieces of tin ore, with which they were fed, and as he drew nearer to watch them, the noise was almost deafening; but all the same he stopped to watch them curiously, and evidently dissatisfied with the primitive nature of the machine.

Farther on he paused to watch where a dozen women and boys were busy directing the flow of a stream of muddy water over a series of sloping boards, so as to wash the crushed ore free from earthy particles and powdered stone, till it fell of its own gravity into a trough prepared for its reception, where it looked like so much coffee-grounds waiting to be taken out and dried.

"Very, very primitive, and full of waste," muttered Geoffrey then, as he noted the ruddy, healthy look of the people who ceased working to stare at the stranger, an example followed by a couple of men whose clothes seemed reddened by some mineral.

The manager welcomed the visitor in the most civil manner, and furnished him with a rough suit of flannel for the descent, as well as a stiff, solid kind of hat, which did duty for helmet, to protect his head from falling stones, and also for holder of a large tallow candle, which was stuck in front, so as to leave his hands at liberty.

The necessity for this was shown as soon as they reached the great square shaft, which was divided by a stout wooden partition into two. Up one of these came and went, by means of a rusty iron chain running over a wheel, a couple of long iron skeps or buckets, one of which, full of tin ore mingled with quartz rock and the ruddy mineral which Geoffrey had noted, came to the surface as they reached the pit.

"We go down here," said Geoffrey's companion, as a man lifted a heavy trap-door in a framework of planks, worn by many feet, and disclosing a dark hole up which came a hot, steaming vapour, which floated away in a thin cloud.

Geoffrey was as brave as most men, but he could not avoid a feeling of shrinking, as he saw what he had undertaken to do. He had expected to step into a cage such as was in use at coalpits, or perhaps have had to make use of the peculiar machine which lowered the miners from platform to platform ten or a dozen feet at a time; but here, as he gazed down into the dark, misty heat, he found that he would have to trust entirely to his own nerve and strength, for the descent was by a series of wet, greasy, nearly perpendicular ladders, placed zigzag from platform to platform, and with very little to save him from a fall too awful to contemplate.

The manager watched him narrowly before asking if he was ready, and on receiving an answer in the affirmative, he went down to the first wet, rotten-looking platform, where he stopped, and on being joined by Geoffrey he struck a match, and lit the candles in their caps.

"How deep is the mine?" asked Geoffrey.

"Two hundred fathom," was the reply.

"Twelve hundred feet!" said Geoffrey. "A good long descent by ladders. How is it you have no chain and cage?"

"Money!" was the abrupt reply, and after a warning to him to hold tight, the manager, a rough-spoken Cornishman, continued the descent, Geoffrey following, and finding every thing of the most primitive character. The ladders were clumsily made, splashed with candle grease, and terribly worn; the platforms so old and rotten that they seemed unsafe; and yet down for twelve hundred feet stretched these ladders, one after the other, in apparently interminable length.

Geoffrey Trethick's nerves were strong, but they were well put to the test, for every now and then a step of the ladder gave, or rattled beneath his weight. Now he would find a round so greasy that his foot would slip, while his candle sputtered, and several times nearly became extinguished, as they passed some shower of water that forced itself out of a vein in the rock.

"Rather rough work," said the manager, and his voice sounded echoing and strange in the gloomy shaft, seeming to whisper past him, and die away amidst the maze of ladders overhead.

"Rather!" replied Geoffrey, who was beginning to be drenched with perspiration. "How much farther?" he continued.

"Farther! Oh, we are not half-way down yet, sir—nothing like it," was the reply. "Like to rest?"

"No. Go on."

Down—down—down—lower and lower, in one apparently endless descent, with the noise of the trickling water growing louder and louder, and ever and again a hoarse, rattling, clanging noise as the chain bore buckets up and buckets down, and the great pump worked its mighty piston to free the mine from the water collected in the sump.

At times it was impossible not to feel that the bucket coming rushing through the darkness was descending upon the heads of those who laboriously climbed down, or that the enormous piston-rod would crush them to death at its next movement, instead of working steadily on the other side of the stout dividing boards. But the rod worked on, and the chain rattled as the buckets rose and fell, and with the trickling and plashing of the water growing louder, the ladders more wet and coated with grease, the platforms more slippery and rotten, Geoffrey sturdily kept on descending, but with the thought always forcing itself upon his brain that every ladder would have to be climbed before he could see the light of day.

But Geoffrey possessed all the stubborn determination of a true Englishman. He was truly one of those who did not know when he was beaten, and he was ready to go on with a task he had begun until brain and muscle completely gave way, and then only would he have paused and waited for strength before beginning again.

They had stopped on one of the platforms to snuff the flaring candles, a supply of which the manager carried in a tin box slung from his shoulder, when once more from the other part of the shaft came the rushing noise of the ascending and descending buckets, and so close did they sound that Geoffrey involuntarily shrank, feeling that they must strike against him and crush him on the narrow platform where he stood. But after this his ears grew more accustomed to the sound, and he began again plodding steadily downward, the frantic desire to cling tightly to the ladder and ask for help growing weaker as he became more used to the task.

At last the manager stopped, and pointed to a black opening before him like a little arch in the side of the shaft.

"Here's one of the old galleries," he said. "Would you like to see it?"

"Are the men at work here?"

"Work? No! Nor haven't been these fifty years. But there's enough to see there to give you an idea of the mine, and it would save you from going down farther if you are sick of it."

"I'm not sick of it," said Geoffrey, stoutly. "I'm only warm. Go on down to the bottom, and let's see the workings."

"All right!" said the manager, smiling, as he gave Geoffrey a peculiar look; and a fresh start was made.

"That fellow Tregenna has done this to try me," thought Geoffrey. "He could have given me an introduction to some mine where there was a regular cage. Never mind: I'm not chicken enough to give it up!" and, regardless of the rotten, wet ladders, he steadily went on, his spirits rising and his confidence increasing—for as he kept on noting the primitive way in which every thing was done, he felt more and more satisfied that if science were brought to bear in such a mine as this the profits must be largely increased.

For instance, he reasoned, here were the miners forced to undergo a long and arduous piece of toil before they could reach their work, and when their spell was over they had a fresh task to climb patiently up at a time when they were exhausted with toil, thus spending fruitlessly many hours every week.

"I've come to the right place," he thought, with a feeling of exultation coming over him, "and if I don't make my way it is my own fault."

"Tired?" said the manager, from below.

"No," was the sturdy answer. "Are you?"

A low, chuckling laugh came up to Geoffrey as he glanced down at the descending-light in the manager's hat.

"Well, if you put it in that way, sir, I am; and we'll get a little wind here by this old lode."

He stopped on the next platform, and, Geoffrey joining him, he once more snuffed the candles. There was another opening going horizontally into the bowels of the earth, where a lode of tin had been followed until it had become worthless. The roof glistened with huge crystals, which flashed in the light of the candles as they were held inside what looked like a subterranean passage into a castle, the abode of some giant of the nether world.

"I suppose the workings below are just like this?" said Geoffrey.

"Just the same, sir," was the eager reply; "and if you'd like to give up now, we could inspect this drive for a few hundred yards, and then go back. It's rather dangerous, though, for there have been some falls from the roof, and the galleries are like a net."

"But I don't want to give up," said Geoffrey, laughing, "and am ready as soon as ever you like."

"I never got any one to get down farther than this," said the manager, who started again, descending in silence, broken only by the occasional echoing whirr of the ascending and descending buckets, and the hiss and splash of the falling water. The heat seemed to increase, and the depth might have been miles, so endless seemed the ladders, and so tedious the descent.

"Give me a word if you feel likely to let go," said Geoffrey's guide just when they were on one of the wettest, weakest, and most slippery ladders of the descent. "There was a man once fell off this very ladder, and knocked off the man below him as well."

"Were they hurt?" said Geoffrey.

"Don't suppose as they were," was the cool reply. "They broke through platform after platform, for the woodwork was very rotten just then. They couldn't have known any thing after they fell, for they were quite dead when they got them up. It was a gashly job."

"Pleasant incident to relate now," thought Geoffrey. Then aloud— "You don't often have accidents?"

"Well, not very. We get a fall of rock sometimes, or a ladder breaks, or a man falls down the shaft. Now and then, too, there's a bit of an accident with the powder when they are blasting. But we do pretty well. We're not like your coal-mining folks, with their safety-lamps and gas."

"The mines are, of course, free from foul air?"

"Oh, yes; sweet as a nut."

"But how much farther is it?" said Geoffrey. "Surely we've come down a thousand feet."

"Well, yes; I suppose we have," said the man, coolly. "I don't think there's more than a half-dozen more ladders. Yes, seven," he said.

These were steadily climbed down, but seemed the longest of them all. At last, however, they stood beside the great sump or water-cistern, which received the end of the vast pumping apparatus, all of which Geoffrey carefully examined with a look of disgust at its primitive character and clumsiness.

Chapter Fourteen.

Pengelly—Miner.

"I should just like to shake hands with you, sir," said Geoffrey's guide, wiping his hand carefully upon his flannel trousers after using his fingers to snuff both candles. "I never thought you'd come down half-way—that I didn't. You're a plucked un, sir. That's about what you are, if you'll excuse me."

Geoffrey laughed, and shook hands with his guide, finding that he had risen wonderfully in the man's estimation, the manager looking at him quite admiringly.

"My name's Curnow," he said, "Richard Curnow, and I'd like to see you again, sir. Now what can I show you?"

"Every thing!" exclaimed Geoffrey. "Let me see all the workings, and what sort of stuff you are sending up."

"Why, you've been down a mine before, sir?" said the manager, curiously, and he gazed inquiringly in Geoffrey's face with a look of suspicion, gradually growing plainer; but he remained very civil, and led the way through the maze of passages through which for many a generation the ore had been picked out—laboriously hewn out of the solid rock as the veins of tin were patiently followed. Every now and then some dark, echoing gallery struck off at right angles, till Geoffrey felt, as he stumbled on, that a stranger would soon lose his way in such a terrible labyrinth, if not his life through falling down one of the well-like pits yawning here and there at his feet.

Sometimes the way had a lofty roof, and the floor was clear; sometimes they had to stoop and wade through mud and water, and crawl round buttresses of rock to avoid a fall, or to step from sleeper to sleeper of a very primitive tramway.

"Let me see," said the manager. "Amos Pengelly ought to be somewhere about here. Wait a minute, and let's try if we can hear him."

There were only a few distant echoing noises to be heard, as they stood in the midst of that black darkness, their candles just shedding a halo of light round them, and casting grotesque shadows of their forms upon the glistening walls, and they once more groped more than walked along, Geoffrey pausing now and again, though, to examine with his light the various tokens of minerals that could be seen cropping out on wall and roof, to all of which actions the guide gave an impatient shrug.

"They don't mean any thing," he said. "We've pretty well worked the old place out. There's Amos!"

Geoffrey turned from the place he was examining, and could hear a confused sound; but after journeying on for about a hundred yards the manager stopped and touched his arm.

They had just reached a low side passage, at the end of which there was a faint glow, and there, keeping time to the clicking sharp strokes of a pick, came the sounds of a rich tenor voice, whose owner seemed to be throwing his whole soul into what he was singing.

"Hal—le—hal—le—lu—i—jah. Hal—le—hal—le—lu—i—jah."

And so on slowly, every other syllable being accompanied by a stroke of the pick. Then, as the verse of the old-fashioned anthem being sung came to an end, there was a pause, the light seemed to be shifted, and the singer began again, but this time choosing Luther's hymn as an accompaniment to the strokes of his pick.

"Here's a gentleman come to see you, Amos! Creep out, my lad; we can't get in to you."

They had approached the singer till the ceiling was so low that it would have necessitated crawling to where Geoffrey could see by the light of a candle, stuck with a lump of clay against the rocky wall, a dark figure, half lying upon one side, vigorously working a sharp-pointed steel pickaxe, and chipping down fragments of glistening tin-grained quartz.

On hearing the summons, the figure gave itself a roll over and crawled slowly out, when in the short, lame, thick-set miner Geoffrey recognised the man with the piece of conger eel who had explained the fishing to him on the cliff.

"This is our Amos Pengelly," said the manager, as if he were showing one of the curiosities of the mine; "works all week-days and sings psalms; goes out preaching on Sundays."

"Well," said Geoffrey, bluntly, "he might do worse."

Amos nodded and looked curiously at the speaker, who went down on hands and knees to creep to where the miner had been at work; took down the candle from the wall, and examined the vein of glistening tin and the fragments that had been chipped off.

"Very poor stuff," said Geoffrey, as he returned.

"Ah, we work out poorer stuff than that," said the manager, "don't we, Amos?"

"Ay," said the miner, looking eagerly at the visitor. "Was you thinking of buying this mine, sir?"

"No!" said Geoffrey, shortly.

"Surveying it for some one else, perhaps?"

"What's the good of talking like that, Amos," said the manager, "when it is not for sale?"

"I heered as it was," said Amos, still gazing searchingly at the well-built young man before him. "But whether it be or not, sir, if you wants to buy a good working and paying mine, you buy Wheal Carnac."

"Ha, ha, ha, ha!" laughed the manager, a man who had evidently been himself a working miner. "Oh, come, Amos! I wonder at you who call yourself a Christian man trying to persuade a stranger to buy that old swindle."

"I don't care!" cried Amos, excitedly, "Christian or no Christian," and he gave his pick a blow on the rock which made the sparks fly, "I know there's good stuff down that shaft, and if it arn't been found yet it's because they haven't looked in the right place. You go and look at it, sir, and see what you think."

"Don't you do nothing of the sort, sir," said the manager. "It's a gashly old hole, down which thousands of pounds have been thrown, and machinery wasted over. Don't you take any notice of what Amos says."

"All right," said the miner, making the sparks fly again as he smote the rock angrily. "I haven't worked underground man and boy for five and twenty year without knowing something about it, and as I'm a honest man, why Wheal Carnac's a fortune to them as know'd how to work it."

"I'll have another look at the place," said Geoffrey, who was struck by the man's earnestness.

"You just do, sir, you just do, and if that place don't turn out right, I'll—I'll—"

"Swallow your pick heft, eh, Amos?" said the manager, tauntingly.

"Nay, I won't; but I'll never believe in any thing again. But you can't look at the stuff they got up, sir, she's full of water."

"And it would take hundreds of pounds to get her dry, eh, Amos? Don't you worry your head about Wheal Carnac, sir, unless you want a place to work a company, and draw a salary until they are sick of it."

"As some rogues down in these parts do," said Amos, making the sparks fly again.

"I don't know about rogues," said the manager, laughing. "There's always plenty of fools with heaps of money, which they want to invest in mines, and I don't see why the adventurers shouldn't have it as well as any one else."

Geoffrey turned in disgust from the manager, and held his candle so that its light should fall upon the frank, honest face of the miner, whose ways rather won upon him.

"Look here, Pengelly," he said, "you and I will have a chat about Wheal Carnac and a look at the ore together."

"Will you, sir? will you?" cried the miner, excitedly. "I can show you some of the ore. When will you look?"

"Any time you like," said Geoffrey. "I don't suppose any thing will come of it, but I came to see all I can."

"I've—I've waited years upon years to see that mine fairly tried," cried Pengelly, "but every one laughs at me."

"Of course they do, Amos," said the manager, banteringly. "Why, you did trick one party into fooling away thousands."

"Trick? trick? I tricked any one?" cried the miner, who had for the last few minutes been writhing under the lash of the other's tongue. "It's a lie—a cruel lie!" he exclaimed, and in a furious burst of passion he whirled up his steel pick as though it had been a straw, to strike at the cause of his annoyance.

Amos Pengelly's furious burst of passion was but of momentary duration. As Geoffrey made a step forward to seize his arm, the pick dropped from the man's hand, his face became convulsed, and all token of menace had gone. One moment he had been ready to strike down the manager for hinting that he was dishonest; the next his arms fell to his sides, his head drooped, his shoulders heaved, and he turned away into the darkness of the mine, uttering a low, piteous moaning as if torn by some great agony that he wished to hide from the sight of man.

"Come away, sir," said the manager, quietly, "he won't like to face us again to-day," and as Geoffrey rather unwillingly followed him, the manager went on towards the foot of the shaft. "Poor old Amos! I believe he's a bit touched in the head. I haven't seen him in one of his fits of passion like that for months. He's off now into one of the darkest corners he can find, and he'll be down on his knees praying as hard as ever he can. His temper gets the better of him sometimes, and he's such a religious chap that he won't forgive himself for getting in a rage; but when he comes up to grass to-night he'll walk straight to my office, as humble as a child, and beg my pardon."

"And you'll forgive him?" said Geoffrey.

"Forgive him? Oh, yes! poor chap. Why not? He can't help it."

"He seems an honest fellow," said Geoffrey, musingly.

"Honest? Oh, yes! he's honest as the day's long, sir. I'd trust him with all our sales' money without counting it. His failing is that he's gone off religious crazy; and what's as bad, he's in love with a handsome girl who don't care for him. Bess Prawle, down at the Cove, is as straight as an arrow, and poor Amos is quite a cripple, and not the sort of fellow to take the fancy of a dashing girl like she."

"Poor fellow," said Geoffrey, softly, as he followed his guide, who kept on conversing.

"Then, too, sir, poor old Amos got that craze on about Wheal Carnac, and wanting people to believe in it, so that altogether it's no wonder he turns queer. People say that Bess Prawle, who's a bit of a witch, has ill-wished him, but I don't know. One thing I do know, though—poor old Amos is about as good a workman as ever handled a pick."

"Then," said Geoffrey, thoughtfully, "you think Wheal Carnac is worthless?"

"Worthless? Worthless? Ha-ha-ha!" roared the manager. "If you had lived down here you'd have laughed as I do to see what money's been wasted there. No end of people have been took in with that mine. Just you go and have a look at it yourself, sir. You seem to know a bit about mining. Of course you can't do much, but you can turn over a few of the stones and see what was dug out last. Now, sir, what do you say—would you like to see any more of the place?"

"No," replied Geoffrey, who had been in several parts of the mine, and spoken to different men at work, "no, I have seen all I wish to see for one day," and, following his guide to the foot of the shaft, the terrible array of ladders was attacked; and at last, with wearied and strained muscles, Geoffrey reached the mouth in safety, feeling as if he had never seen the sky look so pure and blue, or felt the breath of heaven so sweet.

He was drenched with perspiration, and only too glad to accept the manager's hospitality, and have a wash and rest. But he was well satisfied with his visit, in which he had learned no little, but above all, he could not help dwelling upon the words of the miner, and feeling deeply impressed about the deserted mine—so deeply indeed that what had been merely a visit of curiosity proved to be the turning-point in his future career.

An hour afterwards he was striding back towards Carnac, while Amos Pengelly was still upon his knees in the darkest part of Horton Friendship, the great tears streaming from his eyes as he prayed, in all the sincerity of his great soul, for forgiveness of his burst of anger, and for strength to control the temper that mastered him from time to time, lest the day should come when he should go forth into the world with the curse of Cain upon his brow—for that was the black shadow that haunted the poor fellow's life.

Chapter Fifteen.

Mr Penwynn Makes a Friend.

"I cannot help it, papa. You know how obedient I have always been to you; but in this case I really cannot give way."

"Yes, yes, yes, Rhoda! you obey me in a thousand unimportant things, but now there is something upon which a great deal of our future turns you refuse."

"I cannot—I never could love Mr Tregenna, papa."

"He is a thorough gentleman, is he not?"

"Yes—oh, yes!"

"And handsome, and well-informed, and clever. A thoroughly polished—there, quite a ladies' man."

"Ladies' man!" exclaimed Rhoda, in tones of disgust. "Handsome and well-informed, of course, papa."

"Well then, my dear," said Mr Penwynn, ignoring Rhoda's peculiar look. "What more do you want?"

"Papa! do you think I want to marry a ladies' man?" said Rhoda, scornfully.

Mr Penwynn looked at the bright flushed face, and felt as proud as he did vexed. He was seated at a writing-table, and the blotting-paper before him bore testimony to his annoyance, for it was covered with the initials of unpleasant words, which he kept dotting down to relieve his feelings—a habit in which he indulged sometimes at the office, as Mr Chynoweth was well aware. He nearly spoiled a new quill pen in dashing down another letter, and then went on,—

"No, no, of course not, Rhody; but Tregenna is not a silly dandy. Besides, as I have before told you, he is very useful to me, and an alliance with him would be most valuable. There, there—you must think the matter over."

"I cannot, papa. I have told Mr Tregenna plainly that he must not hope."

"Nonsense, my dear; take time. Let the matter rest awhile. Be friends with him, and in a few months you will be ready to regret this hasty decision."

"No, papa," said Rhoda, decidedly. "Mr Tregenna can never be more to me than an acquaintance."

"You have not heard any thing—any serious—there, any scandal?"

"I, papa? I have heard that he is too attentive—there, it is not that."

"Then try not to be so foolish, my dear. I am going down to the office, and I shall see Tregenna again to-day. Let me tell him that he is not to look upon the matter as finally closed. Poor fellow! I never saw a man look so dejected. I could not have believed that he would take it so to heart."

"Papa," said Rhoda, impetuously, "I have promised Mr Tregenna that we should continue friends. If you lead him to believe that he is to persevere with his suit, I shall absolutely hate him."

Mr Penwynn turned upon her angrily, but as she stood before him, with heightened colour and flashing eyes, gazing full in his face, he felt that she was no weak girl to be subdued by a burst of parental anger, and forced into a course against which her spirit rebelled. For some reason or other she evidently felt an intense repugnance to Tregenna, and, though he would gladly have gained the day, and made the solicitor his ally, he felt that at present there was not the slightest chance for such a consummation of his plans. He knew his child's character only too well, and seeing how hopeless it was at present to persevere, he made a virtue of necessity and gave way.

"Well, well, my dear," he said, quietly, "God knows that I would not force on this affair against your prospects of happiness. There, there," he continued, taking her in his arms, "we must not fall out, Rhody. I can't afford to have clouds come between us. Wicked tyrant," he said, laughing, "and oppressor of the poor as you think me, Rhody, I want your love, my child, and I must have it."

"Papa, papa!" she cried, clinging to him, "pray forgive me. I could not love Mr Tregenna. And why should you wish to rob yourself? I have only enough love for you, dear," she continued, taking his face between her hands, and kissing him passionately. "If I reproach you sometimes about the poor people, it is because I am so jealous of my father's good name, and it cuts me to the heart to think that the people should not look up to, and venerate him as I do myself."

"Tut-tut-tut! my darling. If I were a saint they would still talk. Am I not working for you? I want you to be rich, and to stand as high in the world as I can contrive."

"Yes, yes, I know, dear," she said, with her hand playing about his face and caressing his grey hair; "but I would rather be poor than lose the people's respect."

"Well, well, Rhody, my darling," he said, smiling, "we'll be rich and respectable as well. There, there, I must go. John Tregenna must get some one else to cure his broken heart. Good-by, my dear, good-by."

"And you are not angry with me, papa?"

"Not a bit, Rhody," he said, kissing her affectionately, and looking at her with eyes suffused, but full of pride. "Angry? no! God bless you, my dear! I'm disappointed, but I don't know but what I like you all the better for your spirit."

He hurried away to hide his weakness, for his love for his child was the one soft spot in his nature.

"I'm glad, and yet I'm sorry," he said. "Tregenna would have been a powerful friend, and now what I have to hope is that he will not prove to be a bitter enemy. I must fight it out, I suppose, just as I have fought out far worse troubles."

"Any one been, Chynoweth?" he said to his confidential clerk, as he entered his office.

"Mr Tregenna's waiting to see you, sir."

"Humph! so soon," muttered Mr Penwynn, who was somewhat taken aback; but he put a good face upon it, entered his private room, and shook hands with the solicitor, whose eyes were fixed upon him inquiringly.

"Well," he said, "what news?"

"Bad," replied Mr Penwynn, quietly.

"You have had a long talk with her?"

"Yes—a very long talk."

"What does she say?"

"She is immovable." John Tregenna's face grew very dark, and he rose from his chair to walk excitedly up and down the office.

"Did you—did you ask for time?" he said hoarsely.

"I did indeed, Tregenna."

"Did you tell her that I was your best friend?"

"I did, Tregenna. I pleaded your cause as hard as if it had been my own; but she is as firm as so much granite. My dear fellow, I am very sorry, but I am afraid you must give it up."

"It's a lie—a cursed lie!" roared Tregenna, who could not control his rage and disappointment. "You have been fighting against me all along, and it is by your orders that she throws me over. I see it all now. You have been playing a cursed, double-faced, traitorous part, and I was a fool to trust to your smooth tongue. But mark my words, Penwynn—"

"John Tregenna," said Mr Penwynn, rising and speaking with dignity, "you are now in a passion, produced by what is, of course, a bitter disappointment; but pray in what manner have I failed towards you that you should make such an unfair charge?"

"What have you done?" cried Tregenna, grinding his white teeth. "Did you not lead me on for your own ends to believe that she would accept me, and submit me to the humiliation of this second refusal, which I feel sure now was at your instigation."

"Mr Tregenna," said the banker, quietly, but with anger striving for the mastery, "will you have the goodness to go now. Some other time when you are cool I shall be willing to talk to you. We cannot discuss the matter now, for it would be better that we two should not come to an open quarrel."

Tregenna snatched up his hat, darted a fierce look at the speaker, and strode towards the door, passed out, but in the act of banging it after him he recovered the mastery over his maddened brain.

He came back, closed the door after him softly, threw himself into a chair, and sat down with his forehead resting upon his hands.

Mr Penwynn stood by the table, with one hand in his breast, watching him, and for a time there was an impressive silence in the room.

At the end of a few minutes Tregenna drew a long, deep breath, and rose with his face calm, and a saddened look softening his eyes. He let fall his hands, rose, and advanced towards Rhoda's father.

"Forgive me, Penwynn," he said, humbly. "Let me apologise for what I said just now. Forgive me. You cannot tell the agony I suffered, nor conceive the utter feeling of despair and disappointment, nor the rage which seemed to force me to speak as I did. It is over," he said, as if to himself, "over now. But you will forgive me, Penwynn?"

"Yes," said the banker, quietly, "I forgive you, Tregenna."

"My words," continued the latter, "were as false and cruel as they were undeserved, and I cannot reproach myself enough for my mad folly. Can I apologise more humbly, Penwynn?" he added, with a sad smile.

"You acknowledge, then, that I did my best for you?" said Mr Penwynn.

"I do," cried Tregenna, eagerly; "and I believe that you acted in all sincerity. Penwynn, you and I must not quarrel. As to Rhoda—Miss Penwynn—if I am not to have her love, let me enjoy her friendship and esteem."

Mr Penwynn looked at the speaker coldly and searchingly for a few moments, but he could see nothing to indicate that the man before him was not perfectly sincere, and ready to say and do any thing in reparation of the past outbreak.

"You don't believe me, Penwynn," cried Tregenna, bitterly. "For heaven's sake, have a little feeling for a man. Here am I thrown in an instant from a state of hope that I might realise my fondest wishes into a state of utter, abject despair. I am not an angel, man, that I can bear such a disappointment unmoved."

Mr Penwynn still continued his scrutiny.

"It is a bitter—a cruel overthrow," continued Tregenna, "and a few moments back I feel as if I must have been mad—I was mad. I could have said and done any thing. Even how I can hardly keep calm. Have some pity on me."

"My dear Tregenna," said the banker, laying his hand upon the other's shoulder, "I do indeed sympathise with you in your disappointment, but I want you to believe that I have been perfectly straightforward and honourable."

"Yes, yes," cried Tregenna, excitedly, "I do believe it."

"You know what Rhoda—Miss Penwynn—is. I ask you, is she like an ordinary weak girl?"

"No, you are right. She is not," said Tregenna, mournfully. "If she were, I should not worship her as I do."

"She has a will of her own," continued the banker, "and she can be very firm. At your request I tried to soften her determination—asked her for time, asked her to let you continue your visits as a friend, and renew your proposal six months hence; but it was in vain, and I know her too well not to see that if you continue to press your suit you will not only lose all chance of her intimacy, but excite her dislike."

"Did she say that?" asked Tregenna, with glittering eyes.

"Well, well, not exactly."

"But she said that if I pressed my suit she should dislike me."

"Oh, no!—not so explicit as that. I think not. I—"

"Speak out plainly, Penwynn," said Tregenna, sharply. "Don't play with me."

"Well, it was something of that sort; but she was greatly excited, for I had pressed her home."

Tregenna was silent, and turned away his face, which was slightly convulsed. But he soon mastered his emotion, and at the end of a minute turned back to face Mr Penwynn.

"It is over now," he said, in a low, hoarse voice. "Forgive me my anger, Penwynn. It was very hard to bear, but you see now that I was sincere. You are right—she is very different to other girls. But it would have been the pride of my life to have won her, and whoever does win her I shall hate from the very bottom of my heart."

"Upon my word, Tregenna, I believe that your hatred will die in the bottom of your heart," said the banker, wringing his visitor's hand, "for it will never be called forth. I don't believe that there is a man living who can rouse any love in Rhoda's heart save one."

"And who's that?" cried Tregenna, with flashing eyes.

"Your humble servant," said the other, smiling. "She loves me devotedly—God bless her! And I think that I, too, shall be ready to hate any one who robs me of the slightest smile or look."

"I shall not be jealous of you, Penwynn," said Tregenna, with a strange gleam in his eyes. "There, I'll go now and have a walk on the cliff, so as to get my nerves back in tone. We are friends still?"

"Of course—of course!" said Mr Penwynn, warmly.

"I may call just as usual?"

"Call? My dear Tregenna, if you will take my advice, you will drop in just as of old, after drawing a line between the events of the past few days' proceedings and those which are to come. Bury it all, and forget it as soon as ever you can."

"I will—I will!" cried Tregenna, holding tightly by the banker's hand. "It will be best. If I am a little strange at first, you must both look over it."

"Of course! To be sure. Come soon, and let her see that it is all over."

"I will!" exclaimed Tregenna; and, after shaking hands once more, he left the room.

"Thank goodness," said Mr Penwynn, with a sigh of relief, "that's over. I should not have cared to make an enemy of Tregenna."

"Damn him!" cried Tregenna, as soon as he was alone, and he ground his teeth savagely. "Give her up? Yes, some day, perhaps: a proud, cold-blooded jilt. Wait a little, my proud beauty, for if I do not some day have you in the dust at my feet, my name's not John Tregenna."

He strode on rapidly by the track on the cliff side, leaving Wheal Carnac and the promontory to the left, and making straight for the unused mine on the path to Gwennas Cove.

He was alone now, as he thought, and, in spite of his self-command, he began gesticulating fiercely and talking to himself, without noticing that there was already some one on the track, who drew aside and walked into the unused engine-house to let him pass, and then stood uneasily watching him as he went towards Prawle's cottage.

"Forget it, and give her up. Let it all be as a something of the past—eh, Master Penwynn? Yes, when Rhoda has been mine for some months—wife or mistress, we'll see which. Not till then."

He went on muttering more and more angrily to himself, and the figure that watched limped out to follow; but on seeing Tregenna encounter the rugged old man, Bessie's father, and enter into conversation, he calmly limped away along the path.

"The old man will take care of her," he muttered; "and I don't believe that Bess would listen to him even if she won't listen to me. But he's a bad one—one as wouldn't stop at any thing to have his will, and I don't know as I'd feel very comfortable if I was him as stood in his way."

Chapter Sixteen.

Amongst the Rocks.

Geoffrey Trethick found that his were very pleasant quarters at the cottage, for Mrs Mullion seemed to take quite a motherly interest in his welfare, while her daughter Madge formed an excellent lieutenant, having evidently been won over by the young man's frank, pleasant ways as much as by his looks.

"If there is any thing I can do to make you more comfortable, Mr Trethick, I hope you'll say so," said Mrs Mullion, one morning as Geoffrey was just going out. "Both Madge and I have got so used to waiting on gentlemen that it comes quite natural to us."

"I'm sure you are very kind," said Geoffrey.

"Buttons on and darning, and that sort of thing, of course, we'll see to. I used to do all that for our late clergyman, Mr Owen—a very nice, genuine man. He used to put me so in mind of poor Madge's father. Ah!" she continued, sadly, "very different he was to his brother, Mr Paul—half-brothers, you know. Dear Edward never spoke like Thomas—Mr Paul—does. I don't say but what he would be out of temper sometimes, all gentlemen will be, but he used to say his bad words inside like, so that you could not hear them."

"A very good plan," said Geoffrey, smiling.

"Thomas—Mr Paul, you know—says very strange things sometimes, but he means well, and he is a very, very good man."

"Yes, so I believe," replied Geoffrey.

"Our Mr Owen, too, was a very good man, and they were great friends. I liked him better than this Mr Lee. I went to hear him on Sunday, but I could not really make out what he meant, but I've no doubt he meant well."

"Yes, of course," said Geoffrey, "most clergymen do."

"To be sure," assented the amiable little woman. "Have you seen the Rumseys yet?"

"I've met the doctor," replied Geoffrey.

"A very clever man," said Mrs Mullion, "and his wife means well, but she drills the children so. She's very proud, and thinks they have come down; but, as I say to my Madge, if she would not drill those poor children quite so much, and use a pocket-handkerchief to their noses, it would be so much better. Yes, Madge, I'm coming directly."

Geoffrey wished she would go, for he wanted to write a letter; but the little lady kept prattling on.

"I want to see you get a good colour, Mr Trethick. You look Londony, you know. You must let me cook you a chop or a steak for breakfast—underdone, you know. Dr Rumsey says there's nothing like it. So much better for you than fish; and I will say that of our butcher, he does have good meat. His only fault is that, as Mr Paul says, he seems to have a knife that will cut two pounds when you want one."

"A common failing with butchers, I believe," laughed Geoffrey.

"Yes," said the little woman, innocently. "We get our milk there, and—to be sure! Now, look here, Mr Trethick, before you go out for those early morning walks of yours—"

"Mamma!"

"Yes, Madge, I'm coming! Bless the child! how impatient she is when I'm here. But, as I was going to say, you must let me beat you up a new-laid egg in a glass of fresh milk. Lornocks have got a new cow, an Alderney, with such a beautiful bust, and I never saw richer milk in my life."

"But, my dear Mrs Mullion, I'm not an invalid!" laughed Geoffrey. "The only consumption I suffer from is that of the pocket."

"Hallo! You here?" said old Mr Paul, stumping in.

"Yes, Thomas. I was advising Mr Trethick about his health."

"Stuff! He's all health! Don't take any notice of her, Trethick, or she'll want to put you in a poultice every night! There, be off, woman!"

"Yes, dear, I'm going," said the little woman, gently.

"She'll be giving you beef-tea and arrow-root till you can't see," growled the old fellow. "I believe she was a nurse once."

"Indeed?"

"Yes, before she was born what she is."

Geoffrey stared.

"And that she'll be a hen next, like Mrs Rumsey, to set on eggs and cluck over chickens."

"Metempsychosis?" said Geoffrey.

"Hah! yes! The niggers out in Poonah are right as right about that."

"Very likely," said Geoffrey. "Now, what do you suppose you'll be next?"

"Don't know," said the old man, sharply; "but I've no doubt you'll be a dog."

"May I ask why?"

"Because you're an impertinent puppy now!"

"Just as you like," said Geoffrey, smiling. "But you look cross."

"No, sir; things are not just as I like," said the old man, seating himself upon Geoffrey's table, but only to get off, go quickly to the door, open it softly, and then dash out—to come back disappointed, for there was no one listening. "Look here, Trethick, I want to ask you a plain question."

"Go on, then."

"That niece of mine goes out a great deal now—has gone out a great deal since you've been here. Is it to meet you?"

Geoffrey had hard work to sit unmoved, for he thought of what he knew, and wondered whether he ought to speak out: and he felt that the old man was watching him searchingly.

"No!" said Geoffrey, shortly. "It is not!"

"That's right, I'm glad of it," said the old man, taking a chair, and apparently more at his ease. "She'll be a cat one of these days, hang her! But look here, boy. Don't you look at her. The jade's ready to lead on everybody she sees. If I were not her uncle, I believe she'd set her cap at me. Now, look here: I told you at first, and I tell you again, I'll have no fooling."

"Give me one of those cigars of yours," said Geoffrey, rather bluntly, and apparently without paying any heed to the old man's words. "I want a smoke."

"Humph! Things are going crooked with you, then, are they?"

"Very!" said Geoffrey. "But come out to the summer-house, and let's feel the free air."

"Here, catch hold!" cried the old man, holding out a black cheroot. "That's the only good trait in your character, boy, you do know a good cigar. He, he, he! You should try some I keep for Rumsey, and fellows like that."

"Thanks, no," said Geoffrey.

"Ah! I told you how it would be," continued the old man, as they entered the look-out and took their seats. "I told you how it would be. I knew it well enough. So I did."

They sat looking at each other for a few moments.

"You can't get an engagement then, my lad, eh?"

"No," said Geoffrey, lighting up; "not yet."

"No; nor you won't. That you won't," chuckled the old man, as Geoffrey sat himself on the summer-house table, and, thrusting his hands in his pockets, began swinging one leg backwards and forwards.

"I've tried at twenty mines in the month I've been here," said Geoffrey, "and pointed out ways of saving that would pay me a good salary ten times over, and put money in the proprietors' or shareholders' pockets."

"Yes, and they laugh at you, don't they?"

"Confoundedly," said Geoffrey.

"Keep that leg still," said the old man, poking at the swinging member with his cane.

Geoffrey gave the cane a kick, and sent it flying out on to the grass-plot, making Uncle Paul turn white with rage; but the young man got leisurely down and picked it up, retaining it in his hand as he reseated himself, and began making passes with it at a knot in the wood.

"Give me my cane," said the old man, angrily.

"They're as blind as moles to their own interests," said Geoffrey.

"Do you hear? Give me my cane."

"And treat all my advances as if I were trying to trick and defraud them."

"I say, give me my cane!" cried the old man.

"They flatly tell me that my plans are new-fangled and foolish, and that they'll have none of them."

"Confound you, you insolent puppy! Will you give me my cane?"

"They're as hard to move as so many mules," said Geoffrey, handing the cane, and smiling in the old man's face.

Uncle Paul snatched the cane, and made a threatening gesture as if about to strike, when Geoffrey held out one hand, school-boy fashion, for a cut on the palm, and the old man made as if to give it a vicious blow; but, as the other did not flinch, he checked the fall of the cane, and sat showing his yellow teeth.

"I'm glad of it, very glad," he snarled. "I told you so; and now you may pack up and be off, for I'm sick of you, and want to see your back."

"But I'm not going," said Geoffrey, coolly. "I wouldn't move for the world. You do me so much good."

"I do you good, puppy?"

"To be sure you do. I get as bilious and acid, and put out with my ill-luck as can be, and then I come and take a dose of you, and it seems to put me right again."

"You're—you're the most insolent, cool, impertinent puppy I ever met?" cried the old man; "and—and I wish you all the ill-luck you can get."

"Thanky," said Geoffrey. "Well, good-by for the present. I'm going to take a walk down to the Cove."

"Of course," snarled Uncle Paul. "Hi! here. Madge! Madge!"

"Yes, uncle," she cried, running eagerly out of the porch, and across the grass-plot.

"Yes, uncle," he snarled. "You jade. You were listening, and waiting for a chance for another look, or a word, with this puppy here."

"Oh, uncle!" cried the girl, colouring up, for the old man had guessed the truth.

"Pray don't protest, my dear Miss Mullion," said Geoffrey, coolly. "Say you were. There's no harm in it."

"Harm in it?" cried the old man, fiercely, "harm? Why, you don't suppose I'm going to let you, a mining adventurer, flirt and play tricks with my brother's child, and then go off and never come back?"

"Youth is the time for folly, Mr Paul."

"Yes; but there shall be no follies here, sir. Look here, Madge, this fellow's not to be trusted. He's always going over to the Cove, to make eyes at handsome Bess Prawle; so don't you listen to him."

Madge looked at Geoffrey inquiringly.

"It's quite true, Miss Mullion," said Geoffrey, bowing assent to the old man's words, "I am going over to the Cove; and I dare say I shall see Miss Prawle the pretty. By the way, Mr Paul, are women any the better for being pretty?"

"You—you impudent jackanapes! You, you—There, ha, ha, ha! Look at her!" he cried, chuckling at the effect of his words. "She's run indoors in a huff, and she'll cry as soon as you're gone."

"Then I hope you feel happy, sir?"

"I do," said the old man, rubbing the ivory top of his cane. "Look here, boy, do you mean any thing by being so civil to that girl?"

"What girl, sir?"

"Don't aggravate me, boy. Her—Madge—that smooth-faced, good-looking cat."

"I don't mean any thing but to be civil."

"Not marriage?"

"Well, seeing that I can barely keep myself," said Geoffrey, laughing, "no."

"Marry Miss Pavey, then," chuckled the old man, maliciously. "Sweet creature. False teeth, false hair, false ways, false voice—falsetto. Lovely woman. See what a dresser she is. What a useful piece of furniture for a house."

"Marry her yourself," said Geoffrey; "you are an old bachelor."

"Bah!" exclaimed the old man. "But look here, sir. My niece!"

"Still harping on my daughter."

"No, I'm not, Polonius Junior; but upon my niece. You say she don't go out to meet you."

"No, she does not."

"Then don't be civil to her. Marriage is folly. My brother married Jane Mullion there, and she worried his life out with being so stupid, and then he died and left her and her child paupers."

"Hang that word!" cried Geoffrey, warmly. "How I do hate it."

"Then don't go and make a race of paupers," said the old man. "Bah! A young fellow has his work cut out in life, and starts on his journey by sticking a load of woman on his back. Then she sticks a load of baby on her back, and most likely goes on banging children all over him till the burthen gets too heavy to be borne, when the poor wretch breaks down and dies. Look at me, sir. I never married; but saved enough to live on, and keep other people. Follow my example."

"And grow as cantankerous."

"Do you want to quarrel, puppy?"

"Not I. I haven't time."

"What are you crying about?" said the old man, roughly, as he found that Mrs Mullion, attracted by his loud voice, had come to see what was the matter, and had heard a part of his last speech.

"At what you said, dear," sobbed the poor woman.

"Don't you mind what he says, Mrs Mullion," said Geoffrey; "he doesn't mean it. I'll be bound to say he's got a very soft spot in his heart somewhere."

As he spoke Geoffrey walked out of the garden, whistling, and made for the cliff path, drinking in the deliciously-fresh sea-breeze as he went along.

"This place keeps one from having the dumps," he said to himself, "it is so fresh and bright; but really, in spite of my vainglorious boasting, I'm afraid I am wasting time here. *Nil des*, though; I'm not beaten yet. Old Paul is glorious as a dose of bitters, if he didn't give one quite so much about Brown Maudlin. Pretty girl, very; but wants ballast horribly. Hang the old man, he goes just the way to make a fellow think about her. But he's a fine old boy. Now I'll go and have a dose of resignation from poor old Mrs Prawle.

"That old lady always does me good," he said, as he went on. "What sane man could grumble who has all his faculties, just because he cannot make filthy lucre, when he has that patient old lady ready to face him with her calm, subdued ways. Hang it, there's a very pathetic side to her life!"

He did not see that he, too, was watched, as he went swinging along; but went right ahead in his thorough way, setting his mind on a certain goal, and hardly heeding any thing else; but he had not passed one clump of rocks far, when Amos Pengelly came out, and stood watching him till he disappeared, and then followed slowly, to make sure that Geoffrey went down to the Cove.

The rough miner's face was very white and drawn, and he uttered a low moaning sigh as he satisfied himself that the man whom he was watching had gone straight to the Cove, and then he limped back some little distance, and, with a heavy frown settling on his massive face, he seated himself on a rock waiting for Geoffrey's return, his fingers crooking and clenching into fists, and the ruined mine shaft not far behind.

Chapter Seventeen.

At Gwennas Cove.

Bess Prawle was leaning against the rough granite door-post, very handsome, picturesque, and defiant, as she knitted away at a coarse blue worsted jersey which she was making; looking up from time to time to watch her father, who, pipe in mouth, was weeding the little patch of garden, of which he seemed to be very proud, while every now and then he paused to speak.

Just then the old man raised his nose and sniffed.

"There's your mother burning again, Bess. Go and see," he growled.

The girl ran in to find poor old Mrs Prawle evidently greatly exercised in her mind lest a jersey of her husband's should be put on damp, and hence she was scorching it against the fire.

"Oh, mother!" cried Bess impatiently, "how you frighten me. Pray do take more care."

"Yes, yes, Bess," cried the poor woman querulously, as she turned and re-spread the article of clothing on her knees, "but some one must see to the things being aired;" and Bessie returned to where the old man was at work, when he stood up and drew his hand across his mouth.

"I don't care, lass; I arn't lived to sixty without finding that when a young fellow keeps coming to a cottage like this, it isn't only to see an old woman who's sick."

"Stuff, father! you're always thinking young men come to see me."

"Am I?" grumbled the old man. "Well, I know what I know, and I know this—that if that London chap keeps coming here to see you, I'll break his gashly head, or shove him over the cliff as I would have done to Jack Lannoe if Amos Pengelly hadn't thrashed him instead."

"Then I'll tell him what you say, father—no, I won't," cried Bess, sharply, "I'll tell mother what you promise to do."

She made a movement as if to go in, when her father caught her by the skirt of her gown, and drew her back.

"I'll never forgive you, Bess," he said, in a hoarse whisper; "I'll never forgive you if you do."

"I will tell her," cried the girl, looking angry and flushed, "unless you promise never to touch Mr Trethick."

The old man held on to her and drew her farther away, so as to make sure that no words of their altercation should be heard inside the cottage.

"Look here, Bess," he said hoarsely, "doesn't he come to see you?"

"To see me?" said the girl, scornfully. "Isn't he a gentleman, and arn't I a witch, as the people say, and arn't you the worst character in these parts?"

"So they say," said the old man, grimly. "The fools!"

"Is it likely that a gentleman like him would come after me?"

"That Tregenna did," said the old man, suspiciously.

"Yes, till you threatened to break his neck," said Bess, laughing.

"And I'd have done it too," said the old man, with his eyes lighting up fiercely; "and so I will to this one."

"He don't come to see me, father," said Bess, quietly. "You watch him next time he's here. He's not the sort of man to care about women at all, and—hush, father! here he is."

There was the sound of a heavy foot on the stones above, and Geoffrey Trethick came into sight, looking fresh and breeze-blown as he strode along.

"She knows his step," muttered the old man, grinding his teeth, "and I won't have it."

He glanced at his daughter, and saw that her warm colour was a little heightened as Geoffrey came up with a hearty "Good-morning."

"Why, Bess," he cried, "you look as fresh as a rose. Ah, Father Prawle, how are you? Look here, I've brought you an ounce of prime tobacco," and he held out the little roll to the old man.

Prawle took it, looking vindictively at him, and made as if to throw it over the cliff into the sea, but jerked it back at the giver's feet.

"I don't want your tobacco," he said, roughly. "I could buy you and yours up a dozen times over if I liked."

"You are precious poor if you can't," said Geoffrey, stooping and picking up the tobacco. "Well, if you won't smoke it I will. But look here, Prawle, what's the matter with you? What have I done to offend you?"

"I don't like your coming here, and I won't have it," cried the old man.

"Do you want to frighten poor mother?" exclaimed Bess, hastily. "Don't mind what he says, Mr Trethick," she continued; "mother is so glad for you to come—it makes such a change; but father won't believe you come on purpose to see her."

"Then what does he suppose I come for?" said Geoffrey, sitting down on a rough bench by the path. "Does he—Oh! I see," he said, laughing; "he thinks it's to see you, Miss Bess. Why, Prawle, Prawle," he continued, getting up and clapping the old man on the shoulder, "what a queer set of people you are down here!"

Bess changed colour a little as she heard the visitor's half-contemptuous tone when he alluded to her, but she forced a smile, and spoke out firmly,—

"Yes, Mr Trethick, that's what he thinks."

"Then he was never more mistaken in his life," cried Geoffrey. "Here, come and sit down, old man, and we'll smoke a pipe together till mother wakes, and then I'll buy some sweets and be off again; but I want a talk with you. Amos Pengelly says you know more about the mines here than most men."

"Maybe I do, sir," growled Prawle, surlily, and apparently only half convinced.

"Sit down then, man, and speak out honestly. What do you know about Wheal Carnac?"

"Wheal Carnac!" said the old man, starting. "What do I know about it? Nothing at all—nothing at all."

"Fill your pipe. Sit down and light up."

Prawle hesitated for a moment, and glanced at his daughter, then back at their visitor, and ended by sitting down on the bench and knocking the ashes from his pipe to refill it from the tobacco brought by his visitor; while Bess, in whose eyes the tears were gathering, turned away and softly peeped into the cottage.

"That's better," said Geoffrey, as both pipes were lit, and they sat under the grey and purple cliff facing the sparkling sea. "Amos Pengelly says he believes you have a good deal of faith in that mine."

"Amos Pengelly's a psalm-singing, chattering fool," said the old man, angrily.

"No he isn't," said Geoffrey; "he's a very good, honest, sensible fellow."

Bess turned sharply round and looked curiously at him.

"Bah! what does he know 'bout what I think?" growled Prawle.

"I don't know; but he tells me you worked in it."

Prawle nodded.

"Well, you must have seen a good deal of what the rock is like."

"Like rubbish," said the old man, hastily. "Thousands have been wasted there, and thousands more will be by anybody who's fool enough to work it."

"Humph?" said Geoffrey, between two puffs of smoke, "perhaps so. Is that your honest opinion?"

As he spoke he gazed full in the old man's eyes, which met his without flinching for a few moments, but only to sink before the searching gaze and take refuge on the ground.

"Never you mind what's my honest opinion. I'm not an Amos Pengelly to go and chatter about my affairs."

"A still tongue makes a wise head, Master Prawle," said Geoffrey, "even about little smuggling and wrecking jobs."

"What do you know about smuggling and wrecking?" cried Prawle, angrily.

"Very little," said Geoffrey, "only this cove looks to me about as convenient a place as well could be for any little job of that sort."

"Mother's awake, Mr Trethick," interposed Bess, as she saw her father's wrath rising at Geoffrey's bantering comment.

"I'll come directly," said Geoffrey, as he saw her appealing look. "There, I won't joke you about your private affairs, Master Prawle. So you won't tell me any thing about Wheal Carnac?"

"Not a word," said the old man, angrily.

"Not this time," said Geoffrey, rising, "but think it over. Now, Miss Bessie, how is our invalid to-day?"

Mrs Prawle's face lit up as Geoffrey's form darkened the door, and she held out her thin white hand eagerly, as, in his bluff way, her visitor asked after her health.

"Very sadly, sir, very sadly," she said, turning a fresh article of attire and spreading it upon her knees; "but do you—do you want—I'm so glad to do a little to save being a burthen to them."

"Want sweets?" said Geoffrey. "Yes, I've got a commission to spend a whole sixpence; and see here, Miss Bessie, above half are to be those transparent red gentlemen."

He looked merrily in the girl's face, little thinking of the pain he gave her, and how her woman's vanity was touched by his utter indifference. She smiled back, however, filled a paper bag with what he required, and went out to resume her knitting by the door, while Geoffrey sat on chatting, and listening to the poor woman's plaints.

"She's such a good girl, my Bess," she said, proudly, as her mother's heart throbbed high at the thought of what a thing it would be if this well-spoken gentleman from London should take a fancy to her child, and raise her to his position.

"Yes, she seems to be," said Geoffrey, little suspecting her thoughts.

"So patient and so good; and you will not heed what they say about us, sir?"

"Not I," said Geoffrey.

"They say, you know, that she's almost a wise woman; and they've been very bitter against us ever since Mrs Polwhyn's cow died."

"Indeed!"

"Oh yes," said the poor woman, earnestly; "they say Bess ill-wished it, and that she has ill-wished Mrs Vorr's boy, who is a cripple."

"You are a curious set of people down here," said Geoffrey; "but do you mean to tell me that they believe such things as that?"

"Indeed they do," said the poor woman, with tears in her eyes.

"And about witches?"

"Oh yes," she said, laying her hand on the big Bible by her side; "and, of course, that is true, sir. You know King Saul went to see the witch of Endor."

"Yes," said Geoffrey, dryly.

"But it is too bad about my poor Bess, who is such a good and patient girl, and waits upon me day and night. He'll be a lucky man who wins her for a wife!"

"I'm sure he will," said Geoffrey.

"Then they say such cruel things about Prawle, and call him wrecker and smuggler."

"Well," said Geoffrey, laughing, "I wouldn't swear he has never helped the landing of any thing in the cove."

"Don't ask me, please sir," said the old woman, looking terribly troubled; "but he is the best and truest of men, and, though he's very rough, never a hard word has he said all these weary years that I have been nothing but a burthen and a care."

"Oh, come, come!" said Geoffrey, taking her hand, as he saw the tears trickling down her furrowed face, "don't talk like that; there's always a pleasure in doing things for those we love. Hallo! who's this?" he cried, starting up as the doorway was shadowed, "Miss Penwynn!"

"Mr Trethick!" cried Rhoda, flushing slightly, "you here?"

"Yes," he said, laughing frankly, as he shook hands, "I've come to buy some sweets. Mrs Prawle's an old friend of mine. Let me recommend the transparent red fellows, with acid in them," he continued, merrily. "Miss Bessie, here's a fresh customer."

Rhoda laughed and looked pleased at the way in which he kept up the pleasant fiction, as he immediately resigned his seat in her favour, and after a few cheery words about the weather and the like, he bade the invalid good-by, asked after. Mr Penwynn, and left the cottage.

"He's a brave, good young man, my dear," said Mrs Prawle, wiping her eyes, "and he often comes over and spends a sixpence here."

"Does he?" said Rhoda, quietly.

"Yes, very often; but Prawle don't like it, though I can't see why, my dear, for no young man could be nicer; and if he has took a fancy to our Bess, and should marry her, it would be the happiest day of my life."

"But—do you think—"

"Well, I don't know," said the invalid, glad of an opportunity to prattle on; "she's a good and a handsome girl, as she showed in the way she sent that Mr Tregenna about his business, and it was a merciful thing that Prawle never did him a mischief; he's that violent, and Mr Tregenna was always hanging about to see our Bess."

"Yes, yes," said Rhoda, colouring, "I know about that;" and then, her woman's curiosity prevailing over her dislike to hear gossip, she continued, "but you don't think Mr Trethick comes to—"

"See our Bess, my dear? Well, I can't say. He's quite a gentleman, and I'm sure if he does he means honourable to her."

"Yes, yes, of course," said Rhoda, hastily, "but he is quite a stranger."

"Yes, my dear, and it may be all my fancy; but gentlemen do sometimes marry poor girls—not that my Bess is poor, or will be poor," she said, proudly. "There's many a farmer's or captain's daughter will be worse off than she."

"But I thought," exclaimed Rhoda, "that Bess had a sweetheart—that lame man, Pengelly?"

"No," said the invalid, "I don't think that's any thing. He's a good young man—so religious, and sings and prays beautifully. He prayed here by me one Sunday for a whole hour; but it is not nature that my Bess should care for the likes of him, even if he does worship the ground she walks upon."

The old woman prattled away, but Rhoda did not hear her, for somehow her mind was busy running on with Geoffrey Trethick's career, and she was thinking how strange it would be if he married the old smuggler's handsome daughter, who, it was reputed, would have plenty of money when her father died, but was to be avoided on account of the possession of the evil eye.

At last the visit was brought to an end, Rhoda promising, somewhat unwillingly, to come soon again; when Bess was summoned to come in, with her fearless erect carriage, to do up the parcel of sweets that the visitor purchased.

As they were taken, the eyes of the two girls met, each gazing searchingly at the other, and to Rhoda it seemed that there was a calm, triumphant smile on the face of Bess, who almost looked at her mockingly, though there was a bitterness in the curl of her lip.

Somehow Rhoda grew very thoughtful as she slowly made her way back. Geoffrey Trethick was nothing to her, but he had been their guest, and it seemed to be almost an insult that he should know them, and yet stoop to the pursuit of this common peasant girl.

"But why should I trouble about it?" she said, merrily; and all thought of what had been said was chased away upon her seeing the object of her thoughts upon the cliff track, in company with the Reverend Edward Lee.

Meanwhile Bess Prawle had gone out, knitting in hand, to where her father was busy in his garden, and stood beside him for some time in silence, till he looked and saw her gazing at him, with a settled frown upon her face.

"Well, father," she said rather huskily.

"Well, lass."

"Do you think now that Mr Trethick comes over to see poor me?"

Chapter Eighteen.

Meeting a Volcano—and a Placid Lake.

Geoffrey came swinging along the path, with his head thrown back and his chest forward, smiling at something that crossed his mind, when he stopped short, for Amos Pengelly suddenly stood in his way.

"Ah, Pengelly," he said, heartily, "how are you, my lad?" and he stretched out his hand.

To his astonishment, the miner struck it savagely aside, closed with him, caught him by arm and waistband, and by a clever Cornish wrestling trick, and the exercise of his iron muscles, literally lifted him from the ground.

Geoffrey was powerful, and full of youth and vigour, but his antagonist's dwarfish legs gave him another advantage, and he could have thrown the young man heavily to the ground, but in the very act of dashing him upon the rocks he relented, and let him recover himself.

"Have you gone mad, Pengelly?" cried Geoffrey, warmly. "Hang it, man, if you don't control that confounded temper of yours you'll be on your trial some day for murder."

"Maybe it'll be yours," cried Amos, fiercely. "What have I done to you that you should serve me in this way?"

"I? Serve you?" cried Geoffrey, in astonishment, for he had resumed his unruffled manner. "What's the matter, Amos?"

"Where have you been, master?"

"Been? Down to Gwennas Cove."

"There, you own it," cried Amos, with his passion rising again.

"Look here, master, there are things that make me mad. I've fought like men with beasts at Ephesus, as holy Paul says, and my beasts are the beasts of passion that rise up in me. I've fought and I've prayed, and I've mastered them again and again, but there's one thing lets them loose, and I can't keep them down."

"Look here, Pengelly," said Geoffrey, quietly, "I had hoped when the day came that I could get a good engagement to have you as one of my best men; but, hang me! if I can trust a fellow who has always got a volcano in him ready to burst out."

"Then why do you cross me like this?"

"Cross you, my good fellow?" said Geoffrey, as he fixed the miner with his eye. "I'm not going to cross you. There, come along back to Carnac, and let's talk about yonder mine."

"I want no dealings with such a treacherous man," cried Amos, fiercely. "But, look here, I warn ye. You're well-shaped and good to look upon, while I'm only a cripple; but I can't—there's that in me that won't let me—stand by and see another man take up with her as flouts me for what I am."

"Flouts? Take up with her?" said Geoffrey, wonderingly, while the miner's breast heaved as he seemed to be battling hard to contain himself.

Then a light burst upon Geoffrey, and he was ready to burst into a fit of laughter; but he saw that the subject was too serious for mirth, and he exclaimed, in a tone of vexation once more,—

"Are all you people mad here upon questions relating to the sexes? Why, my good fellow, where do you think I've been?"

"You said—to Prawle's."

"Yes, of course; but what for?"

"You've been to see her. You've been again and again, master, till I can bear it no more. Oh! Master Trethick," he cried, piteously, "it may be play and trifling with you, but it's killing me."

"Amos Pengelly," cried Geoffrey, laying his hand on the miner's shoulder, "if you think I go over yonder to see Prawle's daughter you, never made a greater mistake in your life."

Amos drew back and looked full in his eyes, which never flinched for a moment, but frankly returned the gaze.

"Say that again," said the miner, hoarsely.

"I won't," cried Geoffrey. "Hang it, man! there are bounds to every thing. It's absurd, it's—"

He stopped short as he saw the man's emotion, and said kindly, as he held out his hand,—

"Pengelly, my lad, as I am a man, I never bestowed a thought on Bessie Prawle, but have been there to sit half-an-hour with her poor sick mother."

The miner's face changed, and he was about to speak, but he turned sharply round, and limped away with wonderful activity, disappearing amongst the rocks; and, after waiting a few minutes to see if he would return, Geoffrey gave himself a shake, and then stooped to pick up something that fell tinkling on the granite path.

"That's one of my brace buttons gone," he said pettishly. "Hang the fellow! he's as strong as a horse. It was enough to break all one's buttons. So that's Cornish wrestling, is it? I thought myself pretty clever, but he could have thrown me like a baby."

"Poor fellow, though," he said to himself, as he went on, "I suppose he did feel cut up and savage with me. But what a set they are—down here, to be sure. Seems to me that they think of nothing but love-making, and that it isn't safe to look at a woman in the place. What a blessing it is that I am so constituted that all women seem to me to be mothers and sisters—mothers and sisters—sisters—yes, sisters," he mused, as he looked at his right hand, opening and closing the fingers gently, as he seemed to feel within it a soft, shapely white hand, and traced each tapering finger where Rhoda's had so lately been.

"She would have been a very sweet sister to a man. Full of firmness, and ready to advise and help a fellow in his troubles. It must be very nice to have a sister—such a one as she."

He walked on very slowly, growing moment by moment more thoughtful, and somehow his thoughts were of Rhoda Penwynn; but they were all chased away by the sight of the Reverend Edward Lee coming along the track.

"Ah, Mr Lee!" he cried, holding out his hand, "how are you getting along?"

The young clergyman started and looked confused. There was a shrinking manner about him as he unwillingly put out his hand to be heartily pressed; but somehow Geoffrey Trethick's will seemed always to master his, and he replied nervously to his inquiries.

"I've been going to call upon you over and over again," said Geoffrey. "Coming for advice, and that sort of thing; but I suppose you are terribly busy over your new cure?"

"I am—very busy," said the other, with a half sigh, as he recalled some of the difficulties of his task; and he looked nervously in Geoffrey's eyes, and felt constrained to say that he would be very glad to see him.

"That's right," said Geoffrey, "I shall come. One has not too many cultivated acquaintances down here. And I'm a parishioner, you know."

The Reverend Edward Lee grew bolder for this suggested duty.

"And I have not called upon you," he said. "I have been remiss."

"Ah, well, you'll make up for that," said Geoffrey.

"Is—is that why I have not seen you at church?" he said.

"Oh, no!" said Geoffrey. "That's because I have been remiss and—ah, here's Miss Penwynn."

His companion started, and a slight colour came into his pale cheeks as Rhoda came round one of the rocky buttresses of the cliff, and, in spite of himself, as his keen eyes detected the change, Geoffrey felt a suspicion coming upon him that the Reverend Edward Lee had had some idea that Rhoda was walking in this direction, and had turned his steps that way so as to meet her.

"Why, she's blushing, too!" said Geoffrey to himself, as Rhoda came up and shook hands with Mr Lee.

"I need not shake hands with you again, Mr Trethick," she said. "By the way, it is very kind of you to call and talk to that poor Mrs Prawle."

The vicar darted a quick glance from one to the other, and then, without making any pretence of going further, he turned round, and walked back beside Rhoda towards Carnac, Geoffrey coming behind, for the path did not admit of three abreast. The consequence was that he only came in for a stray word here and there, and told himself that being the third party he was *de trop*.

All the same, though, he found himself taking note of Rhoda's figure, the carriage of her head, and her free, firm step on the rugged path. This path seemed to trouble the young vicar, who, being short-sighted, more than once caught the toes of his thin boots against some irregularity in the granite, as he talked on in his smooth, easy-flowing way, only interrupted by Rhoda turning her head occasionally to point out some place of interest in the distance.

"Parson's like the rest!" said Geoffrey to himself, as he turned off to the cottage. "He's touched. I wonder whether she knew that he was coming to meet her, for that he went on purpose, I'll swear. I wonder whether any thing could be made of Wheal Carnac? What a nice sister she would make! Hallo! Pengelly, you here again? No, no; stand off, my lad: I've no more brace buttons to spare. One of your hugs is enough for a day. What?"

"I beg your pardon, Master Trethick," said the miner, humbly; and he stood with his hat off in the track, "I beg your pardon humbly, sir; I do indeed."

"Oh, tut—tut, man, that's all past," said Geoffrey, heartily.

"No, sir, it arn't," said Amos. "I feel that shamed o' myself that I haven't got words to speak it. Only please say that you forgive me, and won't think of it any more."

"Forgive you! Yes, Pengelly, of course; but next time you suspect one of any thing wrong, just bark out aloud before you bite, will you?—it will give a fellow a chance to get out of your way."

"Ah, sir, you don't know how foolish I feel."

"Do you? Then don't feel so any more. And now look here, my lad, I want to have a few words with you again about Wheal Carnac."

"Yes, sir—when?"

"Oh, soon—say to-morrow morning. I'll meet you there at your own time."

"Say six, sir. I'm not on at the mine till nine," said Amos, with his face lighting up; and they parted, for Geoffrey to become aware, as he entered the gate, that Madge Mullion was at the window ready to smile at him as he went in, and a shrewd suspicion smote him that she had been watching for his return.

Chapter Nineteen.

At Wheal Carnac.

"I've got Wheal Carnac on the brain," said Geoffrey, as he leaped out of his bed soon after five o'clock, made a great deal of noise and splashing over a tub, and ended by standing up fresh, healthy, and dressed, and calling himself a fool. "Why, I might have taken a towel and had a dip in the sparkling waters," he said, as he gazed out, to see the ripples stained with blood-red and gold, orange and brilliant topaz with the rising sun. "Why, it would have been a bath in Falernian wine! Never mind—live and learn."

"By George, what was I dreaming? Oh! I remember: that I fell down the old pit-shaft and went on falling into infinite space, with some one like that Tregenna laughing at me the while."

He went softly out of his room and down-stairs, so as not to disturb the other occupants of the house, to find, to his surprise, that the door was open; and, on stepping out into the garden, he came suddenly upon Madge, looking very bright and rosy, with her rich auburn hair taking a fresh tinge from the early morning beams.

"Ah, Miss Mullion! Good-morning. You up so soon?"

"Yes," she said eagerly, "I often go out for an early walk down to the sea."

"Not to play at mermaid, and sport in the briny wave!" he asked laughingly.

"Oh, dear, no!" she cried with a shiver, "I'm so afraid of the water."

"Are you?" he said, smiling. "Well, it would be a job to get all that pretty hair dry again."

Madge coloured with pleasure.

"It is so nice walking over the rocks quite early," she said.

"Yes, I suppose so. Well, I must be off."

"Are you going for a walk?" she said naïvely.

"Yes, but only on my way to work. Good-by for the present. I say, Miss Mullion, a nice bit of brown fish for breakfast, please. I shall be as hungry as a hunter when I come back."

He walked sharply off, not seeing that uncle Paul's blind stirred slightly, and Madge stood gazing after him.

"He's as cold as a stone," said the girl, petulantly. "I declare I hate him—that I do. But I'll pique him yet, see if I don't, clever as he is. He'll be sorry for this some day. A great, ugly, stupid thing!"

The tears of vexation stood in her eyes, but they disappeared almost directly.

"He did say it was pretty hair," she said, with her face lighting up, "and if I don't make some one jealous yet it's strange to me."

She hesitated for a few moments as to whether she should take the same path as Geoffrey, and ended by flinging herself petulantly round and entering the house.

"It's a glorious morning," said Geoffrey, as he went down the steep, stone-paved pathway, drinking in the fresh salt-breeze. "I declare, it's like living a new life here," and his chest seemed to expand, and his muscles and nerves grow tense, as the life-blood bounded through his veins.

At times he felt as if he would like to rush off and run, like a schoolboy, from the full tide of vitality that made his veins throb; but he went on soberly enough, exchanging a nod with different fishermen at their cottage doors, for most of them had come to know him now, and showed their white teeth in a friendly smile as he swung along.

He glanced at his watch as he neared the slope up which the mine chimney crawled, like a huge serpent, to the perpendicular shaft on the hill, and found he was an hour before his time; so walking sharply down to a little sandy stretch only bare at very low tides, he slipped off his boots, tied the laces together, and hung them over his shoulder, and then drew off his socks, which he thrust into his pocket, turned up his trousers, and had a good wade; after which, being without a towel, he began to walk along the dry sand so as to let sun and air perform the part of bath attendants, finally taking a seat upon a stone to put the final polish to his toes with a silk pocket-handkerchief.

He was bending down, seriously intent upon a few stray particles of sand, when a shadow fell athwart him, and looking up sharply, there stood Rhoda Penwynn.

"Oh! I beg your pardon, Mr Trethick," she cried, colouring.

"Beg yours," he said bluntly, as he started up and held out his hand; for it struck him that under the circumstances the better plan was to ignore his pursuit.

"It's only a matter of custom," he said to himself; "bare feet are no more indelicate than bare hands or bare shoulders, and if ever she goes to sea she won't see many sailors wear socks and shoes."

So in the coolest manner possible he walked by Rhoda's side, as calmly as a barefooted friar of old, and as free from guile; while she felt half-annoyed, half ready to blush, and ended by smiling at her companion's matter-of-fact ways. For he chatted about the place, the contents of the rock-pools, and the various weeds, and ended in the bluntest way by holding out his hand.

"Good-morning, Miss Penwynn, I have an appointment now. Let me say good-by though, with a compliment."

"Please don't," said Rhoda.

"But I will," he said, laughing, "I only wanted to say that I admire your early rising ways."

Then nodding in his frank, cheery way, he started off back towards the ruined mine, walking quickly till the acorn barnacles upon the rocks suggested the advisability of putting on his socks and boots, which he rapidly did.

"What a Goth she must have thought me!" he said, laughing. "Well, can't help it if she did."

Then starting off once more, he turned a corner and could see a short, thick-set figure advancing, and waved his hand, to see a cap held up in return.

"Morning, Pengelly," he cried, as he met the miner. "Did you bring a pick?"

"No, sir, it looked too business-like," said Pengelly, "and I thought we'd keep the matter quiet. But is that all over, sir?"

"What?" said Geoffrey.

"That last night work, sir. I haven't slep' a wink for thinking of it."

"Tut, man! I never thought of it again. But, as you have spoken, just look here, Pengelly; you people down here seem to be all mad about marriage."

"Well, I don't know about mad, sir," said the miner, apologetically; "but folks do think a deal about coming together."

"So it seems," said Geoffrey, grimly.

"Comes natural like, sir," said Amos, in a quiet, innocent way; "I think it no shame to say I think a deal of Bessie Prawle, and that's what made me so mad last night."

"Well, I suppose it was natural, Pengelly. But hang it, man, you must keep that devil of a temper of yours chained."

"I do, sir; I do," said the miner, piteously. "I fight with it hard; but you, a fine straight man, don't know what it is to love a handsome girl like my Bessie, and to feel that you are misshapen and unsightly in her eyes."

"Well, but they say pretty girls like ugly men, Pengelly," said Geoffrey, smiling.

"Foolish people say many foolish things, sir," said the miner. "I can't believe all that. She's a handsome girl, and she's as good as she's handsome, and waits upon her mother hand and foot. I wish I could bring her though to a better way, for they don't do as they should; and old Prawle makes a mock at all religious talk. Then people say Bess is a witch, and can ill-wish people, and it worries me, sir, knowing as I do how good she is at heart."

"Well, never mind, Pengelly," said Geoffrey, cheerily. "Some day, perhaps, Miss Bessie yonder will find out that you are like one of the sea-shells, rough outside but bright and soft within. Eh? But come along, let's see if we can't find out something worth our while. I want to get a good mine going, my lad."

"And so do I, sir," cried the miner. "I want to save money now; and—and—"

"Well, what?"

"You don't think it foolish of me to talk, sir, as I have?"

"Not I, my lad."

"It was all owing to that upset last night, sir."

"Which we will both forget," replied Geoffrey, "for I've got work on hand that I mean to do, and have no time for such nonsense. Now then, how are we to examine these stones without a pick?"

Amos Pengelly smiled, and opened his waistcoat, to show, stuck in his trousers' waistband, the head of a miner's hammer, and a crowbar with a piece of wood, tied in the form of a cross, to keep it from slipping down his leg.

"That's capital," cried Geoffrey. "Give me the hammer; you take the bar. First of all let's have a look at the shaft."

There seemed to be nothing to see but darkness, but Geoffrey gazed long and earnestly down its rocky sides, and as he let a stone fall down to get an approximate idea of its depth he felt a strange shudder run through him, as he thought of what a man's chance would be did some enemy throw him down.

"Ugly place!" he said, as he saw Pengelly watching him.

"I never think of that, sir," was the reply.

A glance round at the buildings sufficed, and then the miner led him to the bottom of a slope where hundreds of loads had been thrown down as the *débris* was dug out of the shaft, and, patiently clearing off the grass that had sprung up, Pengelly kept handing up pieces of rock for Geoffrey to break and examine.

"Yes," said Geoffrey, as he inspected scrap after scrap, even examining the fractures with a magnifying glass, "yes, that's paying stuff, Pengelly."

"Iss, sir, isn't it?" cried the miner, eagerly.

"Paying, but poor."

"But it would be richer lower down, and we should hit the six-foot lode by driving."

"May be," said Geoffrey. "Humph, mundic! There's copper here too," he said, examining a piece of stone that glistened with the yellowish metal.

"That there be," cried Pengelly; "I'm sure Wheal Carnac would pay, sir; I always believed it; and old Prawle there at the Cove, though he's close, he knows it's a good pit."

"Yes," said Geoffrey, "I believe it would pay, well worked, and on economical and scientific principles."

"Pay, sir? Yes, I'm sure she would," cried Pengelly. "You look here, sir, and here, at the stuff."

He plied his crowbar most energetically, and Geoffrey worked hard, too, breaking fragment after fragment, and convincing himself that, though under the old plans it would not have paid to powder, wash, and extract the tin from the quality of ore lying thrown out from the mouth of the pit; yet under the system he hoped to introduce he felt sure that he could make a modest return.

"And there's such a chance, sir," cried Amos, with whom the working of Wheal Carnac was a pet project. "Look at the money laid out, and how well every thing was done."

"What became of the machinery?" cried Geoffrey, abruptly.

"It was sold by auction, sir; all beautiful, fine new engines, and boilers, and wheels, and chains—not old-fashioned ones, but new casts, and they bought it at Tulip Hobba."

"Where they work with it?"

"No, sir, it's stopped; and they do say as it could all be bought back for very little."

"Your very littles all mean thousands of pounds, Master Pengelly," said Geoffrey, thoughtfully.

"But they'd all come back, sir, and you'd have the machinery still. Do buy it, sir, and get her to work once more."

"Why, you don't suppose I've got the money to invest?" cried Geoffrey.

"Haven't you, sir?" said Pengelly, in a disappointed tone.

"Not a penny, my man."

"Never mind, sir; you get them as has, and we'll turn out such an output of tin to grass as'll make some of the clever ones shake their heads."

"More copper," said Geoffrey, picking up a piece of stone.

"Yes, sir, a bit by chance; but I don't think there's much. This pit was sunk for tin."

"Copper pays better than tin," said Geoffrey, as he went on from spot to spot. "You don't think any of this stuff was brought here from anywhere else?"

"Oh, dear, no, sir."

"Not thrown down to make the pit seem more valuable than it is? Such tricks have been played."

"Oh, no, sir. Besides, I wouldn't begin till she'd been pumped out, and some more stuff got up to try her."

"No," said Geoffrey, "of course not;" and he went on with his examination, finding nothing to cause him great elation, but enough to make him soberly sensible that there was a modest career of success for the mine, if properly worked.

Who was to find the money, and give him the charge?

That was the problem he had to solve, and as he returned the hammer to Pengelly, and walked slowly back, he wondered whether he should be fortunate enough to find any one with a sufficiency of the speculative element in him to venture.

He was so deep in thought that he nearly ran up against Rhoda Penwynn, returning from her early walk, and in conversation with the Reverend Edward Lee, evidently also on a constitutional bout.

Rhoda gave him a smile and a salute, and the young vicar raised his hat stiffly; but Geoffrey's head was too full of tin ore, pounds per ton, cost of crushing and smelting, to give them more than a passing thought; and he was only aroused from his reverie by a peculiar odour at Mrs Mullion's door, where that dame stood, buxom, pleasant, and smiling, to hope he had had a nice walk, and tell him that breakfast was quite ready, and Uncle Paul already having his.

Chapter Twenty.

Geoffrey is Foolish.

Time glided on, and Geoffrey had very little to encourage him. He investigated Wheal Carnac a little more, and then stopped because he could go no farther. He found life, however, very pleasant at the far western home. He was invited to several houses; and played whist so well that he became a favourite, especially as he generally held bad cards. Then he sat a good deal with old Mr Paul, and bantered him when he was cross; while with Mrs Mullion he became an especial favourite, the pleasant, patient, innocent little body delighting in going to his room to tell him of her troubles, and about what a good man brother Thomas was, though she did wish she would be more patient.

"He gets more impatient as he grows older," she sighed; "and if his paper isn't on the table it's dreadful. You see, Madge is so fond of getting it to read down the list of marriages, while, when her uncle has it, the first thing he does is to look and see if any one he knows is dead. I always peep to see if any one I know is born."

Poor Mrs Mullion used to blunder on in the most innocent way possible, to her half-brother's great delight, while Geoffrey had hard work sometimes to refrain from a smile.

The young man's life was one of disappointment, but it was not unhappy; and more than once he found himself thinking of what it would have been had he had a sister, and that sister had been like Rhoda Penwynn. Then came thoughts of Madge Mullion, who seemed to be developing more and more a desire to enlist him in her train of admirers. Rumour said that she was fond of flirting, and her uncle angrily endorsed it. Now Geoffrey began to think of it, he recalled the fact that he received many little attentions at the girl's hands such as an ordinary lodger would not get. Fresh flowers were always upon his table, both in sitting and bed room; books were left in conspicuous places, with markers in tender passages; he had caught Madge several times busy with needle and thread over some one or other of his articles of attire that needed the proverbial stitch in time; and one night, as he lay in bed thinking, he suddenly recalled the fact that he had said in her hearing that if there was any colour in the universe that he liked, it was blue.

"And, by George! she has worn blue ever since. The girl's a regular man-trap, and old Paul's right."

"Well," he said, getting up, and giving his pillow a vicious punch, as he lay thinking of her more than usual, "she may go on till all's blue, for I sha'n't put my foot in the trap. Why, confound her impudence! she's carrying on with that smooth-looking fellow Tregenna, or else my ears deceived me, and—bother the wench! she's very pretty, and *piquante*, and attractive, and all that sort of thing, and I wish she was at the bottom of the sea—a mermaid combing her golden hair—not drowned. Stupid wench!"

He then turned over, and mentally went down Horton Friendship mine, discussed to himself the losses that the slovenly manner of carrying on the work must entail to the proprietary; and then absolutely writhed over the contemptuous indifference his proposals received from those whom he looked upon as common-sense people.

"Hang them!" he growled. "The old cry. What did for our great-grandfathers will do for us. The farther you go back, the wiser people were; so that if you will only go far enough into antiquity there you find perfection.

"Now take my case," he said. "I don't propose any extraordinary new invention that shall take men's breath away. I merely say you are getting your ores in a costly, wasteful manner. That you are digging out of the ground vast quantities of mundic and throwing it away. Well, I say to them that mundic is pyrites, and contains so much sulphur; that, by a process, I can utilise that, so as to supply sulphur as a heat producer, to the great saving of fuel, besides which, I can give you metallic results as well, and make a large profit.

"Result: they shake their heads and laugh at me."

"Hang them! They're as obstinate as—as—well, as I am, for give up I will not."

Then, in a half-dreamy manner, he mentally went to the edge of the shaft at Wheal Carnac, and, as he had often done in reality, he picked up and examined the *débris*, lying where it had been thrown when the shaft was dug, and ended by going to sleep after half determining to try and get some apparatus fitted to allow of a descent, as far as he could go for the water, to examine the shaft and the adits, when if he could conscientiously feel that there was any prospect of the place being profitably worked he would make an effort to get a few enterprising capitalists together to take advantage of what was already done, and carry the mine on to prosperity.

The first person on whom Geoffrey's eyes rested the next morning as he entered his room was Madge Mullion, in a neat blue gingham dress, arranging a bunch of forget-me-nots in a little blue vase upon his breakfast-table, and ready to look very bright and conscious, as she started up to smile pleasantly in his face.

"Why, hang the girl! she has blue eyes, too," thought Geoffrey, as he nodded, by way of good-morning.

"Uncle Paul down?" he said.

"Yes, Mr Trethick, I heard him come down just before you, and—"

"The old rascal's got something good for breakfast," cried Geoffrey, with a pronounced sniff. "What is it?"

"Curried lobster, Mr Trethick," said Madge, pouting her pretty red— perhaps already too pouting—lips at the lodger's extremely mundane views.

"I love turned lobster," said Geoffrey, "especially such lobsters as you get down here. I shall go and attack him for a portion."

"Don't, please, Mr Trethick," said Madge, earnestly. "There is a delicious sole for you. It came from the trawler this morning, and—and I cooked it myself."

"Egged and crumbed; Miss Mullion?"

"Yes," she said, eagerly.

"Humph! Well, I think I'll compound for the fresh sole, and let Uncle Paul have his lobster in peace."

"You shall have it directly, Mr Trethick," cried Madge, looking brightly in the young man's face. "I—I brought you some forget-me-nots this morning."

"Yes," he said, smiling, "I was admiring them. They are beautiful; just like your eyes."

"For shame! Mr Trethick; what nonsense!"

"No," he said, "it's a fact, and you've got the downiest of cheeks, and the reddest of lips that pout up at one as if asking to be kissed; and really, Madge, if they ask like that I shall be obliged to kiss them."

"I'd never forgive you if you did," said Madge, with a look that bade him go on.

"Well, I'm afraid I must chance the forgiveness," he said, merrily. "It's a great risk, but you may be merciful," and he playfully caught her in his arms and kissed her, Madge making a pretence at resistance as she triumphantly told herself that she knew she could pique him and master his coldness.

"Oh! Mr Trethick!" she exclaimed.

"Madge! Here, I say, Madge!" cried the old man, whose door was heard to open sharply.

"Yes, uncle," cried the girl, reddening.

"Oh, you're there, are you," he said, stumping across the little passage. "What are you doing there, madam?"

"Defending your curried lobster, most bravely, old gentleman," said Geoffrey, coming to the rescue, but asking himself how he could have been such an ass, and whether he had not caught the complaint so prevalent in Carnac.

"How the devil did you know I had got curried lobster?" cried the old man.

"Smelt it," said Geoffrey, curtly. "Is it good?"

"No, it isn't good," cried the old man, "and I want to know why—why my niece can't let the girl wait upon you."

"Why, you're jealous, old boy," cried Geoffrey. "Hang it all! are you to have all the good things, and best attention in the house? Let me have my sole in the next room, Miss Mullion. Your uncle's low-spirited this morning, and I'll go and keep him company. Come along, old fellow."

To Madge's great relief, and Uncle Paul's utter astonishment, the result being a grateful look from the one and an angry snarl from the other, Geoffrey thrust his arm through that of the old man, marched him into his own room, and half forced him into his chair.

"There, begin your breakfast," cried Geoffrey; "it's getting cold."

"It's always getting cold, and how the devil am I to eat my lobster without salt? Every thing's forgotten now, so that you may get what you want."

"Rubbish!" said Geoffrey, taking a chair.

"It is not rubbish, sir. Didn't I see that jade exchanging glances with you just now? and she's always in your room."

"Let the poor girl alone, and don't worry her into hysterics, at all events not until I have got my sole," cried Geoffrey; "and don't talk stuff about what you don't understand. What paper's that?"

"*Times.* What I don't understand?" cried Uncle Paul, who was foaming with rage at being so unceremoniously treated.

"Yes, what you don't understand. Thanks, Miss Mullion, that will do. But there's no salt."

"I do forget so now," said poor Madge.

"Yes, and what can you expect, if you stuff your brains full of other things?" snarled Uncle Paul, with the result that Madge beat a hasty retreat, and the maid came in with the salt and the rest of the breakfast.

"Now look here, Uncle Paul," said Geoffrey, as the old man, after growling and snarling a little over his curry, took a liqueur of brandy in a very small cup of coffee, and seemed to calm down, "you are a shrewd old fellow."

"Shrewd?" he cried, "I'm an old fool, a lunatic, an ass, or I should never have brought you up here."

"Ah! we all do foolish things sometimes."

"Yes, even to running after artful, coquetting jades of girls."

"Well," said Geoffrey—"By George! what a capital sole, flaky and creamy as can be. Try a bit."

"Curse your sole!" snarled the old man, with his mouth full of curry.

"You mean the fish, I hope," said Geoffrey, laughing. "Let's see; what was I saying? Oh! I know, about doing foolish things. I've done a great many in my time, but running after coquettes was never one of them."

"Nor yet indulging in mine moonshine?"

"Moonshine, eh? Well that brings me to what I was going to say. Now, look here, Uncle Paul."

"Confound you, sir, don't stick yourself on to me as a relative. You'll want to borrow money next."

"Very likely," said Geoffrey.

"Ha-ha-ha! he-he-he!" chuckled the old man, with his face lighting up. "I should like to see you doing it. You're a clever fellow, Master Trethick, but I don't quite see you getting the better of me there."

"That's right," said Geoffrey. "Now you look yourself again." Uncle Paul's face was transformed on the instant by an aspect of wrath, but Geoffrey took no notice, only went on with his breakfast and talked.

"Look here, old gentleman, from what I hear, some fifty thousand pounds went down that Wheal Carnac?"

"Quite. Fool's money," said Uncle Paul. "Give me that thick bit of the sole with the roe in."

"I don't know about fool's money," said Geoffrey, helping him to the choice piece of fish. "Now I've had some good looks at that place, and I'm beginning to be convinced that a little enterprise freshly brought to bear would result in good returns."

"Exactly," said Uncle Paul, grinning, "and you'd like me to invest a thousand pounds, and nine other fools to do the same, and to appoint you manager, with a salary of three hundred and fifty pounds a year, and Amos Pengelly, the mad preacher, as your foreman, at a hundred. I saw you through a glass, you two, poking and picking about."

"Well, I should like a hundred a year for Pengelly," said Geoffrey, "and he'd be well worth it."

"Oh! I did not go high enough then," said Uncle Paul, with a sneer. "Suppose we must make it five hundred a year. Will that enlist your lordship's services?"

"I should spend a hundred pounds first," said Geoffrey, quietly; "that would be ten pounds apiece for ten shareholders, in carefully examining the mine and testing the lodes, and then, if I thought it really would be a good venture, I'd give my services for fifteen per cent on the profits, and take not a penny besides."

"Wouldn't you really?" said the old man, with an aggravating sneer, as he threw himself back in his chair. "Ha-ha-ha! There, I'm better now. Look here, Master Geoffrey Trethick, I mean some day to buy Wheal Carnac for a building plot, and to turn the engine-house into a cottage, where I can live in peace, and not be aggravated to death by seeing that jade of a niece of mine running after every good-looking, or ill-looking, fellow she sees. I've got a bit of money, but before I'd put a penny in a mine, I'd cash the lot, and go and sit on a rock and make ducks-and-drakes with it at high water. As for you, my lad, I don't like you, for you're the most confoundedly impudent fellow I ever met; but I'll give you this bit of advice: if you can find any fools to venture their money in an adventure, fix your salary and have it paid. No percentage. There, now I'll give you one of my best cigars."

He got up and unlocked a desk, out of whose drawer he took a couple, and relocked the holder, when, just as he was in the act of offering one to Geoffrey, the door opened, and Madge came in, looking flushed and pleased.

"What the dev—"

"It's a letter for Mr Trethick," cried the girl, hastily, "from Mr Penwynn, and it says 'important.'"

"Then you should have sent it in," cried the old man, shaking his fist at her.

"Penwynn—to see me this morning—important business," read Geoffrey, flushing with pleasure. "Then," he said aloud, "the tide has turned."

"Oh, Mr Trethick! I'm so glad," cried Madge; but her uncle made as if to throw something at her, and she ran out of the room, while Geoffrey hastily re-read the letter.

"Do you see that?" cried the old gentleman. "You've been talking nonsense to her, and you promised not."

"I? no! Hang the girl!" cried Geoffrey, joyously. "Uncle Paul, old man, the tree's going to bear fruit at last?"

Chapter Twenty One.

The Vicar is Shocked.

Geoffrey read it that he was to go up to. An Morlock, where he was informed that Mr Penwynn was engaged, but would be at liberty in a few minutes, and he was shown into the drawing-room, where he found the young vicar and Rhoda, who rose eagerly, but the next moment seemed rather constrained.

"The vicar has been discoursing of spiritual love," said Geoffrey to himself, as he declined to notice, either Rhoda's constraint or the young clergyman's stiffness, but chatted away in his free-and-easy manner.

"By the way, Miss Penwynn," he said, after a few moments' conversation, during which he felt that he was in the way, "I saw you were at church last Sunday."

"I was very glad to see you there, Mr Trethick," interposed the vicar, hastily.

"Thanks," said Geoffrey, bluffly. "I shall come—sometimes. Don't you set me down as a heathen. I went to the chapel in the evening."

"Indeed!" said the vicar, gazing at him in a horrified way, his looks plainly saying—"You a University man, and go to that chapel!"

"Yes," said Geoffrey, "and heard a capital sermon."

"Indeed!" said the vicar again, with a slightly supercilious smile.

"Capital," said Geoffrey, "by a miner—a rough fellow—one Pengelly."

"Yes, yes. I know Amos Pengelly," said Rhoda, hastily.

"Then you know a capital preacher, Miss Penwynn," cried Geoffrey, nodding to her. "He's as rough and uncultivated as can be—rather illogical sometimes; but the fellow's earnestness, and the way he swayed the congregation, were something startling."

"He is one of the local preachers," said Rhoda, "and, I believe, a very good man."

As she spoke Rhoda involuntarily glanced at her visitor's feet.

"With a most awful temper," said Geoffrey, laughing. "He got quite angry with the people's sins while he was preaching."

"I must confess," said the vicar, flushing, and speaking rather warmly—"hem! I must confess, Mr Trethick, that the way in which the people down here usurp the priestly office is very shocking, and—and really gives me a great deal of pain."

"Yes," said Geoffrey, coolly, "I dare say it would. But I do not see why it should. Here, for instance, is a truly earnest man who finds his way right to the hearts of the people, and he does what you do—prays that they may be led into better ways. His language is rough, I grant, but they understand its homeliness; and if they wouldn't be so fond of groaning and shouting out 'Glory' and 'Hallelujah' at incongruous times I should not care. One thing is very evident: he rouses people out of what your clerical gentlemen would call their sinful lethargy."

"I must say," said the vicar, "that this is all very terrible to me."

"Well, I suppose so," continued Geoffrey. "You see, Mr Lee, you view it all from a University and High Church point of view."

"And pray, sir, how would you view it?" said the vicar, with his usual nervousness dropped, and speaking like a doughty champion of the church militant, while Rhoda's lips parted, and a slight flush came into her cheeks, as she grew quite excited over the verbal battle.

"How would I view it?" said Geoffrey. "Why, from a common-sense point of view—matter-of-fact—human nature."

"Mr Trethick," cried the vicar, "you—but I beg pardon, Miss Penwynn; this is not a discussion to carry on before you. Mr Trethick, we may talk of this again."

"Oh, go on!" cried Rhoda, naïvely, with her excitement flashing out of her eyes. "I like it."

"Then I will speak," said the vicar, angrily. "Mr Trethick, you pain me by your remark, and I feel it my duty to say that your words savour of most heterodox opinions."

"Yes," said Geoffrey, "I suppose they do. I am decidedly unorthodox. I've studied nature too much to hold to many of our old college notions."

"Perhaps you would advocate free thinking?" said the vicar, with a slight sneer; and Rhoda flushed a little more, as she eagerly looked at Geoffrey for his reply.

"Free thinking? Not I. 'Pon my word, Mr Lee, I believe I'm too religious for that."

"Religious?"

"Yes! Why not? Cannot a man go to chapel, or, in other words, leave off going to church sometimes, without being taxed with irreligion? Look here, Mr Lee, you and I are about contemporaries, and do you know I think if we want to get on here in our different lines of life, the first thing we have to do is to learn of the people."

"My duty here, sir," said the vicar, coldly, and growing very pale and upright, "is to teach."

"So is mine," said Geoffrey, laughing; "yours spiritual, mine carnal; but, my dear fellow, the first thing we have to do, it seems to me, is to learn the right way to the people's hearts."

Rhoda glanced from one to the other, and her pulses began to beat, as she clasped her hands on her lap and excitedly listened for more.

"Perhaps so," said the vicar, coldly, and he glanced at the door, as if to bring the interview to an end, and yet not liking to leave Geoffrey there the master of the situation.

"For instance, take your sermon last Sunday."

"Mr Trethick!" cried the vicar, half rising.

"Don't be offended, I mean no harm," said Geoffrey, smiling, "and I am not talking to an elder, but a contemporary, as I said before. Besides, Miss Penwynn heard it, and she shall be judge."

"I beg, Mr Trethick," began the vicar, but on glancing at Rhoda's eager face, he determined not to be mastered in argument, especially upon his own ground.

"I maintain," said Geoffrey, coolly, "that your sermon was a masterly bit of logic."

The vicar stared.

"A capital line of argument."

Rhoda nodded.

"Most scholarly."

A faint flush began to appear in the vicar's cheeks.

"In fact, an excellent sermon," said Geoffrey.

"Then why do you allude to it?" said the vicar, rather warmly.

"Because I maintain that it was perfectly unsuited for a simple-minded, ignorant congregation of fishermen and miners. What do they care about how Saint Augustine wrote, or Polycarp thought, or the doings of Chrysostom the Golden Mouthed? Your words about the heresies and the Gnostics and Manichaeans were all thrown away. The early days of the Church don't interest them a bit, but they can understand about the patriarchs and their troubles and weaknesses, because the masterly hand that wrote their lives painted them as men similar to themselves."

"Mr Trethick!"

"All right; I've just done," said Geoffrey. "There was another sermon of yours too, I heard you preach, a well-meant one, but somehow you did not get hold of them. You had taken the text about the apostles becoming fishers of men, and the rough fellows could not see that it was their duty to give up their boats and nets, and forsake their wives and little ones, as you downright told them they ought."

"I hope I know my duty, Mr Trethick," said the vicar, sternly.

"I hope you do, sir; but somehow, as I say, you don't get hold of them. Now Pengelly seems to fit what he says to their everyday life, and shows them how to follow the apostles' example in their self-denial and patience. Why, my dear sir, the people here care no more for the early fathers of the Church than—than I do," he added, at a loss for a simile.

"Mr Trethick, you surprise me," gasped the vicar, "you pain me."

"Do I?" said Geoffrey. "Well, I don't want to do so. Now that man on Sunday night; he took for his text—"

"Miss Penwynn, Mr Trethick," said the vicar, rising, "I find—the time—I must say good-morning."

"I'm afraid I've been too free-speaking," said Geoffrey, earnestly, as he held out his hand. "It's a bad habit of mine to get warm in argument; and I dare say I've been preaching most heretically."

The vicar hesitated for a moment, but Geoffrey's manner disarmed him, and besides, Rhoda was looking on.

The result was that he shook hands warmly, and said, with a smile, "Mr Trethick, we must have a few more arguments. I am not beaten yet. Good-morning."

"Beaten? no," said Geoffrey. "Good-morning. Miss Penwynn, I'm afraid I've shocked you," he said, merrily, as soon as they were left alone; and as he spoke he could not help admiring the bright, animated face before him; for after the vicar's smooth, flowing speeches that morning, Geoffrey's brisk, sharp way had seemed to her like the racy breeze of the sea, fanning her spirit, and making her very pulses tingle.

"Shocked?" she said, eagerly; "I liked the discussion. I do love to hear a man speak as he really feels."

"Do you?" said Geoffrey, showing his white teeth. "Well really, Miss Penwynn, if we ever meet much in the future you will invariably hear me speak as I feel. I always did it, and invariably got myself into trouble."

"For being honest?" said Rhoda.

"Yes, for being honest. We're a strange people, Miss Penwynn. Every one advocates the truth, and straightforwardness, but, as a rule, those two qualities find very little favour."

"I'm afraid there is a great deal in what you say," said Rhoda, thoughtfully.

"I'm sure there is," exclaimed Geoffrey. "It's a queer world altogether, but I like it all the same."

"I hope we all do," replied Rhoda, smiling.

"Of course; and we do all like it," said Geoffrey, in an imperious way; "and when next you hear any one, my dear young lady, calling it a vale of tears, and wanting to be somewhere else, you set that person down as an impostor or a fool."

Rhoda raised her eyebrows, feeling half-annoyed at his freedom, half amused.

"It's a splendid world, and it's half bitters, half sweets."

"Indeed?"

"Yes, and wisely so. The bitters make us like the sweets. I find old Mr Paul up yonder do me no end of good when I'm put out. He's all bitters."

"And Madge Mullion supplies the sweets," thought Rhoda.

"Don't you think I ought to have gone into the Church, Miss Penwynn?" said Geoffrey, abruptly.

"No. Why?"

"Because I'm so fond of preaching. Somehow it always sets me going if I come across a man with about two notions only in his head, which he jumps to the conclusion will do admirably for the north and south poles of the world, and that he has nothing else to do but set the world turning upon them; and gets cross if some one tells him the world is really turning the other way. But I'm preaching again. There, I frightened the parson away, and if I don't change my tone, or Mr Penwynn does not soon send for me, I shall scare you as well."

"I am not so easily alarmed," said Rhoda, laughing; "but I hope you are meeting with success in your efforts, Mr Trethick?"

"Success, my dear madam?" replied Geoffrey, laughing outright. "Why, I have been hammering away ever since I came down, months now, and have not succeeded in any thing but in making the people harder against me."

"I am sorry to hear that."

"Thank you. Sympathy's nice," said Geoffrey. "But I'm not beaten yet, Miss Penwynn, and now I think the sun is going to shine, for Mr Penwynn has sent me a line asking me to come and see him; and I have a shrewd suspicion that it means business."

"Mr Penwynn will see you, sir, in the study," said a servant, opening the door; and, after a frank good-by, Geoffrey swung out of the room, Rhoda's eyes following him till the door closed.

But she did not sigh, she did not go to the glass and look conscious, she did not begin to commune with her spirit, she only said, quietly,—

"There is a something about him that I like!"

Chapter Twenty Two.

A Business Interview.

"Ah, Mr Trethick!" said the banker, quietly, as Geoffrey was ushered into his handsome study, crammed with books that he seldom read, "I hope I have not brought you up from any important engagement."

"Well, yes, I was going to be very busy," said Geoffrey, "I had an appointment on the cliff."

"I am very sorry," said the banker, "I thought—"

"That I had nothing to do, and would come down directly. You were quite right, sir, and here I am."

"But your engagement?"

"Was with myself—to go and loaf about and stare down deserted mine shafts, and growl at the obstinacy of proprietors who refuse to be made rich."

Mr Penwynn had begun to look disappointed; he now brightened a little.

"You are quite at liberty then, Mr Trethick?"

"Quite, sir."

"And willing to earn a few guineas?"

"Most willing, sir. When shall I begin? I'm growing rusty from disuse."

Mr Penwynn sat thinking for a few moments, gazing at Geoffrey, and then he began,—

"Rundell and Sharp spoke most highly of you, Mr Trethick."

"I thank them for their good opinion, sir."

"They said that you were a man most thoroughly to be trusted, and that you were conscientious to a degree."

"Indeed, sir," said Geoffrey, sharply. "When did they say that?"

Mr Penwynn was a little taken aback, but he recovered himself, and said with a smile,—

"In a letter that I have received from them."

"Then you have been writing to make further inquiries about me, Mr Penwynn."

"Well—yes, I have."

"Good!" said Geoffrey, quietly. "Then I presume you are satisfied, Mr Penwynn?"

"Yes, I am," was the reply, "and on the strength of their recommendations I am about to try and throw something—just a trifle—in your way."

"Mining, I hope?"

"Yes, Mr Trethick, mining; but on one condition."

"And what is that, Mr Penwynn?"

"That I have your whole and sole effort to work for my interest to the best of your ability."

"Why, of course, sir," said Geoffrey, "I should be taking your pay."

"Yes, Mr Trethick; but I have known cases where a man takes pay from one employer, and works in the interest of another."

"Mr Penwynn!"

"I don't for a moment hint that you would do such a thing, Mr Trethick. I merely say to you, I trust you to do for me the best you can, and not let yourself be tempted away from the path of rectitude by any of the scoundrels you may encounter."

"Mr Penwynn," said Geoffrey, warmly, "you ought not to speak to me like that after the letter you say you have had. But now, sir, suppose we proceed to business?"

"Exactly?" said Mr Penwynn, drawing his chair a little nearer.

"The fact is, Mr Trethick—this in confidence, mind, and for the present I don't want to appear in the matter at all—I have been offered at a price a mine over which two or three companies have failed. I want to know whether it is worth my while to buy that mine, and I am going to act upon your Report."

"A tin-mine?" said Geoffrey.

"Yes; a disused mine."

"Not Wheal Carnac?"

"Yes, Wheal Carnac," said Mr Penwynn, starting. "What of it?"

"Buy it!" said Geoffrey, sharply.

"Buy it?" said Mr Penwynn, frowning. "What do you mean?"

"What I say," said Geoffrey, eagerly; "buy it."

"You are not long in giving in a report, Mr Trethick," said the banker, suspiciously. "May I ask what you know of Wheal Carnac?"

"More than you suppose, sir," was the reply. "I have been looking about that place a good deal, and I am of opinion that with capital I could make it pay."

"Oh, yes! so I suppose," said the banker; "but you are going much too fast, Mr Trethick. What I want to know is whether the mine is worth buying at a price."

"What price?" exclaimed Geoffrey.

Mr Penwynn hesitated, bit his nails, tapped the table, and looked again and again at his companion's searching eyes.

"Well," he said at last—"this is in confidence, Mr Trethick—eight hundred pounds!"

"Why the land's worth it," cried Geoffrey; "there can be no doubt about that."

"Possibly," said Mr Penwynn.

"The buildings—the material," cried Geoffrey. "Why really, Mr Penwynn, I could give you a decisive answer at once. The place is worth buying."

The banker sat gazing at him in a curious, searching way, and he made no reply for a few minutes; but it was evident that he was a little infected by Geoffrey's enthusiasm.

"Are you willing to go down the mine as far as you can go, Mr Trethick—I mean for water—and to see what tokens you can find of tin ore?"

"Yes," said Geoffrey, "I'll go down again if you like."

"Again?"

"Yes; I've been down as far as I could go."

"You have, Mr Trethick?"

"Yes, sir," said Geoffrey, smiling, "I have."

"But right down to the water?"

"Right down into it, sir," replied Geoffrey, laughing. "I had a regular ducking, for my companion let the rope slip."

"Do you mean to tell me, Mr Trethick, that you made the descent of Wheal Carnac?"

"To be sure I do, sir. Look here, Mr Penwynn, I took rather a fancy to that place. Every thing is so thorough and well done. Then I met with a rough mining fellow, one Amos Pengelly. Know him?"

Mr Penwynn nodded.

"He is sanguine about the mine, and asked me to examine it. I did so as far as I could, and then one night we procured a rope, and I rigged up a ship's block on a stoutish cross-beam, took a lantern, and Pengelly let me down."

"By himself?"

"Oh, yes! sir; he's as strong as a horse. But he did duck me."

"Mr Trethick," said the banker, pulling out his pocket-handkerchief, "do you mean to tell me that you trusted to one man to lower you down that pit?"

"I do, Mr Penwynn, and a precious black pit it is; and, as I tell you, he let me down rather too far, but not till I had had a good look round."

"And what did you discover?" said the banker, wiping the palms of his wet hands.

"Nothing," said Geoffrey, bluntly. "No more than I could find out on the heap of *débris*. No thorough examination could be made without the mine were pumped out."

"And that would cost?—"

"Fifty or a hundred pounds, perhaps two," said Geoffrey. "Principally for carriage of pumping apparatus, fixing, and taking down again."

"You have been thoroughly into the matter, then," said Mr Penwynn, who was growing more and more interested.

"Thoroughly," said Geoffrey, bluntly, "I don't play with what I take up, sir."

The banker shifted his position, got up, walked about the room, sat down again, and began tapping the table with his fingers.

"Will you have a cigar, Mr Trethick?" he said, unlocking a drawer.

"Thanks, no," said Geoffrey. "I don't smoke over business."

There was another pause, during which Geoffrey sat patiently awaiting the banker's orders, while that gentleman was evidently turning the affair well over in his mind.

At last he spoke.

"Mr Trethick," he said, "what remuneration should you ask to undertake to examine that mine?"

"Can't be done without pumping out, sir."

"Supposing I place the necessary funds at your disposal?"

Geoffrey drew his chair closer.

"Do you mean this, Mr Penwynn?"

"I never joke over business-matters, Mr Trethick," said the banker.

"Mr Penwynn," said Geoffrey, rising, and by his words chasing away from the banker's mind any lingering doubt of his energy, "I have so much faith in making that mine pay, that I'll do what you ask for nothing, but be content with a percentage on future profits."

"No, Mr Trethick, I never work in that way," said Mr Penwynn. "I ask your services on what I suppose to be a fortnight or three weeks' task. I want your best energies, and a truthful and just report, not highly coloured, rather the reverse. If you will do this for me, I will give you a fee of five-and-twenty guineas. Will that do?"

"Do? Yes!" cried Geoffrey, flushing. "When shall I begin?"

"When you please," said the banker, smiling at his earnestness.

"And you place funds at my disposal?"

"Yes, to the amount of a hundred pounds. If that is not enough, you may spend another fifty. Then stop. But mind you are doing this under orders. I do not wish to appear in the matter yet. If it were known that I was going in for such a mad venture, as people would call it, I should lose all credit in the place. Not that it would much matter," he added, with a contemptuous smile. "Well, Mr Trethick, shall we draw up a memorandum to the effect that you will give me your best services in this commission? I trust to you, implicitly."

"If you like," said Geoffrey, grimly, as he once more rose and took an excited stride up and down the room. "Mr Penwynn," he exclaimed, stopping short before the banker, "you have given me new life in this display of confidence. There's my memorandum and bond, sir," he cried, stretching out his broad, firm hand, and gripping that of the banker. "You sha'n't repent it, come what may."

"I hope not, Trethick," said Mr Penwynn, smiling, "but time tries all."

"Oh, no!" said Geoffrey, sharply. "That's an old saw, and I put no faith in saws. Time will try me, Mr Penwynn; there's no doubt of that. And now I'm off."

"It's close upon one o'clock," said Mr Penwynn, glancing at his watch. "You'll stay and have lunch?"

"No, thanks," said Geoffrey; "I'm going to work off some of this rust. But how am I to let you know how I am getting on?"

"Don't you trouble about that," said Mr Penwynn, laughing. "You don't know Carnac yet. Why, every step you take will be known all over the place, and people will be asking what madman is finding the money."

"I see," said Geoffrey, nodding.

"Give me a written report when you have done. Mr Chynoweth shall send you a cheque-book, and your cheques will be honoured to the sum I name."

Geoffrey looked him full in the eyes for a moment or two longer, and then strode off, Rhoda, who was at the window, seeing him pass, evidently deeply intent upon something, for he paid no heed to her, but made straight for Horton mine to see Pengelly, while Mr Penwynn walked up and down his study with a satisfied air, as if he considered that he had done a good morning's work.

"He's the right man," he said, rubbing his hands. "He's as true as steel!"

Putting on his hat, he walked down to the office, he knew not why, but taking a deeper interest in the affair each moment, and passing Tregenna on the opposite side of the way.

"Send Mr Geoffrey Trethick a cheque-book, Chynoweth," he said, as he entered his office, and spoiled a most interesting game of whist.

Mr Chynoweth took down his slate, and made an entry.

"Honour his cheques to the amount of a hundred and fifty."

This entry was also made upon the slate, and Mr Penwynn walked back to his lunch.

Mr Chynoweth became thoughtful. He had played out a hand at whist in his desk that morning; and he had written an offer of marriage to

Miss Pavey, who had won five and sixpence of him the previous night at whist; but this was a very important matter, and thinking that he could remain a bachelor a little longer, he took out his letter, opened, read it, sighed, and, striking a match, carefully burned it on the hearth.

"Tregenna here—Trethick to draw cheques—what's that mean?" said Mr Chynoweth, thoughtfully. "What does the governor mean by that? I hope he is not going in for mining. If he is—"

He paused for a few moments.

"I wouldn't bet a crown he is not going to try Wheal Carnac."

Chapter Twenty Three.

How Tregenna Hooked his Fish.

There was, of course, a reason for the banker's actions.

John Tregenna had at once taken advantage of the proposal that he should still be on friendly terms with the Penwynns, and, calling frequently and dining there, set himself, in a pleasant, frank manner, to remove any unpleasant feeling that might exist in Rhoda's mind.

To her he was gentlemanly and courteous, without formality, showing in every way that it was his desire that the past should be forgotten. With Mr Penwynn he resumed his old business relations, and, as the banker's confidential solicitor, he finished and carried through a tiresome law case, which ridded Mr Penwynn of a good deal of anxiety, and put five hundred pounds in his pocket.

"By the way," he said, on the morning when he had brought in the news of the satisfactory settlement, and it had been discussed, "they want to sell Wheal Carnac."

"So Chynoweth told me some little time back," said Mr Penwynn. "I wish they may get a customer."

"Well, so do I, if it comes to that," said Tregenna, "because I am to have a hundred if I effect a sale."

"And where will you get customers? Why, they've wasted no end in putting it up for auction in London, advertisements and one way and the other."

"Yes, and that makes them willing now to part with the place for a mere song."

"Bah!" said Mr Penwynn. "The place is worthless. The money wasted there is enormous."

"Yes, they were pretty extravagant; but do you know, Penwynn, I've got hold of a man who used to work there."

"Yes?"

"A man of the name of Lannoe."

"Lannoe, Lannoe? Why, that was the man who summoned a miner for half killing him."

"To be sure, yes, so it was. I remember now. Some quarrel about a girl."

"Of course. That scoundrel Prawle's wench down at the Cove. Well, what about him?"

"He swears to me that when the company broke up, and the owners would advance no more money, they had just got to good paying stuff."

"I don't believe it," said Mr Penwynn sharply.

"Well I don't put much faith in it myself, but they say where there's smoke there's fire."

"Not in this case, Tregenna, for Wheal Carnac was all smoke."

"Ha, ha, ha! That's not so very bad, Penwynn," said the solicitor, laughing; "but I cannot help thinking there may be something in it."

"Well, I tell you what I'd do then," said Mr Penwynn, looking very serious; "you're pretty warm, Tregenna; buy Wheal Carnac, and then buy up the machinery from some other mine that is in difficulties, work the concern on your own hook, and land a fortune."

Tregenna half-closed his eyes and tightened his lips into a dry smile of derision, as he looked at the banker, and then the two men burst into a hearty laugh.

"Not exactly," said Tregenna. "I don't quite see myself performing such an act of lunacy at present; but really, seriously though, I do think there is something in that mine."

"Yes," said Mr Penwynn, picking his teeth, "water!"

"Yes, that's the devil of it. Else they want so little for the place that I'd go to the expense of having it tested. In fact, they ask so small a sum now that a man might venture to buy it for nothing else but a spec, to sell again."

"Like me to buy it, perhaps," said the banker, laughing.

"I don't know," said Tregenna seriously; "but I wouldn't mind going in for spending a little money in testing the place."

"Now look here, Tregenna," said Mr Penwynn, "what is your game here?"

"My game? Oh, that's soon said. I want to make a hundred pounds commission on the sale, and get an account against the vendors for another fifty."

"Do you think there is any thing in that man's words?"

"Heaven knows," said Tregenna; "but if they are true, the place, instead of being worth eight hundred pounds, would be worth more than as many thousands."

Mr Penwynn thrust his hands very deeply into his pockets and whistled softly, as he gazed searchingly at the other. For, though Tregenna had thrown some hundreds latterly in his way, he was still upon his guard.

"I should estimate the land and foreshore as being worth the money," said Tregenna. "There's a good deal of it, and the building material in squared granite is worth a trifle. There's plenty to build a couple of good houses."

"Ah! you want to make that hundred and fifty pounds, Tregenna."

"Yes, I do, certainly; but I don't think the buyer could be much out of pocket unless he began mining on his own account. Of that I wash my hands. By the way, though, that would not make a bad building site."

"Too exposed," said Mr Penwynn, thoughtfully.

"Well, yes, it is exposed, certainly."

"What do they want for it?"

"A thousand, but between ourselves they wouldn't refuse eight hundred."

"No, I suppose not," said Mr Penwynn, dryly. "Look here, Tregenna, what will you spring towards having the place pumped out, quietly you know, to see if there's any truth in your fellow's assertion?"

Tregenna sat tapping the table with his fingers, and he did not reply.

"You don't seem to rise at that fly," said Mr Penwynn, laughing.

"I was thinking whether I could get them to advance fifty pounds for the purpose; but they're so poor, and if they would it could only be on some undertaking to buy. I tell you what, Penwynn, I haven't much faith in the fellow's statement proving correct—I believe, mind you, he's an honest fellow, but he may have been mistaken—in fact I haven't much faith in any thing now," he continued dismally; "but I tell you what I'll do; I'll stand fifty to your fifty to examine the place properly before you do any thing else, on one condition."

"What's that?"

"That if it turns out a failure and you don't buy, you'll make that fifty up to me out of something else—that you won't let me be the loser."

"What else?"

Tregenna laughed.

"There's no doing you, Penwynn, with an assumption of modesty. There, frankly, I want something more off it. If it turns out a good thing you will come down handsome."

"I will," said Mr Penwynn. "You leave that to my honour, and I will."

Tregenna screwed up his face a little.

"That's rather vague, my dear sir," he said.

"Well, vague or no, what do you want?"

"A thousand pounds."

"A thousand grandmothers," said Mr Penwynn, pettishly.

"Well, that's not unreasonable," said Tregenna. "I suppose—well, we won't suppose, but put it in plain figures—if that mine should turn out well—"

"Which it will not."

"Well, it is the merest chance, but I say if it does turn out well, I shall have ten per cent of its market value two years hence."

"Done," said Mr Penwynn, holding out his hand.

"Agreed," said Tregenna, grasping it. "Now write a memo to that effect."

"Isn't it premature rather, seeing that I have decided nothing?"

"Well, perhaps it is," said Tregenna, taking out his watch. "I must be off. Think the matter over for a few days. Shall I keep it quiet, or try elsewhere?"

"Try elsewhere if you like," said Mr Penwynn, carelessly.

"All right. Good-morning," said Tregenna. "My kind regards at home."

Mr Penwynn nodded, and Tregenna went out, nodded to Chynoweth, who was shutting down his desk-lid over a hand of whist, and then walked swiftly away, muttering one word—

"Hooked!"

Chapter Twenty Four.

Hunting a Witch.

Geoffrey strode right across the heather and stones to Horton mine, bent upon, if possible, securing the services of Pengelly if they were to be had. If not, he felt bound to take counsel with him, and let him know his every step.

The manager was at his office, and welcomed Geoffrey in a very friendly way.

"Want Pengelly, eh!" he said, looking at the speaker, inquiringly. "He won't be here to-day. But look here, Mr Trethick, I like you. You're a man with some stuff in you. Let me give you a word of advice."

"Thank you," said Geoffrey. "What is it?"

"Don't let Amos Pengelly lead you into any scrape. He's mad, that's what he is; and if you don't look out he'll persuade you to take up some mining spec, such as that old fly-blown Wheal Carnac, and ruin you. The fact is, Mr Trethick, between you and me, Cornwall's about pumped out. You understand."

"Yes, I understand," said Geoffrey, who felt much amused.

"You take care of yourself, and wait till something turns up. Don't you be in too great a hurry. As for Amos Pengelly, he's religious crazy, and half his time don't know what he's about."

"Where do you suppose he is to-day?"

"Dressed up in his black satin waistcoat and long togs, gone preaching. There's a revival meeting somewhere."

"All right; thanks," said Geoffrey, and, with a bluff "good-morning," he strode off back again; but before he had gone many yards he determined to try and make a short cut across to the cliff, west of Carnac.

"I can have a good look at the old mine, and call in at Pengelly's cottage and leave word that I want to see him," thought Geoffrey.

"That chap'll get himself into a scrape with Amos Pengelly, if he don't look out," muttered the manager, as he watched his visitor out of sight. "He's one of your jolly, honest sort, he is, and Amos Pengelly's one of your religious kind. If them two put their heads together there'll be a nice mess made of it."

After delivering himself of this prophecy, the manager went back into his office to begin a laborious process of making up accounts; while Geoffrey, with the brisk sea-breeze making his pulses throb, crossed rough scraps of pasture, leaped the quaint Cornish stiles of parallel blocks of stone, heavily-laden slopes of granite, stony track, and rugged ravine, with a tiny stream at the bottom, overhung with ferns.

He had meant to make a bee-line for the cliff, but the country was more rugged than he anticipated. Then, too, he had to follow a path here and there formed on the top of the low granite walls that separated various plots; and the result was, that instead of striking the cliff just west of the town, he found himself beyond the older ruined mine, and nearly as far as Gwennas Cove.

"Might as well go and see the old lady," he said to himself, as he scrambled down the steep face of the cliff, and reached the shelf-like path. "No, I'll get on with my work now," he continued; and, turning at once for the town, he had not gone a hundred yards before he became aware of a loud shouting and yelling, as if something was being hunted along the cliff.

"Why, what could they hunt here?" he said to himself. "Foxes? seals? Nonsense, they couldn't get up the cliff. It must be—why, by George! it's a woman."

He ran along the cliff towards where a woman, in a bright-coloured petticoat, seemed to be coming towards him, half surrounded by at least fifty people—men and women, and great fisher lads, some of whom seemed to have headed the fugitive, who, as Geoffrey came up, had taken refuge in a narrow cleft that ran up from the track, where there was one of the quaint old Cornish crosses, and now stood at bay.

In less time than it takes to describe it, Geoffrey Trethick had seen that the fugitive was Bessie Prawle, with her hair dishevelled, wild-eyed, her clothes torn, and fouled with mud and fish refuse, some of which had bespattered her face, now bleeding quite profusely; but she uttered no sound, only turned her fierce defiant eyes on the crowd, who yelled, hissed, and pelted her with any thing that came to hand, some of the rough mining women, in their excitement, tearing up scraps of heath and grass for an impotent fling.

"Yah! witch! witch!" reached Geoffrey's ears as he dashed up, just as a great lout of a fisher lad, in a blue jersey, had picked up a lump of granite, and was about to fling it at the wretched girl.

"Heave hard, my son," cried several. "Don't look at her eyes, or she'll ill-wish you."

The lout raised the piece of stone, took good aim, and then struck heavily against a companion, who cannoned against another, and all three staggered over the cliff edge from the shelf on which they stood, to fall half-a-dozen feet, scrambling, on the granite slope below.

For the impetus with which Geoffrey Trethick had thrown out one of his fists, driven by the full weight of his body, would have upset a giant, and coming as he did like a thunderbolt amongst them, the people divided right and left, some staggering, some falling, as he made his way up to where Bessie Prawle stood, in time to receive a dirty, half-rotten dog-fish right across his chest.

"Who threw that?" he roared furiously.

"I did," cried a great stupid-looking young fisherman, "but it warn't meant for you. Come away; she's a witch. She'll ill-wish you."

"I'll ill-wish you and break every bone in your cowardly thick hide," roared Geoffrey. "Call yourself a man," he cried, "and throw at a woman!"

"She's a witch—a witch! We're going to douse her," shrieked a wild-looking woman, a regular bare-armed virago. "Now gals, have her out. Lay hold of the man, lads; have him away."

Urged by the woman's words the big fisherman uttered a shout to his companions, and made at Bessie Prawle's defender; but somehow, they did not know how, the little crowd saw the young fisherman go down, crash, and Geoffrey stamp one foot upon his chest and hold him there.

This checked them, and the three lads who had gone over the cliff edge now scrambled back, furious, and ready to pick up stones or any thing that came within their reach.

But they did not throw them, for Geoffrey's angry eyes, and the prostrate man beneath his foot, had a wonderfully calming effect upon their angry passions.

"Get back home—all of you," he cried. "Shame upon your ignorance!"

"She ill-wished Nance Allion's gal, and she's pining away," cried one woman, angrily.

"She ill-wished Mrs Roby's gal, too, and she's in a 'sumption," cried another.

"And she's ill-wished my mother, so as she hasn't any inside," cried a great lubberly lad.

"Ill-wished!" cried Geoffrey, in tones of contempt. "Get back, I say, all of you who call yourselves women; and as for you," he raged, "you, you cowardly louts that stand here, I'll hurl the first man or boy over the cliff who flings another stone."

There was a loud murmur here, but the *émeute* was over, and the women and lads began to shrink away; while Bess Prawle, her defiant aspect gone, had sunk down now, panting and overcome, looking piteously up at Geoffrey, as he went upon one knee beside her, after letting the prostrate man shuffle away, and applied his handkerchief to her bleeding face.

Poor Bess could not speak, but she caught the hand that helped in both of hers, and with a hysterical sob pressed it firmly to her lips.

"Come, come," he said, gently; "there's nothing to mind now. Try and get up, and lean on my arm."

"Let me come, Mr Trethick," said a voice that made Geoffrey start; "she is fainting."

Rhoda Penwynn, who had been walking on the cliff with Miss Pavey, had come up in time to hear Geoffrey's furious words, and see the brave way in which he had defended poor Bessie. She had seen, too, the passionate kiss the poor girl had bestowed upon her defender's hand, and, she knew not why, a feeling of sorrow seemed for the moment to master her alarm.

Geoffrey made way for her on the instant, as she knelt down and loosened Bess's throat and held a little vinaigrette to her nostrils, just in the middle of which acts Geoffrey's services were again called into requisition, for Miss Pavey looked at him piteously, uttered a cry, and would have fallen but for the ready arm extended to help her gently down upon the heathery bank.

The crowd had stood back, muttering menacingly; but the coming of the banker's daughter had the effect of sending half the men shuffling farther off in an uneasy fashion, the others following, and soon after the little group was left alone.

"Poor lass!" said Geoffrey, whose interest in Bessie was far greater than in fainting Miss Pavey, who lay back for the moment untended. "Do you know how this occurred, Miss Penwynn? Your people here seem to be half savages."

"I saw it all, Mr Trethick," said Rhoda. "She is coming to now. Poor Miss Pavey has fainted, too. Pray hold the vinaigrette to her nostrils."

Geoffrey caught the little silver case, and held it so vigorously to the poor woman's nose that her face, in spite of her efforts, became convulsed; and she uttered a loud sneeze, after which she faintly struggled up, wished that they had been alone, when she would have essayed to kiss Geoffrey's hand out of gratitude, as she had seen Bess Prawle. As it was, she had to be content to look her thanks.

"Thank you, miss—thank you," said Bess, rising. "I felt sick and giddy. I'm better now. Thank you, too, sir. The cowards would have killed me if you had not come."

"Oh, don't talk about the savages," cried Geoffrey, who was full of sympathy for the poor ill-used girl. "But you are very weak still: here, take my arm, and I'll see you home."

"I will go home with her, Mr Trethick," said Rhoda, coldly.

"Better still," he said.

"I—I think I can manage by myself," said Bess, hoarsely.

But the difficulty as to who should see her home was solved by the appearance of old Prawle himself, approaching at a trot, armed with a short steel-armed boat-hook, which looked a formidable weapon in the hands of the fierce-looking old man, who came up half-mad with rage, a boy having carried him the news that they were "going to douse Bess Prawle for a witch."

"What's this? What's all this?" he cried, savagely; and he looked from one to the other, as if in search of some one to assault.

"Take me home, father—take me home," said Bess, faintly. "Thank you, miss," she continued, turning to Rhoda. "Mr Trethick, sir: I shall never forget this."

The fierce-looking old man glared at all in turn; but in spite of his savage aspect, Geoffrey noted that there was something inexpressibly tender in the way in which he drew his child's arm through his, and directly after parsed his arm round her to give her more support, walking gently by her as the others watched them till they turned a corner of the cliff.

"Miss Penwynn," said Geoffrey, excitedly, breaking an awkward silence, "I could not have believed that such superstition existed in these later days."

"Superstition dies hard, Mr Trethick," said Rhoda, rather coldly. "Shall we say good-morning here? Miss Pavey and I are going across the fields."

Geoffrey raised his hat, and took the very plain hint that he was to go, by passing on along the cliff, while Rhoda and her companion took to the upland path, which Geoffrey had so lately left.

"Oh, my dearest child!" cried Miss Pavey, as soon as they were alone, and she could burst into a fit of ecstasies, "isn't he noble—isn't he grand—isn't he heroic? Ah! Rhoda, Rhoda, if my heart were free it would fly from my bosom to such a chivalrous knight as he. It quite puts me in mind of the olden times."

Rhoda did not reply, for the scene she had witnessed had agitated her.

"I declare I never saw any one behave so gallantly and well," continued Miss Pavey. "He is quite a hero!"

Still Rhoda did not reply, for there was an uneasy feeling in her breast, and, in spite of herself, she could not help recalling Bess's act as she raised and passionately kissed Geoffrey Trethick's hand.

It was nothing to her, of course, and she hated to think of the things in which her companion would have gloried; but still old Mrs Prawle's words and Geoffrey's frequent visits to the Cove floated back, and a feeling of irritation and anger against him they had just left kept growing stronger and stronger.

"I declare," exclaimed Miss Pavey, suddenly, with quite a girlish giggle, "neglectful as he was to me, I feel smitten—absolutely smitten."

"What?" exclaimed Rhoda, harshly.

"Oh! my dear child," cried Miss Pavey, "don't for goodness' sake snap a poor creature up like that. But oh, you naughty, naughty girl! Have I touched the tender chord at last? Oh, Rhoda, my darling child, don't be jealous; you have no cause!"

"I—jealous?" cried Rhoda, frowning.

"Not the slightest cause, dearest," said Miss Pavey, simpering. "I would not confess such a thing to any one but you, dearest; but if Mr Trethick went down on his knees to me at this moment, much as I admire him, I should have to say *no*!"

"My dear Martha, what do you mean?" exclaimed Rhoda, half angrily.

"I can't help it, dearest," sighed Miss Pavey. "That scene has made me feel hysterical and low; and I cannot help confessing to you, dearest Rhoda, that I love him."

"Love Mr Trethick?" cried Rhoda, whose eyes contracted.

"No, no, dear! what a naughty, foolish girl you are, and how you do betray yourself."

"Betray myself?"

"Yes, dear, your head is always running on this Mr Trethick. I was talking about Mr Lee—he is so pure, and saint-like, and sweet."

"Oh, yes, I had almost forgotten," said Rhoda, dreamily; "I had almost forgotten that he lodges with you."

"Boards with me, dear; and I try to help him in his efforts with these dreadful people here. But tell me, dear, don't you think it was very imprudent of Mr Trethick to go and lodge at Mrs Mullion's?"

"No," said Rhoda; "why?"

"Because of Madge, dear."

"I do not see why it is more imprudent than for Mr Lee to go and lodge with a lady I know."

"Board, my dear," said Miss Pavey, with dignity. "But Mr Lee is a guest."

"But guests are men," said Rhoda.

Miss Pavey shook her head as if she did not agree; and as Rhoda had turned very silent since Mr Lee's name had been mentioned, Miss Pavey came to the conclusion that her companion's thoughts were of the young vicar, and felt a pang of pain.

"Ah! Rhoda," she said, with a sigh, "love is a strange thing, is it not?"

Rhoda uttered an ejaculation that evidently meant disgust; but poor Miss Pavey did not understand it, and went prattling on by her companion's side till they reached the town, where they separated, Rhoda gladly seeking her own room, to be alone and think, telling herself that the scenes she had witnessed—the words she had heard, had unstrung her more than she cared to own.

Chapter Twenty Five.

Tom Jennen's Opinion.

"Poor lass!" said Geoffrey, as he walked in the direction of Pengelly's cottage. "They'd have half killed her. I wish I had hit those fellows harder. It will frighten the poor old woman to death."

He then went on thinking a little about Rhoda Penwynn.

"She must have seen me flourishing my fists," he said, laughing. "I must have looked gentlemanly. I like that girl somehow, but by George, she's as proud as a peacock. Pea-hens are not proud. I wonder whether she will marry that Tregenna after all."

He was brought back from surmise to reality by the sight of the people clustering about the cottages on the cliff, as he entered the little town and noted that a variety of ominous scowls awaited him. There were plenty of women about, and they had stones and stale fish in their hands. The rough lads had increased in number, and a number of the fishermen, among whom was Tom Jennen, were standing by the rails as if to see some expected sight.

"Hang me if I don't think they are getting up a warm reception for this respectable individual. That's pleasant! A sort of running marine pillory. What shall I do? Go back?"

"Not this time!" he said, setting his teeth, and taking a very shabby old black meerschaum from a case; he closed the fastening with a loud snap, pulled out an india-rubber pouch, filled the pipe, deliberately walking slowly and calmly along gazing in the most unruffled way in the faces of the women, and not deigning to notice the rough lads, all of whom seemed to be only waiting for a signal to begin showering their missiles upon his head.

Suddenly the great stupid-looking fisher lad whom Geoffrey had knocked down, strode out in front of him, spread his legs apart, set his arms akimbo, and pretty well barred the narrow granite-paved way.

A low buzz of excitement arose, the lads grasped their missiles ready to throw, but the women dropped their arms to their sides or behind them, as they gazed at the fine, manly young fellow, who looked at them with a half-mocking smile upon his lip as he passed.

Geoffrey did not flinch. On the contrary, a red spot appeared in each of his cheeks as he put the amber mouth-piece of his pipe between his lips, strode forward, laid one strong hand upon the fellow's shoulder, and, apparently without effort, swung him round.

"Stand aside, you cowardly hound!" he cried aloud; went on three or four yards, and stopped in front of Tom Jennen and the group of men who stood staring with all their might.

"Give us a light, fisherman!" said Geoffrey, bluffly.

"Light? Ay, my lad," was the reply, and the rough fellow brought out a brass box of matches, and handed it to Geoffrey, who coolly opened it, struck a match, and sheltered light and pipe between the hollow of his hands, drew vigorously, and puffed out clouds of smoke between his fingers, after which he returned the box with a bluff "Thanky!"

"Where does Amos Pengelly live?" he said then.

"Up yon turn, ninth house, with a green door," said Tom Jennen. "There's a gashly old bit o' rock opposite."

As he spoke, he pointed to a narrow steep path which Geoffrey had passed, and which necessitated his running the gauntlet again, as it were.

But he was equal to the task.

"I say, fisherman," he said, addressing Tom Jennen, but meaning it for the group, "If I were you I should use the rope's-end there, and try to make those cowardly young lubbers men!"

Then thrusting his hands into his pockets, he walked coolly back, looking woman after woman in the face, turned up the passage, and was gone.

No sooner was his back turned, than the boys uttered a yell, and made as if to throw, but the women turned upon them fiercely, and Tom Jennen and his mates cleared the road by making a menacing charge.

"Well, of all the smart young chaps as ever I set eyes on," said one woman, "he's about the best. Put that there gashly old fish down, Jan Dwiod, or I'll give you a smack i' th' mouth."

"That's pluck, that is," said Tom Jennen, with his hands very far down in his pockets. "That's the sorter stuff as men's made on. That's pluck, that is," he continued, nodding at every one in turn, and then at intervals repeating the words—"that's pluck!" Geoffrey did not know it then, but his cool treatment of the party lying in wait for him, had made him, as it were, a king, and in place of menace on his next appearance in the streets there was a smile on every lip, and he might have had the help of all for the holding up of a hand.

Meanwhile he had reached Pengelly's cottage to knock and be told by a woman next door that the owner was gone out preaching, and wouldn't be back till night.

"Ask him to run up to Mrs Mullion's when he comes," said Geoffrey, and the woman promising to convey his message, he went back to his lodgings to dine and complete his plans.

Chapter Twenty Six.

A Night at the Mine.

As Geoffrey rattled the garden gate he heard a rustle at one of the windows, and, looking up, there was Madge ready to welcome him with a smile.

"Oh! you're there, are you, madam," he said to himself. "How are you?"

He nodded to her civilly enough, and was going on to the house, when from out of the look-out there came a rough "Hallo!"

"Hallo, old gentleman!" said Geoffrey, and, turning aside, he entered the summer-house, where Uncle Paul sat smoking, cane in hand, with which he pointed up towards the window where Madge had been.

"Why didn't you kiss your hand at her, eh?" snarled Uncle Paul.

"Didn't think of it, old fellow," replied Geoffrey, coolly.

"I've warned you about it, you know," said the old man, angrily. "Well, have you seen Penwynn?"

"Yes."

"And what has he got to say?"

"Given the instructions."

"To go back to London? Well, I'm glad of it; very glad of it."

"Thank you," said Geoffrey, lighting his pipe. "No, old gentleman, I've got my first job, and now I'm going to work."

"What, smoking?"

"Yes, engine-fire smoking soon, I hope."

"What, are you going to spend somebody's money over a mine?"

"Yes."

"Then it will be smoke. Whose money—a company's?"

"Business is business, Mr Paul," said Geoffrey. "I can't tell you whose money is going to be spent, for I don't believe I know. But I'll tell you this much, I'm going to open out Wheal Carnac."

"Wheal Carnac?"

"Yes, and at once."

"Then—but bah! it don't matter, you'll be paid. My hundred's gone, so its nothing to me."

They sat smoking in silence, for Geoffrey returned such short answers that the old man was offended, and scarcely a word was said. After a time, Geoffrey took out a note-book and began to make entries and draw, without noticing how intently his companion was watching him, and this went on till Mrs Mullion came and announced that the young engineer's composite tea-dinner was ready, to which he went in without a word.

"Nice company he's getting," said Uncle Paul, sourly. "Humph! he can be busy enough, now I want him. Here, hi! Trethick!" he shouted across the passage when he went in, "I'm going down to Rumsey's to-night. We're going to play whist. Come with me?"

"No, thanks," said Geoffrey. "I've got other cards to play now."

"Hang him and his independence! What a nuisance! And he plays such a good hand. I meant to have him for a partner. Well, never mind, if he's busy like that it will keep him from thinking about Madge. Hallo!" he exclaimed, as he heard the gate click, "that girl's off again. I wonder where she's going now?"

He returned to his own tea, and before it was finished there was another click, when, on looking up curiously, it was to see Pengelly come limping up the path.

"Humph! we shall have the house full of miners now, I suppose. Ah, well, thank goodness, it isn't my money that's going to be sunk."

Pengelly was admitted, and his first act, on being left alone with Geoffrey, was to catch his hand, and hold it tightly between both of his.

"Why, Pengelly man, what's the matter?" cried Geoffrey, wondering at his strange manner.

"I've heard all, Mr Trethick, every word. I've heard all."

"All? All what?" cried Geoffrey.

"About those wretches—those blind, weak wretches—and my poor injured Bess."

"Oh!" cried Geoffrey, "I'd forgotten all about it, man. Bah! that's nothing."

"Nothing?" cried Pengelly, with the tears standing in his eyes, "nothing? Mr Trethick, sir, if you'd let me be your dog, I'd follow you to the world's end."

"Oh, come, come, Pengelly! don't think any more of that. How is she, though?"

"Better now, sir, and she told me all about it, and how brave you had been. God bless her! she spoke kinder to me than she had ever spoke before."

"I'm glad she was not much hurt, Pengelly. Poor weak-minded fools, what a charge to get up against her! But come, pass that over. I've news for you, Pengelly. I'm going to pump out Wheal Carnac."

"You are?" cried Pengelly, joyfully.

"I am."

"Then your fortune's made."

"Is it?" said Geoffrey, laughing. "Well, my lad, can you leave your present work for a week or two, and come and help me a little?"

"If you'll have me to help you, Mr Trethick, there's no work in the world shall keep me back; and, what's more, I swear to you that I'll never leave you till Wheal Carnac's the greatest paying mine in West Cornwall."

"Come, that's cheering, Pengelly," said Geoffrey, laughing. "Why, you are more sanguine than ever."

"Sanguine, sir? No, it's sureness, that's what my feeling is;" and, sitting down at Geoffrey's request, he was soon going into business-matters with him—where to obtain temporary pumping gear, chain and buckets, wheels, and the like, their planning taking so long that it was past nine when Pengelly rose to go.

"I should like to stretch my legs too, Pengelly," said Geoffrey. "I'll walk down with you. What do you say to getting a lantern, and having a look round the place to-night?"

"I can get a lantern," cried Pengelly, eagerly; and they went out together, meeting Madge just outside the gate, and she hurried by them with bended head, but Geoffrey hardly noticed her, being intent upon his mission.

A lantern was obtained, and matches, and they were soon down upon the shore, climbing along the rough path towards the promontory upon which, just dimly seen against the sky-line, stood out the dark, weird-looking engine-house. The foam that broke upon the rocks at the promontory's base was all aglow now with phosphorescent light, which rose and fell, and flashed with a wondrous brilliancy.

"Poor night for the fisher lads, sir," said Pengelly.

"Indeed! why?"

"Their nets will be all a-light with the brime, sir, and every thread will stand out in the deep water, as if afire, and not a fish will go near."

They clambered on, higher and higher, till they reached the engine-house, into which they proposed to go, and there light the lantern.

"If they see us from the harbour, what will they think?" said Geoffrey.

"That we are ghosts or demons, the weak creatures," cried Pengelly, scornfully. "It will keep them away: not a man will come near if they see our light. Keep this way, sir, you are getting too near the shaft."

Geoffrey hastily altered his position, and closely following Pengelly he entered the great engine-house behind him, and then stood waiting while the lame miner struck a match, which blazed up, and then he dropped it, for there, plainly seen in the momentary glare, stood a dark, strange-looking figure, within a few feet of a heap of stones.

In spite of his manhood, Geoffrey felt a chill run through him, for seen in that momentary light the aspect of the figure was so weird and strange.

"It's only a man!" exclaimed Pengelly, rapidly striking a second match, and holding it to the candle in the lantern. "Hey, Master Prawle! what are you doing here?"

As he spoke he threw the light full upon the old smuggler's rugged features, Prawle growling the while as he began to fill a blackened pipe.

"What am I doing here, Amos Pengelly? Why, filling my pipe."

"And playing ghost to frighten honest men, Prawle, eh? I say, old fellow," cried Geoffrey, "we've got you on the right spot, so you may as well speak out all you know."

"All I know?" said Prawle. "I don't know nothing, only that I come for a walk, and stepped in here to light my pipe."

"Light your pipe, eh?" cried Geoffrey, laughing.

"Yes," said Prawle, spitefully, "and found you courting."

"Found me?" exclaimed Geoffrey. "Why, I've been with Amos Pengelly these two hours. Eh, Amos?"

"Ah, well, if it warn't you it were somebody else. What do you want here?" growled the old fellow.

"Oh! we've come in to light our pipes," said Geoffrey, laughing.

Prawle growled, and, after a furtive look round, turned to go.

"Warn't you two here 'bout two hour ago?" he said, sharply.

"No; neither of us," replied Geoffrey. "But come, Prawle, let us two be a little more friendly. Why can't you speak out? If you will be frank and honest with me, I'll make it worth your while."

"I don't want you to make it worth no whiles of mine," growled Prawle. "I can get my living, I dessay."

"Of course you can, man; but other people have got to get theirs. Sit down now, and let's have a talk. Let's hear all you know about the mine."

"What mine? This mine? Wheal Carnac?" said Prawle, quickly. "Nothing; nothing at all. Only everybody's ruined who takes it. Why?"

"Only that I'm going to work it," said Geoffrey, "and it might be worth your while to tell me all you know."

"Work it? You going to work it?" cried Prawle, eagerly. "You?"

"Yes: I," said Geoffrey. "Now then, what do you say? Will you help me?"

The old man stood scowling and blinking at them in the dim light shed by the lantern, and as his eyes rested upon Geoffrey they seemed less fierce in their gaze; but his face grew very rugged again, as he exclaimed,—

"I can't help you. I know nothing about the place. What are you going to do? When are you going to begin?"

"My dear Mr Prawle," said Geoffrey, "I invited you to cooperate with me, and you declined. Now will you allow me to show you the door. Pengelly, let me hold the lantern for Mr Prawle to see his way. Pray take care, Mr Prawle, and don't make a mistake about the shaft. It is not fenced in. Your life is valuable, you know. Good-night."

Geoffrey smilingly held the lantern for the old man to see his way, and Prawle looked at him in a puzzled fashion, as if not knowing what to make of his speech. One moment he seemed disposed to resent it; the next he took it in good part, and, as he got outside, after looking suspiciously from one to the other, he said, hastily, as if ashamed of his weakness,—

"I don't want to quarrel, but don't you have nothing to do with this pit. It's a bad un—a bad un, and has ruined scores. Thanky for helping my Bess."

The next moment he was gone.

"Pleasant style of man, your father-in-law-to-be, Pengelly," said Geoffrey, coolly, as he returned with the miner into the engine-house. "What was he doing here?"

"I can't quite make out, sir," said Pengelly, thoughtfully. "He always was fond of hanging about here of a night, as if jealous that any one should notice the place."

"Bit of smuggling—hiding-place?" suggested Geoffrey.

"I've thought that sometimes, sir, and sometimes I've thought there was another reason. He's a strange old fellow in his ways."

"Yes, there's no doubt about that," said Geoffrey. "But what have you got there?"

Pengelly had just stooped and picked up a fragment of stone, which glittered as he held it to the lantern.

"Bit o' tin, sir, and I was wondering how it come here."

Geoffrey took the piece of rough ore and examined it.

"Why, it is perfectly fresh," he said. "That fracture has been made quite lately."

"Yes," said Pengelly, nodding, "it's quite new, sir. The old man knows more than he'll own to. He's been chipping about here to-night with a hammer; I know, and this is some of his work."

They looked about amongst the *débris*, but could find nothing more for some time, till, climbing a little way up the heap of granite scraps that had been evidently dislodged when the machinery was moved, Pengelly uttered an exclamation.

"What have you found?" cried Geoffrey, as he saw the miner hold down the light.

"It's what I said, sir," exclaimed Pengelly. "Look, sir, he's been chipping and hammering here. Depend upon it the old man knows the mine's rich."

"But he wouldn't be chipping the old stones here," said Geoffrey, examining the fragments, which looked as if some one had been hammering up some pieces of ore.

"It's some he found and brought in," said Pengelly. "He's a regular old fox, sir, and you see by and by when he finds we are going right, if he don't come to us—to you I mean, sir—and offer to sell what he knows."

"And, perhaps, by that time we shall have found it out. Eh, Pengelly?"

"We'll try, sir," replied the miner; and then together they had a good look round the place, making plans for the fixing of the necessary machinery, Geoffrey growing more and more satisfied with the earnestness and sagacity of his companion, who seemed to throw himself heart and soul into the work in hand. Then, after appointing to meet in good time the next morning, they made their way back to the cliff and separated.

"This has been an eventful day," said Geoffrey, as, after softly letting himself in with the key that he had taken, he quietly took off his heavy boots, and, slippers in hand, stole up-stairs to his bedroom.

As he reached the door, however, a faint sob reached his ear, and as he stood listening it was very evident that some one was in grievous trouble, sobbing and crying as if her heart would break.

"That must be Miss Madge!" said Geoffrey to himself. "Poor wench! the course of her true love does not seem to run very smooth. Well, I can't comfort her, and they say that a good cry always does a woman good. So, my dear, you must have your good cry and get better. I'm afraid that women are very silly things if they are not sisters or mothers."

He said the words rather cynically, but, after undressing, he lay there thinking a good deal about Madge Mullion and her love affairs; then about Bess Prawle and her witchcrafts, laughing so heartily at the people's folly that the bed rattled; then, lastly, Wheal Carnac filled his mind, and, sleeping or waking, he could think of nothing but pumping machinery, the emptying of the shaft, and the coming of the hour when he should be the first to go down to inspect the place, and then was it to be fortune or disappointment, success or failure?

In this instance it was to be sleep, for at length his regular, low breathing told of a weary man's rest; while, just at the end of the passage, Madge Mullion's flushed face was full of pain, her soft auburn hair was tangled, and the pillow soaked with tears.

Chapter Twenty Seven.

Two Visitors at An Morlock.

They were busy days which followed for Geoffrey Trethick, and his interviews with Mr Penwynn, in consequence of the latter's desire to keep his name out of the project, were of an evening at An Morlock, where he more than once encountered Rhoda, who pleased him by the way in which she entered into the spirit of his plans.

The first time he met her was when, after a couple of visits to the mine where the Wheal Carnac machinery had been taken, and some long discussions with Pengelly, he had gone up to An Morlock to ask Mr Penwynn whether he would buy it back from the trustees of the bankrupt estate.

"But that will take quite a heavy sum, Trethick," said Mr Penwynn. "What I want to do is to have the mine emptied and thoroughly tested without further expense."

"Exactly so, sir," replied Geoffrey; "but, working in your interests, I felt it my duty to lay this before you. Here, to pump out, a certain amount of money must be spent in fixing hired machinery. If the mine proves good all that money is wasted. On the other hand, if you are willing to buy back this original machinery, which is, I guarantee, to be had for a fourth of its value, it will do the work better, and you have it ready to carry on future proceedings, when a vast amount would be saved."

"And suppose the venture—I mean the testing—proves a failure?"

"You have a valuable lot of modern machinery to sell, and cannot lose."

Mr Penwynn sat thinking, and Rhoda raised her head from her work.

"Well, my dear," said her father, smiling, "what should you do?"

"I think I should take Mr Trethick's advice, papa," she said quietly; and she had hardly spoken when the servant announced Mr Tregenna, who came in smiling, and shook hands warmly all round.

"I thought I'd just drop in for a chat," he said, looking meaningly at Mr Penwynn. "Why, the place is ringing with the news that you are going in for mining."

"Confound them, how did they know that I was at the back of the affair?" said Mr Penwynn, irritably; and he looked sharply at Geoffrey.

"Not from me, sir," he said, smiling. "I've been as silent as an oyster."

"Oh, from your clerks, I'll be bound," said Tregenna. "You sent for Mr Trethick here, didn't you?"

"Yes, of course," said Mr Penwynn.

"Well," said Tregenna, laughing, "that was quite enough. I'll be bound to say the ladies of Carnac know to a penny how much that charming costume of Miss Penwynn's cost—the one she wore last Sunday."

Rhoda looked up, and nodded, and smiled, feeling set at her ease by the quiet, matter-of-fact way in which Tregenna had put aside the past.

"Well, they'd have been sure to know it sooner or later," said Mr Penwynn. "You've just come opportunely, Tregenna. I want a bit of advice."

"*Viva!*" said Tregenna, laughing, and taking out his memorandum-book. "I came in for half an hour's relaxation, and I shall earn a guinea in consultation. I am all attention."

"You charge for your advice, and you see how I'll charge in the way of discount for the next bill you present," said Mr Penwynn, laughing. "Well, look here, Tregenna, Cropper and Grey want to sell the old Wheal Carnac machinery."

"*New* machinery, you mean," said Tregenna.

"Well, yes, it is nearly new," said Mr Penwynn. "Mr Trethick here advises its purchase and refixing to pump out the mine."

"But that would run into a lot of money," said Tregenna.

"Yes," replied Geoffrey; "but it all fits the place, and it is to be got for a fourth of its value. Even if the whole venture proved a failure, the machinery would be worth the money. It seems to me a chance."

Tregenna sat back in his chair, tapping his teeth with the end of his pencil.

"That machinery costs a tremendous deal of money," he said, thoughtfully.

"Yes, and is in admirable order," said Geoffrey, "or I would not suggest such a thing."

"What do the trustees ask for the lot?" said Tregenna, at last.

Geoffrey mentioned the sum.

"Well, that must be very moderate," said Tregenna, "as far as I understand such things. But business is business," he continued, laughing. "I am growing very sordid. Look here, Mr Penwynn, I know Cropper and Grey, the trustees, of course. If you decide to purchase that machinery, which certainly, on the face of it, seems a wise stroke, especially as you want it, and it would always be worth its money, I'll undertake to get it for you two hundred and fifty pounds below the sum named on condition of received a cheque for fifty pounds commission."

"Certainly. Agreed," said Mr Penwynn; "but I have not yet made up my mind."

"Oh, of course not!" said Tregenna, making a note in his book.

"Advising you on the purchase of machinery. Long consultation—thirteen and four," said Geoffrey, dryly.

"Oh, no, Mr Trethick," said Tregenna, closing the book with a snap, "I shall be satisfied with my fifty pounds cheque."

"When you get it, Tregenna," said Mr Penwynn, laughing.

"When I get it—cashed," replied Tregenna.

"By the way, Tregenna, would you mind coming into the study a minute or two? There's one little point I should like to discuss with you," said Mr Penwynn, rising. "Rhoda, my dear, Mr Trethick would, perhaps, like a little music."

"I think I'll be going," said Geoffrey, rising.

"No, no, don't go yet," said the banker.

"I'm going your way presently," said Tregenna; and Geoffrey sat down again as the banker and the solicitor left the room.

"I hope you are beginning to like Carnac better, Mr Trethick," said Rhoda quietly.

"I always did like it," said Geoffrey. "It is one long study of character; and, now that I have something to do, I quite love the place."

"It is very beautiful and wild," replied Rhoda, thoughtfully. "By the way, Mr Trethick, do you think there is a good prospect of this mining affair succeeding?"

"It is impossible to say," replied Geoffrey, looking full in the large, earnest eyes before him. "Every step for some time to come must be tentative. I really think, though, that there is a good hope of success."

"Hope? Mr Trethick."

"Well, I might say certainty of clearing expenses—hope of making a large profit."

"Papa has always said that he would never enter into a mining speculation, and now he seems to have been drawn into this. I should not like it to cause him trouble."

"Honestly, I do not believe it will, Miss Penwynn," replied Geoffrey. "It shall go very bad with me if it does."

"I trust that you will do your best for him, Mr Trethick," said Rhoda, earnestly.

"You may take it for granted, Miss Penwynn," said Geoffrey, "that if only out of selfish considerations I shall leave no stone unturned—that is likely to contain tin," he added, laughingly. "No, my dear young lady, I have had to wait too long for this opportunity to be careless. I shall, and I will, make Wheal Carnac pay."

He got up as he spoke, and Rhoda watched him as he walked up and down the room.

"Many an earnest man has been damped over these wretched mining speculations, Mr Trethick," said Rhoda sadly, her eyes following him the while.

"Oh, yes," he said cheerily, "there are plenty of failures in every thing. Fellows read for honours and plenty of them fail, but the men who stick to the work the best generally get somewhere on the list. I'm going to stick to Wheal Carnac, Miss Penwynn, and if one is only last on the list it will be something."

"To be sure," said Rhoda, smiling. "Well, Mr Trethick, I wish you every success."

Geoffrey stopped short to look at her in a bold, straightforward manner that made Rhoda lower her eyes.

"Thank you," he said frankly. "I'm sure you do. And look here, Miss Penwynn, the first rich vein we strike shall bear your name."

Rhoda smiled.

"Find it first, eh?" he said. "Well, I will if it is to be found, and I am supplied with the sinews of war. I say, Miss Penwynn, has that Mr Tregenna any thing to do with this affair?"

"Oh, no, I think not!" replied Rhoda, looking at him wonderingly.

"I'm glad of it," said Geoffrey bluntly.

"May I ask why, Mr Trethick?" she said, watching his earnest face.

"Because I don't like him for any thing more than an acquaintance—that's all," he said; and then suddenly recollecting his suspicions that Tregenna had proposed to Rhoda on the night of the dinner, he flushed slightly, and exclaimed, "Really I beg your pardon. My antipathies ought to be kept private."

Rhoda bowed and walked to the piano, where her voice was rising and falling in a well-known ballad, when Tregenna and the banker re-entered the room, the former darting a quick, suspicious look from one to the other, but without finding any thing upon which his suspicions could feed.

Whatever the business had been, Mr Penwynn seemed perfectly satisfied, and the conversation became general till Trethick rose to go, Tregenna following his example; but Mr Penwynn laid his hand upon the solicitor's arm, and asked him to stay for a few minutes longer.

"Good-night, Mr Trethick," he said. "I will sleep on that affair, and give you an answer in the morning."

"Going to consult Tregenna a little more," said Geoffrey, as he walked homeward. "Well, he is not a man whom I should trust, and I'm very glad I have no dealings with him whatever."

He stopped at a corner to fill and light his meerschaum.

"There's some pleasure in having a pipe now one has got to work," he said, as he puffed the bowl into a glow, and then, as he went on—"that's a very nice, quiet, sensible girl, that Miss Penwynn;" and then he began to think of Tregenna.

Just at the same time Rhoda had said to herself,—

"Mr Trethick is very frank, and manly, and natural," and then she began thinking about Madge Mullion and Bess Prawle, and then—she could not tell why—she sighed.

There was a long talk that night in Mr Penwynn's study, and when at last Tregenna left he was thinking to himself about mines and mining.

"That's a splendid fellow, that Trethick," he said. "I did think of trying to mould him, but he wants no touching, only leaving alone. Once set a man on the mining slide, there is no stopping till he gets to the bottom; and I think friend Penwynn will find the bottom of Wheal Carnac very deep."

Chapter Twenty Eight.

A Chat with Uncle Paul.

They were busy days for Geoffrey Trethick and his factotum Pengelly, who hardly gave himself time to rest. The visit to Mr Penwynn that next morning had resulted in the information that he had commissioned Mr Tregenna to offer a certain sum for the machinery.

"And mind this, Trethick," the banker said, "you have led me into this affair, and you will have to make it pay me well."

"Never fear, sir," said Geoffrey, "I'll do my best."

Visits to Gwennas were rare, and Geoffrey went to and from the cottage with an abstracted air, too busy to notice that Madge looked pale and careworn, and that Uncle Paul seemed a little changed.

The old man would waylay him though sometimes, poke at him with his cane, and get him into the summer-house to smoke one of the long black cheroots.

"Well," he said one morning, "how are you getting along, boy? Swimmingly I suppose? I saw the water coming out at a fine rate."

"Yes," said Geoffrey, "we've got all the machinery fixed as far as was necessary, and the pumping has begun."

"And you are going to make my hundred pounds come back to me, eh?"

"Well, not very likely," said Geoffrey, "unless you buy fresh shares of the new proprietors. What do you say?"

"Bah!" exclaimed the old man; and they smoked on in silence for a time.

"Might do worse," said Geoffrey.

"Rubbish! I tell you it will all end in a smash-up. You get your money regularly, and don't let them have any arrears."

"Oh, that's all right," said Geoffrey. "So you think there will, be another failure?"

"Sure of it I shall buy that piece of ground yet for a house. Sure to fail."

"So old Prawle says."

"Oh, old Prawle says so, does he?" continued Uncle Paul.

"Yes; and I told him the Indian file thought the same."

"The *what?*" said Uncle Paul.

"The Indian file—you," said Geoffrey, coolly.

Uncle Paul thumped his stick on the floor, and looked daggers.

"Look here, young fellow," he said, sharply, "you go a deal too much to Gwennas Cove, and it don't look well."

"Haven't been half so often lately," said Geoffrey, coolly.

"You go ten times too much. Look here, boy, have you seen how pale and ill that jade, Madge, looks?"

"No. Yes, to be sure, I did think she looked white."

"Fretting, sir, fretting. Now look here, boy, it isn't square."

"What isn't?" said Geoffrey, coolly.

"So much of that going to Gwennas Cove, and rescuing young women from infuriated mobs, and that sort of thing. Lady very grateful?"

"Very."

"Humph! Bewitched you?"

"Not yet."

"Humph! Going to?"

"Don't know."

"Damn you, Geoffrey Trethick," cried the old man, "you'd provoke a saint."

"Which you are not."

"Who the devil ever said I was, sir? Now, look here, you dog, I warned you when you came that I'd have no courting."

"*You* can't stop courting," laughed Geoffrey. "It would take a giant."

"None of your confounded banter, sir. I told you I'd have no courting—no taking notice of that jade—and you've disobeyed me."

"Not I," said Geoffrey.

"Don't contradict, puppy. I say you have."

"All right."

"The jade's going about the house red-eyed, and pale, and love-sick—confound her!—about you, and now you make her miserable by playing off that brown-skinned fish-wench with the dark eyes."

Geoffrey's conscience smote him as he thought of that day when he playfully kissed Madge, and asked himself whether she really cared for him now, but only to feel sure that she did not.

"Does this sort of thing please you?" he said.

"Confound you! No, sir, it does not. Act like a man if you can, and be honest, or—confound you, sir!—old as I am, and old-fashioned as I am—damme, sir—laws or no laws, I'll call you out and shoot you. You sha'n't trifle with the girl's feelings while I'm here."

Geoffrey's first impulse was to say something banteringly; but he saw that the old man was so much in earnest that he took a quiet tone.

"Uncle Paul," he said, "why will you go on running your head against a brick wall?"

"What do you mean, boy?"

"Only that you have got a notion in your head, and it seems useless for me to try and get it out. I'm busy and bothered, and have a deal to think about, so, once for all, let me tell you that I have hardly ever paid Miss Mullion the slightest attention, and, what is more, I am not so conceited as to believe she is making herself uncomfortable about me."

The old man glared hard at him and uttered a grunt, for the eyes that met his were as frank and calm as could be.

"Then all I can say is that if what you say is true—"

"Which it is—perfectly true," replied Geoffrey.

"Then it's very strange," grumbled the old man. "She never went on like this before. Have another cheroot, Trethick?"

"Now that's the most sensible thing I've heard you say to-day," said Geoffrey, smiling, as he took one of the great black cheroots. "I say, old fellow, these are very good. What do they cost you a-box?"

"Five pounds a hundred," said the old man, quietly.

"What?" cried Geoffrey.

"Shilling apiece, boy."

"Why I—'pon my word, sir, really I'm ashamed to take them."

"Bah! stuff!" cried the old man. "Do you suppose, because I live here in this quiet way, that I'm a pauper? Smoke the cigar, boy. Here's a light."

Geoffrey lit up, and inwardly determined that in future he would keep to his pipe, while the old man sat watching him.

"So you mean to make the mine pay, eh, Trethick?" he said.

"Yes, I believe I shall, Mr Paul," said Geoffrey, quietly. "I'm not starting with the idea of a fortune, but on the principles of which I have often told you of getting a profit out of a mine by economy, new means of reducing the ore, and living where others would fail."

"Humph!" said the old man, looking at him thoughtfully, and they smoked on in silence.

"I was a bit bilious this morning," said Uncle Paul at last, in an apologetic tone.

"Yes," said Geoffrey, "I saw that."

"Parson called and upset me. Wanted me to go and take the chair at a missionary meeting for the Hindoos, and I told him that the Hindoos and Buddhists ought to send missionaries to us. But don't take any notice."

"Not I, old gentleman," said Geoffrey, laughing. "I rather like it."

"Humph! I rather like you too, boy. You seem to do my biliousness good. You can stand a bullying without flying out. I haven't found a fellow stand it so well since I left the coolies."

"Mutual admiration," laughed Geoffrey. "I like you, old gentleman, because you do fly out. It's quite refreshing after a lot of disappointments to have some one to quarrel with."

There was another pause.

"I say, Trethick," said the old man, "then Penwynn and Tregenna are hand-and-glove in this job, eh?"

Geoffrey looked at the old man wonderingly, for he was evidently beating about the bush.

"I don't know. There, don't ask me questions, old gentleman," was the reply. "I'm not at liberty to chatter."

There was another silence.

"Madge isn't a bad sort of girl, Trethick," said the old man at last.

"No," said Geoffrey; "she's pretty and amiable, and I believe, poor lassie, she is very good-hearted. I often think you are too hard upon her."

"Hard be hanged, sir! I've been her's and her mother's support these ten years."

"Very likely," said Geoffrey, dryly; "but a dog doesn't like his crusts and bones any the better for having them thrown at him."

"Humph!" ejaculated the old man, thoughtfully. "Well, perhaps I am a little hard upon her sometimes; but she aggravates me. Trethick, you are quite conceited puppy enough, I know, but that girl is fretting about you."

"Ignorance is bliss, sir. I was not aware of it."

"Ignorance is a blister, sir," cried the old man, sharply. "But," he added, more gently, "she is, I tell you. Trethick, she is a nice girl, and you might do worse."

"Stuff, stuff, my dear sir!" cried Geoffrey, laughing. "You are mistaken, and I am not a marrying man. There, I must be off;" and, starting up, he swung off along the path, and away down towards the mine buildings, where steam was now puffing, water falling, and several busy hands were at work.

Uncle Paul watched him thoughtfully as he strode away, and then sat back thinking, as he gazed out to sea.

Chapter Twenty Nine.

Bess Prawle's Secret.

Time goes by rapidly with the busy. To Geoffrey it went like lightning; to Madge Mullion it hung heavy as lead. When they met, which was seldom now, and he spoke a few kindly, cheery words to her, she looked at him rather piteously, but said little in return.

Once or twice there was a twinge of pain in Geoffrey Trethick's conscience, but he said nothing, only went on with his work busily and well. The water was all out of the mine, and he had carefully examined and reported upon it—a carefully worded report, promising nothing more than a moderate return upon a small capital; and, not satisfied, he persuaded Mr Penwynn to have down an experienced mineralogist to give his opinion.

"Whom would you recommend?" said Mr Penwynn, and Rhoda watched Geoffrey anxiously for his reply.

"No one, Mr Penwynn," said the young man. "Get somebody I don't know—a reliable man whom you can trust, and don't let me see him."

He happened to turn his eyes upon Rhoda as he spoke, and there was such a bright, eager look in the glance that met his that it made him thoughtful.

"Quite right," said Mr Penwynn, "it would be better;" and the next day Mr Chynoweth was set to write to a mining engineer in town.

That night there was a game of whist at Dr Rumsey's, and Chynoweth and Tregenna were there. Tregenna lost heavily for such play as they had. Chynoweth was in high delight, and Tregenna and he walked home together.

The next day Mr Tregenna had business in London, and the day following the mining engineer and mineralogist came down, inspected Wheal Carnac, and made his report afterwards to Mr Penwynn, with the result that the banker said nothing to Geoffrey Trethick, only bade him go on, feeling satisfied that his venture was to be a great financial success.

A month later it was known that a new company had bought the mine, and that shares were to be had.

The matter was chatted over at An Morlock, and, as sometimes happened, Geoffrey and Rhoda were left together for a time; their talk being generally of the mine; and when he was gone, Rhoda got into the habit of sitting silent and thoughtful, in judgment upon Geoffrey Trethick's character.

Her line of argument took somewhat this form—she did not know why she should argue out his cause—but somehow she felt compelled to do so. Scandal had made pretty free with his name, and, in spite of her efforts, Rhoda seemed obliged to hear, through Miss Pavey, all that was said.

And the sayings were these—that Geoffrey Trethick was young and gay; that he had gone so much to Gwennas Cove that old Prawle had threatened his life if he went there again, and that upon one occasion the old man had lain in wait for him with a hammer at Wheal Carnac, only Pengelly was with Trethick and had saved him; then Trethick had promised that he would go to Gwennas no more, and the matter at once ended.

"False on the face of it!" said Rhoda, with spirit. "Geoffrey—Mr Trethick," she said quickly, "told me that he had been twice to see old Mrs Prawle this week, and begged me to go soon."

The next indictment was that Geoffrey had become so intimate with Madge Mullion that old Mr Paul had ordered him to leave the house, and that he was going at once.

This was Miss Pavey's news, and she added that Mr Trethick would have to leave the town unless Mr Penwynn took compassion upon him.

"Of course, my dear," she had said, maliciously, as she blew her nose in a gentlemanly way as if it were a triumphant note of defiance, "after what we are hearing you have quite cast him off?"

Rhoda looked at the speaker steadily, but made no reply.

But of this charge?

"Well," Rhoda argued, "Madge Mullion is pretty and attractive, and she would probably throw herself open to the attentions of such a man as Geoffrey Trethick. But, if this were true, would Geoffrey behave as he had behaved at An Morlock of late? He seemed to be the soul of honour, and his words always had the ring of truth in them. No: it was one of the Carnac petty scandals; Geoffrey Trethick was no trifler."

There was another long, dreamy time after this, and there were moments when Rhoda felt angry with herself for thinking so much about the man who now came to lay bare his plans, to consult her, so it seemed, when he was asking counsel of her father. And all at once she seemed to awaken to the fact that, by some means, the life of

Geoffrey Trethick had become interwoven strangely with her own—that his success was her success, his failures hers; and yet he had spoken no word, given her no look. He was different to any man that she had ever met, and he even annoyed her sometimes by his quiet assumption of authority as the stronger in thought. For he would ask her advice, and often enough show the fallacy of what she had said.

Then she would think that they were becoming too intimate, and blame her father for encouraging the presence of this stranger; but Mr Penwynn seemed, after a life of immunity, to have taken the mine fever badly, and the thought of Geoffrey Trethick pretending to his daughter's hand never occurred to him.

"No," thought Rhoda, "papa thinks of nothing now but this speculation; and why should he? Geoffrey Trethick has never behaved otherwise than as a visitor working in my father's interest;" and as she said this to herself, a curious feeling of pique arose, but only to be crushed at once.

Finally, Rhoda Penwynn's verdict on Geoffrey Trethick was that he was a gentleman—a man of unstained honour, whom fate had placed in a town full of petty scandal.

The next day Rhoda endorsed her verdict, and it was in this wise.

She granted, as she started, that it was due to Geoffrey's request, for otherwise she might not have gone. As it was, she started in the afternoon to walk over to Gwennas Cove, passing along the cliff, and looking somewhat eagerly down towards Wheal Carnac, where figures were moving and shaft smoking, while the great beam of the pumping-engine went steadily on with its toil.

She was half-startled to see how the wreck had been transformed into a busy scene of industry, and, in spite of herself, she felt a glow of pride as she recalled whose hand had brought about the change.

Her face turned hard directly after, as she thought of her father, and of how he had seemed to become inoculated with Geoffrey Trethick's enthusiasm. He did not want for money, and yet he had entered upon this mining speculation—he of all men, who had laughed at the follies of those who embarked upon such ventures. What was to be the end?

She walked on, and soon after reached the spot where Bess Prawle had been driven to bay by the superstitious crowd; and, as the whole scene came back, with Geoffrey's gallant behaviour, and the girl's display of gratitude, Rhoda stopped short, with her eyes contracting, her brow ruffled with emotion, and her lips half parted. For she was startled at the pang of misery that shot through her. The contemptible scandal she had heard forced itself upon her, and she seemed obliged to couple with it the weak wanderings of poor old Mrs Prawle about Geoffrey and her child.

It was horrible! What had she been doing? How had her fancies been straying, she asked herself, as she awakened to the fact that imperceptibly her interest in Geoffrey had grown so warm that the thought of his caring for another caused her misery of the most acute kind.

She shook off the feeling, calling herself weak and childish, and, gathering mental strength with the walk, she at last reached Gwennas Cove.

Old Prawle was busy overhauling a long line, and binding on fresh hooks, a task from which he condescended to raise his eyes, and give the visitor a surly nod as she spoke.

His voice brought out Bess, looking handsomer than ever, Rhoda thought, in her picturesque dress and carelessly-knotted hair.

For a moment the two girls stood gazing in each other's eyes, and a cold, chilling feeling ran through Rhoda as, in spite of herself, she felt that it would be no wonder if Geoffrey Trethick did love this bold, handsome girl.

The next moment the thought was gone, and Rhoda had held out her hand.

"I hope there is a good stock of sweeties, Bessie," she said, with a frank smile. "How is Mrs Prawle?"

Bess's breath came with a catch, as she returned the smile; and, leading the way into the cottage, the pleasant little fiction was gone through, and the invalid made happy in the thought that she had added the profits of a shilling's-worth of sweets to the general store.

But there was no conversation this time about Geoffrey Trethick, for Bess stayed in the room, and then followed Rhoda out on to the cliff path when she left.

"Why, Bessie," said the visitor, smiling, "I have hardly seen you since that day when those mad people behaved so ill."

"I very seldom go into the town now, miss," said Bess, whose colour came as she recalled the conclusion of that scene.

"It's very sad," continued Rhoda, "that the people should be so ignorant. Well, good-by, Bessie," she continued, holding out her hand, "you will not ill-wish me?"

"No," said Bessie, softly, as she watched the tall, well-dressed, graceful figure slowly receding. "No, I will not ill-wish you; but there are times when I feel as if I must hate you for being what you are."

She let Rhoda go on till the fluttering of her dress in the sea-breeze was seen no more, and then, moved by some strange impulse, she followed, avoiding the track; and, active and quick as one of the half-wild sheep of the district, she climbed up on to the rugged down above the cliff path, and kept on gazing below at Rhoda from time to time.

She went on nearly parallel with her for a quarter of a mile or so, and then stood motionless for a time, gazing down, before, with a weary wail of misery, she threw herself amidst the heather, her face upon one outstretched arm, whose fingers clutched and tore at the tough plants and grass, while her whole frame quivered with her passionate sobs.

"Bess!"

At the sound of that hoarse voice she started up into a sitting position, but shrank away as she gazed up into her father's fierce, rugged face. The old man was down on one knee beside her, and his gnarled and knotted hand was pointing in the direction of the cliff path a hundred feet below.

"Is—is it come to this, Bess?" he said.

"What—what, father?" she cried, catching at his hand; but she missed it, and he gripped her arm.

"Is that smooth, good-looking villain thy lover, too?" he said, in a vindictive whisper.

"Oh! no, no, no, father," she gasped.

"I knew it would come to it," he cried. "Curse him! I'll crush his false head again the rocks."

"Are you mad, father?" she whispered, throwing her arms round him.

"Mad? No," he cried; "but do you think I'm blind as well as old? Bess," he continued, "I wish before his gashly face had darkened our door—"

"Oh father, father, dear father," she moaned—and she crept closer and closer, till her arms were round his neck, and her head in his breast; "kill me, but don't hurt him."

"Then he has been trifling with thee, girl? I knowed it; I was sure it would come."

"No, no, no," moaned Bess; "he never said word to me but what you might hear."

"Is—is this gawspel, Bess?" cried the old man, dragging up her convulsed and tearful face, and gazing in her wistful dark eyes.

"Can't you see, father?" she said, with a low, despairing sigh. "I'm not good enough to be his wife, and he's not the man to trifle and say soft things to me. You see down yonder," she added, pitifully, as she waved one brown hand in the direction of the path.

"Nay, it's along of Madge Mullion," said the old man, wrathfully. "Yon's nothing, and will come to naught. They say old Paul's niece—"

"It's a lie, father, a cruel lie," cried Bess, starting from him. "I heard it, and it's a lie. Mr Trethick's a gentleman, and he's as noble as he's good."

"Curse him for coming here," cried the old man fiercely.

"God bless him!" said Bess, simply, as, kneeling there, she let her joined hands drop into her lap. "God bless him for a good man, and—and—may he be very—very happy in the time to come."

Bess Prawle's face dropped into her hands, and she sank lower and lower, with the tears of agony growing less scalding, and falling by degrees, as it were, like balm upon her burning love—a love which she had held unveiled before her father's gaze, while the old man bent over her, the savage roughness of his face growing less repulsive, and a look of love and pride transforming him for the time.

He knelt down and kissed her bright black hair; then he put his arms round her, and drew her to him, and at last held her to his heart, rocking to and fro as he had nursed her a dozen or fifteen years before.

"My pretty flower," he cried hoarsely, "my Bess! He don't know—he don't know. You not good enough for he? Harkye, my girl. He shall marry you—he shall be proud to marry you—for I know that as will bring him to you, and put him on his knees and ask you to be his wife."

"Father?" said the girl, looking at him wonderingly.

"Yes," he said, nodding his head exultantly, and kissing her broad forehead. "I can make you as fine a lady as any in Cornwall, my lass, and I can bring him to you when I will."

"No, no, no," moaned Bessie, with a piteous smile.

"But I say yes," cried the old man. "I haven't had my eyes open all these years for nothing. Let's go home, Bess; I'll talk to thee there. Get up, my girl, and I'll bring him to thy feet whene'er thou wilt."

Bess rose sadly, and put her hand in her father's, but, as they took a step forward, the nook in the cliff where she had stood at bay opened out beneath them, and they both saw that which made Bessie Prawle feel as if her heart would break.

Chapter Thirty.

Making a Victim.

Breakfast-time at Dr Rumsey's, and Mrs Rumsey, in a very henny state, clucking over her brood, for whom she was cutting bread and butter.

Her name too was Charlotte, but no Werther fell in love with her when she was ingeniously trying how many square inches of bread two ounces of butter that had been warmed into oil by the fire would cover. For Mrs Rumsey was not handsome, being a soft, fair, nebulous-looking lady, who had been in the habit of presenting her husband with one or two nebulous theories of her own regularly once a year; and the "worrit" of children had not improved her personal appearance.

Her face was, as a rule, white, and soft, and heavy, dotted with dull branny freckles, while the possession of a soft *retroussé* nose that seemed loosely attached to her skin, and travelled a good deal out of place whenever she twitched her countenance, as she often did spasmodically, did not add to her attractions.

Unfortunately for Dr Rumsey, his wife's notable care of her children did not extend to herself, for as she grew older she also grew more and more unkempt. While he, as he saw it, would sigh and thrust his hands into his pockets all but his thumbs, which stood out and worked as she unfolded to him her family cares, giving them the aspect of two handles in the mechanism by which he was moved.

"Any thing will do for me," was her favourite expression; and, in the belief that she was lessening the burthen on her husband's shoulders, she made herself less attractive in his eyes year by year, and grew more dowdy. How the fact that his wife's hair was not parted exactly in the middle, and left unbrushed, could affect his income, Dr Rumsey never knew; neither could he see that it was any saving for a hook on a dress front to be inserted in the wrong eye, or for his wife's boots to be down at the heel and unlaced. Such, however, was the state in which Mrs Rumsey was often seen, though, to do her justice, the children were her constant care, in both senses of the word.

He saw all this and sighed, giving his ears a pull now and then, telling himself that they tightened his skin and drew the wrinkles out of his face; while, when his lady was extra sensitive and nervous—in other words, disposed to blame—he would shrug his shoulders, button up his coat, turn up his collar; and upon one occasion he even sent the good lady into a passionate fit of hysterics, by putting up an old umbrella to shelter him till the storm had done.

"Ah, Rumsey!" she would say, "I don't know what you would do without me. If you had not me to take care of you and yours, you would be lost indeed."

The lady did not seem to consider it a case of his and hers, but went on behaving as if she were a kind of upper servant or nursery governess, while he wanted a companion and help. Certainly she opened his clean pocket-handkerchiefs for him, for fear he should look dandified; and she taught his children well according to her lights, though her teachings certainly had the appearance of what Mrs Mullion called drilling, for she was very strict.

But somehow the doctor was not happy, and spent as little of his time as possible at home. When a wet day compelled him to stop in, as the streams were flooded, he amused himself by going over his fishing-tackle, or making weather-cocks to place out in his garden to scare away the birds, which were supposed to be tempted by the fruit.

On this particular morning, with her cap awry, and looking more unkempt than usual, Mrs Rumsey was very lachrymose and very busy, carving away at the bread and butter, and rocking the cradle with one foot, while at times she cast an occasional eye out of the open door at her twins, Billy and Dilly, two sturdy little boys a couple of years old, fair, fat, and so much alike that it required study to avoid mistakes. They were toddling up and down the pebble garden-path, each with a feeding bottle tied to his waist, the long india-rubber pipe reaching upwards, and the mouth-piece between his lips, the pair looking like a couple of young Turks enjoying a morning hookah in the open air.

The other children were already in their places, sniffing occasionally and looking longingly at the pile of bread-and-butter mounting high, what time mamma gave them torture lessons during the preparation for the meal.

"Why don't your father come?" she said, dolefully, as she looked impatiently at the door. "He always will stay with his patients so much longer than he need. Who's that coming?"

"Madge Mullion, ma," cried the eldest-born, a long, thin girl, whose face lit up as there was a bang of the garden gate and a rustling of skirts; and, after bending down to kiss the children, Madge, looking very pale and pretty, came in without ceremony.

"How are you?" she cried, kissing Mrs Rumsey.

"Very poorly, my dear," whined the doctor's wife. "These children will worrit me into my grave."

"No, no," cried Madge, as she faced round. "Have you any news?"

"No, my dear, there's never any news down in this lost out-of-the-way place. Dr Rumsey always would persist in leaving London, or he might have been having his guinea fee from every patient, and keeping his carriage by now."

"Then it isn't true!" said Madge, with a sigh of relief.

"What, my dear?—Priscilla, if you will persist in sniffing so, I certainly will slap you."

The young lady addressed immediately began tugging at a pocket-handkerchief, secured by one end to the waistband of some undergarment, and bent her young body like an arc to get a good blow.

"I have been to the shop, and heard that Mr Tregenna was taken ill in the night."

"Oh, yes, my dear, he was. Papa was called up at two o'clock, and he hasn't come back yet."

"Oh!" ejaculated Madge, turning paler.

"That he has, ma," cried the eldest boy. "I got up at five to see what time it was, and pa was just going out with his fishing-rod; and he told me to go back quietly to bed and not wake anybody."

"Then you're a naughty, wicked boy, Bobby, for not saying so sooner," cried Mrs Rumsey, angrily. "Don't make that noise, or you shall have no breakfast."

Bobby was drawing a long breath for a furious howl, but he glanced hungrily at the bread and butter, smoothed his countenance, and put off the performance for the present.

"I declare it's too bad," continued mamma; "he knows how anxious I am when he's away, and yet he comes creeping back at daybreak, like a burglar, to steal his own fishing-tackle, and goes, no one knows where, after a few nasty trout."

"Then Mr Tregenna must be better," said Madge.

"Oh, yes, my dear, he's better," said Mrs Rumsey, petulantly. "What a silly girl you are to think of such things. I'm sure I ought to be a framing to you. Look at me!"

Certainly, as an example against entering into the marriage state Mrs Rumsey was a warning; but, like most other such warnings, ineffectual.

"I couldn't help calling just to try and hear a few words," said Madge; "but you won't betray me, dear?"

"Oh, no, I won't tell, Madge," said Mrs Rumsey, a little less grimly, and evidently greatly delighted at being made the repository of the young girl's love affair. "But I do wonder at you, Madge," she said, in a whisper, with a slice of bread and butter half cut. "John Tregenna's all very well, and certainly he has a noble nose, but you've got somebody far nicer at home."

"Yes, isn't he nice?" whispered back Madge.

"I've only seen him once, dear, but I thought him far before John Tregenna."

"Yes," said Madge, sighing.

"Yes, I know, my dear. John Tregenna has such a way with him."

"He has indeed," said Madge, sighing again.

"Ah, well, my dear," said Mrs Rumsey, finishing the slice, and laying it in its place upon the pile, "I ought not to say any thing against it, if you are set upon such a wilful course, for John Tregenna is papa's patient, and of course you would be; and what with measles, and chicken-pox, and scarlatina, your family would be a help."

"Oh, Charlotte dear!" exclaimed Madge.

"Ah, you may say, 'Oh, Charlotte dear!' but it must come to that; and a good thing too, for I'm sure our income's limited enough, and—Oh, here he is at last, and his boots wet through. There, now: if there ever was an unreasonable man, it's my husband. He's bringing that Mr Trethick in to breakfast."

"Oh, what shall I do?" cried Madge, to her companion. "Let me go without his seeing me."

"You can slip out at the back," said Mrs Rumsey, "and he won't see you."

But Madge thought it would look so cowardly, and, after a glance at the glass, determined to face Geoffrey, who was half pushed into the room by the doctor.

"Ma, dear, here's Mr Trethick. We've had a couple of hours up the stream."

"And there's nothing but bread and butter, papa," said Mrs Rumsey, in an injured tone. "I didn't know you were going to bring company."

"Company? I am not company," said Geoffrey, merrily. "I'm a patient in prospective, and the doctor prescribes bread and butter. I was brought up on that happy animal and vegetable combination. Ah, Miss Mullion, good-morning! Who'd have thought of seeing you here? I say, I want to have a good laugh at those two little Turks out in the front."

"Yes, Mr Trethick," said Mrs Rumsey, pitifully, "indeed they are young Turks; but won't you sit down?"

"Don't let me disturb you, Miss Mullion," he cried.

"Oh, I'm going, Mr Trethick," said Madge, giving Mrs Rumsey a wistful look, which she interpreted aright, and acted accordingly.

"How is Mr Tregenna?" she said to her husband.

"Tregenna? Oh, ah, yes, to be sure! I had forgotten him. He's all right again. Called me up in the middle of the night; said he was dying. Fit of indigestion; lives too well. I am always telling him so. He's getting a liver as bad as old Paul. He works it too hard, and then it strikes, and telegraphs messages all over the body even to the toes, and then there's a riot, for all the other organs strike too."

"Then he was not seriously ill, papa?" said Mrs Rumsey, after another glance from Madge.

"Not he. Guilty conscience, perhaps. Sent for me for nothing. I told him he'd cry 'Wolf!' once too often, and I shouldn't go."

As Madge heard this she glided out of the room, and made her way unperceived to the front, and out into the street, in sublime unconsciousness that Miss Pavey was at her window, with a a very shabby little tortoise-shell-covered opera-glass, by means of which she had been intently watching the doctor's house.

"Ah, me! Poor Rhoda!" she said to herself; "but it's not for me to say any thing, only to pity the poor deluded girl. Oh, these men, these men!"

Meanwhile, after a few words to his guest, Dr Rumsey turned an eye to business.

"Ah, Tregenna!" he said; "must not forget him. Prissy fetch me the day-book. I'll enter that while I remember it."

"No, papa," said Mrs Rumsey in an ill-used tone, as she frowned the little girl back in her place, "leave that till Mr Trethick has gone. If you will expose our poverty by bringing visitors to breakfast, don't forget all the past, and let Mr Trethick go away thinking we have quite degenerated into Cornish fishermen and miners."

"Oh, Trethick won't think that," said the doctor heartily.

"Indeed I should not," said Geoffrey merrily. "How about the trout, doctor?"

"To be sure," cried the doctor, "we must have them."

"Don't, pray, say you have brought home any nasty trout to be cooked for breakfast, my dear," cried Mrs Rumsey imploringly. "I really could not get them cooked."

"Oh, never mind, my dear," said the doctor, rubbing his ear in rather a vexed way. "You won't mind, Trethick; you shall take them home with you."

"Mind? Not I," said Geoffrey.

"Of course if Mr Trethick particularly wishes trout for breakfast, I'll go and broil a brace myself," said Mrs Rumsey in an ill-used whine.

"I protest against any such proceeding," cried Geoffrey, who had been brought home by the doctor on purpose to partake of their spoil. "In fact, I rather dislike fish for breakfast," he added mendaciously. "There, that's capital. I'll sit here between these two young rosy-cheeked rogues," he cried, "and we'll have a race and see who'll eat most slices of bread and butter."

Mrs Rumsey stood with the coffee-pot in one hand, looking at him aghast.

"And we'll cut for ourselves," said Geoffrey, smiling.

Mrs Rumsey was thawed, especially as papa fetched the loaf and butter, and placed them on the table.

"There, Trethick, make yourself at home," he said; "we can't afford ceremony here."

"Glad of it," said Geoffrey, making one of his little neighbours laugh. "Why, Mrs Rumsey, you ought to be proud of your children. What a jolly, healthy little lot they are."

"Little?" cried Rumsey, pausing with his cup half-way to his lips.

"I mean in size, not number. Miss Prissy, if you look at me so hard with those blue eyes I shall think you are counting how many bites I take."

"Oh, I'm very proud of them," said Mrs Rumsey in a tone of voice that sounded like a preface to a flood of tears, "but it is a large family to care for and educate."

"Yes, it is," replied Geoffrey. "Mr Rumsey tells me that you educate them entirely yourself."

"Yes, quite," cried Mrs Rumsey, brightening a little. "Priscilla, say your bones."

To Geoffrey's astonishment Miss Priscilla put her hands behind, and began, with her mouth full of bread and butter—

"Flanges and metacarpals, hands and feet; tibia, fibula, femur, scapular, clavicle, ulna, radius, costa—vertebra—maxillary—minimum—Please, ma, I don't know any more;" and Miss Priscilla sat down suddenly and took another bite of her bread and butter.

"Bravo!" laughed Geoffrey. "Well, young lady, I don't think I could have remembered so many."

"She knows her muscles too," said Mrs Rumsey.

"Yes, but we won't have them now," said the doctor, quietly.

"Ah," sighed Mrs Rumsey, who felt injured, "but it is a very large family."

"Yes, but they look so healthy," continued Geoffrey. "Eh, coffee not strong enough, Mrs Rumsey? It's delicious. What beautiful butter?"

Mrs Rumsey seemed softened by her guest's homeliness.

"I wish I was as healthy," she sighed.

"So do I," said Geoffrey. "I'll be bound to say papa does not waste much medicine on them."

Dr Rumsey screwed up his face a little at this, and laughed.

"Dr Rumsey is very clever," said Mrs Rumsey, who—in her efforts to supply wants, cast an eye at the cradle, and see that the children behaved well before company—got into such a tangle that she besugared some cups twice, and some not at all. "I always say to him that he is throwing himself away down here."

"You do, my dear, always," said the doctor uneasily.

"There is so little to do," continued Mrs Rumsey, who got nothing to eat herself. "Priscilla, take your spoon in your right hand."

"Please, ma, my coffee's got no sugar," observed Bobby.

"There is no sugar in my coffee," said mamma correctively, as she gave her nose a twitch which sent it half an inch on one side. "Tom, sit up, sir. Yes, Mr Trethick, if my husband had his dues as a medical man, he would be in Harley Street, or in Brook Street, Grosvenor Square."

"As a specialist, eh?" said Geoffrey.

"Yes, Mr Trethick. Esther, my dear, why will you fill your mouth so full?"

"Still, life down here is very jolly, Mrs Rumsey," said Geoffrey, handing bread and butter to two or three hungry souls. "See how the little rascals eat."

"Yes," said the doctor, "that's just what they do do."

"Yes," said Mrs Rumsey, endorsing her husband's words, "their appetites are dreadful; and the doctor has so little business."

"Yes, there isn't much, only a mining accident now and then, or a half-drowned man or two to attend," said Rumsey.

"My pa brought a man to life again," said Bobby, gazing round-eyed at the visitor.

"Did he though?" said Geoffrey.

"Bobby, hold your tongue."

"Tom Jennen said he did," whispered the boy; "and my pa's very clever."

"Yes," sighed Mrs Rumsey, "he is clever."

"Hero worship," said the doctor to Geoffrey, with his eyes twinkling.

"That's your great fault, dear," said Mrs Rumsey, giving her nose a twitch in the other direction. "It was that which kept you so back in London. You know you are very clever."

"I'm setting a good example to my neighbours in having my house well garrisoned," said the doctor dryly. "I'm not at all ashamed to speak to my enemies in the gate—except when they come with their bills," he added softly.

"For shame, dear," cried Mrs Rumsey, "what will Mr Trethick think?"

"Think, ma'am," cried Geoffrey, "that he ought to be proud of his children. I never saw any better-behaved at table."

"He is proud of them, I must say," said Mrs Rumsey, who was beginning to forgive her visitor for coming to breakfast; "and if he had justice done to him people would own how clever he is."

"Clever at throwing a fly, Trethick, that's all."

"Well, I shall have to tumble down a shaft, or get blown up, or catch a fever, or something, to try him some day, Mrs Rumsey."

"Ah, a few more patients would be a godsend," said the doctor.

"My papa cut a man's leg right off once," said Bobby, sententiously.

"Then your papa must be a clever man," said Geoffrey, looking amusedly at the stolid little face.

"Bobby, you must not say such things," cried Mrs Rumsey. "Little boys should be seen and not heard. Prissy, my dear, you are swinging your legs about again."

"And he's got a wooden leg now—like an armchair," whispered Bobby, very softly, as soon as he saw his mother's attention taken up.

"There was no chance in London, Trethick," said the doctor. "I'd no capital, except children, and the rents were ruinous. Besides, you have to keep up appearances to such an extent."

"But the people there were not barbarians, my dear," sighed Mrs Rumsey.

"Well, my dear, and they are not here. We live, and manage to pay our way—nearly; and when they come to know you, the people are very sociable. We do have capital whist parties."

"But you know I detest whist, dear," sighed Mrs Rumsey. "Let me send you another cup of coffee, Mr Trethick."

"Thanks," said Geoffrey. "The fact is, I suppose," he continued to his host, "there are not enough inhabitants to give you a good practice."

"That's it, so I fill up with catching trout, and making a few shillings at whist."

"Yes, dear, you always would play whist," sighed Mrs Rumsey; and, to Geoffrey's horror, her nose this time went right up, as if to visit her forehead.

"Capital game too," said the doctor. "That and fishing often keep me from having the blues."

"Why don't you try and invest in some good mining speculation?" said Geoffrey.

"First, because I've got very little to invest; secondly, because where there is a good spec, there's no chance of getting on."

"Try Wheal Carnac," said Geoffrey.

"Do you mean to tell me, as man to man, that that is going to turn up trumps?" said the doctor, with a little more animation.

"I do indeed," said Geoffrey; "and if I had any money, I'd invest the lot."

"What, after so many people had been ruined in it?"

"Look here, doctor," said Geoffrey. "Suppose you go and take a house in, say Grosvenor Street, and start as physician."

"That's just what he ought to do," cried Mrs Rumsey, who began to think Geoffrey full of sound common-sense.

"Well, you would be sure to get some connection."

"Of course, but it wouldn't be enough to keep me."

"Exactly. Then another man, still retaining your plate on the door, comes, because you give it up in despair—fail, so to speak."

"Oh, dear no!" sighed Mrs Rumsey; but her attention was taken off by her children, two of whom were having a silent quarrel, and indulging in furtive kicks and pinches beneath the table.

"Go on," said the doctor.

"Well, he next fails, after increasing the connection, and another takes the place, and another after him."

"Yes."

"Well, the last one has some connection to start with, adds his own efforts, and goes on and prospers, like a son succeeding his father."

"You mean to say then that you succeed to something in Wheal Carnac."

"I say that we succeed to all the work the others have done. There is the shaft sunk and the buildings ready, and with our machinery fixed, all that was needed was that we should go to work with plenty of enterprise."

"But suppose it don't succeed—suppose you can't bring your patient back to life?"

"My papa brought a man back—"

"Be quiet, Bobby, when your papa's talking," cried Mrs Rumsey, who had to go out then to use the family handkerchief upon the noses of the hookah-smoking twins.

"But I shall bring it back to life," said Geoffrey, firmly. "As you would say, the organs are all sound, and all it wanted was a stimulus to send the life-blood throbbing through the patient's veins."

"Veins of tin, eh?" said the doctor.

"Perhaps of copper too," said Geoffrey. "If you have a hundred or two to spare—"

"I've got four or five hundred of my wife's money, but not to spare," said the doctor. "Brings us in three and a half per cent."

"I wouldn't promise," said Geoffrey, enthusiastically; "but I sha'n't be satisfied if I don't make that mine return its company thirty, forty, perhaps fifty, per cent."

"Dr Rumsey," said the lady, whose nose had been travelling in quite a circle round the centre of her face, "it is your duty to invest that money in this mine."

"But it isn't a regular company, is it?"

"No," said Geoffrey, "but it is in my power to get a little interest in the affair for a friend."

"If I could feel sure," said the doctor, dubiously.

"I would not advise you against your good," said Geoffrey, earnestly. "I am certain the mine will pay."

"Thirty, forty, or fifty per cent?"

"No," said Geoffrey. "I only hope that; but I'll warrant six or seven, perhaps fourteen."

"It would about ruin us," said the doctor, "if it was like most mines—a failure."

"My dear, I'm ashamed of you," cried Mrs Rumsey. "You always would fight against every chance of advancement. It is my money, and I say it shall be invested. There?"

The way in which Mrs Rumsey's nose twitched at this juncture was something surprising, and made Geoffrey quite uncomfortable.

"Well," he said, rising, "I must go. Mrs Rumsey, thank you for a charming breakfast. Rumsey, you think over that, and, look here, if you do think of it seriously, come up to me—soon."

"He shall, Mr Trethick," said the lady, decidedly.

"I will—think over it," said the doctor. "But, look here, if I do play and lose the rubber, don't you come to me when you are ill, or I'll give you such a dosing."

"My papa keeps it in a bottle," said Bobby, in a whisper.

"Does he? Well, we'll hope the stopper is never removed on my behalf," said Geoffrey. "But, look here," he cried, as he remembered something. "I've got two paper bags in my pocket;" and he dragged out the effects of his two last visits to Mrs Prawle, leaving the children in a high state of delight, and Mrs Rumsey telling her husband that if he had had the energy of Geoffrey Trethick he would be keeping his brougham, and she sitting in silk and satin, instead of having to wash up the breakfast things, while their one servant made the beds.

Chapter Thirty One.

Geoffrey Makes Love.

A long morning in the mine, now thoroughly cleared of water, and where, under the leadership of Dicky Pengelly, the picks were ringing merrily. Geoffrey had little good news to report, for the lode of tin was excessively poor; but all the same he felt that he could work on at a profit, and at any time they might strike a good rich vein. There was nothing, then, to mind.

He had reported every thing to Mr Penwynn exactly as it occurred, and that gentleman seemed not only perfectly satisfied, but encouraged him to go on.

"I have made the venture, Trethick," he said, "and I will not play with it. I look to you to pull me up if it is going to be a losing affair; but it seems to me that to withhold capital would be a miserable policy: so go on. Do you think it can become worse?"

"No," said Geoffrey, firmly, "that I do not. The fact is, Mr Penwynn, I am disappointed in the mine."

"Disappointed? You don't mean—"

"No, no, sir, I'm not beaten," said Geoffrey, laughing. "I mean I am disappointed in the mine, and I have found out two or three things about it."

"What sort of things?" said Mr Penwynn, uneasily.

"Trickeries—sharpings," said Geoffrey. "It is very evident that to sell that mine, or may be to impress shareholders with its value, the place has been more than once salted, as miners call it."

Mr Penwynn nodded.

"Tin ore from other mines has been thrown down, and, of course, I saw through that directly; but in several places right at the end of drifts, Pengelly and I have found great pieces of ore fitted into the solid rock in the most artful manner, so that it needed no little care to find out that it was a trick."

"But are you sure that it is a trick?" said Mr Penwynn.

"Certain, sir. It would have deceived an ordinary miner or owner."

"But did not deceive you?"

"Well, sir, I take no credit to myself for that. I went through a course of mining study, and it is as simple as A B C."

"How so?"

"Why, look here, sir. Only yesterday Pengelly called me to show me a rich place he had found."

"Yes. Well?"

"I had to crush the poor fellow's hopes at once. The thing was most artistically done, a quantity of tin-bearing quartz, evidently *in situ*."

"Yes."

"But I always carry this with me, Mr Penwynn," said Geoffrey, pulling out a pocket-lens; "and that showed me at once that the quartz was veined with a different mineral from that all around, and also that the granulations of the stone were such as are found in the strata on the other side of the county, and not here."

Mr Penwynn said nothing, but looked hard at his manager.

"They've spent a good deal of time and money to successfully swindle people, and cleverly too, where the same energy and outlay would have made a poor mine pay."

"Then you consider it a poor mine, Mr Trethick?"

"Very, sir."

"But the report I had said that it was rich."

"Then the reporter was either a fool or a knave," replied Geoffrey.

"Humph!" ejaculated Mr Penwynn, "and you think then that we had better stop."

"Certainly not," said Geoffrey, flushing. "It cannot give a poorer yield, for there are thousands of tons of such ore as we are now sending to grass, and which I can make yield at least five per cent dividend, while at any time we may 'strike ile,' as our friends the Yankees call it."

"Thank you, Trethick," said Mr Penwynn, quietly; and he drew a long breath. "Go on, I leave myself in your hands."

Geoffrey did go on working most earnestly, and on this particular day he had come up out of the mine, weary in body and mind, gone to the cottage and changed, and then started off along the cliff for what he called a blow.

"I'll go and see poor old Mrs Prawle," he said to himself; and in that disposition he went on till he came to the nook where he had interposed in Bess Prawle's defence; when, seeing an inviting place, he sat down, and as he did so the whole scene came back.

He did not know how it was, but there was a curiously uneasy sensation at his heart, and he found himself recalling Bess Prawle's looks, her way of expressing her gratitude, and ended by taking himself to task.

"I can go there often enough and chat with the poor old woman—poor soul, there's a very pathetic side to her patient, uncomplaining life; but why should I go when it may cause uneasiness to others? Poor Bess! she's a fine, handsome lass. I shall have her father making suggestions like Uncle Paul about poor Madge. 'Pon my soul, I must be a very fine-looking fellow," he cried merrily.

Then he laughed, took out a cigar, lit it, and sat smoking.

"The people here have too much time on their hands," he thought, "and it makes them scandalous. I wonder they don't have the impudence to couple my name with that of—"

"Bah! nonsense! what an idiot I am," he said, sharply; and the next moment he was self-communing, and asking why he should be so uneasy at such an idea.

For answer Rhoda's face seemed to rise before him, quiet, earnest, and trustful. He seemed to hear her sweet, pleasant voice, not thrilling him as whispering of love; but it seemed to him now that she had given him encouragement, that her suggestions had been of endless value to him, and that she was always so kind and sisterly to him, that—that—was it sisterly this? Was his feeling brotherly?

His brow grew rugged, and then as he thought on he began to feel startled at the new sensations that seemed to be springing up within his breast. He looked inward, and he obtained a glimpse of that which he had before ignored.

"Oh, it's absurd," he said, half aloud; "I should be mad. I should be a scoundrel."

Then he stopped, for the face of Rhoda, with the large, searching eyes, was gazing full into his, and this time it was no fancy. She was returning from Gwennas Cove, and she had turned into the nook to see once more the spot that had aroused such envious feelings in her breast.

"You here, Mr Trethick?" she said, quietly. "I did not expect to see you."

"I did not expect to see you here," he said, as quietly; but his voice sounded different, and Rhoda looked up at him for a moment, and then let her eyelids fall.

She had not held out her hand to him, neither had he offered his, and they stood there in that nook amidst the granite, surrounded by a solemn silence which neither seemed disposed to break.

Nothing could have been more simple. They had met as they might have met at any time, and they might have walked back quietly to the town. It was the most everyday of occurrences, and yet it was the most important moment of their lives.

They had both been blind, and now they were awakened, Rhoda to the fact that her heart was at length stirred to its deepest depths, Geoffrey to the knowledge that with all his strength of mind, his determination, his will, he was a man with all a man's weaknesses, and, if weakness it could be called, he loved the woman who stood with him, face to face.

He was dazzled, blinded at the revelation that had come like a lightning's flash, and then a feeling of horror came upon him, for he felt that he had been treacherous.

Then that horror seemed to be swept away by the stronger passion, and he looked earnestly in her face till the blue-veined lids were raised, and her eyes looked deeply and trustingly in his.

How long was it? Neither of them knew, before Geoffrey said quietly the one word,—

"Rhoda!"

She looked up at him again, and then stood hesitating, for the thoughts of the petty scandal she had heard flashed before her; but she shook them off as if they had been venomous, and, looking him full in the face, she placed her hand in his with an air of such implicit faith as stirred him into speech.

"I did not know this—I did not think this," he said hoarsely; "and I feel as if I were acting the part of a treacherous villain to the man who has given me his confidence and trust."

"And why?" she said.

"Because I know that I love you," he said; "love you with all my heart. Rhoda, I must leave here. I ought not to have spoken as I did."

She looked up at him timidly, with a half-flinching fear in her face as she met his eyes, but it turned to a look of pride, and she laid another hand upon his arm.

"No," she said, "you must stay. Geoffrey, I could not bear it if you were to go."

He must have been more than man if he had not clasped her to his breast at that, and in that embrace he felt her head rest upon his shoulder, and knew that fate had been very kind to him, and that he had won the love of a woman who would be part and parcel of his future life.

"And I had laughed at love," he said, little thinking that there were witnesses of what was passing; "but now I know. Rhoda! Oh, my love!"

He clasped her in his arms again, and for a moment her lips met his. Then with one consent they stood there hand in hand.

"I will tell him at once," said Geoffrey. "I know it will seem to him like madness; but I dare not meet him if I could not look him in the face. It is unfortunate, Rhoda, but yet I could not go back a moment of my life now."

"Unfortunate?" she said gently.

"Yes. Have you thought what it may mean?"

She shook her head.

"The end of a dream of success. Mr Penwynn will say, what right have I to think of you? He will call me adventurer, ask me how I dared to presume, and bid me never enter his house again. I am his servant, and it will be just."

"My father will be just," said Rhoda, gazing in his face; "and if he is surprised and angry at first, he loves me too well to cause me pain. Geoffrey: I am not ashamed of my choice."

He held her hands, looking down at her proudly, wondering that he had not loved her from the first.

"You will succeed, Geoffrey," she continued, "and we can wait, for we are young yet. My father, I know, already likes you for the same reason that you first won my esteem."

"And why was that?" he said, smiling.

"You are so different to any one we ever knew before."

"Yes," he said at last, "we can wait."

And so they were pledged one to the other. Geoffrey never seemed to know how it had happened; Rhoda could not have told when it was she began to love; but they both knew, as by a sudden inspiration, that they loved the deeper and stronger for the calmness upon the surface of their lives.

There was no passionate wooing, there were no vows of constancy, all was simplicity itself; but the foundation upon which their love had been reared seemed firm as the granite around promised to be lasting; as the sea whose ripples were now golden in the setting sun, whose warm glow seemed to glorify the face of Rhoda, and intensify the love-light that glanced from her eyes. It was a time of calm, and peace, and rest, and as in the midst of this new joy, the quaint idea suggested itself that their love seemed somehow associated with the scent of the wild thyme they crushed beneath their feet, they stood there in silence, drinking in deep mental draughts of the new sensation, and wondering at their happiness the while.

Chapter Thirty Two.

Within Touch of Wealth.

"Thank you, Trethick," said Mr Penwynn, the next morning, and he looked very calm and stern as he spoke, "I expected this, for my daughter told me all last night. I might have known this would happen, though I confess to having been very blind. Now go on, what have you further to say? But, first of all, you are a man of sense and some experience in the world. You do not, you cannot, expect me to sanction your addresses?"

"No, sir, not now. I only ask you to put no pressure upon either of us, but to let us be free."

"In other words, give you the run of my house, and ample time for follies. You don't want to come and live upon me?"

"No, sir," said Geoffrey, sternly. "I am somewhat of a man of the world. I tell you that my declaration to Miss Penwynn took me by surprise; but there are times when we cannot command ourselves. All I ask now is your indulgence towards me, knowing what I do, and time. I shall come very rarely to your house, and our business relations I hope will continue the same. I mean to succeed, sir," he cried, striding up and down the banker's room—"here if you will let me stay, elsewhere if you say to me go."

"If I say to you go?" said the banker, thoughtfully.

"Yes, I give you my word of honour, Mr Penwynn, that I will not attempt to see Miss Penwynn again, and I will leave every thing at the mine so that my successor can carry on without a hitch."

"And if I say stay," said the banker, coldly, "what then?"

"I am your manager, Mr Penwynn, and I shall remember that I am your servant until you bid me come to your house as a friend. You may trust me, sir," he said, gazing frankly in the banker's eyes. "I had ambition to spur me on before; I have a far greater incentive now."

Mr Penwynn sat thinking for a few minutes, and then said quietly,—

"Mr Trethick, I ask you, *as my manager*, to stay."

"And if I succeed, sir, what then?"

"Succeed first, and then we'll talk."

There was considerable emphasis upon a portion of the banker's speech, and Geoffrey rose, and, without another word, left the room.

"I am to stay," he thought exultingly, and his first idea was that he should go and tell Rhoda; but he recollected that he must henceforth look at her from a distance. It was only reasonable, he felt. What right had he, a penniless adventurer, to aspire to Rhoda's hand? It was madness, he owned; but time was before him, and he had her love.

He had the indorsement of her love when he returned from the mine that evening, for Madge Mullion brought him a note that he saw at a glance was in Rhoda's handwriting, and a throb of joy ran through him as he caught the envelope.

Then, looking up, he saw the bearer's eyes gazing wistfully at him, and he noted, more and more, how pale and wan she looked.

"Why, Madge," he said, "are you unwell?"

She shook her head, and hurried away.

"Poor girl," he muttered, "I cannot have made her look like this. She must be ill, and fretting about some one else."

He was opening the letter as he spoke, and his eyes flashed as they ran over the few simple lines the note contained.

They were very short. They only told of the interview between father and daughter, and bade Geoffrey remember that though they would seldom meet now, the future was before them, and Rhoda added, "My daily prayer will be for your success."

"For my success," said Geoffrey, firmly, as he placed the letter in one particular fold of his pocket-book. "Then now I am going to work."

Rather a curious declaration for one whose labours had for months been almost herculean, but it did not seem to occur to Geoffrey that it was strange; and, after partaking of his tea, he was about to go in and see Uncle Paul, when there was a step outside, and directly after the girl came in to say that Amos Pengelly wanted to see him.

"Show him in, girl," said Geoffrey; and directly after there was a heavy limping step; the miner entered, and, without a word, banged down a great lump of granite quartz upon the table.

"There," he cried excitedly, "that's not salt."

Geoffrey looked at him wonderingly, took up the piece of granite, which sparkled with black grains in a band of ruddy mineral running through the piece, and turned it over and over by the light.

"That didn't come from nowhere else, master," said Pengelly.

Still Geoffrey did not reply, but continued to examine the piece of rock, the miner's excitement being so great that he could hardly contain himself.

"Where did you get this?" said Geoffrey, at last.

"In the four-east drive."

"Under the sea?" said Geoffrey, sharply.

"Yes, sir."

"When?"

"Not an hour ago."

"You staid down then, Pengelly?"

"Yes. Iss, my son. I knew there was good stuff down there somewhere, and I've hit it now."

"Have you been searching much, Pengelly?"

"Every night, master, since the mine was opened," said Pengelly, proudly, "I felt that my character was at stake. I would find it. I prayed and wrastled that I might find it, master," he cried, with flashing eyes, "and my prayer is heard."

"Pengelly," cried Trethick, "there's thirty per cent of metal in that rock—thirty? Perhaps more," he cried excitedly.

He caught up his hat, and together they hurried down to the mine, where, in spite of the lateness of the hour, the engine was going, and a stream of water pouring forth, for it needed some effort to keep the galleries dry.

Mining garments were soon donned, lamps taken, and, to the surprise of the man in charge of the engine, the manager announced his intention of descending; and, stepping into the cage, Pengelly and he were soon rushing down into the bowels of the earth, to step out at last six hundred feet from the surface, and then thread their way along the dark stone passages of the silent place.

For the mine was deserted now for the night, and there was nothing for company but their own shadows thrown grotesquely on the sparkling walls and floor.

Pengelly led the way with no little agility, making light of lumps of refuse remaining from the old working of the mine, and even yet not removed, for Geoffrey's venture had been in quite another direction.

As they went on, Pengelly pointed here and there to freshly chipped places where he had been, pursuing his investigations without success, and at last he stopped short at the end of the gallery, facing the rock.

"They had got to success," said the miner, hoarsely. "Only another foot, and they would have reached the lode. Look here, master."

"Give me the pick," cried Geoffrey, excitedly; and, snatching the tool, as Pengelly held the lamp, he made the gallery echo and send long, loud reverberations along its course. The rock spat forth a shower of sparks, while Geoffrey proceeded to cut out a goodly-sized fragment of the stone from the bottom of the new fracture where Pengelly had been at work.

It was a strange scene, and the shadow of the young man, as it was cast here and there upon the rock, looked like some hideous spirit of the mine waving its arms, and menacing him with a monstrous pick. There was something awful too, in the harsh, clanging noises repeated from the stony walls; and every stroke of the implement he wielded seemed to draw forth threatening flashes of light, as the toiler smote on at the hard rock that had lain there virgin from far back in those distant ages whose dim vistas are so full of awe to the inquiring mind.

But neither Pengelly nor Trethick thought of aught but the value of the ore that the latter was hewing, till he had detached a far larger lump than that brought to him by his follower.

"Take hold, Pengelly," said Geoffrey, excitedly, as he picked up the dislodged fragment, and, thrusting it into the miner's hands, he took the lamp, which made the dew upon his forehead glisten; and then, with trembling hands, he held the light close to the wall, examining it carefully here and there, right in where the pieces had been cut and at the side. Then, not satisfied, he took the pick, and cut here and there at the dripping, slimy sides that had been coated with a curious growth while under water for years, and against which the newly-cut portions flashed out bright and clean.

A cut here, a few chips there, ceiling, floor a few yards back, in all directions, and the result was the same, namely, that the quartz rock was similar to that where the grand rich vein of tin was running; and, after full five hours' hard toil, patiently lighted the while by Pengelly, it was literally forced upon Geoffrey that trickery had no existence here; that the rock had never been tampered with by speculators, but was virgin and pure as it had been from the beginning of time, and he knew that the old proprietory had ceased their efforts in this direction when riches were within their grasp.

Then, and then only, did Geoffrey draw out a pocket-lens for his final look, close it, throw down the piece of ore, and catching Pengelly's hands in his, shake them with a hearty grip.

"Right!" he cried, "there is no salt here, Pengelly. Wheal Carnac is a great success."

He stopped short, listening to a sound that had at first been but a faint murmur, but had increased by slow degrees to a heavy roar, and he realised that which he had for the time forgotten—that they were beneath the sea, and that the crust of rock between them and the mighty waters must be very thin.

Chapter Thirty Three.

Too Fast.

It was too late to go up to An Morlock on the night of the discovery; but Geoffrey Trethick was there by breakfast-time, to find Rhoda in the morning-room, and Mr Penwynn not yet down.

Rhoda read his face as he entered and threw a heavy bag on the table to catch her hands in his.

"Half the distance got over!" he exclaimed enthusiastically. "Wheal Carnac is a success."

"Is this keeping your word, Mr Trethick?" said a stern voice; but Geoffrey and Rhoda did not start apart.

"I could not keep back my news, Mr Penwynn," cried Geoffrey, going to the table and seizing the bag.

"News! What news?"

"That you own one of the richest mines in Cornwall, Mr Penwynn," cried Geoffrey. "Look here."

The banker looked at him to see if he was sane; then at the piece of ore that had been brought, which he inspected again and again through his glasses.

"Very, very rich stuff," he said at last. "But is this from Wheal Carnac?"

"Yes, sir, as I had hoped. We have struck an enormously rich lode. The poor fellows must have been within inches of it years ago when they left off; and, yes, of course," he said, as he recalled the noise of the water heard on the previous night, "they must have been afraid to go any farther on account of the sea."

"And," said Mr Penwynn, whose customary calmness was swept away by the news, "do you mean to tell me, Trethick, that Wheal Carnac is going to turn out a very valuable property?"

"I tell you, Mr Penwynn," said Geoffrey, proudly, "that unless some strange, unforeseen accident occurs to spoil the project, Wheal Carnac *has* turned out an enormously valuable property."

The banker glanced at the rich ore and then at Geoffrey, who had no hesitation in sitting down to breakfast, and drinking in with the mundane coffee the proud and joyous glances of his love.

Over the meal he told them of Pengelly's researches, and of his announcement on the previous night; then of his visit and careful examination of the gallery.

"There's nothing to fear," he said, "but the water; and I dare say I can guard against that."

The banker became very silent, and sat after Geoffrey had ended, glancing from one to the other, reading as plainly as if it were writ in plain English of his daughter's love for the enterprising, manly young fellow at his table.

Mr Penwynn was weighing matters of the heart in his own mind, just as he would have weighed any business speculation; and when from time to time his matter-of-fact worldliness bade him treat Geoffrey in a plain business-like manner, a look from Rhoda seemed to master him, and he felt as yielding as so much modelling-clay.

"It seems a great folly," he thought. "He is a stranger, an adventurer, and yet his first venture brings me wealth. There," he said to himself, at last, "I'm rich enough, and I'm getting old very fast; let me see her happy if I can."

There was something so frank and friendly in his way of speaking to Geoffrey afterwards that, without a word, Rhoda came to him, laid her hands upon his shoulders and her cheek upon his breast.

She let it lie there for a minute or two, and then, with a glance at him full of affection, she left his side, and, half-timidly, in a way so very different to her usual self, she crossed to Geoffrey and placed her hands in his.

"This is going on fast, Trethick," said Mr Penwynn, smiling, and looking half-perplexed; "but we have only a hint of success yet. I am a man of the world, recollect, and I want to see a big banking balance to the credit of the mine."

"Never fear, sir, that shall follow. Only give me time."

"Well, Trethick," said Mr Penwynn, after a struggle with self, in which, after sordidness and avarice had nearly won the victory, a look from Rhoda's transformed, happy face turned the scale, "what am I to say to you about a share in the prosperity?"

"Let's get the big balance in the bank first, sir," said Geoffrey, laughing. "We will not divide a castle in the air."

"But it would be more business-like and careful if you made your bargain now."

"So I should have thought a month ago, Mr Penwynn," said Geoffrey, holding out his hand. "Our interests ran together then. Now—I think—I hope—they are one, and I cannot strike bargains with the father of the woman!—"

He stopped and looked at Rhoda, who slowly raised her eyes to his, and then her hands, which he took softly, reverently, and kissed. Then he turned to Mr Penwynn and finished his sentence—"most dearly love."

The banker watched them very thoughtfully, for it seemed hardly real to him. In fact, at times he asked himself if it were not a dream.

He was roused from recollections of his own career, some five-and-twenty years before, by Geoffrey turning to him abruptly.

"Mr Penwynn," he said, "I leave myself in your hands. I am working in our mutual interests."

"And suppose I play false?" said Mr Penwynn.

"You can't, sir," cried Geoffrey, "with Rhoda here. If you treated me hard, you would be behaving ill to your daughter, and that you will not do. Now, good-morning. When will you come down and see the lode?"

"I'm not fond of going down mines," said Mr Penwynn.

"But in this case you will, I think," said Geoffrey.—"I'll answer for your safety. Miss Penwynn—Rhoda?"

"Yes," she cried, answering his unspoken question, "I will come down too. I shall not be afraid, and I want to christen the Rhoda vein."

"To be sure," cried Geoffrey, "the vein that is to bring us all wealth and happiness."

He hurried away, and Rhoda ran to the window to see him pass; while Mr Penwynn picked up the piece of tin ore, balanced it in his hands, and, recalling certain rumours of tricks that had been played upon mine-owners, he said to himself,—

"Suppose he should play me false?"

And directly after, when he saw Rhoda's hand waved to Trethick, as he glanced back,—

"Suppose he should play her false?" for certain other rumours came to his mind. "Poor girl, it would break her heart."

Just then, bright, flushed, and animated, Rhoda turned to him.

"No," he said to himself, "she has too much pride."

Chapter Thirty Four.

A Bargain.

"What?" roared Tregenna, furiously.

"It'll turn out the richest mine in Cornwall, sir."

"You're a fool! Absurd! Ridiculous!" cried Tregenna, biting his nails, and then making his teeth grit together as he glared at the rough miner before him.

"Dessay I be," said the man, surlily; "but I've been at work in the gallery all day, and I never see such tin ore before."

"And I've let this go for a paltry few hundreds—a thousand or two at most," muttered Tregenna. "But it can't be true. Are you sure?" he said aloud.

"Sure enough, sir, and I thought you'd like to know. I didn't expect to be called a fool for my pains."

"No, no, of course not, Lannoe," said Tregenna, hurriedly. "I was put out. I've heard the gossip all day, but I thought it exaggerated. I'm glad you've come."

"Oh, there's no 'zaggeration 'bout it," said the man. "I've kept an eye on it all ever since the mine was dried, just as you wished, and they was getting nothing but rubbish, till Amos Pengelly, who was always picking about, hit upon this vein."

"Damn Amos Pengelly!" cried Tregenna, savagely.

"To which I says 'Amen,'" said the miner.

"Then the place will turn out immensely rich, and that fellow Trethick will make quite a fortune."

"Iss, sir, that's so," said the miner. "Master Penwynn and young miss come down in the cage to-night to see it, and young miss took hold of a pick that Master Trethick held for her, and chipped off a bit or two, and there was a lot of smiling atween 'em."

Tregenna's face turned ghastly white, and he changed his position so that the man should not see it; but the miner was keen enough to read him, and he went on, evidently glorying in the torture he was inflicting.

"Master Trethick took 'em back to the cage, and helped young miss in again, and went up with them, and him and Master Penwynn seemed wonderful thick together."

Tregenna's face was ashy now, and he made a motion with one hand for the man to desist, but he went on.

"It do seem hard, sir," he said, "when, after planting the mine on to Master Penwynn, believing it would half ruin him and do for that there Trethick, it should turn out all t'other way."

"How did you know I had any such thoughts?" cried Tregenna, fiercely.

"How did I know?" said the man, chuckling. "You know I arn't a fool, Mas'r Tregenna, or you wouldn't have set me to get work in that there mine, and report every thing to you."

For answer Tregenna unlocked a drawer in his table, and took out a packet of papers, neatly endorsed, and tied up with red tape.

"Look here, Lannoe," he said, shaking the papers at the man, "your tongue runs too fast, and you forget your position. You are a man of bad character whom I got off at the assize for a crime that would have given you penal servitude. You can be a useful man; and when you came to me begging I gave you money and I got you work. Suppose, on further consideration of your case, I should find out that there was a little evidence left out that would convict you, and feel it my duty to make it known, so that the prosecution could have a new trial?"

"You wouldn't do that, Mas'r Tregenna, sir," growled the man. "I'm too useful to you. There, I'll hold my tongue."

"You had better," said Tregenna, who had now somewhat recovered himself. "And so this mine's going to be enormously rich?"

"Not a doubt of it, sir, unless the water breaks in."

"Water breaks in? What, is the vein near the sea?"

"Goes right under it, sir," said the man, watching intently where the packet of papers was placed, Tregenna seeing it, and resolving to place them elsewhere. "You see, the people who failed seem to have driven right in there, till, finding nothing, they were afraid to go farther for fear of the sea breaking through."

"And might it not break through now?"

"Well, it might, sir; but Master Trethick's one of your clever, careful sort, and he'll take care that nothing goes wrong. He had the men busy with props, and struts, and planking all day long. There'll be no water break in there."

"Curse it, it's most unfortunate!" cried Tregenna, biting his nails. "I'd have given any thing sooner than it should have turned out as it has."

"Hundred pound, p'r'aps," said Lannoe, looking at him sidewise.

"Yes, I'd have given a hundred pounds if the mine had turned out a failure."

"Hand it over," said the miner, abruptly.

"What do you mean?"

"You said you'd give a hundred pounds if that there mine turned out a complete failure, and I say hand it over."

"Look here, Lannoe," cried Tregenna, unable to contain his excitement, "can you—do you know—curse it, man, speak out!"

"What for? What's the good?" said the man, hoarsely. "Hundred pounds—hundred pounds. Give me the hundred pounds and you'll see."

Tregenna looked at him strangely.

"I don't pay for work until it's done," he said.

"And I don't work unless I'm paid," said the man, roughly.

"And suppose you break faith?"

"And suppose you get me tried all over again?" said Lannoe. "Look here, Master Tregenna, you're a gentleman, and I'm only a rough miner, but we are both on the same road. I arn't blind, so you may just as well speak plain. I know, you know, and speak plain, and don't hide it from you about Bess Prawle, and my being kicked off and threatened. You don't suppose I let Amos Pengelly half kill me when he threw me on the rocks without owing him for it and wanting to pay it back, even if I do work with him now all smooth? Why can't you speak plain too? I know, you know, about your wanting young miss, and the old man saying you shouldn't, and your Amos Pengelly—this here bullying, ordering Londoner—coming and throwing you. There, master, you'd better hand over that hundred pounds."

"And if I do?" said Tregenna, leaning forward, placing his elbows on the table as he faced Lannoe, and joined his hands carefully as if he were going to say his prayers.

"Wait and see," said the man. "You don't want to know, sir. You want to hear that Wheal Carnac's a failure, and I'm the man as can make it one. Now what do you say?"

Tregenna remained thinking for a time, with hate and revenge against cautiousness fighting for the mastery.

It was two to one, and cautiousness was beaten.

"I'll give you the hundred pounds, Lannoe," he said; "but I warn you that if you play me false I'll have the police on your track at once. You may think think you could get away, or throw it back in my face that I set you to do something; but you could not get away, and my character would be set against yours if you brought any charge against me."

"Who's going to?" cried the man.

"And if it cost me a couple of thousand pounds, man, I'd have you in the dock."

"Don't I tell you I'd do any thing to pay Amos Pengelly, master. Hand over that money."

"I have not got it here," said Tregenna.

"What?"

"You don't suppose a gentleman keeps a hundred pounds always in his pocket, do you?"

"I should," said the man, grimly, "if I'd got it. Give us a bit o' paper then to take to the bank to-morrow."

"Shall I tell the crier to go round and shout that I have given you a hundred pounds for some reason or another? Don't be a fool, man!"

"Give me notes, then," said Lannoe.

"Every one of which, if I had them, would be numbered as having been paid to me. No, Lannoe, I have given you my word that I will pay you; and, what is more," he cried, excitedly, "if—if, I say—you understand? I'll give you another fifty."

"Shake hands," said the man; and Tregenna unwillingly placed his white beringed fingers in the miner's horny paw, to take them out afterwards red and crushed.

"I'll trust you, Lannoe, and you must trust me."

"Right, master," said the miner. "Then look here. Where—"

"That will do," said Tregenna. "I want to know nothing. I'll hear nothing. Come to me some day when you think it wise, and there is the money for you."

He pointed to the door, and the man nodded and went away.

Chapter Thirty Five.

Under the Sea.

Busy times in Wheal Carnac. There had been plenty of visitors in the shape of managers of different mines, to whom the news had come; and all went away astounded at the wealth of the new vein. The demand for shares was enormous, but there were none to be had. Tregenna had had the last, taken to blind Mr Penwynn, and he had sold them to Dr Rumsey, who had invested the whole of his wife's little fortune in the mine, and the next morning after the news had spread, the doctor had hurried up to the cottage, where Geoffrey was seated at breakfast with Uncle Paul, an unusually fine sole from the trawler having brought them together.

Madge opened the door to the doctor, who shook hands with her in a friendly way; and then, as their eyes met, Madge's friendly smile changed into a look of fear, under the doctor's searching gaze. She flushed, then turned deadly pale, and ended by shrinking back with a piteous look, and holding up her hands in a pleading way.

Dr Rumsey's lips tightened, and he said quietly,—

"Tell Mr Trethick I am here."

"Come in, Rumsey," cried Geoffrey's hearty voice. "You're in time for breakfast, man. You are just right. Uncle Paul's as bilious as—as himself."

Madge was forgotten for the moment, and the doctor shook hands warmly with the young man and with Uncle Paul, as a chair was placed for him, and the bell rung for a cup and saucer and plate, for, truth to say, though the doctor had partaken of the morning meal, he sometimes rose from it with a better appetite than was quite necessary for a proper fulfilment of the digestive functions.

"My dear Trethick," he cried, with the tears in his eyes, "God bless you for the hint! The news about the mine is glorious."

"That's right," said Geoffrey. "Eat your sole, man, before it gets cold," for a hot plate had been brought in by Madge herself, who seemed very eager to attend upon the visitor.

"You—you don't mean to say that you have been investing in mining shares, Rumsey?" cried Uncle Paul.

"Indeed, but I hope he has," said Geoffrey, heartily.

"I have: every penny we had," cried the doctor.

"More fool you!" cried Uncle Paul. "Why, Rumsey, how can you expect a man to trust you with his internal management if you go and do such insane things?"

"Uncle Paul don't believe in the mine even yet," said Geoffrey, laughing. "That will do, Miss Madge," he said; "I'll ring for more hot water if we want it."

The doctor saw Madge's appealing look at him, and a half-frightened glance at Geoffrey, and he saw too, as the girl left the room, that Uncle Paul was watching him very narrowly.

When he spoke again his manner was changed, and there was quite a coldness about it, which Geoffrey noticed.

"You hold on," he said, attributing it to nervousness caused by Uncle. Paul's attitude—"you hold on, Rumsey, and don't you be tempted at any price to sell. I warrant, my dear fellow, that you've made by that one stroke a handsome provision for your wife, more than you could have made by doctoring the whole county."

"Then why don't you invest?" snarled Uncle Paul.

"Because I've got no money," said Geoffrey, coolly. "Why don't you, who have?"

"Because I'm not quite such an old fool as you think."

The doctor warmed up again under the sunshine of Geoffrey's cheery ways, and soon after they were walking down towards the cliff, the doctor thanking Geoffrey again heartily as they parted, the one to make his rounds, the other to go to the busy mine.

Geoffrey had not gone half-way before he met old Prawle, coming direct from Wheal Carnac.

"Hallo, old man!" he cried. "How's poor mother? By Jove, I must come and see the dear old lady again."

"Better—better," said Prawle, hastily.

"That's well; and Miss Bessie?"

"Yes, yes, quite well," said the old man, hastily. "I want to see you."

"Come along down to my office. Been to the mine?"

"Yes, yes. I've been down."

"Ah, you old fox!" cried Geoffrey. "You wouldn't tell me, but you see we found it out."

"Yes, yes," said Prawle, still speaking in a hasty way, contrary to his wont. "I'll buy some shares."

"No, you won't," said Geoffrey, laughing.

"Why not, eh? You'll let me?"

"There isn't a share to be had, old man. No, sir, you are too late. You, knowing what you did, Prawle, should have made friends, and taken your share of the good things."

The old man looked at him with a curiously sly expression of countenance.

"None to be had?" he said, dubiously.

"Not a share, Father Prawle: for those who hold them know their value now, and will not part."

The old fellow hesitated as if he half meant to say something, but he did not say it, and went his way; while Geoffrey went on to the mine, busied himself a little about some fresh arrangements for stampers and improved crushing apparatus, and then descended the mine to seek out Pengelly.

He found him hard at work superintending a gang of wielders of the pick, eager to make a goodly show of ore to send up to grass, and Geoffrey stopped about till the men went off to their dinners, when he and Pengelly had a long conversation about the state of the mine at this place.

"I've been measuring and calculating, Pengelly, and I find that you are so near the water here that not an inch must be cut on the face of the drive, rich as it is. We must go down, and trust to finding the lode right away."

"What, and leave this?" said Pengelly. "Why, it's madness."

"Madness or no, I shall not have it touched, Pengelly," said Trethick, firmly. "Lay your ear against the rock. You can almost feel the beat of the water. I make it that we are right out four hundred feet under the sea at high water. We must run no risks."

For answer Pengelly began to ply his pick vigorously on the floor of the gallery, marking out the portion to be sunk so as to be deeper down in the rock, and where there would be no risk of the sea breaking in.

Geoffrey had well made his plans by night, and was the last, as he thought, to leave the pit, and he then went straight to his rooms to refresh himself before writing to several engineers for various necessaries that would be required for the greatly increased output from the mine.

Chapter Thirty Six.

Despair.

There was the sound of angry words in the back part of Mrs Mullion's house that night, and more than once Geoffrey fancied he heard Uncle Paul's voice raised high, but he had so often heard the old man storming about some trifle that he paid little heed to it, but finished the work he had on hand, thought how he would have liked to go up to An Morlock for an hour or two, and ended by bidding himself be patient, and all that would follow.

It was not yet nine, he found, and the house being very silent, he concluded that the old man had gone off somewhere for a rubber of whist.

"I wouldn't half mind a rubber myself," he thought. "I wonder where he has gone?"

"No. It won't do. No rubbers. I'll go and have a stroll on the cliff side and stretch my legs, or else I sha'n't sleep, for my brain is all in a buzz."

In this intent he put on his hat, lit his pipe, and went out, fancying he heard a sob in the farther room, but, not being sure, he attached little importance thereto.

"What a lovely night," he mentally exclaimed, as, thrusting his hands deep into his pockets, he descended the rugged lane, turned to the right, and went off along the cliff.

He had come out for repose, but his brain refused to be at rest, for now came back the sounds that he had heard in the cottage that evening.

"The old man's been rowing that poor girl," he thought, "finding out something concerning her carryings-on with somebody or another. Well, poor lass, I suppose she likes him; and, heigho! I feel very lenient now with people who go in for the commodity called love.

"I suppose it is Tregenna," he continued. "If it is, he is a thorough-paced scoundrel, or he would acknowledge her openly. He's playing fast and loose with her, and that's what makes her look so pale and ill."

He walked on, trying to enjoy the beauty of the starlit night, and the glittering of the smooth, heaving sea, but in vain, for the thought of the sobbing and angry words kept coming back and haunting him, as it were, no matter how fast he walked.

"Now, why the dickens should I make it my business? And yet it seems to be, through knowing the girl and living in the house. I can't interfere, of course, and tell what I know; but, really, if the fellow is trifling with her it ought to be stopped. Why don't the old man know and settle it? He don't, of course, or he would not behave to me as he does, and it would be too mean to put him on the scent. If it's as I think, and the old man does get to know of it, he'll half kill Tregenna. Hang the fellow! he's enough to make one believe in metempsychosis, and think he was once a serpent. I suppose he's the sort of fellow some women would like, though. But not all."

He went on more slowly, for his thoughts now were pleasant, and as he glanced down at the sea, which was one dark sheet of spangled star-drops, playing and shimmering in the ebon blackness, he began to plan how he would carry on the mine, and to think of how suddenly a great change had come over his life.

"What a turn of fortune's wheel!" he exclaimed; and then back went his thoughts to Mrs Mullion's cottage and poor Madge.

"Poor little lassie, if he's behaving badly to her—whoever the *he* may be, for, after all, it was fancy. She is not fretting about me. It is very hard upon her to be bullied at home as well. There's something about her I like. Ought I to tell old Paul what I know?

"Then there would be a row. Tregenna would turn upon me and say it was a lie, and a cowardly attack. He'd, of course, ask for proof, and I have none.

"Oh, confound it all! it's no business of mine. They must settle it amongst themselves. Hallo! what's that?"

A figure passed by him so rapidly that he was half-startled. Then, seeing that it was a woman, and hearing the rustling of the dress on ahead, he took a step or two forward as if in chase.

"What on earth am I doing?" he muttered petulantly. "Who in the world could that be? It couldn't be Bessie Prawle going home. No; I'm sure it was not her walk, and yet nobody else would be likely to be going along here at this time of night. Who could it be?"

He stopped short, took off his hat, and began to fan his forehead.

"I'm as hot and excited to-night as can be," he said, half laughing. "Well, no wonder. It's enough to turn a stronger brain than mine. Such good fortune does not fall to every man's lot in so short a time. Now suppose I behave like a rational being?"

Just then there was the rattle of stones on one of the rough paths that led from the cliff to the beach.

"Whoever it was has fallen," he cried. "Why, what madness to attempt to go down there in the dark! I shall break my own neck going after her."

Risk or none, he began to descend the steep path, but only to find that whoever had fallen had risen, and was making for the beach.

"Why, what folly," thought Geoffrey, as he stopped in the semi-darkness. "It must be some one who knows her way pretty well."

For a moment he thought of calling to her, but there seemed no reason for such a proceeding, and he felt that he might frighten whoever it was; and at last, concluding that there was no occasion for him to follow, he was about to turn back, when a thought flashed across him which made him tremble.

"Good heavens!" he ejaculated, "it's Madge!" and full of the horrible thought that in her trouble she could have come there but for one purpose, he began rapidly to descend the rest of the way, falling heavily twice in his haste to reach the beach, and running no little risk of serious injury.

There was about a hundred yards of wave-worn granite between the cliff foot and where the calm sea heaved gently, and fringed the rocks with a soft phosphorescent light; and here, in the shadow, he paused to try and make out in which direction the figure had gone. His heart was beating wildly, as much from excitement as his exertion, and his sole thought now was to over take and prison the hand of the poor girl he believed it to be.

It was a horrible sensation that of standing helplessly there, eager to stay the wretched girl, but ignorant of the way she had taken. The faint wash of the sea drowned her footsteps, and as he gazed in every direction the dark, rocky beach looked weird and strange, the faint gleam of the phosphorescence adding to the wildness of the scene.

"Madge—Madge Mullion—Madge!" he shouted hoarsely, troubling himself little now who might hear; but there was no reply, and, cautiously making his way amongst the rocks and over the slippery patches of bladder-wrack and broad slimy-fronded weed, he narrowly escaped a fall.

Was it fancy after all, or had he really seen some one come down?

It could not be fancy, he felt sure, and as the minutes glided by he was the more convinced that he was right in his conjecture, and that it was Madge.

"Poor lass!" he exclaimed. "Heaven help her! has it come to this?"

Feeling sure that if his surmise was right, she would be down by some rocks that ran out like a rugged pier into the sea, he crept cautiously on, and strained his eyes to try and make out the figure of her he sought, but in vain; and he was about giving up in despair, mingled with a hope that he was mistaken, when his heart seemed for the moment to stand still, for there was a wild cry from a spot some fifty yards away, followed by a splash; and as he dashed on, regardless of rock and slippery weed, he saw the phosphorescent sea ripple and play about where the poor girl had plunged into the deep water, from quite at the end of the natural pier.

Geoffrey did not hesitate for a moment, but as he reached the brink he plunged in, striking himself against a mass of rock, but fortunately without injury; and, in spite of being dressed, he swam strongly and well in the direction where he had seen the luminous water in agitation.

The distance was farther than he anticipated, and the tide was against him; still this was something in his favour, for it swept the figure of the drowning girl towards him, and as he rose he caught sight of a faint splash or two, making the water flash as she feebly beat the surface with her hands.

But for the unusually luminous state of the sea that night, Geoffrey Trethick's effort must have been in vain. As it was, his sturdy strokes took him to the side of the drowning girl, and catching her dress, he transferred a stout fold to his teeth, and swan; for the shore.

It was a harder task than he anticipated, and when at last he reached the rocks, rough here with limpets, slimy there with anemones, like clots of blood, and long strangling weeds, it required no little effort to climb to a place of safety.

At last, though, he staggered amongst the rocks and stones with his dripping burthen, and then paused with her, resting on one knee to press the streaming hair from her face, and try to bring her back to life.

Dark as it was he could see that it was Madge, and he paused, wondering what he had better do.

To leave her while he went for help meant, perhaps, leaving her to her death; while to carry her up the rugged cliff path was almost impossible in the dark.

While he was hesitating, a low moan from his burthen's lips told of returning consciousness, and he roused her a little more.

"Why, Madge, my poor child," he said, "has it come to this?"

She uttered a wild cry, and burst into a passion of sobbing.

"Let me go—let me die," she cried passionately. "Why did you get me out?"

"Hush, Madge! Hush, girl!" he cried. "Are you mad?"

"Yes, yes," she wailed, "and there is nothing for me but to die."

"Nonsense, girl?" he cried, half angrily, for her unreason annoyed him. "Here, can you walk? Take hold of my arm, and let me help you home."

"Home!" she wailed. "I have no home. My uncle has driven me away."

"Then I'll take you back," cried Geoffrey, angrily. "The old man is mad."

"No, no, no," she cried passionately; and she struggled from his grasp, and made a desperate effort to get back to the sea, but he caught her and held her fast.

"Be quiet," he cried angrily. "You foolish girl Madge, you'll come home at once."

"No, no, Mr Trethick; no," she sobbed hoarsely; and her strength astonished him. "I cannot—dare not go back. You don't know. Oh, God, forgive me! Let me die!"

"Not know?" cried Geoffrey. "I know quite enough. Look here, you silly girl, I don't want to hurt you, but you make me angry. You shall come home."

"No, no, no," she cried; and she struggled with him till he lifted her from the rocks, threw her down and held her, he panting almost as heavily as she.

"You'll repent all this to-morrow," he said. "If I let you have your way there'll be no repentance. Do you know what you are doing?"

"Yes," she moaned. "I cannot live; I want to die."

"Then, my good girl," cried Geoffrey, "you'll find that you can live, and that it's of no use to want to die. There, there, Madge, my poor lass, I'm speaking like a brute to you, but you have made me angry with your struggles. Come, come, my poor child, let me help you home, and you'll find your mother ready to forgive you and take you to her heart."

"Me? me?" cried the wretched girl. "No, no, never again. Let me—pray let me, dear, dear Mr Trethick, pray let me go."

"Yes," he said sternly, "home."

"No, no; I have no home now. You are cruel to me," she cried, with a fresh struggle.

"Madge," said Geoffrey, after easily mastering her this time, "I want to help you in your trouble, my poor girl. Come, let me help you up. Will you let me take you to Prawle's? It is nearer than the cottage, and, if I ask her, Bessie Prawle will give you shelter at least for the night."
"Oh, no, no, no," moaned the poor girl.
"Yes, my child, yes. There, come, get up. That's well. I tell you, I want to help you. There, you will go with me there."
Poor Madge! she had let him help her to her senses, and as she heard his kindly voice she sank down, clasped his knees, and laid her face against them, sobbing wildly.
"There, come, come," he said, "or we shall be having you ill. There, that's well. There's a path up here farther on, and we shall soon be at the cove."
She made no further resistance, but, leaning heavily upon his arm and moaning piteously the while, she let him half lead, half carry, her up a cliff slope farther from the town than that which they had come down, and the road to which lay by the dark arch of the adit running to the shaft of the old mine on the way to Gwennas.

It was almost a riddle to Geoffrey afterwards how he led the poor girl up to the path and along to Gwennas Cove; but at last, nearly tired out, he descended the steep slope, saw with joy that there was a light in the cottage, and, on knocking, Bessie came to the door with a candle, to stand staring in wonder at the sight which met her eyes.

"Quick, Bessie! for heaven's sake?" cried Geoffrey, "or she will be dead."

"Miss Mullion!" cried Bess, flushing; "and here!"

"Bess Prawle, if you have a woman's heart, take this poor creature in," cried Geoffrey, sharply; and, giving him one quick, half-upbraiding look, Bess took his helpless burthen in her arms, and helped to carry her to the old sofa beneath the window-sill.

"What can I do?" cried Geoffrey, as he gazed in the stony face. "Good heavens! Is she dead?"

"Nigh to it, sir," said Bess, in a low, sad voice; but ere she had well finished Geoffrey was running up the path on his way to Carnac.

Chapter Thirty Seven.

An Eventful Night.

It was four o'clock the next morning before Geoffrey went softly up the gravel path to the cottage, and, weary and sick at heart, let himself in.

His clothes had partly dried upon him during his walk, for he had fetched Dr Rumsey from his house to attend poor Madge, the doctor being very quiet and saying little, Geoffrey thought, after hearing a few explanations.

"She seems to have been very unhappy at home," said Geoffrey, "and they quarrelled with her, I think. She must have been half-mad."

"And did she really try to drown herself?" said the doctor.

"I wouldn't answer the question," replied Geoffrey; "but you, being a doctor, ought to know all—so I tell you, yes. She really did, and—pray hurry, old fellow: we may be too late."

"I am hurrying all I can, Trethick," said the doctor; "but I must get in with some breath left in my body."

"Yes, of course; but could I do any good if I ran on first?"

"No, not a bit. Bessie Prawle, you say, is with her. Poor lass—poor lass!"

"So I say, with all my soul, doctor. But I would not put it abroad what has happened."

"These affairs tell their own tale, Trethick," said the doctor.

"Yes, yes, of course; but I'd keep it as quiet as I could."

"I am no scandal-monger, Trethick," said the doctor, dryly; and they hurried on, Geoffrey waiting outside, and walking up and down with old Prawle while Mr Rumsey went in.

At the end of a quarter of an hour he came to the door with a paper.

"Prawle," he said, "will you go to my house and give that to my wife?"

"I'll take it," said Geoffrey, eagerly. "I'm going home."

"You will have to bring something back," said the doctor.

"All right: I'll lose no time," he said, cheerily; and he started off, and had to wait while Mrs Rumsey obtained the bottles from the surgery, sending them and a graduated glass for the doctor to mix himself.

This done, there was the walk back to Gwennas, and then Geoffrey waited for the doctor, who kept coming out for a stroll in the cool starlight, and then returning.

"I've been thinking that I ought to send you for Mrs Mullion, Trethick."

"What! Is she in danger?"

"No; oh, no, poor lass; she'll be better soon. You are going to wait about, I suppose?"

"Oh, yes," said Geoffrey; "you may want me to fetch something more, and I'll wait to walk back with you."

The doctor went in, and old Prawle came up from below and touched him on the arm.

"Come and sit down here," he said, gruffly. "I've lit a fire below."

"Well, I am cold," said Geoffrey; and he followed the old man down into a rough cave in the rock, where he kept old nets, a boat, and various pieces of fishing gear. A bright fire of wreck-wood was burning, and to this, with a shiver, Geoffrey walked up, whereupon the old man took a bottle out of a battered sea-chest, whose outside was splintered by the rocks in coming ashore, and poured him out a little spirit in a chipped and footless glass, frosted by the attrition of the sand in which it had been found.

"Smuggled?" said Geoffrey, with a smile.

"Drink it, and don't ask questions, my lad."

"Your health, Father Prawle," said Geoffrey, tossing it down. "It was rude. By George! what nectar. It puts life in a fellow. Shall we hear the doctor when he comes out?"

"Yes, don't be afeard, man, sit down," said the old fellow. "I'm going to smoke."

"I'll join you," said Geoffrey, "if you have any tobacco. Mine's soaked."

"Oh, yes," said the old man. "I've passed many a night in sea-soaked clothes, but it won't hurt you, my lad. Here's some tobacco."

"I hope not," said Geoffrey, taking the tobacco, filling, and lighting his pipe.

"You got her out of the water then, eh?"

"Yes," said Geoffrey, shortly.

"Poor lass!"

Geoffrey nodded acquiescence, and they smoked for some time in silence.

"It is very kind of Miss Prawle to take her in and attend her," said Geoffrey at last; "but I'm sure poor Madge Mullion will be very grateful."

"My Bess arn't made of stone," said the old man, gruffly, as he sat staring hard across the ruddy fire, whose smoke went up through a rift. Then, re-filling the glass, he handed it to Geoffrey, who drank gladly of the spirit at the time; after which the old man refreshed himself, put on some more driftwood, and stared at his visitor.

"I should have liked to hold some shares in that mine," he said.

"Yes, you ought to have had some, Father Prawle. Hush! was that the doctor?"

"No, only the washing of the sea in the rock holes. Maybe you'll get me some of those shares. I can pay for them."

"There is not one to be had, Father Prawle," replied Geoffrey.

"Maybe you'll sell me some of yours, Master Trethick. I'll pay you well."

"Mine!" cried Geoffrey, laughing. "I don't hold one."

The old man looked at him very keenly, and then let his eyes fall.

"If you would really like to have some," said Geoffrey, "and I see a chance, I'll secure them for you."

"Do, my lad. I'm doing you a good turn here without asking questions."

"And I'm very grateful to you," said Geoffrey; "very grateful."

"Then do me a good turn."

"Because you were so free in telling me all about the mine?"

"Let that bide, Master Trethick," said the old man. "But, look here, I will tell you now, if you'll get me a lot of shares."

"It's too late, man—too late."

"Nay, but it isn't. You get me shares, and you'll see. I worked in yon mine."

"And did not make the proprietors' fortune," said Geoffrey, with a smile.

"Nobody tried to make mine," growled the old fellow, "and they treated me like a dog. I had to think of self. Look here, Mas'r Trethick, I hated you when you come here, for I thought you meant my Bess."

"I know you did," said Geoffrey.

"But I don't think so now, and I tell you this. You get me shares, and it'll be worth thousands to you. Get shares yourself too; and mind this, you've got to take care of your enemy."

"And who's that?"

The old man chuckled, and pointed with his pipe-stem out of the mouth of the cave, looking curiously weird and picturesque in the glow of the fire, with the black, uncouth shadows of the pieces of wreck-wood and boat-gear behind.

"I don't understand you," said Geoffrey.

"The sea, boy—the water's your enemy, so look out."

"I will," said Geoffrey; and then they smoked and chatted on, the old man going up three or four times to see if the doctor was ready to go; and at last, soon after three, he came back, looking more grim than ever, and not to trim the fire this time.

"Doctor will come in five minutes," he said, gruffly. "Will you have any more brandy?"

"No, thanks, no," said his visitor.

"There, mind this, boy, get me shares, and get some yourself, but keep it secret from every one."

"I'll help you if I can," said Geoffrey, "for old acquaintance' sake; but your promise of news comes too late."

"Nay, nay, we'll see, we'll see," said the old man. "But look here, Master Trethick, are you going to marry that gal?"

"What, Miss Mullion? No."

"Ho!" said the old man, gruffly.

"Now, Trethick," came from above; and Geoffrey hastily made his way up the rugged steps to where the doctor was waking.

"How is she?" he cried eagerly.

"Better: going on well," said the doctor, shortly.

"And in no danger?"

"None whatever, if she is kept quiet, and her mind set at ease."

"Poor lass, I'll do all I can," said Geoffrey, earnestly. "I'll have a long talk to Mrs Mullion and Paul in the morning—well, it is morning now—after breakfast. I'll soon set it right. I think I can."

"That's well," said the doctor, as they walked on along the dark path.

"You seem tired," said Geoffrey, for the doctor was singularly reserved.

"Very."

"So am I."

There was another silence for some time.

"What are you thinking about, doctor?" said Geoffrey, at last.

"About Madge Mullion. Look here, Trethick, I like you—"

"Thanky, doctor, I like you, and I'm glad you've taken my hint about those shares."

"Hang the shares!" said the doctor. "Let me finish what I was going to say."

"Go ahead."

"Damn it, man, don't be so cool and unconcerned."

"All right," said Geoffrey.

"I say I like you for some things, Trethick, and I'm by profession tolerably hard and callous; but it frets me, sir, to have seen that poor girl lying there, after trying in her despair to throw away her life, and you as cool and cavalier as can be."

"Well," said Geoffrey, laughing, "I may be calm, but I was not, though, when I fetched you. As to my coolness, I haven't changed my wet things after getting nearly drowned to save her, and I'm cheery because you told me there was no danger."

"No, but she's very ill. And as to your saving the poor lass, it was no more than your duty. You needn't brag about that."

"I don't brag, doctor, so you need not be so peppery. I say, calling you up in the night don't improve your temper."

"Hang it, Trethick, don't be a brute," cried the doctor. "I've known you nearly nine months, and I never liked you less than now."

"Thankye, doctor, but you'll be better when you've had your breakfast. Come, don't let's part huffily. I am sorry I had to call you up, but you must charge extra."

"Look here, Trethick," said the doctor, who was now regularly roused by the other's coolness, "we don't set ourselves up out here for a particularly moral people, but, hang it all, we have got hearts, and when a wrong is done to any one we try to repair it."

"Yes, and a very good plan, too," said Geoffrey. "Why, doctor, you're as huffy as can be."

"Trethick! There, I can't keep it back," cried the doctor, the last words having let loose the flood of his wrath. "How a man who is not a callous scoundrel can treat this affair so coolly, I don't know."

"I don't treat it coolly," cried Geoffrey, surprised at the other's warmth.

"You do, sir; your conduct is blackguardly—cruel in the extreme. Have you no heart at all?"

"Plenty, I hope," cried Geoffrey, now growing warm in turn. "Look here, doctor, I don't allow any man to call me a scoundrel and blackguard, without saying a word in reply. Please explain what you mean."

"What do I mean, sir; why, that poor girl."

"Well, what about her?"

The doctor stopped short in the dark upon that shelf of cliff, and faced Geoffrey.

"Look here! are you a fool, or a knave, or a scoundrel, Trethick, or all three?" he cried, angrily.

"If you dare to say—Bah?" cried Geoffrey, "I won't quarrel. You're hipped, doctor—tired—upset—but don't call a man names. It stirs up a fellow's bile, as old Paul says."

The doctor panted in his anger, for calm, peaceable Dr Rumsey seemed quite transformed.

"And you can talk like this?" he cried, "with that poor girl, the mother of your new-born child, lying an outcast from her home!"

"*What?*" roared Geoffrey, catching at the doctor's arm.

"He is a fool!" exclaimed Dr Rumsey; and, wrenching away his arm, he strode off towards the town, leaving Geoffrey staring as if he were stunned.

He was stunned mentally, and for a few minutes he felt as if he could not collect his thoughts. Then his first impulse was to run after the doctor.

"Oh, it's too absurd," he cried; and at last, sick at heart, uneasy, and disgusted with his late companion, and not even yet fully realising his position in the tragedy of the night, he walked stiffly up to the cottage, hesitated for a few moments as to whether he should enter, and ended by letting himself in, and going to his room, to try and secure a few hours' rest.

Chapter Thirty Eight.

A Stormy Interview.

Geoffrey Trethick's slumbers were very short and disturbed, and, after tossing about for some time, he got up to think out his position. The events of the past night seemed dream-like now, and there were times when he was ready to treat them as hallucinations; but the sea-soaked suit of clothes thrown over a chair were proof positive of the reality of poor Madge Mullion's attempted suicide, and his brow contracted as he thought of the wretched girl's state.

"Poor lass!" he muttered; and by the light of the doctor's charge he read a score of trifles which had been sealed to him before.

"I'll go straight down to him, and have it out as soon as he's up. An idiot! What the deuce does he mean? However, I'll soon put that right."

He looked at his watch and found it was only seven, so that it would be of no use to go down yet to Rumsey's. He could not sleep, and he did not feel disposed to read, so he determined to go for a walk till breakfast-time, and then he would have a talk to Mrs Mullion and Uncle Paul.

But he had no sooner made up his mind to speak to them on the poor girl's behalf than he began to realise the delicacy of his position.

Suppose they took the same view of the case as Dr Rumsey?

"Confound it all!" he cried. "How absurd, to be sure."

He finished dressing, opened door and window, and went down, meeting the servant girl looking red-eyed and dishevelled, as if she had not been to bed all night.

He had seen that Uncle Paul's bedroom door was wide open, but did not note that the bed had been unoccupied; and he was, therefore, not surprised to hear the old man's cough as he entered his own room.

"Trethick! Trethick!" he called, and Geoffrey crossed the passage, meeting Mrs Mullion, who ran out with her handkerchief to her eyes, and her face averted.

"Ashamed of being so hard on her child," thought Geoffrey; and then he started, shocked at the old man's aspect, as, with his hat on, he sat there, looking yellow, wrinkled, sunken of eye and cheek, with all his quick, sharp ways gone, and with generally the aspect of one just recovering from some terrible shock.

"Good heavens, Mr Paul, how ill you look!" cried Geoffrey, anxiously, as the thought struck him that he had not been to bed all night.

"Yes," said the old man, "I feel ill."

"Let me run down and fetch Rumsey. Stop, I'll get you a little, brandy first."

"No, no. I don't want brandy," said the old man, gazing at him wildly, and with his face now cadaverous in the extreme. "Rumsey can't help me. Help me yourself."

"Yes. What shall I do for you?"

"Sit down, Trethick."

He took a chair, looking intently at the speaker.

"Trethick, will you smoke a cheroot?"

"No, not now."

"Not now? Well, another time, then," said the old man, whose voice seemed quite changed. "I'm afraid, Trethick, I have got a dreadful temper."

"Horrible—sometimes," said Geoffrey, smiling.

"But my bark is worse than my bite. I'm not so bad as I seem."

"I know that, old fellow. I always have known it."

"You went out about nine last night, and didn't come back till four this morning."

"You heard me come in then?"

"Yes. We have not been to bed all night. I have been out looking for Madge."

"Indeed!" said Geoffrey, quietly, as he bit his lips to keep back a little longer that which he knew.

"I'm not speaking angrily, am I, my boy?"

"No. I never saw you so calm before."

"It is a calm after the storm, Trethick. I was in a terrible fit last night. Mrs Mullion, my sister-in-law, confessed it all to me, and I was mad with the disgrace. I—I struck her. Yes," he continued, pitifully, "I was a brute, I know. I—I struck her—that poor, weak, foolish girl, and drove her from the house."

"You—struck her, Mr Paul?" said Geoffrey.

"Yes, my boy. I was mad, for she did not deny her shame, only begged me to kill her, and then—then, she uttered a wild cry, and ran out of the house. I seem to hear it now," he continued, with a shudder. "I've been out searching for her, but—but I have not told a soul. We must keep it quiet, Trethick, for all our sakes. But tell me, did she—did she come to you?"

"No," said Geoffrey, sternly.

"But you have seen her? Don't tell me, boy, that you have not seen her. We felt that as you did not come back she had come to you."

Geoffrey was silent for a few moments, thinking of his position; for here, in spite of his quiet way, was a fresh accuser, and poor Mrs Mullion's silent avoidance had only been another charge.

"The poor girl did not come to me," said Geoffrey, at last. "Your cruelty, Mr Paul, drove her away, and but for the fact that I happened to be on the cliff and saw her go by, she would be floating away somewhere on the tide—dead."

"Did—did she try to jump in?" cried the old man, hoarsely.

"She was nearly dead when I fetched her out. A few seconds more would have ended her miserable life."

The old man shrank back in his chair, trembling now like a leaf, his jaw dropped, and his eyes staring.

"And I should have murdered her," he gasped. "But you jumped in and saved her?"

Geoffrey nodded.

"Thank God!" cried the old man, fervently. "Thank God!"

"Poor girl! it was a narrow escape," continued Geoffrey. "She has suffered cruelly, and you must forgive her, Mr Paul, and take her back."

"Yes, yes," said the old man, "we'll talk about that. But shake hands, Trethick. You're a brave fellow, after all. That wipes off a great deal. Poor Madge: poor child!"

The old man held out his hand, but Geoffrey did not offer to take it.

"You saved the poor girl then, Trethick. We felt that you must be with her. Where is she now? Why didn't you bring her back?"

"She would sooner have gone back into the sea," said Geoffrey, sternly. "I took her on to Prawle's cottage, at Gwennas."

"And she is there now?"

"Yes, sir, with her helpless infant."

The old man sank back again with a harsh catching of the breath, and they sat in silence gazing one at the other, as if trying to get breath for the encounter to come.

Uncle Paul was the first to speak.

"I'm—I'm not angry now, Trethick. I'm going to be very humble, and appeal to you."

"Indeed!" said Geoffrey, over whose countenance a very stern, stubborn look began to make its way.

"Yes, yes. I'm going to appeal to you. I beg your pardon, Trethick, if I have said or done any thing to hurt your feelings. I'm very, very sorry I was so cruel to the poor child last night, but it came upon me like a shock, and the disgrace seemed to madden me. I have a hot, bad temper, I know; but, poor child, I'll forgive her—forgive you both."

"Thanks," said Geoffrey, mockingly; and he was about to speak, but refrained, as the old man made an effort and rose from his chair to go behind Trethick, and stand there silently for a few moments as if to master his voice before laying a hand upon the young man's shoulder.

"I did wrong, Trethick, when I brought you up here—very wrong. I ought to have known better, but I did it in a mean, selfish spirit to save my own money, when I had plenty for all."

"Indeed!" said Geoffrey, coldly, and a set frown came upon his brow.

"Yes, it was an ill-advised step, and I am punished for it. But, Trethick, my lad, in my rough way I do love my poor, dead brother's wife and child, and, God knows, I would sooner have been a beggar than have seen this disgrace come upon them."

"Mr—"

"No, no, hear me out, Trethick," cried the old man, imploringly. "I don't blame you so much as I do poor Madge. She was always a foolish, light, thoughtless girl, fond of admiration; and I know she has always thrown herself in your way; but I said to myself he is too sterling and stanch a fellow to act otherwise than as we could wish."

"Look here, Mr Paul," said Geoffrey, sternly. "Once for all, let me tell you that you are labouring under a mistake. Do you accuse me of this crime?"

"No, no, we won't call it a crime," said the old man. "But hear me out, Trethick. I am not angry now. I want to do what is for the best. I don't ask you to humble yourself or confess."

"Confess!" cried Geoffrey, scornfully. "Mr Paul, you insult me by your suspicions."

"But the poor girl, Trethick. Her poor mother is heart-broken. Oh, man, man! why did you come like a curse beneath this, roof?"

"Look here, Mr Paul," cried Geoffrey, whom the night's adventures and loss of sleep had made irritable, "when you can talk to me in a calm, sensible way, perhaps I can convince you that you are wronging me by your suspicions."

A spasm of rage shot across the old man's face, but he seemed to make an effort, and mastered himself.

"Don't be heartless," he said, "I implore you. There, you see how humble I am. There, there—let bygones be bygones. I know you will act like a man by her. Never mind the shame and disgrace, Trethick. She loves you, poor child, and amongst us we have made her suffer cruelly. I have been brutal to her for being as true to you as steel."

"True to me, eh?" said Geoffrey.

"Yes, poor child, she kept your secret, though she could not keep her own. She felt that she might injure you in your prospects."

"You are arranging it all very nicely in your own mind, Uncle Paul," said Geoffrey, quietly, for he was touched by the old man's battle with self.

"Don't ridicule me, Trethick," he said, piteously. "I want to make amends for a great wrong. I feel I have been to blame. But be a man, Trethick, and you sha'n't suffer for it. Look here, I am very old now, and I can't take my money with me. Come, be reasonable, Trethick, for the poor child's sake. We'll forget the past and look at the future."

"At my expense," said Geoffrey.

"No, no, my boy. We are both men of the world, and can afford to laugh at what people say. Let's make both those poor souls happy. There, I'll sink all differences, and I'll give her away; I will indeed. I haven't been in a church these fifteen years, but I'll come and give her away; and look here, my lad," he cried, pulling out a slip of paper, "there's a cheque on the Old Bank for a thousand pounds, payable to you—that's Madge's dowry to start with. Now, what do you say?"

"Humph! a thousand, eh?" said Geoffrey, looking admiringly at the speaker.

"Yes, a thousand pounds," cried the old man.

"Will you make it two?" said Geoffrey.

An angry flush came in the old man's face, but he looked across Geoffrey, and saw that poor broken Mrs Mullion was peering in at the doorway, and his rage went with his hesitation.

"Yes," he said, "for her sake I'll make it two."

"Not enough," said Geoffrey. "Will you make it five thousand down, and all your money bequeathed to us by will?"

The old man's breath seemed to be taken away, and he stood gasping angrily; but once more the piteous aspect of the poor woman at the door disarmed him, and he said, in a low, hoarse voice,—

"I haven't long to stop here. You shall have what you say, Trethick, only remove this cloud from the poor girl's life."

"Uncle Paul," cried Geoffrey, turning upon him eagerly, "I always liked you, for I knew that you were a stanch old fellow under that rough bark, but I never thought you were so true a man as this. Five thousand pounds, eh? and you make me your heir? Give me your hand."

The old man's hand was slowly stretched out, and Geoffrey seized it.

"Yes," said Uncle Paul, "and the past shall all be forgotten;" but a look of disgust, in spite of his efforts, came across his face at the mercenary spirit displayed.

"Five thousand pounds down?" said Geoffrey, "eh?"

"Five thousand pounds down."

"As you say, Uncle Paul," said Geoffrey, probing the old man to the quick, "you cannot live much longer. You have had your spell of life, and you will give that by deed of gift at once to save poor Madge's fame, and the rest when you die?"

The old man nodded.

"Suppose I say make it ten thousand down?"

"Take—take it all," said the old man, piteously; and then, in a low voice, "God help me to do one good act before I die."

As he spoke he tried to withdraw his hand from Geoffrey's.

"Take what I have," he said again, "but wipe away the stain from that poor girl's life."

"God bless you, Uncle Paul," cried Geoffrey, wringing the old man's hand. "You're a noble old fellow, but if your money was millions, instead of thousands, not a penny could I touch. Go and see the poor girl, and then you must see another, and come back and tell me that you ask my pardon for what you have said."

The piteous look, the air of weakness, and the trembling of the hands passed away as if by magic, as Uncle Paul tore his fingers from Geoffrey's grasp; and, in place of his mingled appeal and disgust, passion flashed from the old man's eyes.

"Dog—coward—scoundrel!" he cried, shaking his cane threateningly. "Your success at the mine, and your hopes of wedding Rhoda Penwynn, have blinded you to all that is honourable and true, but you shall repent it."

"Oh, hush, hush!" cried Geoffrey. "Mr Paul!"

"Silence, scoundrel!" he roared. "You shall live to see your mine a wreck; and as to that Rhoda Penwynn—"

"Silence, yourself, old man," cried Geoffrey, in a rage. "How dare you mention her name?"

"How dare I, dog?" he cried; "because she is too good, and pure, and virtuous for such a libertine as you. Out upon you for your worthlessness! I tell you, that girl will turn her back upon you in shame and disgust. You don't know of what stuff our Cornish women are. I meant to keep this silent if I could. Now the town shall know you for what you are; and as for my poor niece—Heaven forgive her!—I would sooner see her in her coffin than the wife of such a heartless, cold-blooded, mercenary wretch."

"You will repent all this when you are cool," cried Geoffrey, whose own rage was driven away in dread lest the old man should fall before him in some fit.

"Out of my sight, dog! Leave this house."

"Uncle Paul, you are mad. Will you listen to reason?"

"Go!" cried the old man panting, as he threatened the tall, sturdy young fellow with his stick; "go, and present yourself at Penwynn's, and be shown the door. Out! Go! I cannot breathe the same air with so heartless a villain."

"If I leave this house," said Geoffrey, "it is for good. No apologies will bring me back."

"Apologies," cried the old man. "Oh, if Heaven would give me back my strength but for one short hour! Scoundrel!" he cried, sinking back in his chair, "if I were but a man instead of such a poor old wreck—"

"Mrs Mullion! quick!" cried Geoffrey, for the old man's appearance alarmed him; but the poor woman had heard all, and was already at her brother-in-law's side. "What shall we do?"

"Let him leave the place," panted the old man. "Don't let him touch me—don't let him come near me—let him leave the place. He tortures me. Why did I bring him here?"

"Fate, I suppose," said Geoffrey, coldly. "I thought she had been too kind. Shall I fetch Rumsey, Mrs Mullion?"

"No, no, no. Pray go—pray go," sobbed the poor woman. "Oh, Mr Trethick! Mr Trethick! what have I done that you should treat me so?"

"There, for heaven's sake, don't you begin," cried Geoffrey. "I can bear no more. You people here are mad. There, I'll rid you of my presence, Mrs Mullion. I'll go and put up some where else till you have come to your senses, and then perhaps—no, I cannot come back here. I'm going down to Rumsey's, and I'll send him up. Poor old fellow?" he said; and he came a step towards where, with half-closed eyes, Uncle Paul sat back, panting heavily; but at the first step forward he shrank away with such a look of loathing that Geoffrey strode into the passage, seized his hat, and went off across the garden, and down the cliff path to send up Dr Rumsey to the stricken old man.

Chapter Thirty Nine.

More Unpleasantries.

Dr Rumsey was in, Mrs Rumsey said, but he was engaged. She would give Mr Trethick's message, and she turned sharply round and shut the door.

"Confound the woman," exclaimed Geoffrey, frowning, and he went off towards the mine.

His way lay through the principal street, and as he was passing the hotel it suddenly struck him that he had had a terrible night, and that he was half-starved.

"The engine won't work without coal," he said, with a bitter laugh. "I must have breakfast," and, going in, he ordered the meal, ate heartily, and then, feeling refreshed and brighter, he hesitated as to what he should do—go down to the mine or walk across to Gwennas.

He stopped, thinking,—

"If I go to Gwennas, people will say that the case is clear against me.

"If I don't go they will say that it is clearer, for I stop away because I am a coward, and that my conduct is cruel.

"Well, I won't be brutal, at all events; so here goes to see Father Prawle, and to know how the poor girl is."

He started off walking fast, but just then who should come round the corner but a thin figure in black, half-way between a sister of mercy and a lady in deep mourning.

"Miss Pavey, by all that's wonderful!" he exclaimed. "What a transformation. What has become of the rainbow?"

"Ah, Miss Pavey," he said. "Good-morning."

To his astonishment and disgust, the lady darted a look of horror at him and crossed the road.

"This is pleasant," he cried, angrily. "Why, that woman must know of it, and—"

He felt a chill of horror run through him, for he knew that she would go, if she had not already been, straight up to An Morlock and acquaint Rhoda with the events of the night, no doubt pleasantly dressed up.

"She must have seen the Rumseys this morning!"

He hesitated for a moment, and then turned to go straight up to An Morlock.

"I'll go and tell Penwynn all about it."

"Pooh! Absurd," he cried. "What's come to me? Am I to go and deny a scandal before I have been accused by my friends? Ridiculous."

Laughing at himself for what he called his folly, he went right off along the cliff, looking with pride at the smoking of the Wheal Carnac chimney shaft, and pausing for a moment or two, with a smile of gratification upon his lips, to watch the busy figures about the buildings and to listen to the rattle and noise of the machinery.

Going on, he came to the slope down from the cliff path to the beach, and he could not help a shudder as he saw how dangerous it was even by daylight.

"I wonder we did not break our necks," he thought, as he went cautiously down, and then amongst the granite boulders and weed-hung masses to where he had leaped in and swum to poor Madge's help, for there it all was plainly enough—the long spit of rocks running out like a pier, the swirling water, and the waving masses of slimy weed.

"It's a good job it was night," he thought. "Hang me, if I shouldn't have hesitated to dive in now."

All the same he would not have hesitated a moment; but it was a wild, awesome place, and the chances of a swimmer getting easily ashore, after a dive from the rocks, were not many.

He went on picking his way as nearly as he could to follow the steps taken on the previous night towards the farther sloping path, pausing again as he came opposite to the adit of the old mine up on the cliff.

It was an ugly, low archway, fringed with ferns, and whose interior was glossy with what looked like green metallic tinsel, but proved to be a dark, glistening, wet lichen or moss.

The place, like all others of its kind, had an attraction for Geoffrey, and he went in a short distance to peer forward into the gloom of the narrow passage through the rock, and to listen to the dripping, echoing sounds of the falling water.

It was a part of the working of the old mine, and, doubtless, had been driven in first by the adventurers in search of a vein of tin or copper, after striking which they had sunk the perpendicular shaft on the cliff—the one by the path where he had had his encounter with Pengelly; and, by a little calculation, he reckoned that this adit or passage would be about a hundred yards long.

"I'll have lights some day, and Pengelly and I will explore it."

He went no farther, for there was always the danger of coming upon one of the minor shafts, or "winzes" as they were called, which are made for ventilating the mine, and joining the upper and lower galleries together. In this case the winzes would have been full of water, like the great shaft, up to the level of the adit, which would run off the surplus to the beach.

More by force of habit than for any particular reason, he threw a great stone in, to make a crashing noise, which went echoing and reverberating along the dripping passage, and then he went on.

"Poor lass, she would have had a poor chance," he said, "if she had thrown herself down the old shaft up yonder. I don't think I dare have dived down there. Nay," he added, laughing, "I am sure I dare not."

He went on fast now, noting the difficulties of the pathway up which he had helped Madge in the dark; and then, pausing half-way up to take breath, he uttered an exclamation.

"I shouldn't have thought it possible," he said. "Why, it seems almost madness now. Well, I got her there safely, and I have been thanked for my trouble."

Old Prawle was hanging about, busy, as usual, with a fishing-line, as Geoffrey went down into the Cove, nodded, and tapped gently at the door.

"Well, Bessie," he said, in his light, cheery way, "how is she?"

"Better, Mr Trethick," said Bessie coldly; and the bright look passed from his face as he saw the girl's distant manner.

"Has the doctor been?"

"Yes, Mr Trethick."

"What does he say?"

"That she is to have perfect rest and quiet."

"And your mother?"

"Better, sir. Will you speak to her?"

Geoffrey hesitated a moment, and then seeing that Bessie was misinterpreting his looks, he said sharply,—

"Yes, I will;" and following Bessie in, he found the invalid in her old place, airing and burning more things than usual, but there was such a reproachful, piteous look in her eyes, that he was quite taken aback.

"It's of no use. I can't argue with them," thought Geoffrey.

"Here, Mrs Prawle," he said aloud, "will you kindly see that every thing possible is done for that poor girl. You will be at some expense, of course, till Mrs Mullion and her uncle fetch them home. Take that."

He laid a five-pound note on the table, and walked straight out, Bessie drawing on one side to let him pass, her face looking cold and thin, and her eyes resting on the floor.

"Pleasant," muttered Geoffrey, and with an abrupt "Good-morning" he went out to where old Prawle was at work.

"Here, walk part of the way along the cliff with me," he said. "Come away from the cottage."

The old man looked up at him from under his shaggy eyebrows, and then followed him for a couple of hundred yards, and stopped.

"Won't that do?" he said. "Are you going to give me some money for them two?"

"I've left five pounds with your wife," said Geoffrey, sharply.

"Oh, come, that's handsome," said the old man. "But you couldn't have done less."

"Look here," said Geoffrey, sharply, "you know what I told you last night."

"Yes, I know," said the old man, grimly.

"You tell them the same. I couldn't talk to them. Undeceive them about it, and be kind to the poor lass. I'll do all I can for you, Prawle, about the shares."

The old man nodded and uttered a growl that might have been "All right," or "Thanks," or any thing else, and then Geoffrey went on towards Carnac.

"Tell them the same," said the rugged old fellow, with a grim chuckle. "Why, I might preach to 'em for a month, and then they wouldn't believe it any more than I could myself."

Pengelly was anxiously awaiting his principal at the mine, ready to lay certain reports before him about the drive that was being made, and he did it all in so stern and distant a way that Geoffrey could not help seeing that his right-hand man had heard the report, and, what was more, believed it. The result was that it raised up a spirit of resentment in the young man's breast that made him retire within himself snail fashion; but with this difference, that he left his horns pointing menacingly outside; and for the rest of that day he was not a pleasant person to consult upon any matter.

For in spite of the contempt with which he treated the whole affair, and his determination to completely ignore the matter, it was always torturing him, and there was the constant thought in his mind that Rhoda must sooner or later hear of it, if she had not already been apprised by Miss Pavey or some other tattling friend.

"Let them. If she's the woman I believe her, she'll write to me in a quiet indirect way, not referring to it, of course, but to let me see her confidence in me is not shaken."

The amount of work he got through on that day was tremendous, and as he worked his spirits rose. He strengthened his plans for guarding against the breaking in of the sea; and at last, completely fagged out, he ascended from the mine, changed, and washed in the office, and, without speaking to Pengelly, went straight to Dr Rumsey's.

The doctor saw him coming, and came to the door.

"Find you apartments, Mr Trethick?" he said, coldly. "In an ordinary way it would be impossible. Under the present circumstances it is doubly so."

"Very good," said Geoffrey, sharply. "You persist, then, in believing that?"

"I would rather not discuss the matter, Mr Trethick," said the doctor. "Good evening."

"I must go to the hotel, then, that's all," said Geoffrey to himself. "Confound them all! They will find that I've Cornish blood in my veins, and can be as pig-headed in obstinacy as the best."

Chapter Forty.

Something Wrong.

They were civil enough to him at the hotel, but Geoffrey could not help noticing that there was a peculiar something in his reception.

Of course it was strange his going there, and it led to talking about him; of this he could not help feeling sure.

"Let them talk," he muttered, "if it pleases them;" and, after a late dinner, and spending an hour or two in writing, he made up his mind to go to bed and have a good night's rest, to make up for the losses of the previous night.

He felt that he would like to know how old Mr Paul was, but he could not send or ask with any degree of comfort, so he went to bed at ten.

But it was not to rest. His nerves had been so unduly excited by the events of the past twenty-four hours that, try how he would, he could not get to sleep.

As a rule, strong, healthy, and hearty, no sooner was his head upon his pillow than he dropped off into a deep slumber. But this night his mind was in a continuous whirl. He tossed, he turned, got up and bathed his beating temples and burning forehead, scrubbed himself with a towel, and lay down again, but there was no sleep.

Now he was following poor Madge along the cliff, and plunging into the sea to save her. Then he was facing Bessie Prawle, whose eyes looked reproachfully at him. Again, he would be back at the cottage going through that pitiful scene with poor old Mr Paul; and when at last he succeeded in dismissing that from his mind, he was haunted by the face of Rhoda gazing at him with such a look of scorn and contempt that he was obliged to sit up in bed to make sure it was not real.

"Upsets a man's nerves, no matter how strong he may be," argued Geoffrey; and he once more threw himself down, wishing that he was back at the cottage, for, as it was comparatively early, there were noises in the hotel that helped to keep him awake.

At last, about midnight, he seemed to have successfully laid the whole of the unrestful spirits that had been haunting him, and, feeling calmer, he uttered a sigh of satisfaction, and felt that he was going now to enjoy his well-earned rest, when a fresh thought leaped to his brain, and that was about Wheal Carnac.

He had been down the mine that evening, and every thing was progressing admirably. The machinery was in perfect order, the men settling down more and more to their work, and they were in a high state of delight at the success that had attended Pengelly's investigations. Why then should he trouble himself about Wheal Carnac?

He argued with himself that it was imagination, due to the excited state of his nerves and the worries of the day. He felt that it was that; but, in spite of his reasoning, he could not rest. Sleep seemed to be out of the question, and yet he would be terribly unfit for the next day's work.

At last he could bear it no longer, and, feeling that rest would not come unless he could satisfy himself that the place was safe, he got up and dressed.

"I'm growing a wise man," he said, mockingly. "I wonder whether any one has run away with the mine? Perhaps there is a burglary on, and they are breaking into the boiler."

At the same time he felt that a walk in the cool night air would calm his nerves, and he prepared to descend, when a new difficulty assailed him.

It was past midnight now, every one in the place had retired, and no doubt he would have some difficulty in getting out.

"I say the people here are mad," he thought; "they will think me mad. Well, let them."

He went down as cautiously as he could, and found that his difficulty about getting out was only imaginary, for the door was easily opened, and, as he closed it behind him, and felt the cool night air upon his forehead, he uttered a sigh of relief.

His plans were soon made; he would go first to Pengelly, and knock him up and hear his report: for the manager was going to stay there a couple or three hours after his superior had left the mine.

He felt some compunction in this; but he knew Pengelly's interest in the works, and how willing he would be to answer questions; so he walked on, thinking over two or three plans which he had been revolving in his mind to propose to Mr Penwynn for Pengelly's benefit, and as a reward for his discovery.

Every thing was very still under the brilliant starlit sky, and as Geoffrey reached the narrow lane where Pengelly lived, he again felt some little compunction at arousing him; but, as he had gone so far, he determined to proceed.

The slight tap he gave on the door was quite sufficient to waken the miner, and Geoffrey plainly heard him leap out of bed. The next moment the casement just above his head was opened.

"What's the matter?" he said quickly.

"Nothing, I hope, Pengelly."

"Oh, it's you, sir!"

"Yes, it is I, Pengelly. Tell me, did you leave all right?"

"Yes, sir; quite right."

"At what time?"

"I was there till nine, sir. Have you been since?"

"No, Pengelly; but I have got an uneasy feeling upon me that something might be wrong. I couldn't sleep, so I came on to you."

"Guilty conscience," thought Pengelly.

"I think," continued Geoffrey, "I'll walk on down there to see if every thing is right. Good-night."

"No, sir, stop a minute, and I'll come too."

Geoffrey protested, but as he protested Pengelly jumped into his flannel trousers and frock, and in the time that a modern gentleman would have taken to unbutton his eyelids and think about his bath, the miner was dressed and coming down.

"It's a shame to rouse you up, Pengelly, about such a fancy as mine," said Geoffrey. "I was restless, and that made me fidget about the mine."

"Well, sir, she's worth fidgetting about," said Pengelly. "Let's go down. It won't do any harm. There's the two engine-men on, and it will show them that we may we expected at any time, and teach them their duty."

Geoffrey longed to say something in his own defence to the miner, as they went along under the starlit sky, but his pride kept him silent; and, gradually growing calmer and at his ease as the fresh breeze from the sea blew upon his face, they went on and on till they began climbing the rugged path to where the engine-house stood up dim and gaunt against the sky, with its lit-up windows and door having a grotesque resemblance to the face of some fiery monster, who was uttering a low, panting roar.

They found the engine steadily working, raising and lowering the enormous rod of the series of pumps, and a steady, rushing noise told that the water was running fast.

"They're both fast asleep," said Pengelly. "Hallo! who's that?"

"Where?" said Geoffrey. "I don't see any one."

"I'd be sworn I saw some one go away," exclaimed Pengelly, leaping forward, but only to return to where Geoffrey stood.

"I expect it was fancy, sir; but let's go and rouse them up. They've no business to be asleep."

He led the way into the engine-house, where, by the glow from the stoke-hole fire, the two men on duty could be seen lying back on the stone bench that formed their seat, fast asleep; and, though Pengelly shook them again and again, he could only evoke a deep stertorous snore from each in turn.

"I don't like this, sir," said Pengelly. "Let's take a look round."

Geoffrey took a lantern from a rough shelf, and together they visited office, stables, and the various buildings, ending by going towards the shaft, when Pengelly suddenly uttered a cry.

"What's wrong?" cried Geoffrey, excitedly, though the knowledge had come to him at the same moment as to his man.

"She's burst in, sir. Oh, listen! She's burst in!"

And as Geoffrey bent over the shaft, the fearful sound of the rushing water flooding the mine rose from the echoing depths upon his ear.

Stunned by the nature of the catastrophe, Geoffrey Trethick stood clutching the framework of the shaft, and leaned over listening to the surging roar of the water as it seemed to him to come bursting up through the winzes in fountains and rushing in triumph through each gallery and drive.

As for Pengelly, he had thrown himself upon the ground, and for a time neither spoke.

"Is this treachery or accident, Pengelly?" cried Trethick at last in a hoarse, changed voice.

"Call it judgment, sir—call it judgment," groaned the miner. "If we sin, the punishment must find us out."

"Pengelly?" cried Geoffrey, as he turned upon him in his rage. "There, I cannot argue with you now. What can we do?"

"Do!" cried Pengelly, piteously. "Do nothing. What can we do but pray and ask for mercy and help, sir, from above."

"Help!" cried Geoffrey. "God helps those who help themselves. Let us be up and doing, man alive."

"It's no time to be up and doing now, sir," replied Pengelly solemnly. "Listen, sir; do you hear? Hark at the water, as if the fountains of the great deep were broken up. Mr Trethick, sir," he continued, incongruously, "we may stop the engine, for a dozen such could not master the water gathering there."

"The wall was too thin to stand the pressure," groaned Geoffrey, "and yet it seemed so safe. Is it possible that any tricks can have been played with the mine? Yes; I see it now," he cried passionately. "That man you saw—those two fellows drunk—yes, of course. Look! the cage is down. Some one must have gone below to-night."

Pengelly, roused by his companion's words, seemed now to grasp their meaning, and, gazing from Geoffrey to the space where the cage should have been, he ran into the engine-house, and, turning the bars, threw the wheels in gear, when, after what seemed to be an interminable space of time, the dripping cage came up empty to the mouth.

"Some one has, been down," said Pengelly, hoarsely; "but whoever it was has not come up;" and without another word, the miner walked slowly back into the engine-house, sat down, and buried his face in his hands.

For a time Geoffrey stood there, holding by the iron rail that protected the shaft, listening to the rushing water, for even yet he could hardly realise the appalling nature of the affair. A short time back it would have been a very serious loss! but now, just as prosperity in fullest tide had come upon them, sweeping away all doubts and fears, the calamity seemed greater than he could bear.

And Rhoda? Mr Penwynn? What was he to say to them?

Well, the former would pity and sympathise, and he must begin again.

The latter would help him no more.

It was horrible, and if he could only bring it home—

He shuddered, for he recalled Pengelly's words.

Perhaps the cause of that mischief was below.

Then, like an icy blast, came the recollection of that other trouble—the suspicion that had been laid at his door; but he laughed that off with contempt, and turning at last, he followed Pengelly into the engine-house, where the fire burned ruddily, the two men slept, and, as if in mockery, the vast engine kept up its solemn, heavy thump, bent, apparently now, so Geoffrey thought, upon the task of pumping the Atlantic Ocean dry.

"Blow off the steam, man; throw open the furnace bars," cried Geoffrey, suddenly, "and stop that cursed engine clank. The game's up for the present. I'm going home to bed."

Even as he spoke the words he recalled that he had no home, and Pengelly laid his hand upon his arm.

"I'll do your orders, master," he said sadly, "and then I'm going back to pray, for it's a judgment on us, master, a judgment for our sins."

He was about to say *you*, for in his simple breast the poor fellow believed the tale that was the talk of the little place.

"But he's my master," he had said; "and I'll serve him true, for who knows but what I may some day make him sorrow for his sin, and see the light."

Geoffrey turned upon him angrily, but Pengelly's face disarmed him; and as the miner obeyed his orders and the clank of the great pump ceased, he threw himself upon the stone bench, and, staring in at the flaming furnace-fire, asked himself how he was to face the coming day.

Chapter Forty One.

How Lannoe Earned his Hundred Pounds.

Miner Lannoe had well made his plans, and, after abiding his time, he had arranged with a confederate to be at the shaft mouth ready to lower down the cage, when he should give the signal, and draw him up.

On second thoughts he told his confederate to lower down the cage first, and then to be ready to touch the handles of the engine in due form, and draw him up.

They had both worked at mines long enough to be quite conversant with the lowering and raising of a cage, and a promise of half a sovereign and unlimited beer was quite enough to enlist a man he knew in his service—a convenient kind of man, who was stupid enough to do what he was told without asking questions.

But this would necessitate the agreement of the two men who would be on duty keeping the engine pumping all night, for the mine was still very wet.

But Lannoe knew how to manage them. A bottle of smuggled brandy, which he knew how to get, was quite sufficient for the purpose, especially when drugged with tobacco, and thoroughly fulfilled his wishes, doing more too than he anticipated for his employer's service.

He was obliged to trust to his confederate, for he had made up his mind to stay down, but his orders were simple in the extreme. The man had only to stroll into the engine-house, when he had seen every one off the premises, with the bottle of brandy under his arm, propose a drink, and not drink himself.

"If he don't keep all square it will be awkward," thought Lannoe, as he hung back when the other men left the pit; and, pulling out some bread and cheese, sat down in the dark and made a hearty meal.

"That'll give a fellow strength," he muttered, when he had done. "Now let's see what's what? Ugh! it's a gashly job; but a hundred pound's a big lump, and it may be a hundred and fifty."

He took out a box of matches, lit a lantern, and walked cautiously towards the foot of the shaft, to find that the cage had been lowered down since the men went up—Pengelly with the last batch; and from that he argued that his confederate was on the watch.

To make sure he uttered a low whistle, which went up, seeming to increase as it rose, and an answer came back.

"That's right," he muttered. "I should stand awkward if he wasn't there."

He felt a strange sense of hesitation come over him, and a tremor of dread that made him flinch from his task, till he thought of Pengelly, and the money that was to be his reward.

"There's nothing to be scared about," he muttered. "If he wasn't there I could get up the winze, and then up to the next gallery by the ladders, so I'm all right."

Satisfying himself that he had nothing to fear on his own account, he turned and went on along the dark galleries, all of which were pretty familiar to him, till he reached the place where the new workings were going on, and stopped by the end of the passage where Geoffrey had marked out the portion that was not to be touched.

The man's face looked very stern and grim as he took out of his pocket along cartridge, ready for blasting purposes, one which he had filched from the receptacle, and three fuses, which he tied together, end to end, so as to make one of extraordinary length.

Laying these upon a ledge ready, he went off to a niche in the rock some distance off and returned with a miner's tamping-iron, and slipping off his frock, and turning up the sleeves of his tight jersey shirt, he paused for a few moments to consider.

As he stood listening, the stillness of the mine was awful, and the sweat stood out upon his forehead as he glanced timorously round; but, nerving himself with the thoughts of revenge and reward, he poised the bar, and the next minute the galleries were echoing to the strokes of the tamping-iron, while the sparks flew thick and fast from the stone.

He was an old and practised hand, knowing full well how to wield the implement so as to bore a hole big enough to hold the cartridge, and he toiled steadily on, forgetting his fear in his work, determined to go in a certain distance, and then insert the cartridge, light the fuse, and escape.

He calculated pretty well what the consequences would be. The thin wall at the end of the gallery would have a goodly piece blown out, and the water would rush in, flooding the mine beyond possibility of redemption.

Stroke, stroke, stroke, with the sparks flying fast, and once more the light from his lantern, as in the case of Geoffrey, cast that strange, weird shadow, as of the evil genius of the mine waving its arms, and threatening the intruder upon his realms.

Now the man paused and examined the edge of the tool he used, and wiped his forehead that was bedewed with sweat. Then he worked on again, till the sparks flew faster and faster, and he grimly laughed as he thought of what would be the consequences should one reach the cartridge.

"No fear of that," he said, half aloud; and he worked on again for quite an hour before he stopped to rest.

"It's gashly work all alone here," he muttered, and he stood listening, but the only sound he heard was the regular thumping beat of the great pump, and the rushing noise of water, which came to him softened by the distance through which it travelled.

Another long attack upon the rock, with the tamping-iron going in deeper and deeper, till, with a grim look of satisfaction, he finished his work, and wiped and stood the tool aside.

"That's long habit," he said, half aloud. "That tool won't be wanted any more; and, perhaps, a lad named Lannoe, with a hundred pound in his pocket, and a place where he can get more if he wants it, may stand better with old Prawle than a lame, preaching hound as ain't so rich after all."

"I wonder what time it is," he muttered, with a shiver; and, having now completed one stage of his work, he hesitated, thinking of his means of escape; and, taking up his lantern, he went rapidly along to the foot of the shaft, listened for a few minutes, and then uttered a low whistle, which went reverberating up the long shaft to the still night air, and another whistle came back in answer.

"One whistle, make ready; two, draw up," muttered Lannoe; and once more he threaded his way along the galleries, till he reached the spot where he had been at work.

Here a shrinking sensation seemed to come over him again, for he took the cartridge and fingered it about, held the lantern up to the hole he had made, and asked himself whether he had not better go on and drive it through to the water, so as to let it run in, though he knew all the while that a small pump would easily master as much water as forced its way in through such a hole.

Then he tried the fuse.

Yes, there was plenty of that to burn till he reached the foot of the shaft. Perhaps he might be up before the charge exploded. There was nothing to fear, then.

But still he hesitated, and a word or two would have made him give up his task and escape for his life.

It was not to be: for the thought of the money mastered him. He could easily force more from his employer, who dare not refuse; and, to make matters better, he would be having a rich revenge upon Pengelly.

Was it safe to trust his mate about the drawing up?

Bah! What matter! He could escape without his help if he failed; and, rousing his courage to the sticking-point, he vowed he would wait no longer.

The rest was done in desperate haste and with his hands trembling. The tamping was bold, manly work, but he had to deal now with a great cartridge of gunpowder, he told himself, and he must be careful.

He was careful as he thought, but he would have exercised more care if he had known that the stolen cartridge was not gunpowder, but formed of one of the newly-discovered explosives, made by Geoffrey's own hands.

He laid his fuse ready for attachment, and placed the lantern a little farther back.

But no: that would not do; his shadow was thrown right across the hole, and he had to change the position of the lantern.

That would do well, and there was no danger; but still he hesitated, and he drew his arm across his wet forehead.

Of course—yes—he must not forget that. He must not leave his jacket behind; and, laying down the cartridge once more, he leisurely put on his frock and cap, hesitated a few minutes longer, and then, with the thoughts of the yellow gold blinding his eyes, he seemed to nerve himself to desperation, picking up the cartridge, and trying to fit it into the hole he had bored.

It went in easily enough for a part of the distance; but the action of the tool had made the hole slightly funnel-shaped, and the cartridge would not go in so far as he wished.

True, he might have fired it where it was, but then he would not have been sure of the result. The wall of rock was comparatively thin, he knew, but unless the cartridge was well in, a sufficiency might not be brought down, and his wish was to make so terrible a gap that no pump ever made, or likely to be made, could keep down the water in the deluged mine.

How it would rush in, carrying all before it, as soon as the shot was fired. He had seen dozens of such blastings, and he knew what great chasms were blown out of the solid rock. Here, where the wall was thin, the whole side would be blown back into the sea, and then where would rich Wheal Carnac be?

John Tregenna would say, at all events, that he had well done his work, he thought; but how was this cartridge to be forced farther in?

He laid it down for a moment, and took up the iron, thinking to enlarge the hole, but he knew it would be an hour's work, and now he was strung up he wanted it done.

He tried the cartridge again. It nearly fitted; a good drive with the back of the tamping-iron would force it in. So, twisting it round and round, he screwed the paper-covered roll in for so goodly a distance that it was well placed in the wall, and needed, he thought, but a slight thrust or two to send it home.

He was ignorant, and blinded by his desire to finish the task he had undertaken; desperate, too, with the fear that was beginning to master him; and catching up the iron once more, he hesitated for a moment as he turned it round, and then, placing the butt end in the hole, he gave the cartridge a sharp blow.

In the act of striking he moderated the blow, so as not to strike fire from the rock; but no fire was needed there, the percussion was sufficient to explode the mighty imprisoned force, and, as that blow fell, there was one deafening crash, a pause, and then an awful rush of water that swept off the shattered fragments of the dead miner from the floor, and wall, and ceiling, and churned them up and bore them along through the galleries of the ruined mine.

For Lannoe's blast had been a success. He had blown out so great a mass of the thin wall that the pump had not been invented that could master such a rush of water as that which poured in to flood the mine.

The explosion was sharp, and it roared through the galleries, but the rush of water seemed to drown it, so that the noise which reached dead Lannoe's mate did not startle his drink-confused brain. He only wondered why Lannoe was so long; and at last, when quite wearied out, he saw Geoffrey Trethick and Pengelly come, he thought it was a good excuse for going, and he ran away.

Chapter Forty Two.

An Unkindly Stroke.

Rhoda Penwynn felt suspicious of Miss Pavey as she entered her room, blowing her nose very loudly, and then holding her handkerchief to her face, where one of her teeth was supposed to ache.

There was a great change in Miss Pavey's personal appearance, and her bright colours had given place to quite a sister-of-mercy style of garb, including a black crape veil, through which, on entering, she had given Rhoda quite a funereal kiss, as if to prepare her for her adverse news—news which she dreaded to communicate, for she felt afraid of how Rhoda might compose herself under such a trial.

"Why, Martha," said Rhoda, smiling, "surely there is nothing wrong—you are not in mourning?"

"Oh dear, no, love. It is the festival of Saint Minima, virgin and martyr."

Here Miss Pavey sighed.

"Oh!" ejaculated Rhoda, quietly. "How is Mr Lee?" she added, after an awkward pause.

"Not well, dear—not well. He works too hard, and troubles himself too much about the wicked people here. Poor fellow! how saintly are his efforts for their good. But what do you think, Rhoda, dear?"

"I don't know."

"He has taken to calling me Sister Martha!"

"Well," said Rhoda, smiling, "as you are working so hard with him now in the parish, it is very kindly and nice, even if it does sound formal or ceremonial—Sister Martha."

"I must confess," said Miss Pavey, "that I don't like it. Of course we work together—like brother and sister. But I don't think it was necessary."

"Neither do I," said Rhoda, smiling.

"I do not agree with Mr Lee, of course, in all things," continued Miss Pavey, "but he is very good."

"Most energetic," assented Rhoda.

"You know, I suppose, that we are to have a new harmonium?"

"I did not know it," said Rhoda, looking curiously at her visitor, who kept down her veil, and whose conscious manner indicated that she had something particular to say—something unpleasant, Rhoda was sure.

"Oh, yes; a new and expensive one; and I am to play it," continued Miss Pavey. "We disputed rather as to where it should stand. Mr Lee wished it to be in the north-east end, but I told him that it would be so much out of sight there that I was sure it would not be heard, so it is to be on the south side of the little chancel."

"Yes," said Rhoda, who was waiting for the object of Miss Pavey's visit; "that seems to be a good place."

"Yes, dear, he willingly gave way; but he would not about the babies."

"About the babies?" exclaimed Rhoda.

"Yes, dear. It was only this morning. We were discussing baptism and infant-baptism, and I don't know what possessed me, but it was in the heat of argument. Babies are so soft and nice, Rhoda, dear. I'm not ashamed to say so to you, because we are alone—but they really are—and I do like them; and it horrifies me, dear, to think of what the Church says about them if they've not been baptised. Poor little things! And really, I'm afraid I spoke very plainly. But, oh, Rhoda! my love, how shocking this is about Madge Mullion."

"About Madge Mullion?" cried Rhoda, excitedly, for she knew now from her visitor's manner that her disagreeable communication had come. "What do you mean?"

"It's too shocking to talk about, dear—about her and Mr Trethick, and—"

Here she got up, raised her veil above her lips, and whispered for some moments in Rhoda's ear.

"I'll not believe it," cried Rhoda, starting up with flaming face and flashing eyes. "How dare you utter such a cruel calumny, Miss Pavey?"

"My dearest Rhoda," cried her visitor, whose red eyes and pale face as she raised her veil, bore out the truth of her assertion, "I have been crying half the night about it for your sake, for I knew it would nearly break your heart."

"Break my heart!" cried Rhoda, scornfully. "I tell you it is impossible. For shame, Martha Pavey. I know you to be fond of a little gossip and news, but how dare you come and insult me with such a tale as this?"

"My dearest Rhoda, my darling Rhoda," cried the poor woman, throwing herself at her friend's feet, and sobbing violently, "you don't know how I love you—how much I think of your happiness. It is because I would not have you deceived and ill-treated by a wicked man that I come to you and risk your anger."

"You should treat all such scandal with scorn," cried Rhoda. "Whoever has put it about deserves—deserves—oh, I don't know what to say bad enough! You know it is impossible."

"I—I wish I could think it was," sobbed Miss Pavey. "That Madge was always a wicked girl, and I'm afraid she tempted him to evil."

Rhoda's eyes flashed upon her again; and, without another word, she left her visitor, and went straight to her own room.

Martha Pavey stood with clasped hands for a few moments gazing after her, and then, with a weary sigh, she lowered her veil and was about to leave the house, when she encountered Mr Penwynn.

"Have the goodness to step back into the drawing-room, Miss Pavey," said the banker, whose face wore a very troubled look; and, in obedience to his wish, she went back trembling, and took the seat he pointed out, while he placed one on the other side of the table, and began tapping it with his fingers, according to his custom.

Miss Pavey looked at him timidly, and her breath came fast, for she was exceedingly nervous, and she dreaded that which she felt the banker was about to say.

He hesitated for some few moments, glancing at her and then out of the window, but at last he seemed to have made up his mind.

"Miss Pavey," he said, "you are a very old friend of my daughter."

"Oh, yes, Mr Penwynn; you know I am!" she cried.

"You take great interest in her welfare and happiness?"

"More I may say than in my own, Mr Penwynn."

"You are a great deal about in the town too, now?"

"Yes, a great deal, Mr Penwynn."

"In fact, you assist Mr Lee a good deal—in visiting—and the like."

"A great deal, Mr Penwynn."

"And therefore you are very likely to know the truth of matters that are going on in the place?"

"Oh, yes, Mr Penwynn; but what do you mean?"

"Simply this, Miss Pavey. I am a father, and you are a woman of the world—a middle-aged lady to whom I may speak plainly."

"Mr Penwynn?" cried the lady, rising.

"No, no, don't rise, Miss Pavey, pray. This is a matter almost of life and death. It is a question of Rhoda's happiness. I believe you love my child, and, therefore, at such a time, as I have no lady-friends to whom I could speak of such a thing, I speak to you, our old friend, and Rhoda's confidante."

"But, Mr Penwynn!" cried the lady, with flaming cheeks.

"This is no time, madam, for false sentiment. We are both middle-aged people, and I speak plainly."

"Oh, Mr Penwynn!" cried the lady, indignantly.

"Tell me," he said, sharply, "have you been making some communication to Rhoda?"

"Yes," she said, in a whisper, and she turned away her face.

"Is that communication true?"

She looked at him for a few moments, and then said,—

"Yes."

"That will do, ma'am," he said, drawing in his breath with a low hiss; and, rising and walking to the window, he took no further notice of his visitor, who gladly escaped from the room.

A few minutes later he rang the bell.

"Send down and see if Dr Rumsey is at home," he said.

The servant glanced at him to see if he was ill, left the room, and in half an hour the doctor was closeted with the banker in his study.

"I'm a little feverish, Rumsey," said Mr Penwynn, quietly; "write me out a prescription for a saline draught."

Dr Rumsey asked him a question or two, and wrote out the prescription. The banker took it, and passed over a guinea, which the doctor hesitated to take.

"Put it in your pocket, Rumsey," said his patient, dryly. "Never refuse money. That's right. Now I have a question or two to ask you."

"About the mine, Mr Penwynn?" cried the doctor, piteously. "Yes, every shilling of my poor wife's money! Five hundred pounds. But I ought to have known better, and shall never forget it. Is there any hope?"

"I don't know," said the banker, coldly. "But it was not that I wanted to ask you. It was about Geoffrey Trethick."

"Curse Geoffrey Trethick for a smooth-tongued, heartless, brazen scoundrel!" cried the doctor, rising from his general calm state to a furious burst of passion. "The money's bad enough. He swore to me, on his word of honour, that the mine would be a success, and I let myself be deceived, for I thought him honest. Now he has come out in his true colours."

"That report about him then is true?"

"True," cried the doctor, bitterly, "as true as truth; and a more heartless scoundrel I never met."

"He denies it, I suppose?"

"Denies it? Of course: as plausibly as if he were as innocent as the little babe itself. That poor woman, Mrs Mullion, is broken-hearted, and old Paul will hardly get over it. He has had a fit since."

"Is—is there any doubt, Rumsey?" said Mr Penwynn, sadly.

"Not an atom," replied the doctor. "He has been my friend, and I've trusted and believed in him. I'd forgive him the affair over the shares, but his heartless cruelty here is disgusting—hush!—Miss Penwynn!"

Rhoda had opened the door to join her father, when, seeing the doctor there, she drew back, but she heard his last words.

"I won't keep you, Rumsey. That will do," said Mr Penwynn, and, as the doctor rose to go, he turned to the banker,—

"Is—is there any hope about those shares, Mr Penwynn? Will the mine finally pay?" he said, piteously.

"If it takes every penny I've got to make it pay, Rumsey.—Yes," said the banker, sternly. "I am not a scoundrel."

"No, no, of course not," cried the doctor, excitedly, as he snatched a grain of hope from the other's words. "But would you sell if you were me?"

"If you can find any one to buy—at any price—yes," said the banker, quietly; and the grain of hope seemed to be snatched away.

As the doctor was leaving, Rhoda lay in wait to go to her father's room, but the vicar came up, and she hastily retired.

"Mr Lee? What does he want?" said the banker, peevishly. "Where is he?"

"In the drawing-room, sir."

Mr Penwynn rose, and followed the man to where the vicar was standing by the drawing-room table.

"You'll excuse me, Mr Penwynn," he said, anxiously; "but is Mr Trethick here?"

"No. I have been expecting him all the morning, Mr Lee. May I ask why?"

The vicar hesitated, and the colour came into his pale cheeks.

"I want to see him particularly, Mr Penwynn."

"May I ask why?"

"I think you know why, Mr Penwynn. There's a terrible report about the mine. Is it true?"

"Too true," said the banker, coldly. "And you have come to try and rise upon his fall," he added to himself.

"Poor Trethick!" exclaimed the vicar; "and he was so elate and proud of his success. He is a brave fellow, Mr Penwynn."

"Indeed," said the banker, sarcastically. "Come, Mr Lee, suppose you are frank with me. What of that other report?"

"It is a scandal—a cruel invention," exclaimed the vicar. "I cannot, I will not believe it. For heaven's sake keep it from Miss Penwynn's ears."

The banker turned upon him sharply.

"Why?" he said, abruptly.

"Why?" exclaimed the young vicar, flushing. "Mr Penwynn, can you ask me that?"

"Mr Lee," said the banker, "I'd give a thousand pounds down to believe as you do. I have been waiting here all the morning for Mr Trethick to come to me—to bring me, as he should, the bad news of the flooding of the mine, and, if it is necessary, to defend himself against this charge that is brought against him; and he does not come. What am I to think?"

"Think him innocent, Mr Penwynn. I for one cannot believe such a charge to be true. But here is Mr Trethick," he cried, as a hasty step was heard upon the gravel, and, without waiting to be announced, Geoffrey walked straight in.

The vicar started at his appearance, for he was haggard and his eyes red. He had evidently not been to bed all night, and his clothes were dusty and covered with red earth. There was a curious excited look, too, about his face, as he stared from one to the other, and then said, hoarsely,—

"Ruin, Mr Penwynn; the mine is drowned."

"So I heard, Mr Trethick, before I was up," said the banker, coldly.

"I sat by the furnace-fire all night," said Geoffrey, in the same low, hoarse voice, "trying to think it out, for I know—I'll swear this is the work of some scoundrel; and if I can prove it—"

He did not finish, but stood with his fists clenched looking from one to the other.

"I've been asleep," he said, "and I'm not half awake yet. I felt half-mad this morning. I drank some brandy to try and calm me, but it has made me worse."

"There is no doubt about that. We will talk about the mine some other time, Mr Trethick," said the banker. "Will you leave my house now? You are not in a fit state to discuss matters."

"Fit state?" said Geoffrey. "Yes, I am in a fit state; but the accident has been almost maddening. No; it was no accident. I'll swear it has been done."

"Perhaps so," said the banker, calmly; "but will you return to your apartments now. I will send for you to-morrow."

"My apartments?" exclaimed Geoffrey, with a harsh laugh. "Where are they? I have none now. Mr Lee, will you give me your arm; my head swims. Take me down to Rumsey's place. I'm going wrong I think—or something—there was—little brandy in the—in the—what was I saying—the men—bottle—furnace-house—I was—faint—Pengelly gave me—I—I—can't see—is—is it night? Fetch—Rhoda. I—"

He sank heavily upon the floor, for it was as he said. He had remained watching by the dying furnace-fire the whole night, and then, heart-sick and faint, he had taken the little cup of brandy and water Pengelly handed to him, the remains of the bottle from which the two watchers had been drugged, and, little as he had taken, it had been enough to send him into a deep sleep, from which he had at last risen to hurry up to An Morlock—drunk, so the servants said.

"Disgracefully intoxicated!" Mr Penwynn declared.

The Reverend Edward Lee said nothing, but sighed deeply and went his way, and Rhoda Penwynn was fetched down by her father, who took her to the drawing-room door, and pointed to where Geoffrey lay upon the carpet.

"Your idol is broken, Rhoda," he said, in a low, stern voice. "We were both deceived."

"Oh, papa! is he ill?" cried Rhoda; and with all a woman's sympathy for one in distress, she forgot the report she had heard, and was about to make for Geoffrey's side.

"Ill as men are who make brute beasts of themselves, my child. Come away, my girl, and let him sleep it off. Rhoda, you can be brave, I know: so show your courage now."

She was ghastly pale, and she gazed from father to lover, hesitating whether she ought not to take Geoffrey's part against the whole world.

Heart triumphed, and snatching away her hand as she was being led from the room,—

"I'll never believe it, father," she cried. "Oh, Geoffrey, Geoffrey, speak to me. Tell me what is wrong?"

She had sunk upon her knees and caught the prostrate man's hand in hers, with the effect that he roused himself a little, and slightly turned his head.

"Mine's drowned," he muttered. "Don't worry—that brandy."

"Yes, yes; but you will soon put that right."

"Put it right," he said, thickly. "No—sha'n't marry her—poor little Madge—I like little Madge—I'm sleepy, now."

Geoffrey's hand fell from Rhoda's heavily upon the thick carpet, and she shrank away from him as if stung. Then her head drooped, her face went down into her hands, and as Mr Penwynn stood watching her, she uttered a moan, rocking herself to and fro.

This lasted but a few minutes, and then a curiously-hard, stern look came over her pale face, as she slowly rose from her knees, and went and placed her hands in those of her father, looking him full in the eyes; and then, with the air of outraged womanhood lending a stern beauty to her face, she let him lead her to his study, where she sat with him, hardly speaking, till she heard it whispered that Mr Trethick had got up, and gone staggering out of the house.

"Where did he go?" said Mr Penwynn, quietly.

"Down to the hotel, sir."

"That will do."

Father glanced at daughter as soon as they were alone, when Rhoda left her seat and laid her hands upon his shoulder.

"I don't feel well, dear," she said. "I shall go up to my room. Don't expect to see me again to-day, father, and don't be uneasy. You are right, dear," she said, with her voice trembling for a moment; then, flinging her arms round his neck, she kissed him passionately.

Mr Penwynn held her to his breast, and returned her kisses.

"It is very, very hard to bear, father. Oh, don't—don't you think we may be mistaken?"

"No," he said sternly; "I do not."

Rhoda heaved a bitter sigh, and then drew herself up, but bent down and kissed him once more.

"I'm your daughter, dear," she said, with a piteous smile; "but I'm going to be very brave. I shall be too proud to show every thing I feel."

She left the study and went up to her chamber, where she stood gazing from the window at the sunlit sea and glorious view of many-tinted rocks around the bay; but she could only see one thing now, and that was her broken idol as he had lain upon the floor below, and uttered the words, still burning in her ears, full of pity for "poor little Madge."

Chapter Forty Three.

Awakening to the Worst.

Geoffrey Trethick, as the servants had said, rose from the place where he was lying, and stood trying to think; but his brain seemed out of gear, and all he could master was the idea that he was not in a fit state to be at An Morlock. Consequently he groped his way out, staggered along the drive, and began to make for the hotel in a vague, erratic fashion, greatly to the amusement of such people as he met.

Fortunately for him about the sixth person he encountered was Amos Pengelly, who limped up, looking at him with a curious expression of disgust upon his countenance.

"'Wine is a mocker,'" he muttered; "'strong drink is raging.' He's been trying to forget it all."

The stout miner hesitated for a moment, and then took and drew Geoffrey's arm through his own, supporting his uncertain steps, and leading him straight to the hotel, where they were refused entrance.

"No," said Mrs Polwinno, the landlady; "Mr Trethick had better take his favours somewhere else;" and Mr Polwinno, her little plump, mild husband, nodded his head, and said, "Exactly so, my dear."

Amos Pengelly frowned, and the disgust he felt grew so strong that he was ready to loosen his hold upon Geoffrey, and leave him to his fate.

"He is false," he said to himself, "and bad, and now he has taken to the gashly drink, and I've done with him."

But as he spoke he looked in Geoffrey's flushed face and wild, staring eyes, and something of his old feeling of respect and veneration for his leader came back, and with it a disposition to find some scriptural quotation to suit his case.

"'A certain man went down from Jerusalem to Jericho, and fell among thieves,'" he muttered. "Yes, he's fell among thieves, who've robbed him of his reason, and I can't leave him now."

Taking hold of the helpless man a little more tightly, and knitting his brows, Amos Pengelly, in complete forgetfulness now of his scriptural quotation, proceeded unconsciously to act the part of the Good Samaritan, but under far more trying circumstances.

He had not gone far before he met Tom Jennen, slouching along with his hands deep down in the pockets of a pair of coarse flannel trousers, which came well under the arm-pits, and covered his chest, and the sight of those he met made Tom Jennen grin most portentously.

"Why, Amos," he said, "they told me the gashly old mine was drowned, when it was engineer and head miner. Why, Amos, I thought you'd took the pledge."

Pengelly tightened his lips and went on without answering, finding no little difficulty in keeping his companion upright.

"Ah," said old Mrs Trevoil, standing knitting a jersey at her door, and smiling maliciously, "some folk gets up and preaches o' Sundays among the Methodies, and teaches what other folk should do, and can't keep theirselves straight."

"Yes," said a sister gossip, in a loud voice, "that's a nice companion for a preacher. Shame on you, Amos Pengelly! You ought to be took off the plan."

Pengelly's face grew tighter, and he strode manfully on without deigning to say a word, or to make a reply, as he ran the gauntlet of the fisher-folk standing at the low granite doors, though the remarks he heard thrown at his own religious leanings, and at Geoffrey's double fall from the path of virtue, stung him as sharply as if he had been passing through a nest of hornets.

"I'd take him 'bout with me to chapel o' Sundays till you've converted him if I was thee, Amos Pengelly," said one sharp-tongued woman at last, as he turned the corner of the steep lane where he lived; and then his own door was reached. He dragged Trethick inside, and passed his hand across his dripping brow before taking the young man, now terribly helpless, upon his back, after the fashion of a sack, and carrying him up the short flight of steps and laying him upon his own bed, where Geoffrey seemed to go off at once into a deep sleep.

For the drug had had a most potent effect upon him, from the fact that he had partaken of a terribly strong dose in the dregs of the bottle, where it had settled down; the two watchers at the furnace, though they had drunk deeply, neither of them having swallowed one-half so much.

As soon as Pengelly had relieved himself of his load, he sank down in the one chair in his bare bedroom, and sat watching Geoffrey hour after hour, waiting for him to awaken.

"When he's sober, and in his right mind, I'll talk to him," said Pengelly, to himself; and there he sat, hour after hour, comforting himself by singing hymns in a low voice, giving them out first two lines at a time, after announcing number and tune, to an imaginary congregation gathered round; and this he kept up till the afternoon.

Then he went down to the mine, leaving Geoffrey locked in; but, on reaching the cliff, it was only to see so many people hanging about the buildings discussing the accident that he had not the heart to go there and be questioned; so he turned aside, and walked on past the old mine shaft to Gwennas Cove, hoping to find old Prawle outside, for he felt that he could not go to the cottage.

He had his wish, for the old man was there, sitting upon a stone and smoking his pipe.

"Well, Amos," he said, as the miner came up, "so you've flooded the mine, I hear."

"Ay, she's full o' water," said Pengelly, sadly.

"Ah, that's a bad job; but what fools ye must have been."

"Fools, perhaps, not to keep a better look-out; but it's done, Master Prawle, and we must get the water out. How's Bessie?"

"Busy," said the old man, shortly.

Pengelly stood looking down at him for some few minutes, wanting to speak, but flinching from his task.

"Well," said the old man at last, "what is it? Ye're a strange chap, Amos Pengelly. Ye won't drink nor smoke a pipe, only stand and stare and glower, as if you was too good to mix with the like o' me. Now speak out, or else go."

"I want to know if it's all true, Master Prawle?"

"If what's all true?"

"What I've heard up churchtown."

"How do I know what you've heard up churchtown? I was there this morning, and I heard that Wheal Carnac was flooded. Is that what you mean?"

"No, Master Prawle. I mean—I mean about Mullion's lass. Is she here?"

The old man took his pipe from his mouth, and nodded.

"Did Master Trethick bring her here last night?"

The old man nodded again.

"And it is all true about—about the little one?"

"Ay, it's all true enough," said the old man. "But never mind about that. He'll marry her by-and-by, and it will be all right next time. Look here, Amos, what are you going to do about Wheal Carnac?"

"I don't know," said the miner.

"Then get to know," said old Prawle, eagerly. "Look here, Amos, you're fond of coming and hanging about, and I know what you mean, of course. So look here, I say, if you want to be friends with me, Amos Pengelly, you've got to come and tell me what goes on there, and what you are going to do, my lad, about that mine, d'ye hear?"

"Yes, Master Prawle," said the miner, heavily. "I must go back now."

"Yes, you'd better," the old man said, with a leer. "They don't want men folk about here now. My Bessie has turned me out, and I don't seem to belong to the place. I'll walk part of the way back with you, Amos, and talk about the mine;" and, to Pengelly's astonishment, the old man did so, talking eagerly the while about the water, and the best way to clear it off.

"P'r'aps they'll give her up now, Amos," he said, at last. "P'r'aps they won't spend no more over her."

"Very likely," said Pengelly, wearily.

"Then mind this—if you want me to be on your side, Amos, you come over now and then and tell me all."

Pengelly nodded, and they parted, the miner making haste back to his cottage, where he found that Geoffrey had not stirred, neither did he move all that night, while Pengelly dozed beside him in a chair.

It seemed as if he would never wake, and the probabilities are that a man with a less vigorous constitution would never have woke again, so powerful was the drug thrown with reckless hand into the brandy by the ignorant man.

In fact it was ten o'clock the next morning before Geoffrey started up and gazed wonderingly at Pengelly.

"You've woke up at last, sir," said the miner, with a reproachful look.

"At last? What do you mean? Good heavens! How my head throbs."

"It was a sorry trick to do, Master Trethick, and not a man's part, to go and drown your *brain* like the pit."

"Look here, Pengelly, my head's all in a whirl. I'm ill. I hardly know what I am saying. How came I here?"

"I carried you here mostly, Master Trethick, sir, after you come away from An Morlock."

"Did I go to An Morlock?"

"Yes, sir, I s'pose so—to say the mine was flooded."

"Yes, of course, the mine was flooded; but did I go to Mr Penwynn's?"

"Yes, sir, in a state such as I had never believed I could see you, sir—full of drink."

"What?"

"I suppose you had been taking it to make you forget the trouble, sir. That drop I gave you at the furnace—"

"Ah, to be sure," cried Geoffrey, who saw more clearly now—"that brandy."

"Wouldn't have hurt a child, sir," said the miner, bitterly.

"But it sent my two men to sleep. What time is it now—three—four?" he cried, gazing at the window.

"It's ten o'clock, sir, and you've been since two yesterday sleeping it off."

"Then that stuff was drugged," cried Geoffrey. "Here, Pengelly, may I wash here? I must go up to An Morlock directly."

There was a knocking on the door below, and Pengelly descended, while Trethick tried to clear his head by drinking copiously of the cold water, and then bathing his face and head.

"Good heavens! If I went up to An Morlock in such a state what would they think? How unfortunate. Every thing goes wrong."

The cold water did clear his dull brain somewhat, but his lips and throat were parched, and he felt terribly ill. So confused was he still, that for the time he had forgotten all about Madge Mullion, while the proceedings of the previous day seemed to him to be seen through a mist, and the more he tried, the worse confusion he was in. One thing, however, was certain, and that was that he must go up to An Morlock at once, and see Mr Penwynn about the mine.

"Humph! here is a comb," he said. "I'll straighten a little, and then run up home, and—"

He dropped the comb and caught at the window-sill, where a little glass was standing, for as he mentioned that word home, he felt giddy, and back, like a flash, came the recollection of all that had passed.

He had no home to go to. Rhoda must have heard of that awkward incident, and he had been up to An Morlock while under the influence of a drug.

"Feel giddy, sir?" said a voice. "I'll give you a cup of tea before you go away; but here's Mr Penwynn's man been with a letter for you."

Geoffrey caught the letter from the bearer's hands, and, with a terrible feeling of dread oppressing him, tore it open, and read it through twice before he fully realised its meaning.

It was very short but to the point, and Geoffrey seemed to see the stern-looking writer as the words gradually took shape and meaning.

For Mr Penwynn said, in cold, plain terms, that, after what had taken place, of course Mr Trethick saw that he could not call at An Morlock again, and that he was commissioned by Miss Penwynn to say that she fully endorsed her father's words. As to the mine, for the present Mr Trethick must continue his duties there, and in the conduct of their business relations Mr Penwynn called upon him to use his most strenuous exertions to reduce the loss, and to place the mine in its former state.

"Curse the mine!" cried Geoffrey aloud. "What is that compared to my character there? Pengelly," he cried fiercely, "do people believe this scandal?"

"Yes, sir."

"Do you?"

"Yes, sir."

"And yesterday? What about me? How did I seem?"

"Like one, sir," said the miner sternly, "who had forgotten that he was a man, and drunk till he was a helpless beast."

"And I went there like that," thought Geoffrey. "Perhaps she saw me. And she believes all this."

He stood there with his head feeling as if a flood had burst in upon his throbbing brain.

Chapter Forty Four.

Geoffrey's New Lodgings.

Geoffrey Trethick had truly expressed his character when he said that he had Cornish blood in his veins, and could be as obstinate as any in the county. Whether he was descended from the same race as peopled the opposite coast of France, it is impossible to say, but he was as stubborn as any Breton ever born.

The days glided on, and he found that he was disbelieved and doubted; that Mr Penwynn had lost faith in him, and that Rhoda had set herself aloof; and one way and another he was so exasperated that he set his teeth firmly, and swore he would never say another word in his own defence.

"Let them think what they may, say what they like, I'll never protest or deny again; and as for Rhoda, fickle, cold-hearted, cruel girl, I hate her with all my heart—and I am a liar for saying so," he cried. "But that's all over, and some day or another she shall beg my pardon—and I'll tell her so."

Acting on the impulse of the moment he sat down and hastily penned a note to her, without internal address or signature, placed it in his pocket, and kept it there ready for posting when he passed the office. It was very brief.

"I gave you my love in full trust and hope. I believed you gave me yours in return. Trouble came—accident—mishap—and appearances blackened me. You heard much, saw less, and you judged me from hearsay, giving me no opportunity for defence. In other words, you believed me to be as great a scoundrel as ever walked this earth. I accept your washes conveyed in your father's note; but some day you will beg my pardon—ask my forgiveness. I shall wait till that day comes."

Not a very gentle letter to send to a lady, but he sent it just at a time, to use his own words, when his soul was raw within him.

He had seen Mr Penwynn, who ridiculed the idea of the flooding being the work of an enemy, and bade him, imperiously, free the mine from water.

He was too proud to say much, but accepted at once the position of servant, and went his way to examine the mine once more, set the pumping-engine working at its highest pressure, and found at the end of twenty-four hours that he had not sunk the water the eighth of an inch.

Then he had found himself deliberately "cut" by the better-class people in the place, and that his efforts to obtain even the humblest lodgings were in vain. The hotel people excused themselves on the plea of want of room, and for several nights he slept in the office by the mine.

There was one man, though, who seemed to be hunting Geoffrey about from place to place, but he avoided him in his anger.

"I know what he wants to say to me," he cried, "and, by George! I won't have it. I never did strike any one wearing the cloth, but I'm in that aggravated state of mind just now that if he did speak to me, and begin to preach, I should hit him."

It is needless to say that the man he avoided was the vicar.

"Reverend Master Lee has been here again, sir," said Amos Pengelly to him one morning, "and I said you'd be here soon, and he's coming again."

"Then I won't see him," cried Geoffrey, angrily. "Look here, Pengelly, I'm not going to be driven out of Carnac. People are sending me to Coventry, and are trying to aggravate me into going, but I sha'n't go."

"No, sir, I wouldn't go," said Pengelly, quietly. "I'd stay here and put the mine right, and then make amends."

Trethick turned upon him fiercely, but Pengelly did not shrink, and the young man uttered an impatient "pish!"

"Look here, Pengelly, I must have lodgings somewhere. What am I to do? I'm not a dog to live in this kennel of an office."

"You can share my place if you like."

"No, no; I told you I would not."

"I was talking to Mrs Prawle about it last even, sir."

"What! you were over at the Cove?" said Geoffrey, eagerly. "How was poor Madge?"

"Very sadly, sir, they say. You haven't been over for some days."

"I? No, of course not," said Geoffrey, sharply. "What should I do there?"

"Mrs Prawle said that if you could not get a better place, they had their little parlour and the one room out of it to spare; and Bessie said she would tend you if you liked."

"But, hang it, man! I couldn't go there," cried Geoffrey.

"I don't see why, sir," said Pengelly, simply. "I couldn't go there now, or I'd give up my place to you, but you could."

"Oh, no—impossible!"

"They're wonderfully clean people, sir," continued Pengelly, "and, though the furnishing's humble, they'd make you very comfortable, for old Master Prawle's seldom in the house, and it's little you'd want it for except for your breakfast and to sleep."

"But that poor girl's there," cried Geoffrey.

"I don't see why that should make any difference, sir," said Pengelly. "I was talking to Bessie about it after Mrs Prawle had spoken, and I went against it; but she said it would be quite right, and hoped you would go."

"Indeed!" said Geoffrey. "I say, Pengelly, how many times have you been there lately?"

"Every night, sir. It come of my taking a message, and money, and a parcel, from Mistress Mullion up at the cottage; for, though she can't have her child back, because of old Mr Paul, her heart's very sore about her, and she sends there every day."

"And so you and Miss Bessie have been talking matters over, eh?"

"Yes, sir. I'm a poor fellow to go to a woman's eye, but I'd try very hard to go to her heart," said the miner, simply.

"I did not mean that, Pengelly," said Geoffrey, smiling. "I meant about my matters."

"Oh yes, sir, a deal; and if you can't get elsewhere, I'd go there."

The miner went off about his work, and Geoffrey began to think over what had been proposed.

"Oh, no; it would be madness to go there. It would be giving colour to the report;" and he dismissed the idea from his mind. But that evening, as he sat at the office-door upon the bleak, wind-swept promontory, with the remnants of a cheerless meal, brought him by one of the miners' wives, upon the desk behind him, and the prospect of a night upon the bench beside the door, with a rolled-up coat for a pillow, his thoughts went back to the cottage at Gwennas, and he had to light a pipe to try and soothe himself, so bitter were his feelings.

"It's too bad—a thousand times too bad for any thing," he cried, as he gazed out to sea at the ever-darkening waves, now beginning to glitter with the reflections from the stars above.

"'Pon my soul, I'm the most unlucky fellow that ever breathed, and it's miserable living like this. Suppose I go to old Prawle's? I could sit with him down in his cave, and smoke, and drink smuggled liquor. I'm a drunkard by reputation, so why not indulge?

"I like poor old Mrs Prawle—and Bessie. Good lass."

He had a long, quiet think, and then burst out into a cynical laugh.

"What would Carnac say if I went there?"

And directly after, in a hard fit of stubborn opposition,—

"What does Carnac say now? Damn Carnac. I will go, and they may say and think what they will."

He had worked himself up into such a fit of passion, that for fear he should cool down, and let himself back out of what he looked upon as a bit of revenge upon the scandal-loving place, he started off at once, reached the cliff, and walked swiftly along to the Cove, where, as he came to the rapid descent, he stopped short to gaze at the place below.

On a stone outside the door, which was open, and from which came forth a soft flood of light, sat old Prawle, smoking away, with the bowl of his short black pipe glowing in the twilight like a star, while leaning against the door-post, with something in her arms, was Bessie Prawle, rocking herself to and fro, and singing an old Cornish ditty in a sweet, wild voice.

"By George!" said Geoffrey, softly, "I'd forgotten the bairn."

He stood there watching that scene and listening to Bessie's song for some time, and it set him thinking of women and children, and of what strength there is in their weakness to alter the journey of life. Then he thought of the suffering girl inside, lying there helpless and forsaken in her sorest time of need; and lastly he thought he would go back and try and furnish up the office and make it habitable, but just then a gruff voice hailed him with a rough—

"Hallo!"

"Hallo, Father Prawle!" he cried, and he went down, Bessie retiring into the cottage as he came into sight, "What's the news about the mine?" said the old man.

"Bad," was the reply. "Don't go away, Miss Bessie. How is your patient?"

"Not well, Mr Trethick," she said, coming back and standing before him with the baby in her arms, and gazing firmly and unshrinkingly in his face.

"I'm sorry. Poor lass!" he said. "May I come in?"

Bessie drew back, and he stooped and entered the room, where poor invalid Mrs Prawle was seated; and half an hour after the affair was so far decided that he had been referred to old Prawle himself to settle terms.

The old man had descended the rock-hewn steps to his bit of a cavern, from which came up the loud crackling of wood, while a ruddy glow shone out on the darkened rocks.

"Ahoy, there!" shouted Geoffrey.

"Ahoy!" echoed the old man. "Come down."

Geoffrey descended, to find a ruddy fire burning, and a quaint old copper kettle singing in the hottest place.

"I thought you'd come down and have a pipe and a drop o' brandy before you went back, my lad," said the old man, in his grim, gruff way. "Sit down on yon tub. There's some good tobacco there."

"Ah, that looks sociable," said Geoffrey, who was at heart a very gregarious animal. "I want to talk to you about terms."

"What, for the mine?" said the old man, sharply.

"No: for lodgings, if you'll have such a bad character in the house as I."

"Been talking to them?" said the old fellow.

"Yes; and they are quite willing. Are you?"

"Oh, ay, I'm willing enough," said Prawle, roughly. "I like bad characters," he chuckled. "We're all bad characters here—so they say."

"Then I shall be in the right place," said Geoffrey, cynically. "But come, what shall I pay you?"

"Whatever the old woman thinks right, my lad," said the old man, who, in spite of his grim ways, seemed to glance with favouring eyes at his visitor. "Sattle it with that poor soul up yonder, and pay her the bit of money regular. Let her think—hold that glass upright while I pour in the hot water—now help yourself to the brandy. Never paid duty in its life," he whispered, grinning.

Geoffrey poured in the spirit, and helped himself to the sugar. The old man mixed for himself, tasted, nodded, and went on—

"Let her think, poor soul, that she's saving and helping to pay for her keep, and it will make her happy. Better than selling sweets."

"That's settled then, Father Prawle?"

"Sattled," said the old man, holding out a great, gnarled hand, and giving Geoffrey's a tremendous grip. "We don't want the brass, but it pleases her."

"And I may come down here and smoke a pipe when I like?"

"Ay, ay, my lad, and welcome," said old Prawle. "You'll find the brandy in the locker here, and the key's always up on that ledge of rock yonder in the niche, and the matches are over t'other side there in that one. There's always plenty of wreck-wood for a bit of fire, and I keep the breaker there full of fresh water."

"Good," said Geoffrey, smiling. "Then I shall come to-morrow, Father Prawle, and the world may say what it likes."

"That for the world!" cried the old man, contemptuously exhaling a great puff of smoke. "The world's called me wrecker, smuggler, and thief. The world has called my bonnie lass there witch. Let it. I'm a rough old fellow, Master Trethick, and I'd ha' knocked you down at one time—I'd ha' throwed you over the cliff at one time, 'fore I knowed you; but you stood up like a man for my bonnie lass there, and you've said a many kind word to my poor creetur up yonder, and there's my hand."

He held out the great gnarled fist again, and Geoffrey took it and had his own tightly gripped.

"I don't care for what people say," growled the old fellow. "This place is mine, and I could buy a dozen such if I liked. You're welcome, my lad, as long as you like, and when you care to go I can give you as good a bit o' fishing as a man could have, and as good a drop of brandy and bit of tobacco. As to Mullion's lass, that's no affair o' mine, and I sha'n't make it any affair o' mine; but it's as fine a little youngster as I ever see."

Geoffrey's countenance, that had been glowing from the joint effects of the warmth of the fire and old Prawle's hospitable words, grew dark once more; but he sat chatting to the old man for another hour, and then returned to the office by the mine.

The next day Carnac society had another shock right to the centre, and Miss Pavey was outraged in her tenderest feelings by the news which she heard, and which she hastened to take to An Morlock, namely, that that wicked young man had now joined poor lost Madge Mullion at the Cove.

At night old Mr Paul heard the news as well, as he tottered through the place by the help of his stick, and he went back home, and smoked the first cheroot he had smoked for days, to tell Mrs Mullion; and the news had somewhat the colour of hope in the poor, sad mother's eyes.

Chapter Forty Five.

Oak and Willow.

Mr Chynoweth was in very good spirits one morning, for he had composed a letter, offering his hand and fortune to Miss Pavey, entirely to his satisfaction. It was written in a large engrossing hand upon superfine brief paper, and had the legal look that a document of so much importance ought to wear.

"I think that will do it," said Mr Chynoweth. "Her little income and my little income will make a big income; and with rubbers regularly three times a week, we ought to add something to the common fund."

So rubbing his hands with satisfaction, he proceeded to play a quiet game in his desk, which he had just finished as Mr Penwynn came in, when Mr Chynoweth referred to his slate, and told him where Geoffrey had gone to lodge.

"It is nothing to me," said the banker, "so long as he does his work. Any thing fresh?"

"No, sir, nothing. He has been here this morning, and said there was little to report. He says all his efforts to relieve the mine are useless; that hardly any thing can be done."

"Tell him when he comes again that he must do something. I must call in fresh help if he is too ignorant to free the mine from water."

He might have called in the help of half the engineers in England, but they could not have shown him a satisfactory means of battling with the huge rush of water that entered the gap blown out by the wretched man. For beneath the sea there was always a torrent ready to take the place of any that might be pumped out, and, after endless investigations, Geoffrey Trethick and Pengelly gazed at each other in despair.

It was bitterly tantalising. Here was the rich tin ore waiting for them in abundance, but no means of reaching and sending it up.

They examined the shore. Went out in boats and sounded. Took into consideration the possibility of throwing in sand bags over the chasm, but on such a coast they would have been tossed aside by the first storm; and the despair at Geoffrey Trethick's heart grew blacker.

They were bitter times too, for Mr Penwynn. On the strength of the success, John Tregenna had presented himself, made a claim, and been handsomely paid off by the banker, who, wishing to be on good terms with the man he had formerly disappointed and being then in the full flush of triumph, had paid Tregenna double the amount agreed upon, and now he was too proud to demand it back, though it would have been a useless proceeding if he had.

Large as was the sum he drew, Tregenna had been terribly wroth, but when the news came to him of the flooding of the mine he sat and gloated over his success, and laughed to himself till he began to think of the man Lannoe, his tool, and of the possibility of getting rid of him in some plausible way, so as to be sure of being free from demands for black mail.

Then the days passed with more good news. It was certain, he knew, that Geoffrey had been dismissed from visiting at An Morlock, news that was delightful in its way. Then Lannoe did not come, though he was expecting him day after day, till a strange feeling of hope began to grow into a certainty, and at last he felt sure that the man had lost his life in his nefarious attempt.

Lastly came to him the information that Geoffrey Trethick had gone to lodge with the Prawles; and John Tregenna laughed aloud as he thought once more of Rhoda, and of the time when he could renew his pretensions, and this time, perhaps, with better success.

The days wore on, and finding that nothing could be done in the way of pumping out the mine, Geoffrey and Pengelly spent their time in the top galleries, to which the water had not reached, searching in vain for something in the way of reward.

The former found his bad character seemed to have but little effect upon the poorer people of Carnac, even though Miss Pavey in her visiting said that he was a terrible wretch, and ought to be excommunicated by the church. His worst failing in the eyes of the people was his going to lodge at Prawle's, and unwittingly in this he had done poor Madge an ill turn, for the news reached the cottage just at a time when old Paul had settled that Mrs Mullion should fetch her daughter home. When this news came he bade her wait.

So time went on, and from the poorer folk there was always a shake or a nod as Geoffrey passed, and now and then an offering of fish from Tom Jennen or some other rough fellow with whom he had spent a night out in the bay.

He was passing along the road one day, in a very morose humour, when he came full upon the Reverend Edward Lee, and was about to pass him with a short nod, but the vicar stopped.

"How are you?" said Geoffrey, shortly.

"Not well, Trethick," said the vicar, holding out his hand, to the other's great surprise.

"Sorry for it," said Geoffrey, grimly, shaking hands. "What is it—bile?"

The vicar looked at him with a pained expression of countenance.

"No," he said, "I am sick at heart. We don't see one another often, Trethick. May I walk with you?"

"Oh, if you like," said Geoffrey, as the vicar turned and walked by his side. "I was going over the hill yonder by Horton mine, to let the wind blow some of my bad temper out of me."

"I should like to go with you, Trethick," said the vicar, eagerly.

"Look here, Lee," exclaimed Geoffrey, "I'm a man of the world, and rough usage has made me rough. If you want to talk pious platitudes to me by rote, please don't, for we should be sure to quarrel. I am horribly unholy this morning."

"But I do not," exclaimed the vicar, earnestly. "I want to talk to you as a man of the world."

"Come on, then," said Geoffrey; "it's a treat to talk to a civilised being now."

He thrust his arm through that of the young vicar, and hurried him on and on up-hill till the latter was breathless. Then he stopped.

"Now then!" said Geoffrey, "here we are, right out on the top, with heaven above and the free air around; now talk to me like a man of the world."

The vicar followed Geoffrey's example, and threw himself on the short, crisp turf, wiping the perspiration from his forehead, and gazing at his companion with a curiously troubled air.

"Now then," said Geoffrey, "man of the world, make a beginning."

The vicar hesitated, and Geoffrey smiled.

"Well, I'll help you," he said. "You want to know why I have not been at church lately?"

"Yes," said the vicar, eagerly catching at the ball thrown to him, "I did want to speak to you about that for one thing."

"Too wicked!" said Geoffrey. "Mind too much taken up with other things."

"Too much bent upon laying up treasure upon earth, Trethick, thinking too little of the treasure in heaven."

"I thought you said that you were going to talk to me like a man of the world," said Geoffrey, sharply.

"Yes, yes—I am," was the hasty reply, for the vicar saw that a few more words in the same strain would send his companion away.

"Go on then. You said you were heart-sick," said Geoffrey. "What's the matter?"

"I am in a great deal of trouble, Trethick," said the vicar, heavily. "I'm not a man of the world, but you are, and—and—I like you, Trethick, I don't know why, but I wish we were better friends."

"You like me?" said Geoffrey, laughing. "Why, my good sir, you and I are like positive and negative poles; we repel one another."

"But why should we, Trethick? You seem always to exercise a strange power over me. I did not like you at first."

"No," said Geoffrey. "I was too rough and outspoken; too irreligious. I shocked you."

"Yes, yes. That is true," said the vicar.

"Then you found that I was a rival, and you hated me?"

"No: not hated you," said the vicar, sadly. "I felt that we could never be friends. That was all."

"Look here, Lee," said Trethick; "are you a saint, or a humbug?"

"Certainly not the first," said the vicar, smiling. "I sincerely hope not the second."

"No: I don't believe you are," said Geoffrey, shortly. "Well, sir, the game's up. I've failed in my projects, and I've failed in my love. The way is open. I am no rival now."

"Trethick," said the vicar, earnestly, "can't we be friends?" and he held out his hand.

"Oh, yes, if you like," said Geoffrey, bitterly. "But why should you want to be friends with such a blackguard? There, man, go and have your way. I'm out of the race."

"You are speaking very bitterly, Trethick," said the vicar, sadly.

"You are bitterly disappointed with your failures. So am I. It is as Mr Penwynn said that evening: we have not been able to make our way."

"But you are making your way," said Geoffrey.

"No," replied the vicar, shaking his head, "not at all. I cannot move these people. I try all I can; I have done every thing possible, but they prefer to go to that wretched chapel, and to hear such men as Pengelly. Trethick, I speak to you as a man of the world," he continued, growing each moment more earnest, and his face flushing. "I am in despair; that is why I came to you, whom I know to be disappointed, as I am myself. I cannot get at these people's hearts. I yearn to do good amongst them, but I cannot stir them, while you seem to touch them to the core. If I announced that you would preach to them next week, the place would be thronged; as it is, it is nearly empty. Why is this?"

"Because I am the sinner, you the saint," said Geoffrey, bitterly. "There, don't look shocked, man; it is because you are too clever—too scholarly with them; you put on the priest's garment, and with it the priest's mask, and completely hide your nature. Let them know your profession by your ways, sir, and not by your cassock. I believe you are a good fellow at heart. Your words now prove it; but you have grown so full of belief in form and ceremony that you think them all in all. Why, Lee," he cried, lighting up, "I could get these people to follow me like dogs."

"Yes," said the vicar, sadly; "but they shun me."

"No," said Geoffrey; "I am boasting. But still I believe I could move them. Look here, Lee, you are in earnest over this?"

"Earnest?" cried the other. "I'd give any thing to win them to my side."

"Then be more of a man, less of a priest. Don't draw such a line of distinction between you. Mix with them more. Never mind the long cassock and ritualistic hat. Take more interest in their pursuits, and let them feel how much your nature, however polished, is like theirs."

"I will, Trethick. Yes, you are right. I am sure you are right."

"I believe—I hope I am," said Geoffrey.

"I am sure of it," cried the vicar; "and I see now how unsuited much of my teaching has been. But now about yourself, Trethick, let me begin by being more human, and helping you."

"How can you help me?" said Geoffrey, bitterly. "I am a hopeless bankrupt in pocket and morals, so the world says; and I am cut off from all that I looked forward to with happiness. Why don't you be up and doing, man, as I told you?" he cried, with a mocking devil in his eyes; "the way is open—go and win the race."

"I do not understand you," said the vicar, sadly.

"Don't understand? You know you loved Rhoda Penwynn."

"I did love her—very dearly," said the vicar, simply.

"And not now?"

He shook his head.

"Miss Penwynn would never have cared for me," he said, quietly; "I soon learned that. These things are a mystery, Trethick. Don't speak of that any more. It hurts me."

Geoffrey nodded.

"Here, sit down," he cried, "I'm tired, bodily and mentally. I feel as if I want my mother-earth—to nurse me. There," he cried, settling himself upon the turf with a grim smile, "sometimes, lately, I've felt as if I should like her to take me in her cold, clayey arms, to sleep never to wake again."

"Don't talk like that, Trethick," said the vicar, appealingly; "life is too real and good to be carelessly thrown away."

"Right, Lee; you are right—quite right. Well, then," he said, "I won't; but look here, man, you want to win the people to your side—here is your opportunity. That poor girl—Margaret Mullion."

"Yes," said the vicar, eagerly. "I wanted to talk to you about her."

"Go on then."

"I dared not commence," he said, "I shrank from beginning; but that was one reason why I longed to talk to you, Trethick."

"Well," said the other, smiling. "I am all attention."

"I wanted—not to reproach you for your sin, Trethick—"

"That's right," said Geoffrey, smiling bitterly.

"Don't treat it with levity, for heaven's sake, Trethick," cried the vicar. "Think of the poor girl—of her life blasted—of the wrecked fame, and of the expiation that might be made by way of atonement."

"Yes," said Geoffrey, "I have thought of all that."

"But an hour ago I was with the broken-hearted mother, who was sobbing at my feet."

"And she asked you to see me?"

"Yes. Begged me to see you and appeal to you, and I said I would. Mr Trethick, in our great Master's name, think of all this—think of the poor girl's fall, and try to make amends. No, no, don't interrupt me till I have done. I tell you I have knelt and prayed, night after night, that your heart might be softened, and that your reckless spirit might be tutored into seeing what was right, and into ceasing from this rebellion against the laws of God and man."

"Laws of God and man, eh?" said Geoffrey, mockingly.

"Yes; is it not written that the adulterer and adulteress shall be stoned?"

"Yes," cried Geoffrey, fiercely; "and is it not written—'He that is without sin among you, let him cast the first stone'? Damn it all, Lee, I'm sick of this. I've been stoned to death ever since this cursed affair got wind. My mistress—the woman I was to marry—casts the first stone at my devoted head; every one follows suit, and I am battered so that I don't know myself."

"You are mocking," cried the vicar.

"I am not mocking," cried Geoffrey; "but I am half-mad. And you," he cried, passionately, "even you, who call yourself my friend, are like the rest. But what have you done for this wretched girl, abased and heart-broken in her sin—what have you done?—you and the better-class people? Treated her worse than the beasts that perish. One and all. And this is Christianity! Shame upon you! shame!"

The vicar looked at him appealingly as Geoffrey went on.

"Have you been to her and spoken words of comfort?"

"No," said the vicar, humbly.

"Have you taken her by the hand, and bidden her go and sin no more?"

"No."

"Have you tried to lead her to a better way—helped her, and guided others to help her in her sore distress?"

The vicar shook his head.

"And yet you say, How am I to win the hearts of these people?"

The vicar wiped the perspiration from his brow as Geoffrey went on.

"Not one soul of all who knew her came to the poor wretch's help. Cast off by the man who robbed her of her fame, I found her maddened with despair. Rejected by her own people, I found her ready to die. Ready to die? I found her dying, for she had said to herself—'My people—my love—the whole world turn their backs upon me. What is there for me to do but die?' What should you say to the man who, finding the poor girl drowning, leaps into the sea, drags her out, and, like some poor beggarly imitation of a Samaritan, takes her to a home, and gives her help and shelter, in defiance of the world? What would you say to such a man as that?" cried Geoffrey.

"That he was a hero," cried the vicar.

"You lie," cried Geoffrey, leaping up in his excitement. "You lie to my face, for you come and tell me I am a villain; that I wrecked the poor girl's happiness; that the world scorns me; and you bid me, for what I have done, to marry the girl and give her the shelter of my name."

"But, Trethick—Geoffrey, did you do this?"

"Did I do this? Yes, but—damnation! there was a devil of pride rose up within me, when, on top of my reverses with the mine, I found every one turn against me, and my accusers would not let me speak. Even she who should have been the first to take my part, turned from me and made me more bitter still."

"But, Trethick," cried the vicar, excitedly, "is this true?"

"True," cried Geoffrey, throwing up his arms towards heaven, as he stood there now with the veins starting in his brow, and the passion working within him bringing him to such a pitch of excitement, that his companion could see his temples throb. "I scarcely spoke word about it before; but I swear by the God above us I never felt love, thought love, or dreamed of love but for one woman, and, Heaven help me, she has cast me off."

He turned away and rushed headlong down the hill, but the paroxysm of rage was over, the excitement gone; and he returned directly to throw himself upon the turf.

"Did you ever see such a madman?" he cried, bitterly. "There, go on with your lecture; I'll hear you to the end."

"Trethick," said the vicar, quietly; and Geoffrey turned slowly towards him, to find that his companion was kneeling there with outstretched hands.

"Well?" was the harsh response.

"I asked you to let me be your friend. I ask you again, Geoffrey, as I ask you now, to forgive my doubts."

Geoffrey caught his outstretched hands.

"You believe me?"

"Believe you? Yes, every word. Forgive me for wronging you so cruelly. I'll try and make amends."

"Not by taking my part—not by speaking about this?"

"Why not?"

"As the cloud came so let it go," cried Geoffrey. "The poor girl is silent about her lover, but the truth will come out of itself. Till then I am content to wait, and let the world have its say."

"But he must marry her—poor girl!"

"No!" said Geoffrey, sternly. "No! Better let her bear her lot, hard as it may be. The man who could forsake her in her greatest need would never make her a husband worthy of her love. She must accept her fate."

"But you, Geoffrey Trethick. It is unmanly not to clear your fame."

"Maybe," he said, bitterly; "but I don't think I am like other men. I shall wait until Time shall bleach it once more white."

"But why not leave your lodgings?" said the vicar. "Take apartments elsewhere."

"What, make a cowardly retreat?" cried Geoffrey.

"But the world. It was an unfortunate thing for you to do. Why did you go there?"

"Out of defiance," cried Geoffrey.

"But that is past now. Try and make an effort to crush this wretched scandal upon your name. It is a duty, Geoffrey."

"That I will not do," he said, stubbornly.

"And Rhoda?" said the vicar, softly.

Geoffrey started as if stung.

"Let her wait too," he said, angrily. "When she humbles herself and asks my pardon she shall have it, and with it my farewell words. Lee, I loved that woman as strongly as man could love, but that love is dead."

They stood together now in silence for a few moments. Then Geoffrey turned to go.

"I'll drop in on you some day, Lee," he said, in his usual light tone. "Good-by, old fellow. I think we understand each other now."

"I'll come with you," said the vicar, quietly.

"Come with me, where?"

"To see poor Madge."

And they went together down the hill, oak and willow; but the oak growing gnarled and bowed with a canker in its breast, and the willow growing stronger every hour.

Chapter Forty Six.

A Thank-Offering.

Six months had passed since the night Geoffrey Trethick saved Madge Mullion's life, and his character and his ways had become, like the failure of Wheal Carnac, matters of the past.

There had been scores of interesting topics since then. People had talked about Miss Pavey's change, and how she followed the vicar like his shadow. There was that affair which had shaken Mr Penwynn's little local bank, and the forced sales he had had to make to meet his engagements. The carriage had been put down at An Morlock, and there were people who said that no good would come of the banker's great intimacy with John Tregenna, who was up at the house more frequently than he had been for some time past.

Geoffrey was as much at Coventry with the better-class people of Carnac as ever. Dr Rumsey nodded coldly when they met; old Mr Paul looked at him fiercely, and waited; and other people followed suit. There were no pleasant invitations to high tea, with rubbers of whist, and supper after. A man who had settled down as the companion of old Prawle, the wrecker, and made the cottage at Gwennas Cove his home, was not one to be received.

He used to laugh mockingly as he saw it all, and coolly accepted his fate. At the end of three months he had received a curt letter from Mr Penwynn, enclosing a cheque, and saying that his services were no more needed at Wheal Carnac; but Pengelly was kept on as care-taker of the valuable plant.

Then came rumours from time to time of talk of selling the mine, but no buyer could be found; and Geoffrey writhed as he thought of the treasures buried there, and of the impossibility of reaching them unless another shaft were sunk, and even then the prospects were so bad that the capital was not likely to be subscribed.

Old Prawle was generally the bearer of this news, and he took a wonderful interest in the place, though in a secretive, curious way; and after many chats with the old fellow, Geoffrey came to the conclusion that what he knew was of little worth, and the conversation ceased.

Sometimes he thought he would go, but the bitter spirit of obstinacy was in him more strongly than ever, and he stayed on, waiting, he said, for the apology he expected to get. When that came he meant to say good-by to the place forever. As it was he very rarely saw Rhoda, and when he did she refused to meet his eye.

One day there was a bit of excitement down on the cliff.

"Here you, Amos Pengelly, what have you got to say to it?" cried Tom Jennen. "You don't carry on none o' them games at chapel. Why don't you set to and have thanksgiving, and turn chapel into green-grocer's shop like up town in Penzaunce?"

Amos shook his head, but said nothing.

"Why," said Tom Jennen, "you never see any thing like it, lads. I went up churchtown, and see something going on, when there was Penwynn's gardener with a barrow full o' gashly old stuff—carrots, and turnips, and 'tatoes, and apples, and pears, and a basket o' grapes; an' parson, and young Miss Rhoda, and Miss Pavey, all busy there inside turning the church into a reg'lar shop. Why, it'll look a wonderful sight to-morrow."

"They calls it harvest thanksgiving," said another fisherman, "and I see pretty nigh a cartload o' flowers, and wheat, and barley, and oats, go in. Won't be no room for the people."

"I thought the church looked very nicely," interposed Amos Pengelly; "and if I wasn't down on the plan to preach to-morrow at Saint Milicent, I'd go myself."

"Lor' a marcy, Amos Pengelly, don't talk in that way," said Tom Jennen. "I never go to church, and I never did go, but I never knew old parson carry on such games. Harvest thanksgiving indeed! I never see such a gashly sight in my life. Turnips in a church!"

"Well, but don't you see," said Amos, in an expounding tone of voice, "these here are all offerings for the harvest; and turnips and carrots may be as precious as offerings as your fine fruits, and grapes, and flowers."

"Well said, lad," exclaimed one of the fishermen; "and, like 'tatoes, a deal more useful."

"Didn't Cain an' Abel bring their offerings to the altar?" said Amos, who gathered strength at these words of encouragement.

"Yes," cried Tom Jennen, grinning, "and Cain's 'tatoes, and turnips, and things weren't much thought on, and all sorts o' gashly trouble come out of it. Garden stuff ain't the right thing for offerings. Tell 'ee what, lads, here's our boat with the finest haul o' mack'ral we've had this year, and Curnow's boat half full o' big hake. We aren't got no lambs, but what d'yer say, Amos Pengelly, to our taking parson up a couple o' pad o' the finest mack'ral, and half a score o' big hake?"

Tom Jennen winked at his companions as he said this, and his looks seemed to say,—"There's a poser for him."

Amos Pengelly rubbed one ear, and then he rubbed the other, as he stood there, apparently searching for precedent for such an act. He wanted to work in something from the New Testament about the Apostles and their fishing, and the miraculous draught, but poor Amos did not feel inspired just then, and at last, unable to find an appropriate quotation, he said,—

"I think it would be quite right, lads. It would be an offering from the harvest of the sea. Parson said he wanted all to give according to their means, and you, lads, have had a fine haul. Take up some of your best."

"What, up to church?" cried Tom Jennen. "It'll make a reg'lar gashly old smell."

"Nay," said Amos, "they'd be fresh enough to-morrow."

"You daren't take 'em up to parson, Tom Jennen," said one of the men, grinning.

Tom took a fresh bit of tobacco, spat several times down on to the boulders, and narrowly missed a mate, who responded with a lump of stone from the beach below, and then, frowning hugely, he exclaimed,—

"I lay a gallon o' ale I dare take up a hundred o' mack'ral and half a score o' hake, come now."

"Ye daren't," chorused several. "Parson'll gie ye such a setting down."

"I dare," cried Tom Jennen, grinning. "I arn't feard o' all the parsons in Cornwall. I'll take it up."

"Bet you a gallon o' ale you won't," said one.

"Done," cried Tom Jennen, clapping his hand into that of his mate.

"And I'll lay you a gallon," said another.

"And I,"—"and I,"—"and I," cried several.

"Done! done! done!" cried Tom Jennen, grinning. "Get the fish, lads. I arn't afraid o' the gashly parson. I'll take 'em."

Amos Pengelly looked disturbed, but he said nothing.

"What's he going to do with all the stuff afterwards?" said Tom Jennen.

"Give it to the poor folk, I hear," said Amos.

"Then he shall have the fish," cried Tom Jennen. "Anyhow, I'll take 'em up."

There was a regular roar of laughter here, and a proposal was made to go and drink one of the gallons of ale at once, a proposal received with acclamation, for now that the bet had been decided upon, the want of a little Dutch courage was felt: for, in spite of a show of bravado, there was not a man amongst the group of fishermen who did not, in his religiously-superstitious nature, feel a kind of shrinking, and begin to wonder whether "parson" might not curse them for their profanity in taking up in so mocking a spirit such an offering as fish.

"Thou'lt come and have a drop o' ale, Amos Pengelly," said Tom Jennen.

"No," said Amos, "I'm going on."

"Nay, nay, come and have a drop;" and almost by force Amos was restrained, and to a man the group joined in keeping him amongst them, feeling as if his presence, being a holy kind of man, might mitigate any pains that might befall them.

If one only had hinted at the danger, the rest would have followed, and the plan would have come to an end; but no one would show the white feather, and, with plenty of laughing and bravado, first one and then a second gallon of ale was drunk by the group, now increased to sixteen or seventeen men; after which they went down to the boats, the fish were selected, and four baskets full of the best were carried in procession up to the church, with Tom Jennen chewing away at his quid, his hands in his pockets, and swaggering at the head of the party.

It was a novel but a goodly offering of the silvery harvest of the sea, and by degrees the noisy talking and joking of the men subsided, till they spoke in whispers of what "parson" would say, and how they would draw off and leave Tom Jennen to bear the brunt as soon as they had set the baskets down by the porch; and at last they moved on in silence.

There was not one there who could have analysed his own feelings, but long before they reached the church they were stealing furtive glances one at the other, and wishing they had not come, wondering too, whether any misfortune would happen to boat or net in their next trip.

But for very shame, they would have set down the baskets on the rough stones and hurried away; but the wager had been made, and there was Tom Jennen in front rolling along, his hands deeper than ever in his pockets, first one shoulder forward and then the other. He drew a hand out once to give a tug at the rings in his brown ears, but it went back and down, and somehow, in spite of his bravado, a curious look came over Tom Jennen's swarthy face, and he owned to himself that he didn't like "the gashly job."

"But I arn't 'fraid o' no parsons," he said to himself, "and he may say what he will. I'll win them six gallons o' ale whether he ill-wishes or curses me, or what he likes."

The dash and go of the party of great swarthy, black-haired fellows, in their blue jerseys and great boots, was completely evaporated as they reached the church, Tom Jennen being the only one who spoke, after screwing himself up.

"Stand 'em down here, lads," he said; and the baskets, with their beautiful iridescent freight of mackerel, were placed in the porch, the men being glad to get rid of their loads; and their next idea was to hurry away, but they only huddled together in a group, feeling very uncomfortable, and Tom Jennen was left standing quite alone.

"I arn't afeard," he said to himself; but he felt very uncomfortable all the same. "He'll whack me with big words, that's what he'll do, but they'll all run off me like the sea-water off a shag's back. I arn't feard o' he, no more'n I am o' Amos Pengelly;" and, glancing back at his mates, he gave a sharp rap on the church door with a penny piece that he dragged out of his right-hand pocket, just as if it had been a counter, and he was going to call for the ale he meant to win.

There was a bit of a tremor ran through the group of brave-hearted, stalwart fishermen at this, just as if they had had an electric shock; and the men who would risk their lives in the fiercest storms felt the desire to run off stronger than ever, like a pack of mischievous boys; but not one stirred.

The door was opened by Miss Pavey, who was hot and flushed, and who had a great sheaf of oats in one hand and a big pair of scissors in the other, while the opening door gave the fishermen a view of the interior of the little church, bright with flowers in pot and bunch, while sheaves of corn, wreaths of evergreens, and artistically-piled-up masses of fruits and vegetables produced an effect very different to that imagined by the rough, seafaring men, who took a step forward to stare at the unusual sight.

Miss Pavey dropped her big scissors, which hung from her waist by a stout white cotton cord, something like a friar's girdle; and as her eyes fell from the rough fishermen to the great baskets of fish, she uttered the one word,—

"My!"

"Here, I want parson, miss," growled Tom Jennen, setting his teeth, and screwing his mahogany-brown face into a state of rigid determination.

"Hallo, my lads, what have you got here?" cried a cheery voice, as Geoffrey Trethick strode up.

"Fish! Can't yer see?" growled Tom Jennen, defiantly.

"Here—here are the fishermen, Mr Lee," faltered Miss Pavey; and, looking flushed with exertion, and bearing a great golden orange pumpkin in his arms, the Reverend Edward Lee came to the door, laid the pumpkin where it was to form the base of a pile of vegetables, and then, with his glasses glimmering and shining, he stood framed in the Gothic doorway, with Miss Pavey and Geoffrey on either side, both looking puzzled, Tom Jennen and the fish in the porch, and the group of swarthy, blue-jerseyed fishers grouped behind.

Now was the time for the tongue-thrashing to come in, and the roar of laughter from the fishermen, who had given up all hopes of winning the ale, but who were willing enough to pay for the fun of seeing "parson's" looks and Tom Jennen's thrashing, especially as they would afterwards all join in a carouse and help to drink the rest of the ale.

"Brought you some fish for your deckyrations, parson," roared Tom Jennen, who had screwed his courage up, and, as he told himself, won the bet.

There was no answer, no expostulation, no air of offence, no look of injured pride, and, above all, no roar of laughter from his assembled mates.

For a moment or two the vicar looked at the offering, and the idea of incongruity struck him, but no thought of the men perpetrating a joke against his harvest festival. The next moment a rapt look seemed to cross his face, and he took off his glasses, gazing straight before him as visions of the past floated to his mind's eye. To him, then, the bright bay behind the group suggested blue Galilee, and he thought of the humble fisher-folk who followed his great Master's steps, and the first-fruits of the harvest of the sea became holy in his eyes.

Geoffrey Trethick looked at him wonderingly, and Miss Pavey felt a something akin to awe as she watched the young hero of her thoughts, with tears in her eyes; while he, with a slight huskiness in his voice, as he believed that at last he was moving the hearts of these rough, stubborn people, said simply,—

"I thank you, my men, for your generous offering," and he stretched his hands involuntarily over the fish, "God's blessing in the future be upon you when you cast your nets, and may he preserve you from the perils of the sea."

"Amen!" exclaimed a loud voice from behind.

It was the voice of Amos Pengelly, who had stood there unobserved: and then there was utter silence, as the vicar replaced his glasses, little thinking that his few simple words and demeanour had done more towards winning over the rough fishermen before him than all his previous efforts or a year of preaching would have done.

"I am very glad," he said, smiling, and holding out his hand to Tom Jennen, who hesitated for a moment, and then gave his great, horny paw a rub on both sides against his flannel trousers before giving the delicate, womanly fingers a tremendous squeeze.

"I am very glad to see you," continued the vicar, passing Jennen, and holding out his hand to each of the fishermen in turn, hesitating for a moment as he came to Amos Pengelly, the unhallowed usurper of the holy office of the priest; but he shook hands with him warmly, beaming upon him through his glasses, while the men stood as solemn as if about to be ordered for execution, and so taken aback at the way in which their offering had been received that not one dared gaze at the other.

"Mr Trethick, would you mind?" said the vicar, apologetically, as he stooped to one handle of the finest basket of mackerel. "How beautiful they look."

"Certainly not," said Geoffrey, who took the other handle, and they, between them, bore the overflowing basket up to the foot of the lectern.

"We'll make a pile of them here," exclaimed the vicar, whose face was flushed with pleasure; and, setting the basket down, they returned for another, Miss Pavey, scissors in hand, once more keeping guard at the door.

"I am so glad," he continued. "I wanted something by the reading-desk, and these fish are so appropriate to our town."

"Let's go and get parson ten times as many, lads," cried Tom Jennen, excitedly.

"No, no," said the vicar, laying his hand upon the rough fellow's sleeve; "there are plenty here. It is not the quantity, my lads, but the way in which the offering is made."

There was an abashed silence once more amongst the guilty group, which was broken by the vicar saying,—

"Will you come in and see what we have done?"

There was a moment's hesitation and a very sheepish look, but as the head sheep, in the person of Tom Jennen, took off his rough cap, stooped, and lifted a basket and went in on tip-toe, the rest followed, their heavy boots, in spite of their efforts, clattering loudly on the red and black tiled floor, while the vicar took from them with his own hands the remainder of the fish, and placed them round the desk.

"I wish we could have had some pieces of ore, Mr Trethick," said the vicar. "I should have liked to have represented some offerings of our other great industry here."

"I'll bring you some tin and copper, sir," cried Amos Pengelly, who had been staring about, cap in hand, and wishing he might get up in that little stone pulpit and preach.

"And I will send you the first winnings from Wheal Carnac, Mr Lee," said Geoffrey, quietly; and as he spoke he saw that Rhoda Penwynn, who had been grouping ferns by the communion rails, and hearing all, was present, and had heard his words, but she turned away.

"Will you?" cried the vicar, eagerly. "I thank you both, and I pray, Geoffrey Trethick, that your venture may prosper yet."

"Thank you," said Geoffrey, quietly, and he looked smilingly in the young vicar's face till his scrutiny seemed to evoke a womanly blush.

In the mean time the fishermen, hanging close together in a group, stood cap in hand, staring round at the decorations of the church, and, lastly, at the wondrous tints upon the fish, that seemed to be intensified and made dazzling as the sun streamed through a stained glass window and fell upon the glistening heaps. One pointed to this heap of fruits, another to that, but no one spoke, and Tom Jennen furtively removed his tobacco quid, and stuffed the dirty-brown, wet morsel into the secrecy of his trousers pocket, giving his hand a polish after upon the top of one of his high fisher-boots.

"I'll ask them all to come to church to-morrow," whispered the vicar eagerly to Geoffrey, as Rhoda now came up, and a chilly greeting passed between her and the miner.

"No," he said quickly; "don't undo your work. You have moved them more than you imagine. Let well alone."

A slight frown crossed Rhoda's brow—forced there to keep herself from marking her approval of his words; and just then a diversion occurred, for Tom Jennen gave a pull at the crisp hair upon his forehead, muttered something about not hindering the stowage, and went off on tip-toe, his mates saluting the vicar in turn, and going gently out. Miss Pavey smiled as she closed the door behind them, and bowed in answer to their "Good-day, ma'am."

Not a word was spoken as they made their way in a cluster down to the rails by the steep causeway leading to the boats, where they all grouped together, and stared from one to the other, waiting for some one to speak.

That some one proved to be Tom Jennen, who, after hunting out his quid from where it lay, in company with some half-pence, a stray button, and a lucky sixpence that acted as a charm against the evil eye, picked off some pieces of flue, tucked the quid in his cheek, and said gruffly,—

"It's a gashly old job, lads, and we've been sold."

"Ay, we have that," was chorused; and the men nodded and shook their heads.

"I wouldn't ha' done it if I'd knowed he was such a good sort," growled Tom, rather excitedly, "for he is a good sort, arn't he?"

"Ay, lad, that he is," was the ready answer.

"And what I say is this," cried Tom. "I won the bet fair and square, and let him as says I didn't, say so right out like a man."

"Ay, lad, you won it fair enough," was the reply.

"Well then," said Tom Jennen, "let's go and drink parson's health in that there ale;" and he gave his lips, which were very dry with excitement, a hearty smack.

"Ay, lad," was chorused, "we will."

They did; and Amos Pengelly thought it was no harm to join.

Chapter Forty Seven.

A Meeting.

"How's Madge?" said Geoffrey one morning, as he encountered Bess Prawle coming out of the bedroom with the baby in her arms.

"Very poorly," said Bess sadly. "She's wearing away, I think."

"Had I better get Dr Rumsey to call?"

"No," said Bess quietly; "no doctor will do her any good. Poor mother's very ill too this morning. I hardly know what to do first."

"Well, it is precious hard on you, Bessie," said Geoffrey. "We make a regular slave of you amongst us. Why not have a woman to come in and help? Money isn't flush: but I can pay her."

"Oh, no, Mr Trethick, I can manage," cried Bess. "No woman would come here to help."

Geoffrey frowned.

"We're such a bad lot, eh?"

"They don't like me," said Bess, smiling; "and father would not care to have a strange woman here."

"And so you get worked to death," said Geoffrey. "I don't like it, Bess, my lassie," he continued, while the girl flushed slightly with pleasure, as she noted the interest he took in her. "Something must be done, or I shall be obliged to take Madge away and get her lodgings elsewhere."

"You'll—you'll take Miss Mullion away?" cried Bess excitedly, as she laid her hand upon his arm. "No, no: don't do that, Mr Trethick."

"Why not? Would you rather she stayed here?"

"Yes," said Bess softly, "I would rather she stayed here. I'll do the best I can for her."

"God bless you, Bessie!" cried Geoffrey warmly. "You're a good, true-hearted lass, and I shall never forget your kindness. Well, I must see if some help can't be managed for you."

Bess flushed a little more deeply, for his words and interest were very sweet to her. Then, looking up cheerfully, she said that it was only a matter of a day or two.

"Father is quite taking to baby too," she said. "He nursed it for over an hour last night."

"Did he?" cried Geoffrey, laughing. "I wish I had been here. I say, Bessie, does tobacco-smoke make it sneeze?"

"No: not much," said Bessie wonderingly.

"Then look here," cried Geoffrey, "I'm not going to let the old man beat me. I don't see why I shouldn't be able to nurse as well as he. Give us hold. I'm going out to loaf on the cliff, and look at the sea, and smoke a pipe and think, and I'll take the baby."

"Mr Trethick!" cried Bess.

"I mean it," he said, laughing. "Here, come on, young one. Which way up do you hold it, Bessie?"

"Oh, Mr Trethick," cried Bessie. "Don't—please don't take it."

"Shall!" said Geoffrey; and to Bessie's amusement and annoyance, for a something in the act seemed to give her pain, he laughingly took the baby and held it in his arms.

"But you won't take it out, Mr Trethick," protested Bess.

"Indeed, but I shall," he said. "I always say what I mean."

"But you can't, sir. It must be dressed, and have on its hood."

"Bother!" cried Geoffrey; "it has got on too much already, and the sea-breeze will do it good. Come along, young top-heavy," he continued, laughing. "I shall be in the corner where I smoke my pipe, Bessie. Come and fetch the little soft dab when you've done."

He went laughing off, not seeing Bessie's countenance contract with pain, and, talking to the round-eyed, staring infant, he made his way up out of the Cove and along the cliff path, towards Carnac, to where the rock retired in one spot, forming a sunny little nook, full of soft, dry turf, stunted ferns and pink stonecrop, and scented with wild thyme. It was a place much affected by Geoffrey, where he could sit and watch the changing sea, and try to scheme his future. Here he seated himself on the turf, with his shoulders against the rock.

"Well, you are a rum little joker," he cried, as he packed the baby up between his knees, nipping its loose garments so as to hold its little form up steady, all but the head, which kept nodding at him, the tiny intelligence therein seeming to find something vastly amusing in the dark, robust man's face, and laughing merrily every now and then, after a staring, open-eyed inspection. "Keep your mouth shut, you drivelling little morsel, will you?" cried Geoffrey, using his pocket-handkerchief to the fount-like lips. "I enjoy you, young 'un, 'pon my word I do."

Here there were three or four nods and another laugh.

"Hold still, will you?" cried Geoffrey, "or you'll wobble that head off. There now, you're square. Good heavens! what a lot of toggery you have got on. Why don't she give you one good thick flannel sack, instead of all these stringed, and pinned, and buttoned wonders! That's right; go it. I'm comic, arn't I? Why, you jolly young jester, you are always on the grin."

The baby relapsed into a state of solemnity, gently bowing its head forwards and backwards, and making a few awkward clutches at Geoffrey's nose, which was nearly a yard away.

"Shouldn't have thought there was so much fun in a bit of a thing like this," continued Geoffrey, putting his hands behind his head, and resting them on the rock. "My ideas of a baby were that it was a sort of bagpipe that was always playing a discordant tune. Oh, I say, baby! for shame! I'm afraid your digestion is not perfect. In good society we always put our hand before our mouth when we make a noise like that. Here, this is the way. Hold still, you soft little atom. Why, I don't believe you've a bone in your body."

Geoffrey's hands had come from behind his head once more, and he laughingly placed one tiny, clutched fist before the wet mouth, for by no amount of persuasion could the hand be made to keep open.

"There, you fat little pudge, now hold still, and don't keep on laughing like a clown."

Geoffrey resumed his former position, and stared at the baby, and the baby stared at him.

"I suppose this is Geoffrey Trethick?" he said at last; "but if I had been coming along the cliff and saw myself I shouldn't have known him. Well, it is a chance to study human life and its helplessness. I begin to see now why women like babies. They're so soft, and helpless, and appealing. A baby is a something with which a woman can do just as she likes, for I suppose there is nothing a woman likes so much as having her own way."

Here a spasm of mirth seemed to convulse the baby, which threw back its head and laughed, and babbled, and crowed.

"Oh, you agree with that opinion, do you, youngster? Well, that's right. Hold still now. Do you hear? I don't want to take you home to your mother in two pieces. I wonder whether a baby ever did wobble off its head?"

Here there was a pause, during which Geoffrey lay back with half-closed eyes, lazily watching his charge.

"Now of course you don't know it, youngster, and it does not trouble you a bit, but you are one too many in this rolling world of ours. People talk about purity and innocence, and little things fresh from their Maker's hands; but, as my friend Lee says, you're a child of sin and shame: that's what you are."

"Do you hear?" he continued. "Why, you're laughing at it, as hard as ever you can laugh. Oh, it's funny, is it? Well, I suppose you are right, but it's no joke for poor Madge."

The baby laughed and crowed loudly here, ending by coughing till it was nearly black in the face.

"Serve you right too, you unnatural little wretch, laughing like that at your mother's troubles. You're a chip of the old block, and no mistake. I've a good mind to pitch you off the cliff into the sea. Oh, you're not afraid, arn't you?" he continued, with his face close to the baby, who wanted re-arranging after the coughquake from which it had suffered, with the result that the two little hands that had opened during the coughing clutched and tightened themselves in Geoffrey's crisp beard, from which they refused to be torn.

"Well, look here, young one," continued Geoffrey, after freeing his beard with a good deal of trouble, and leaving two or three curling hairs in the little fists. "You seem to have made up your mind to back up public opinion, you do, and evidently intend to adopt me as your father. Well, I don't mind. I feel just in the humour to do mad things, so why not adopt you? I dare say I could manage to keep you as well as myself; but you won't get fat. I don't care. But look here, youngster, can you sit it out if I have a pipe, and not set to and sneeze off your miserable little head?

"Ah, you smile acquiescence, do you?" said Geoffrey. "Well, then, here goes."

As he spoke, he began fumbling in his pocket for his pipe-case, tobacco-pouch, and match-box, all of which, in his laughing humour, he placed before the child, then stuck the match-box in one fist, the pipe in the other, and balanced the soft India-rubber pouch on the nodding head.

"Now then, stupid! Do you want to commit self-infanticide with phosphorus? Don't suck those matches. It's my belief, baby, that if you were thrown down in a provision warehouse you'd prolong your existence to an indefinite extent. Will you be quiet?" he exclaimed, laughing aloud. "Well, of all the funny little beggars that ever existed you are the most droll. There, now you've got your mouth all over the dye from that leather case. Wait a moment. There, if you must smoke you shall smoke, but don't be so hungry after it that you must suck the case."

He took the pipe-case from the little hand, opened and took out the pipe, wiped it, and then playfully closed the tiny fingers round the blackened stem of the old meerschaum, and guided the amber mouth-piece into the wet mouth.

The baby began to suck and rub the mouth-piece eagerly against its little gums, till it had a suspicion of the intense bitter of the pipe, when the look of content upon the soft, round little features gradually changed into such a droll grimace of disgust that Geoffrey lay back and laughed till the tears came into his eyes, and he wiped them away, and laughed heartily again and again.

"Oh, you rum little customer!" he exclaimed; "you've done me no end of good. I have not laughed like that since I came down to Carnac. Why, you've made my ribs ache, that you have—*the devil!*"

For at that moment, briskly walking along the cliff path, Rhoda turned the corner, and came right upon the pair.

Rhoda stopped as if petrified, and a fierce look of indignation flashed from her eyes.

Geoffrey was as much surprised, but he had more self-control, and, returning the indignant glance with one full of defiance, he kept his place in the sunny nook, lying right back, and went on tossing the baby to and fro, balancing it on his knees, and then pretending to make it walk up his broad chest, which, however, seemed to heave up into a mountain beneath the tiny feet.

The silence in that sheltered nook was painful, and the low moan of the restless sea even seemed to be hushed, as the child threw back its little head, and kicked and laughed and crowed with delight.

"Pitiful, contemptible coward!" thought Rhoda, biting her lip to keep down her anger. "And I once cared about this degraded wretch!"

"I wouldn't move to save my life!" thought Geoffrey. "You doubting, incredulous, proud, faithless woman! You shall beg my pardon yet."

He had a wonderful mastery over himself as far as his face was concerned, and he returned Rhoda's angry look with one as bitter, if not worse; but though he could keep smooth his face, he was not wholly master of his emotions, as it proved.

For just as Rhoda was trying to summon up force enough to make her tear herself away with a look of intensified scorn and contempt, Geoffrey's hands, which held the baby, instead of lightly tossing it up and down, involuntarily gripped its little tender ribs so fiercely that the merry crow was changed into a loud wail of pain, and, with a hysterical laugh that jarred through every nerve of Geoffrey's frame, Rhoda rushed away, to burst, as soon as she was out of sight, into a passion of tears.

"You little wretch!" roared Geoffrey, springing up and shaking the baby. "What do you mean by making me look such a fool? Be quiet, or I'll throw you into the sea. Hang me, what an idiot I must have looked," he cried, stamping up and down with the baby in his hands, and then stuffing it roughly in a niche in the rock. "Be quiet, will you," he roared, shaking his fist in the poor little thing's face; "be quiet, or I'll smash you!"

The cessation of the shaking, and the appearance of the fist close to its snub nose had the desired effect. The storm passed, and sunshine burst forth over the little face, followed by a laugh and a futile effort to catch at the hand.

"Poor little beggar?" cried Geoffrey, carefully taking up the helpless thing once more. "There, I don't care, do I, baby?" he cried, laughing and grinding his teeth together as the tiny fists grasped and held on to his beard, while the little eyes laughed in his. "Let her see me, and think what she likes. Come along, young 'un. I'm not cross with you. You couldn't help it. Here, hold your little wet button-hole still, and I'll give you a kiss. No, no—kiss: don't suck, stupid?" he said, laughing; and then the anger passed away, as a convulsion swept over the tiny face, and consequent upon a hair from Geoffrey's beard touching the apology for a nose, the baby sneezed three times.

"Well done, young one," he cried. "Feel better? No? Give us another."

He raised the little thing once more and kissed it, and as he lowered it again something prompted him to look back, and as he did he saw that Rhoda was in full view upon the cliff, that she had turned, and that she must have seen that kiss.

Rage took possession of his soul again, and he nearly made the child shriek in his fierce grip.

"Spying, eh?" he cried. "Well, if you will be a petty child, ma'am, so will I;" and, hugging the baby in his arms, he walked on, kissing it over and over again, till meeting Bessie Prawle, he cried out, "Here; catch!" and tossed the little thing into her arms.

Chapter Forty Eight.

Visitors at Gwennas.

Rhoda Penwynn had no idea of going to Gwennas Cove one morning when she went off, in a dreamy, forgetful way, for a walk. She was low-spirited and wretched. Her father's troubles and heavy losses were an endless anxiety, and, to her sorrow, she saw that he had of late grown reckless. How he was situated, or what he had lost, she could not tell, but there was a grey, wrinkled look about his face that went to her very heart. One thing was very evident, and that was that the banker had become entangled in some venture—John Tregenna had hinted as much one evening when at their house, but he had merely hinted, and she could not ask him more.

One thing was very evident, and that was that people had lost confidence in Penwynn, the banker. Other people might dabble in mines, lose, and begin again; but the man to whom the savings of others were intrusted, must be above reproach—above suspicion of speculation; and the Wheal Carnac affair had been a heavy blow in more ways than one.

Mr Penwynn was not long in finding this out, for it resulted in a quarrel with the principals of the great Cornish bank, of which his was but a branch. Somehow—he never knew by what means—they had become prejudiced against him, and a rapid depreciation of his value in Carnac resulted when it was known that he was no longer over the bank.

Then came demands upon him for amounts trusted to him to invest—a regular continuous drain; and Rhoda awoke to the fact that a change in their position, for the worse, was rapidly coming on.

She bore the knowledge as cheerfully as she could, working hard to comfort her father, bidding him not trouble about her, but to pay to the uttermost farthing every demand.

"I shall not mind being poor," she said to him, but she felt that she did not know all, and after long thought and trouble the feeling would always come upon her that she must leave all to fate, for she could not make her future even if she tried.

There was something very suggestive in John Tregenna's manner to her now. He was never, in the slightest degree, effusive. If any thing, he was rather cold, but at times there was a look in his eye that told her he was waiting his time; and more than once, in the bitterness of her spirit, she had thought of the possibility of his some day asking her again to be his wife.

What should she say if he did?

No! The answer came readily enough, for a pang shot through her as she thought of Geoffrey Trethick, and wondered whether she could forgive him for the wrong he had done. She loved him still. She knew that, and in time—perhaps even now, if he came to her in humbleness and confessed his fault—she could have said forgiving words. Her pride would have forbidden her to listen to him. There was forgiveness.

But that was all. He had been set up in the innermost niche of her heart—an idol whom she had worshipped. From thence he had fallen, and as the idol lay broken she had seen that what she thought sterling gold was but miserable potter's clay.

Still there was her love for him—the love once roused never to be completely crushed out. It burned still upon the altar before the empty niche. The idol was gone, and a soft vapour rose concealing the emptiness of the place—a place made often more dim and indistinct by her moistened eyes.

If he had only come to beg forgiveness she would not have cared, but he had taken up his stubborn stand, and to the very last time they had met his eyes looked at her with an angry defiance that made her heart beat fast with rage.

It was from no curiosity—there was not even a faint hope of meeting Geoffrey—that she took that path, but a trick of fate, and she started and turned pale, on suddenly raising her eyes, to see that she was only some fifty yards from Prawle's cottage.

Bessie was standing by the door knitting, and the blood flushed into Rhoda's cheeks as she saw what was by her side.

She saw that Bessie had seen her, and to have gone back would have looked cowardly; so she kept on, feeling pretty sure that at that time of day Geoffrey Trethick would not be there.

"I have not been to see you for a long time now, Bessie," said Rhoda, making an effort to master her emotion and look calm.

"No, miss. My mother has often said she wished you would come. Will you go in and see her?"

Rhoda hesitated.

"Father's out, miss. He has gone off in the boat with Mr Trethick, to try for pollack. We're quite alone."

At the name of Trethick, Rhoda shrank away, but setting her teeth, she determined not to give up like some weak girl. Geoffrey Trethick was nothing to her now, and, as she thought that, a passionate, angry desire to stand face to face with the woman who had robbed her of his love made her take a step towards the door.

Bessie bent down and picked up the baby, which laughed and kicked as she held it in her arms, but Rhoda snatched away her eyes. She hated it, she told herself; and, following Bessie into the gloomy room, she looked towards where Mrs Prawle was wont to sit, but the chair was empty.

"Mother is lying down in the bedroom," said Bessie. "I'll tell her you are here, miss."

As she spoke, Bessie turned aside to place the baby in a pair of extended hands before leaving the place.

Rhoda had not seen who was seated in the darkened portion of the room, but Bessie's act told her who it was, and turning sharply, her veins tingling, and her head giddy with her anger, she stood face to face with Madge Mullion, the girl she hated in a way that she could not have thought possible.

As she stood there, her fingers clenched together, the spirit was in her to strike the girl—to curse her; but, when she saw the pale, weary-looking face, and the great, staring eyes of the young mother, as she clasped her little one to her breast, all Rhoda's anger seemed to pass away as rapidly as it had come, and in its place there was a feeling of profound pity.

They stood there gazing in each other's eyes for some minutes without speaking, Rhoda proud and erect, Madge weak and piteous in the extreme; and, as if in dread of her visitor, she held her little one between them as a shield.

"Are you not ashamed to look me in the face?" said Rhoda, sternly.

"Am I not weak and suffering enough," retorted Madge, "that you say these cruel words? Oh, Miss Penwynn, let me try and explain—let me tell you how I have suffered for the pain I have caused you."

"Hold your tongue," said Rhoda, coldly. "Don't speak to me. I did not come to see you. Do not speak to me again."

As Rhoda spoke she saw the poor girl's eyelids droop, and a ghastly pallor came over her face. She was fainting, and had not the visitor involuntarily caught the little one from its mother's hands, as she fell back in the corner of the sofa, it would have dropped upon the brick floor.

The child uttered a piteous cry, and seemed to stare with astonishment at her who held it from her, stunned almost at her position. But as the babe looked up in her handsome face, the wrinkles in its little countenance departed, and it began to laugh and coo, trying to catch at one of the long curls pendent above its face.

The little one seemed to disarm her resentment. She held it closer to her, forgetful of its mother, and one of its little pinky hands went up now and clutched at her face.

She could not help it. There was no one to see, and Rhoda seemed forced to obey an uncontrollable impulse. One moment her face was hard and stern; then there was a quiver, a softening of the muscles, the tears gathered in her eyes, and began to fall upon the little upturned face.

"It at least is innocent," she muttered, as she held the little thing in her bosom, and kissed it tenderly again and again.

There was a curious, yearning look in Rhoda Penwynn's countenance during these fleeting moments. Then, recalling her position, she hastily laid the child upon the rug, looking cold, hard, and stern once more, as she took out her vinaigrette, and held it to the fainting girl's face.

"Oh, miss, is she ill?" cried Bessie, entering the room.

"Yes," said Rhoda, coldly; "she has fainted."

"Oh, miss," cried Bessie, reproachfully, "you have not been saying cruel things to her?"

"And if I have, what then?" said Rhoda sternly.

"Why, it's a shame—a cruel shame," cried Bessie, angrily. "Why did you come here to reproach her for what she has done? Don't you see how ill she is, perhaps not long for this world? Oh, Miss Penwynn, it's a shame!"

Rhoda flushed with anger, but she would not speak. She told herself that she deserved what she had encountered by her foolish visit, and, stung by the girl's reproaches, and angry with herself, she hurried out of the cottage and hastened towards home.

She was bitterly angry with herself, more angry against Geoffrey, whom, in her heart, she somewhat inconsistently accused of having caused her the degradation which she told herself she had suffered but now.

She bit her lips as she thought of her folly in going there, for she told herself that every one in Carnac would know where she had been; and hardly had she writhed beneath the sting of this thought than she encountered old Mr Paul walking slowly along the cliff.

She would have passed him with a bow, but he stopped short and held out his hand, in which she placed her own, feeling shocked to see how the old man had changed.

"The old painters were right," he said abruptly, as he retained her hand.

"Old painters? Right?" faltered Rhoda.

"Yes, yes," said the old man, "when they painted their angels in the form of a beautiful woman. God bless you, my dear, you are a good, forgiving girl! I know where you have been."

"Oh, this is horrible!" ejaculated Rhoda, as she hurried away. "I cannot bear it. What am I to suffer next?"

She would have turned out of the path, but unless she descended to the rugged beach there was no other way back home; and, as if to make her miseries culminate, she had not gone another quarter of a mile before she met Miss Pavey, with a thick veil shrouding her countenance, and a basket in her hand.

They stopped and looked at each other curiously, and as Miss Pavey raised her veil there was a red spot burning in each of her cheeks.

"Have you been for a walk, dear?" she faltered.

"Yes," said Rhoda, abruptly. "And you—are you going for a walk?"

Miss Pavey trembled, and it was evident that she was having a battle with her feelings. She was afraid to speak, and she looked supplicatingly in Rhoda's eyes, which were fixed upon her in the most uncompromising way.

For a moment a subterfuge was trembling upon her lips, but honesty conquered, and, looking more bravely in Rhoda's face, she said,—

"Yes, dear. Mr Lee wishes it!—I didn't like it at first; but he says it is a duty, and I will do it, whatever anybody else may say."

She said these last words almost passionately, as she looked defiantly at Rhoda.

"And what are you going to do, Miss Pavey?"

"No, no, dear Rhoda, let it be Martha still," pleaded the little woman.

"Well then—Martha," said Rhoda, with a smile.

"I am going to see, and take a few comforts to poor Madge Mullion," said the little woman, with an apologetic look; and then, after another effort, "I have been twice before. Where have you been, dear?"

Rhoda looked at her half scornfully, and the change that had come over her weak little friend struck her as being almost absurd, as, in a defiant way, she said sharply,—

"I? Where have I been? Where you are going now. I have been to see Madge Mullion and that man's child."

She hurried away with her hand pressed upon her heart, as the words seemed to have leaped from her lips, while she felt that if she stayed there a moment longer she would burst out into a hysterical fit of laughter; and this feeling was still upon her as she passed through the rugged streets of the little town and hastened home.

Chapter Forty Nine.

Old Prawle Wishes to Invest.

The rugged pile of rocks along by the ruins of the old mine was a favourite spot with Geoffrey in these troubled days. From hence, when he had clambered into a sheltered nook, where there was a little natural platform, he could see the track towards the town, and think of that evening when, glorified by the wonderful sunset, he had enjoyed that strange dream of love and hope. Every grey-lichened stone seemed to light up once more as he took his seat there, and reflected those wondrous tints that had for the moment coloured his life before all had turned grey and gloomy once again.

He could see, too, Wheal Carnac from where he used to sit with his back against the natural wall, looking as hard and grim as the rock itself.

There lay the unlucky mine and the stony promontory, with the surges breaking fiercely at its base, as if the tide resented its presence and was always striving to tear down a pile that had served to crush the young man's fortunes.

Time stole on, but his position remained the same; for though the vicar had urged him again and again to make some effort to clear himself, he had sternly refused.

"No," he said, "I shall wait; and if you value my acquaintance, or friendship, if you like to call it so, I beg that you will say nothing to a soul upon my behalf."

The vicar sighed, but he allowed himself to be swayed by Geoffrey, whom he feared to tell of his suspicions concerning the state of affairs at An Morlock, for he could not help seeing how rapidly John Tregenna was becoming Mr Penwynn's master, and how helplessly the banker was drifting to a bitter end.

Geoffrey's old blackened meerschaum used to be brought out, and as he leisurely smoked he used to think of all that had taken place since his first arrival in Carnac, and wonder whether he had been wanting in any way in his duties to those who had intrusted him with so important a task.

He was seated there one morning when, in the midst of the reverie in which he was indulging, he was interrupted by the sound of footsteps, and, looking up, he saw old Prawle approaching and beckoning to him in a mysterious fashion.

"What's the matter?" said Geoffrey, starting up.

"I want you," whispered the old man, though probably there was not a soul within half a mile.

"Well, what do you want?"

"Business—particular business. Come down to my place and talk."

"Why, can't you talk here?" said Geoffrey, gruffly.

"No, no. Come to my place."

Soured, disappointed, and out of humour, Geoffrey was on the point of declining; but the old man had manifested so kindly a disposition towards him of late that he followed him without another word along the cliff to the Cove, where they descended the rough stairs to the bit of a cave; where the old man, instead of producing brandy and tobacco as Geoffrey expected, took down an old ship's lantern, saw that it was well trimmed, placed some matches inside, and then placed it inside his rough jacket.

"Wait a bit," he said, "and I'll show you;" and he laughed audibly. "Look here. You carry this compass," he continued, taking one from a shelf.

"But what do you want? What are you going to do?" said Geoffrey.

"I'll tell you soon," said the old man. "I've been talking it over with my Bessie, and she says I may trust you, and that I am to do it. I haven't lived to my time for nothing."

"I'm much obliged to Miss Bessie for her trust," said Geoffrey bitterly; "but what is it? Are you going to dig up some of your old hoards of money?"

"No, no; no, no," chuckled the old fellow, grimly. "I don't bury my money. I know what I'm about. Come along."

Geoffrey followed him down the rest of the rough way to the rocky shore, where the old man's boat was lying, and between them they ran her out into the tiny harbour, formed by a few jutting pieces of rock, got in, and, after arranging some great boulders as ballast, old Prawle was about to take both sculls, when Geoffrey took one.

"Here, I'll pull as well," he said. "I want work."

"Pull then," said the old man. As soon as he had placed the lantern and compass in the stern of the boat, the oars fell with a splash, and, timing the effort exactly, they rode out on a gently-heaving wave, and then old Prawle kept the boat about fifty yards from where the waves beat on the time-worn rocks.

"Tide's just right," said the old man. "Easy. Pull steadily, my lad. There's no hurry. Hear about old Master Penwynn?"

"No. What?" said Geoffrey, sharply.

"They say things are going very bad with him, and that he'll soon be as poor as you."

"No," said Geoffrey. "I did hear that he had losses some months ago. But is this true?"

"P'r'aps not," said old Prawle, gruffly. "Tom Jennen and some of 'em were talking about it. Amos Pengelly heard it, too."

Geoffrey was silent, and his heart began to throb as he thought of Rhoda, and of how it must bitterly affect her. Only a few months ago, and it seemed as if he had secured for her the fortune of a princess; now she was to be as poor as he, and they were still estranged.

"You oughtn't to mind," said old Prawle, laughing. "Penwynn did not behave so well to you."

"Would you mind changing the conversation, Mr Prawle?" said Geoffrey, sharply, when the old man uttered a low chuckle and went on steadily rowing.

"Are we going to fish?" said Geoffrey, after they had been rowing along in the shadow of the rocks for some time.

"Yes: to fish for money, my lad," said the old fellow. "Pull steady."

Geoffrey obeyed, and after his long days of enforced idleness, during which his thoughts had seemed to eat into his mind like cankers, there was something quite refreshing in the rowing over the heaving sea, and joined to it there was a spice of excitement to know what the old man really meant.

They rowed on and on with the bright waters of the bay on one side, and the weed-hung, weather-worn granite on the other, where every wave that ran beneath them seemed to playfully dash at the rocks, to lift the long, tangled brown and olive-green weeds, toss them, and deck them with gems as if they were the tresses of some uncouth sea-monster, before dashing up the wall that checked their way, and falling back in spray.

After a time, as Geoffrey glanced over his shoulder, he caught sight of the towering chimney above Wheal Carnac, and as he snatched his gaze, as it were, away, he found that old Prawle was watching him, and he uttered a low, chuckling laugh.

"Yon's the mine," he said, looking at Geoffrey curiously, as the young man took so tremendous a tug at his oar that the boat was pulled slightly round.

"Easy, my lad; easy," said old Prawle. "Don't you like the look of the mine?"

Geoffrey did not answer, but pulled away, though with less violence; and so they rowed on till suddenly old Prawle exclaimed, as they were lying now well under the promontory,—

"You'd best give me the other oar."

Without a word Geoffrey obeyed, and watched him curiously as, after taking both sculls now, he turned the boat's head towards the rocks, and waiting his time, as he pulled gently on, he paused till a good wave came in, and then, balancing the little boat on the top, allowed it to be carried right in between a couple of masses of rock, barely wide enough apart to admit of its passing. Then, pulling one oar sharply, he turned round by another mass of rock, and Geoffrey found that they were in smooth water, floating in under a rough arch, so low that they had to bend right down in the boat for a minute; after which the ceiling rose, and he found that they were in a rugged cavern, whose light only came from the low opening through which they had passed. It was a gloomy, weird-looking place, in which the waves plashed, and sucked, and sounded hollow, echoing, and strange, each wave that came softly rolling in, carrying them forward as it passed under them, and then seemed to continue its journey into the darkness ahead.

"Mouth's covered at high water," said old Prawle, as he laid the oars in the boat.

"Then how shall we get out?" said Geoffrey, to whom the idea of being caught by the tide and drowned in such a place as this had, in spite of his troubles, no attraction.

"Same as we got in," growled old Prawle. "'Fraid?"

"No," said Geoffrey, sturdily. "I don't want to be caught though."

"I've been several times," said the old man, with a hoarse chuckle. "It scared me the first time, but I soon found there was plenty of room."

"Bit of smuggling?" said Geoffrey.

"Iss, my son," said the old man, with a laugh. "I don't believe there's a soul ever been in this zorn besides me."

"But you don't smuggle now?" said Geoffrey.

"No, not unless I want a drop of brandy or Hollands gin."

"Then why have you come here?"

"Ha, ha, ha! I'll show you," said the old man, laughing. "I haven't lived here for nothing. Wait till I've lit the lantern, and we'll see."

He took the matches, and as he struck one the roof and sides of the cave seemed to flash with metallic green, but Geoffrey saw that it was only the bright, wet moss that he had found in the adit of the old mine, and he sat there watching the old man, as he lit and closed the lantern, set it down on the thwart, and then proceeded to guide the boat forward along the narrow channel of water, over which the granite roof spread in a low arch, sometimes rising ten or twenty feet, but more often coming down as if to crush them.

They must have gone several hundred yards, and still they went on, though it grew much more narrow, till there was little more than room enough for the boat to go along, but the water seemed deep beneath her keel, and the cavern or rift still wound on.

"What have you got in here, Father Prawle?" said Geoffrey, at length, after sitting for some time watching the strange effects of light and shadow, as the old man forced the boat along by thrusting the boat-hook against the roof or sides.

"Nothing," said the old man, laconically.

"Then why have we come?"

"Wait and see."

"All right," said Geoffrey, and, leaning back, he began to think of Rhoda, and of the news he had heard, wondering the while whether she would ever be brave enough to do him justice, and frankly own that she was wrong.

Then he thought of her being poor, and, looking at it in one light, he did not feel very sorry, though he felt a kind of pang to think that she would miss so many of the old refinements of life.

"Which—*vide* self—any one can very well do without," he said, half aloud.

"What?" growled his guide.

"I was only muttering, Father Prawle. How much farther are we going?"

"Not far."

The old man forced the boat along for quite another hundred yards, and then, taking hold of the painter, he leaped upon a rock and secured the rope.

"Jump out, and bring the lamp and the compass, my lad," said the old fellow, in his rough, grim way; and on Geoffrey landing he said to the old man, sharply,—

"Is there ore in here?"

"Nothing but some poor tin," was the reply. "But look there, my lad. The boat won't go up that narrow bit, but that runs on at least a hundred fathom, for I've waded as far as that."

"What, up that narrow hole?" said Geoffrey, as he peered along a place that looked a mere crack in the rock floored with water.

"Yes, up that narrow place. Now what do you say?"

"I don't say any thing," replied Geoffrey. "Why have we come here?"

"Bah! Take your compass, lad. Which way does that bit of a cut run?"

"Nor-east by east," said Geoffrey, holding the compass flat.

"Well, suppose you drive right through that nat'ral adit, as you may call it, for thirty or forty, or p'r'aps fifty fathom, what would you hit?"

"I see your meaning now," cried Geoffrey, excitedly. "Of course, yes, we must strike one of the galleries in Wheal Carnac which run under the promontory from the other side."

"And if you do drive through, what then?" chuckled the old man.

"Why, you'll have an adit that will clear the water off as fast as it comes in."

"To be sure you will," said Prawle.

"But only to a certain level," said Geoffrey, despondently. "It is of no use, Prawle; the tin would be fathoms below."

"Damn the tin, boy," cried the old man, excitedly; and, as they stood on a narrow shelf of rock there, he gripped Geoffrey fiercely by the arm. "Look here, you, Master Trethick, no man ever did me an ill turn but what I paid him off, and no man ever did me a good turn but I paid him off."

"I never did you an ill turn," said Geoffrey.

"No," said the old man, "but you did me a good one, and I wouldn't have minded now if you'd have had my Bessie; but that's nayther here nor there. If she likes lame Amos Pengelly better o' the two, why she must have him; but you helped her when she was hard put to it, and now look here, I'm going to do you a good turn, and myself too."

"How? I tell you that your adit would be good for nothing," cried Geoffrey.

"Tchah! Look here," cried the old man, pulling a sale bill out of his pocket. "Here it all is—Wheal Carnac."

"Put the thing away; it makes me feel half-mad to see it. I tore one down," cried Geoffrey.

"You be quiet," continued the old man, holding the bill against the mossy rock, so that the light from the lantern fell upon the big letters.

"Here you are, you see—To be sold by auction, at the M, A, R, T, Mart, Token-house-yard, unless pre—vi—ously disposed of by private contract."

"Don't I tell you it half drives me mad to think of the mine being sold?"

"With all the pumping and other gear, nearly new engines, and modern machinery," read on old Prawle.

"Are you doing this to tantalise me, Prawle?" cried Geoffrey. "The whole affair will go for a song."

"To be sure," chuckled the old man. "That's what I've been waiting for, my lad—for a song, a mere song, eh?"

"It's horrible!" cried Geoffrey, despairingly, "when there's tin enough there—"

"Hang the tin, I tell you! It's grand, boy, grand. Look, Mr Trethick, go up to London and buy it."

"Buy it?" said Geoffrey.

"Yes; buy it for as little as you can get it for."

"What, to sell the machinery out of it? No, that I won't."

"Nay, nay, to work it, lad. Buy it, and you and me will make fortunes, eh?"

"I tell you that your plan's worse than useless. The ore is far below the level to which we should get the water."

"Give's your hand, Trethick," said the old man, sharply. "Will you swear that you'll play fair with me?"

"If you like," said Geoffrey.

"I'll take your word without a swear," said the old man. "Shake hands, lad."

Geoffrey carelessly gave him his hand, which the old man gripped.

"Now look here," he said, "I'll trust you, and I'll find you the money to go and buy that mine."

"But it will be throwing your money away," said Geoffrey.

"Then I'll throw it away," cried old Prawle. "I want Wheal Carnac, and I've always meant to have her. Now then, will you go and buy her for me, and work her for me afterwards on shares?"

"Yes, if you like," said Geoffrey, sadly. "We might, perhaps, hit upon something; and anyhow I don't think you will have to pay so much that you would lose."

"Go and buy her for me, then. As soon as we get back you shall go up to London and buy her for me as cheap as you can. You can go to the old lawyer I'll tell you of for the money to pay down, as much as is wanted, and then just you come back to me and I'll talk to you about what I mean to do."

"Very good," said Geoffrey, "I will; but it means a good bit of money."

"You buy it," said old Prawle; "and whatever you do, don't let it go; but buy it as cheaply as you can."

Geoffrey stood looking at the old man for a few minutes, and in those few minutes his whole connection with the mine seemed to pass in review before him; and as it did, he asked himself whether he should be doing right in letting the old man invest his money like this.

"Well," said Prawle, "what are you thinking about?"

"You," he said sharply. "Suppose, when you have spent your savings on this mine, it should turn out a dead failure?"

"Well, what then?"

"You would lose something."

"Well, I know that, don't I? Do you suppose I'm a babby? There, I've bided my time, my lad, and I know what I'm doing. Are you ready?"

"Yes," said Geoffrey.

"And you'll stick to me, my lad, when the mine's my property?"

"I will, Prawle," said Geoffrey, earnestly, as he shook off his forebodings; "and, somehow or another, I'll make it pay."

"That'll do, my lad; we understand one another, and you won't repent it. Just give one more look at your compass."

Geoffrey did so.

"Now then, you feel pretty sure you can hit the workings from here?"

"Yes, I feel certain," said Geoffrey; "and it will relieve the mine without pumping, but not so that we can get the tin."

"That'll do," said the old man, nodding. "Come along."

He led the way to the boat, and once more kneeling in her bows, he directed their way along the subterranean passage, while Geoffrey leaned back in the stern watching him, and thinking that if he had been an artist he would have desired no better suggestion for a picture of Charon ferrying some unfortunate soul across the Styx, so weird and darksome was their way, so strange and gloomy the shadows cast, till once more in the distance appeared a faint gleam of light playing upon the surface of the water. Then the low arch came into view, and soon after they were out in broad daylight once again, and rowing steadily towards the Cove.

Chapter Fifty.

Too Late.

There was no time to lose if he intended to be present at the sale, so hastily putting a few things in a bag, Geoffrey bade Madge good-by, and brought a smile in her thin, worn face as he took up the little one and kissed it, giving it a toss, and setting it off crowing and laughing before replacing it in Bessie's arms.

"Any commission for town, ladies?" he said; "ribbons, laces, or what do you say to a new hood for the squire here?"

Just then the dark face of old Prawle appeared at the door, and, reminding him of his commission, he started off at once to catch the coach.

"It's a rum world," he said, as he gazed at the smokeless chimneys of the great mine as he went on, and then, leaning more to his task, he began to picture the place busy once more, with its panting engines, and the click and rattle of the ore-reducing machinery.

"I'll show old Penwynn yet," he said to himself, "that there's money to be made out of the place. Poor old fellow, though, it will be a grievous disappointment to him, and he will feel it deeply."

He walked on with his eyes still fixed on the promontory upon which the mine was standing, and so immersed was he in thought that he almost ran up against two people before he saw them.

"I beg—"

He would have said "your pardon," but the words froze upon his lips, and he went by feeling half stunned; for the couple he had passed were Rhoda Penwynn and Tregenna, the former looking deadly pale as his eyes encountered hers for a moment, the latter calm, self-possessed, and supercilious.

Geoffrey could not trust himself to look back, but tore along the cliff path at a tremendous rate, feeling ready at any moment to break into a run, but refraining by an effort.

His journey was for the time being forgotten, and he saw nothing but the finale of a life-drama, whose last scene was a wedding, with Rhoda the wife of the man she had formerly rejected, and his heart beat heavily and fast.

He was moved more than he thought it possible under the circumstances; and in the hot rage that took possession of him he could find no palliation of Rhoda's conduct. It was evident, he said to himself, that she was engaged to John Tregenna now, and that the last faint hope that, like some tiny spark, he had kept alive was now extinct.

"Ah, Trethick! Where are you going?"

"Eh? Oh, Lee, is that you?"

"Yes; I'm glad to see you. Why don't you come down to me?"

"What, for Miss Pavey to look horrors, and want to fumigate the house, after the advent of such a social leper?" he said laughingly.

"My dear Trethick, why will you talk like this—and to me?" said the vicar, smiling. "But I am stopping you. Were you going somewhere?"

"I? No. Not I. Yes I was, though," he exclaimed. "I am going up to London. I forgot."

The vicar looked at him wonderingly, his manner was so strange.

"Oh, I'm not going out of my mind, man. It's all right," exclaimed Geoffrey, laughing. The next moment his face became ashy white, and his eyes seemed to dilate as, in the distance, he caught sight of Rhoda and Tregenna coming back into the town.

The vicar saw the direction of his gaze, followed it, and sighed, for he had seen the couple together half an hour before.

Geoffrey coloured as he saw that the vicar was evidently reading his thoughts, and he said lightly,—

"Yes, I'm off to town for a day or two, but you need not say I'm going. Good-by."

He did not pause to shake hands, but strode hastily away, secured his seat upon the coach, and that night was well on his way to Plymouth.

Try how he would, he could not shake off the recollection of his meeting with Rhoda.

It was nothing to him, he kept on assuring himself, but there was her pale face ever confronting him; and the more he strove to call her heartless, cold, and cruel, the more the recollection of their short, happy engagement came back.

He was bound now on a fresh expedition, whose aim was to secure the mine and to make money, and, with a half-laugh, he exclaimed, "What for?"

He frowned heavily the next moment, as he saw that his quick utterance had drawn the attention of a couple of his fellow-passengers; and, determining to master what he called his childish emotion, he thought of Rhoda all the more.

This went on for hours, till he felt so exasperated with what he called his weakness that he would gladly have got out of the carriage at the next station, and walked a few miles to calm himself; but this was, of course, impossible, and he sat there listening to the rattle of the train, as it seemed to make up words and sentences, which kept on repeating themselves with a most irritating effect.

Station after station was passed, and the time glided on till he found it was now half-past ten.

They were due at Bristol half an hour past midnight, and a train left there soon after, reaching London about half-past four in the morning, when, after a few hours' rest, he would be in ample time for the sale.

At the best of times a railway journey by night is trying to the nerves of the strongest; to a man in Geoffrey Trethick's state of excitement it was irritating in the extreme. He tried every position he could scheme to make himself comfortable, and have a few hours' rest, but in vain. Every attitude was wearisome and produced irksomeness, till, in utter despair, he let down the window to gaze at the murky night they were rushing through.

This produced a remonstrance from a fellow-passenger, and he drew the window up again, and tried once more to think only of the mine and of old Prawle's venture; but, as a matter of course, the thoughts of the old wrecker brought up others of his daughter and his invalid wife, when, naturally enough, the other invalid—poor Madge—followed; and then came the whole history of his connection with her family and his dismissal by Rhoda, and then—*crash!*

It was instantaneous—one moment they were going along at a rapid rate, the next there was a sharp, deafening crash; the glass flew in shivers, the strong carriage seemed to collapse like a bandbox, and they were at a standstill.

There were four passengers in the same compartment, and as soon as Geoffrey recovered from the stunning violence with which he was hurled against his opposite neighbour he roused himself to afford help. Fortunately, however, beyond a shaking, they had all escaped, and, after a struggle, they managed to get out through one of the windows on to the line.

Here all was confusion—lights were flashing, steam was hissing, and the shouts of the guards and engine-drivers were mingled with the cries and shrieks of the passengers, many of whom were imprisoned in the broken carriages, and some time elapsed before they could be set free.

It was the old story—a luggage train was being shunted and not sufficient time allowed, with the result that the fast night train had dashed at full speed into the goods trucks, and they and the brake-van formed a pile upon which the engine of the fast train seemed to have made an effort to climb; and then, defeated, the monster had fallen right over upon its side, setting fire to the trucks upon which it had dashed.

Fortunately the speed at which they had been going seemed to have saved the passengers. There were bruises and cuts without number, but no serious injury to person. The train, though, was in a state of chaos; both lines were badly blocked, and when Geoffrey could get an answer to a question, the reply was not encouraging, for he was told that at least six hours must elapse before he could go on.

The six expanded themselves into eight, and the consequence was that all Geoffrey's plans were overset. The probability now was that he would not reach town until the sale was over, and, by a strange reversal, what he had looked upon as worthless the day before, now grew into a thing of such value that he was ready to make any sacrifice to carry out his commission in its entirety.

He was in a peculiar position, for he could not telegraph to the auctioneer to appoint an agent to bid for him, for he was not able to say to what price he would go. Old Prawle had left it to him, but even then he could not say "Bid so much." Every thing must depend on what took place, and, under the circumstances, he felt that there was nothing for it but to make the best of his way there on the chance of being in time; London at last, and, without waiting a moment, he jumped into a cab, and bade the man drive to the city.

It is a long drive from Paddington to the Mart, and when he reached the place and had seen in which room the sale was to take place, he ran up to find another sale going on. Wheal Carnac had been up nearly an hour before.

After a little searching he found the auctioneer.

"Wheal Carnac was bought in, I suppose?" said Geoffrey, carelessly.

"No, sir, not this time," said the auctioneer. "That mine's an old friend here, but it has found a purchaser once more."

"Did it make much?" said Geoffrey, hoarsely.

"Went for a song. Not half the value of the machinery."

Geoffrey bit his lip.

"Who bought it?"

"Can't say, sir. Or, stop a moment. Yes, of course," he said, referring to his books. "It is a firm of solicitors. Agents for the real purchaser, I suppose."

Geoffrey obtained the name of the firm of solicitors, found it was in Serjeant's Inn, and went straight there, asked for the principal, and was shown in.

"Wheal Carnac? Oh, yes," said a little, sharp-looking grey man. "We—that is—an agent from this house purchased it;" and he looked curiously at Geoffrey.

"For a client of yours, I presume?" said Geoffrey.

"Certainly you may presume so if you like, sir," said the little lawyer.

"And possibly he would be ready to part with his purchase for a small profit over what he gave?"

"Possibly he might, my dear sir," said the lawyer; "but I don't think it is very probable."

"May I ask why?" said Geoffrey.

"No, sir," said the solicitor, smiling. "Well, there, I will admit that. Because our client—another admission you see, sir—I say because our client is a gentleman, who would not be tempted by a small profit. If you wish to buy, sir, you will have to give a handsome bonus for the purchase."

"How much?" said Geoffrey, bluntly.

"Impossible to say, my dear sir," said the solicitor. "I do not even know that our client would sell. In fact I do not believe he would. His name? Oh, no, I cannot give you his name."

Geoffrey had the name of the firm down in his pocket-book, and as he stepped out into noisy Fleet Street he felt that he could do no more. There was nothing left for him but to go back to Carnac and tell old Prawle of his ill success. Then, perhaps, the old man would say to what extent he would go, and the place might, probably, be obtained by private contract.

Geoffrey went to an hotel, had a few hours' rest and refreshment, and once more he was being hurried to the little mining town, where he arrived this time without adventure, bitter with disappointment, and seeing endless advantages in the possession of the mine now that it was gone from him forever. So enraged was he at the result of his journey that he could not bear to look at the mine as he walked towards Gwennas, but rigorously turned his eyes aside.

He had walked as far as the ruined pit when he started, for he heard his name pronounced, and, turning, there stood old Prawle, waiting to intercept him on his return.

"Now then," he said, excitedly. "How much did you have to give, my lad? Quick! How much?"

"I have not bought the mine," said Geoffrey.

"What?" cried the old man, furiously; and his weather-beaten countenance turned of a curious hue. "I told you to buy her, no matter what price."

"There was an accident to the train. The mine was sold before I got there."

"Sold!" cried the old man, with an oath. "Why didn't you walk on?"

"Two hundred miles in eight hours," said Geoffrey, grimly.

"Why didn't you write or—or send?"

"I tried all; I thought of all; I spared no pains, Father Prawle," said Geoffrey, commiserating, the old man's disappointment. "You could not have saved it had you gone yourself."

"But it was a fortune; it was a great fortune," cried the old man, stamping with rage.

"No, no," cried Geoffrey. "You might perhaps have made a little by it, or we might perhaps have hit upon some plan to get at the tin; but it was doubtful."

"You're a fool," cried the old man, furiously.

"A terrible fool," said Geoffrey, coolly.

"You don't know," stuttered old Prawle, who was beside himself with rage; "you don't know, I tell you. Not half-way down that pit I could show you veins of copper so rich that your tin you found was not worth half."

"What?" cried Geoffrey, staring at the old man to see if he were sane.

"She's full of copper, Trethick. Do you think I would have spent money unless I was sure? She's worth no end of money, and you've thrown away what would have been a great fortune for you as well as me."

"But the copper? Are you sure?" cried Geoffrey, hoarsely.

"Am I sure?" cried the old man. "Didn't I work in her for years? Of course I know."

"Then why did you not say so before?" cried Geoffrey, angrily.

"Why should I say so?" replied the old man, fiercely. "I have myself to look after. People don't come and give me money, and tell me to live out of that. They hate me, and call me ill names. No. I found the copper, and I said to myself, 'If no one else finds it, that's mine. I'll buy that mine some day;' and now, when the time has come, and we could have been rich, you let the mine go, and it is all for nothing."

"You ought to have told me about that copper, Prawle. It would have been the saving of Mr Penwynn. I could have redeemed that mine from loss, and the water might have been removed sufficient for that."

"Nay," cried the old man; "you couldn't have rid her of water without my plan, and I tell you I found the copper, and it was mine, and you have thrown it away."

Geoffrey felt too much enraged to say much, but the old man went on.

"Helped Mr Penwynn! I suppose you would: the man who threw you over. Helped his girl, who threw you over, too, and who is going to marry John Tregenna some day."

A fierce utterance was on Geoffrey's lips, but this last remark of the old man seemed to silence him; and, prostrated by weariness and misery, he went on to the cottage, threw himself on his bed, and slept for twelve hours right away.

Chapter Fifty One.

Madge Hears News.

Madge Mullion was very ill, and she seemed to Geoffrey to be going back, as he sat looking at her a few days after his return from town.

There was something about the poor girl he liked, for she was simple-hearted and loving to a degree, and he would often sit in the next room apparently busy writing, but watching her intensity of affection for her child.

"Come, Madge," he said to her, "why don't you grow strong again, and be a woman and fight the world?"

Her eyes filled with tears, and he cried out impatiently,—

"Now, look here, Madge, you are going to cry, and tell me how sorry you are for the pain you have caused me, and beg me to forgive you for what you have done; and if ever you say such a thing to me again, I shall run out of the house."

"No," she faltered, "I was not, Mr Trethick. I was going to say, why should I grow well and strong again?"

"For that!" he said abruptly, and he pointed to the sleeping child.

She glided from the sofa to the side of the cradle, and laid her face against the little cheek.

"And, look here," he said, "you are fretting yourself into the grave, Madge!"

"Yes, Mr Trethick."

"You must be a woman, and get well. That little thing must be your reason; so make a brave fight for it."

Madge shook her head, and looked at him piteously.

"No," she said, "I feel that I have not strength now, and as if the greatest kindness I could do to you, Mr Trethick, is to die."

"Nonsense?" he said, kindly. "You have done me no harm—only brought me to my senses, and saved me from an ugly fate."

"Ah! Mr Trethick," she cried, "what bitter words! You do not mean them."

"Oh, but I do, Madge," he said, laughing cynically. "Look here, my lass, I rather like you, and we are a pair of miserable unfortunates. I shall have, to marry you, Madge, and force you to like and take care of your little one. Then we shall be able to go back to the cottage, and Mamma Mullion will bless us, and Uncle Paul will make us rich, and we shall all live happily afterwards, like the good people in the story-books."

"Ah! Mr Trethick," she said, softly, "do you think I cannot read your heart better than that? My trouble seems to have made me wiser than I was in my old silly, girlish days. Why do you say such foolish, bitter things? They only give me pain, and I know you do not mean them."

"Oh," he said, laughing, "but I do."

"No, no, no," she said, sadly. "You love Rhoda Penwynn with all your heart, and always will, and I have come upon your love like some cruel blight."

"Curse Rhoda Penwynn!" he cried, savagely. "I love the woman who is to be John Tregenna's wife?"

Madge started from her knees, and took two steps across the room to catch him by the arm.

"What? What is that you said?"

"That there is no such thing as true and honest love upon the face of this wretched earth," he cried. "It is a puzzle and a muddle. For a wretched error I am thrown overhand—"

"Speak what you said before," she said, wildly; "tell me what you said."

"I said that Rhoda Penwynn is about to marry John Tregenna, or John Tregenna is about to marry Rhoda Penwynn, which you like," he said, almost brutally.

"Is—this true?" she said, hoarsely.

"Yes," he cried, with the veins standing out in his forehead, as, in spite of the calm, cynical way in which he had schooled himself to bear all this, the passion burning at his heart would have vent. "Honesty, integrity, and virtue are to have their reward; long-suffering patience is to win the day; so I say to you again, Madge, you and I had better wed."

"Go—go and leave me," said Madge, hoarsely. "Mr Trethick—I want to be alone."

Her looks brought Geoffrey back to his senses, and the ebullition of the passion was over.

"No: you are ill. Sit down there. Here, let me get you water—spirit—something, Madge. My poor girl, I have given you terrible pain by my mad words."

"Mad words? Mr Trethick," she cried, "were not those words true?"

He did not answer.

"They were true. I know they were; and yet she dared to come here and trample upon me in the midst of my wrongs."

"Who? Who came here?" cried Geoffrey.

"Rhoda Penwynn, and accused me cruelly. She to dare to speak to me as she did," cried Madge, whose face seemed quite transformed. "Half fainting as I was, I saw her take the child into her arms, and kiss and fondle it because it was his; and now she would step into my place. But, sooner than she shall be John Tregenna's wife, I'll stand between them at the altar, and—oh, God help me! what am I saying?—and I swore to him that I would die sooner than confess his shame."

She threw herself sobbing upon the floor.

"What have I said—what have I said?" she moaned.

"Only the simple truth that I was sure I knew," said Geoffrey, looking at her sadly. "Only words that it might have been kinder if you had spoken before."

"But I could not—I dared not. He made me swear. He said it would be his ruin, Mr Trethick, and he promised that even if it was a year past, if I would be silent and help him, as soon as he had arranged his money matters I should be his wife; and I never said a word until now," sobbed the wretched girl.

"And it was your ruin and mine instead, Madge," said Geoffrey, coldly. "But there, my girl, I don't accuse you. I felt sure it was so, and I have only waited for the truth to come."

"And you will never forgive me," she cried, piteously.

"Oh, yes, if my forgiveness will do you good, Madge, you have it freely. But there, I must go. I shall stifle if I stay here longer;" and, without another word, he went out and down amongst the rocks, seeming to take delight in trying to exhaust himself by hurrying over the most rugged parts to calm himself by physical exertion.

Over and over again he vowed that he would go and expose John Tregenna, but he always ended by vowing that he hated Rhoda

Penwynn now, and that he would not stir a step even to meet her half-way.

It was past mid-day when he slowly climbed up once more to the cottage, and encountered Bessie at the door nursing the child.

"Well, Bessie," he said, "you look startled. What's the news?"

"Miss Mullion, Mr Trethick!"

"Well, what of her? Not worse?"

"No, Mr Trethick; she has put on her things and gone out I think she has gone up into the town."

"Madge Mullion? Gone up to the town!"

"Yes, sir, unless—unless—oh pray—pray, sir, go and see."

Chapter Fifty Two.

John Tregenna's Visitor.

Mr Chynoweth was seated at his desk, with the heavy flap resting upon his head. The cards were dealt out in four packs, turned up so as to be beneath his eye, and it seemed as if some very particular hand was being played out; but Mr Chynoweth's thoughts were wandering, and for quite half-an-hour he did not move a card.

"Curse him!" he said; and then there was another long pause, during which Mr Chynoweth's thoughts still went on wandering.

"Hah!" he ejaculated at last; "he seems to hold all the trumps, and beats us at every game. I don't know that I like the governor, but he has always been just to me, and paid me like a man, and trusted me. Yes, he has always trusted me, and I'm growing old in his service, and I can't bear to see things going to the dogs. Yes, he holds all the trumps somehow, and he'll win the rubber."

There was another pause, during which Mr Chynoweth impatiently packed the cards, put them away, and shut down the heavy flap of his desk before taking up his slate, and sadly rubbing it with the piece of sponge attached by a string.

"Win the rubber, that's what he'll do. He's got the governor into a regular hole, and under his thumb, and it seems that he'll marry Miss Rhoda after all. Curse the mines! I wish he'd never touched them. An old fool! Hadn't he had experience enough of what comes to those who dabble in mines? It's wonderful! I shall be throwing my own poor savings down next like poor Rumsey, and—talk of the—Morning, Rumsey."

"Ah, Chynoweth!" said Dr Rumsey, entering the office with his fishing-rod in his hand, and his creel hanging from his shoulder. "Nice morning."

"Beautiful. How many trout?"

"Not a brace," said the doctor, drawing the basket round, and peering in at the hole disconsolately. "One miserable little fellow, that's all. Chynoweth, I'm regularly out of luck."

"Ah, yes," said Chynoweth; "you always do seem to hold bad hands."

"Wretched," said the doctor, with a grim smile; "and the money comes in horribly."

"Always does when you want it."

"Always," asserted the doctor, and there was another pause.

"By the way, Chynoweth," he said at last, as the clerk went on polishing his slate, "I hear that Wheal Carnac was sold in London the other day."

"Yes."

"Who bought it?"

"Don't know. We haven't heard. Deposit's paid, and all that sort of thing. That's all we know at present."

"Do you—do you think that I could get fifty pounds lent me on those shares now?" said the doctor, hesitatingly.

Chynoweth shook his head.

"But I paid down five hundred for them—my wife's money."

"My dear Rumsey," said Chynoweth, "you couldn't raise fifty shillings upon them."

The doctor raised the lid of his basket now, and gazed in at the unfortunate trout.

"It's very hard," he said, as if addressing the fish. "My expenses are so large."

"Ten times mine," said Chynoweth, "I dessay."

"Do you—do you think Mr Penwynn would make me an advance, Chynoweth? I'll deposit the shares with him."

"Spades and aces, no!" cried Chynoweth. "The very name of Wheal Carnac would send him into a passion. I'll ask him to make you an advance, Rumsey—that I will," he continued, busily writing away upon his slate.

"Yes, do please."

"No," said Chynoweth, rubbing it all off again with the sponge. "It's of no use. He hasn't the money."

"Hasn't the money?"

"No; it's hard times with us now, Rumsey, I can tell you, and where it's all gone I can't tell."

"But I'm really in distress," said the doctor. "There are several bills I must pay. I can't put them off."

Chynoweth looked at him, then at the slate, hesitated, thought, wrote "I O U fifty pounds" upon it, and rubbed it out, and ended by laying it down.

"Are you very hard up, Rumsey?" he said.

"I never was so pushed before," said the doctor, dolefully. "Hang it, Chynoweth, I feel sometimes as if it is of no use to keep struggling on. It was bad enough before that scoundrel Trethick deluded me into buying those shares."

"I don't think Trethick is a scoundrel," said Chynoweth, quietly.

"You don't?"

"No; I believe he is as honest as the day."

"Indeed?" said the doctor, in what was meant as a sarcastic tone. "Nice honesty. Let alone my case, look at Madge Mullion."

"Ah, poor lass, he hasn't behaved very well to her. That's what I think. But look here, Rumsey, I've won a few pounds of you in my time."

"Have you? Well yes, I suppose you have, Chynoweth. You always seemed to make more of a study of whist than I did."

"Eh? Yes. Think so?" said Chynoweth, glancing at his desk-lid to see that it was close. "But look here, Rumsey, it's of no use to ask the governor for money now."

"But I must. What am I to do?"

"Well, look here, I'll lend you fifty pounds."

"You—you, Chynoweth?"

"Yes," said the little man, quietly; and, without noticing the excited, overcome look of his visitor, he methodically wrote put an I O U, and placed it before him to sign.

"This—this is more than I expected of you, Chynoweth," said the doctor, huskily.

"Well, do you know, Rumsey, it's more than I expected of myself. But there you are," he continued, taking notes to the amount from his pocket-book, "and pay me back a little at a time."

"If I live I will," said the doctor; and, hastily catching up the money, he hurried away to conceal his emotion.

"Poor old Rumsey!" muttered Chynoweth. "He's a good fellow, and some of these days, I dessay, I shall have to be in his hands. Oh, you're here again, are you?"

"Mr Penwynn in his room, Chynoweth?" said Tregenna, entering unceremoniously, and going towards the door of the banker's sanctum.

"No, sir; not come yet," said the clerk, rising.

"All right, I'll wait. I want to write a letter or two."

He walked in and shut the door, while Chynoweth resumed his place.

"Nice state of affairs," he muttered. "Who's master here now?"

John Tregenna evidently, for he made no scruple about taking Mr Penwynn's seat at his table, and writing letter after letter, ringing twice for Chynoweth to answer some question, and then going on with his work, over which he had been very intent for quite an hour, when there was a tap at the door.

"Come in. Well, Chynoweth, Mr Penwynn arrived?"

"No, sir. Here's a lady, sir, wants to see you. She says she has been up to your house, and they said you were here."

"A lady? Is it Miss Penwynn?"

"No," said a voice which made Tregenna sink back in his chair; "it is not Miss Penwynn;" and Madge Mullion, closely veiled, and looking tall in the thick cloak she wore, walked straight into the room.

Chynoweth hesitated for a moment, and then softly withdrew, nodding his head.

"So the devil is going to get his due, eh?" he said to himself. "I'd give something if I could go down to listening at key-holes, but I can't do it—I can't do it—I can't do it!" and he went back to his desk.

"You here, Miss Mullion?" exclaimed Tregenna, making an effort to recover his composure.

"Yes, I am here," she said, very sternly; and Tregenna noticed that it seemed to be no longer the weak, vain, flattery-loving girl who was speaking, but a woman made worldly and strong by trouble.

"And what can I do for you, Miss Mullion?" he said, coolly. "Will you take a seat?"

She stood gazing at him without speaking—without moving, while his dark, handsome face grew calmer and more composed.

"I came—to ask you—a question," she said at last, in measured tones; and, as she spoke, she pressed one hand upon her breast, as if to aid her in speaking coolly.

"Certainly," he said politely; "but this is not my office, Miss Mullion, and I have no right to transact legal business here."

As he spoke he took a sheet of foolscap paper, and a fresh dip of ink, as if to make notes of her business.

"I came to ask you, John Tregenna," she said at last, in answer to his inquiring look, "whether the report that I have heard is true."

"Report? True?" he said. "Really, Miss Mullion—"

"I have heard," she continued, speaking in a slow, painful way, every word sounding harsh and metallic, while her face was fixed and stony in its immobility—"I have heard a report that you are—to be married—to Rhoda Penwynn."

"Well, really, Miss Mullion," he said, smiling, "this is a strange question;" and he looked at her with an amused, perfectly unruffled expression.

"Is it true?" she said, in a louder voice, which Tregenna knew must reach the outer office.

"Well, really—it is somewhat strange that you should come and ask me such a question, Miss Mullion; but, since you have asked it—yes, I am."

Madge raised her veil as he made this avowal, but it seemed to give her no shock; there was no trace of emotion in her face, as she gazed straight in his eyes.

"And what of me?" she said at last.

"I beg your pardon?"

"What of your child?" she said, in the same harsh ringing voice.

"Really, Miss Mullion, my poor girl," he said, rising, "I fear you are ill."

"Ill!" she said sharply; "very ill, but not so ill but that I can come to you now and ask for reparation for my wrongs."

"Ask me, Miss Mullion? Poor soul!" he muttered; "she takes me for Trethick."

Madge heard his words, and if any spark of love or passion remained for him in her breast, those words crushed it out. The weak girl had indeed become a woman now—a woman and a mother; and if John

Tregenna, in a fit of remorse, had asked her then to be his wife, she would have refused, and gone on bearing the burthen of her shame.

"You pitiful, contemptible snake!" she said, speaking now in a low voice that thrilled him through and through. "I am mad, am I, John Tregenna? No, not now. I was mad to listen to and trust you—mad to believe that you would keep your word—mad, if you will, to take upon my poor weak shoulders the sin that was yours more than mine."

"Miss Mullion!" exclaimed Tregenna, rising. "I must put an end to this painful interview;" and he laid his hand upon the bell.

"Do you wish Mr Chynoweth to hear what I am saying to you—what I intend to say to Rhoda Penwynn to-night when she returns from Truro—what I should have said to her to-day, after I had left you, had she been at home? If so, ring."

Tregenna showed the first sign of weakness; his hand dropped from the bell, and he started as he heard poor Madge's bitter laugh, realising more fully now than ever that the enemy in his path, instead of being a weak, helpless girl, had grown into a dangerous woman.

He had made a false step in his defence; but it was too late to retreat, and he kept boldly on.

"My poor girl," he said kindly, "it would be affectation to pretend that I did not know your troubles, but pray be calm. Let me send some one with you home."

"You pitiful coward!" she said again, and there was an intensity of scorn in her words that thrilled him through; "do you think if I had known you as I know you now that I would have kept your wretched secret?"

"Miss Mullion—"

"Have let insult, misery, and injury fall upon others' heads, till I have been heart-broken over their sorrows, and yet in faith to you I would not speak. But it is over now. Mr Trethick knows the truth. To-night Rhoda Penwynn will know the truth. I came to you now more in sorrow than anger, believing that when you saw me, even if the report was true, that the sight of my poor thin face, and what you could read there of my sufferings, would move you to some show of pity for your miserable victim; but instead—Oh, God of heaven!" she exclaimed passionately, "how could I ever love this man?"

"Is any thing the matter, sir?" said Mr Chynoweth, opening the door. "Did you call?"

"No. Yes, Mr Chynoweth," exclaimed Tregenna, excitedly. "This poor girl. She ought not to be away from home alone. I don't think,"—(he touched his forehead).

"That I am in my senses, Mr Chynoweth," said Madge sharply, as she drew down her veil; "but I am. John Tregenna, I shall keep my word."

She went slowly out of the inner room and across the office, Chynoweth hastening after her to open the door, John Tregenna coming close behind, as if to see that Madge did not speak again; but she went away without a word.

"Poor creature!" exclaimed Tregenna. "I suppose I must not heed a word she said. Of course you did not hear, Mr Chynoweth?"

"No, sir, not a word hardly; only when she spoke very loud."

"Ah, poor thing, her brain is touched, no doubt," he said, as he returned to the inner room, where his countenance seemed to change in a way that, had she seen it, would have made Madge Mullion shrink from him in dread, and, perhaps, hesitate in her intention to go up and see Rhoda Penwynn some time that night.

Chapter Fifty Three.

By the Solemn Shore.

Geoffrey started off along the cliff with a strange feeling of dread in his breast, and as he hurried along it was with his eyes gazing down upon the shore, so that he passed without seeing that some one was seated on one of the blocks of stone by the old mine shaft, enjoying the sunshine and gazing apparently sadly out to sea.

He noted the two descending paths that were connected in his mind with poor Madge's attempt to commit self-destruction, and hesitated as to whether he should descend; but he decided upon going on straight, first, to the town, and as he strode on he could not help sighing as he glanced at the buildings about Wheal Carnac.

"I wonder who bought it," he said; and for a moment or two he mused upon old Prawle's sulky indifference now that his *coup* had failed, and wondered whether it would be of any use to try for a post with the new proprietors.

"A nice character mine to go with," he muttered. "Poor Madge! Where can she be? Has she gone up to Tregenna?"

The more he thought of this the stronger the idea became, and with a curious feeling of hope, that he vainly tried to crush down, rising in his breast, he went quickly on, to utter an ejaculation the next moment, for there was Madge walking towards him along the cliff.

"Why, Madge!" he exclaimed. "You quite frightened me. Where have you been?"

"Don't touch me—don't speak to me, Mr Trethick," she said, in a sharp, harsh voice.

"But I shall speak to you, and I shall touch you," said Geoffrey, with a quiet firmness. "There, let your arm rest there. Hang on to me as much as you like: you are weak and excited, and ready to faint. There, let's walk steadily back. Don't hurry. Take off your veil, and let the sea-breeze blow upon your face; it will revive you."

"Oh—oh—oh!" came softly as a whisper from beneath that veil, as Geoffrey's words seemed to change the spirit that was burning in the poor girl's breast; and, weakly and helplessly enough now, she hung upon his arm, and suffered him to lead her onward towards the Cove.

At the end of a few hundred yards they drew near the opening in the huge cliff where the ruined engine-house and mining shaft were, and here they came suddenly upon old Mr Paul, sitting upon a block of stone, with his hands resting upon the head of his great cane.

The old man looked more himself, and there was a grim air of satisfaction in his face as he saw the couple approaching.

Geoffrey felt his companion give a spasmodic start, and she stopped short as if her legs had failed her, uttering at the same moment a low moan, as she saw her uncle rise from his seat and come towards them, looking first at one and then at the other. Then he just nodded his head at them gravely, and walked on in the opposite direction.

Geoffrey gave an impatient stamp with his foot as he turned and saw the old man disappear.

"Poor old boy!" he said. "There's something about him I like, Madge, and I'm bursting with eloquence now—full of things I want to say to him, but hang me if I could speak when he was here."

"Take me home," said Madge, softly; "I mean to the Cove."

Geoffrey saw she was weak and half fainting, so he hurried her along as fast as she could bear the effort until he had reached the descent to the cottage, where he had to lift her in his arms and carry her down the rest of the way.

In the afternoon, though, she revived rapidly, and Geoffrey noticed that she seemed none the worse for her unwonted effort, but rather, on the contrary, better and more energetic than she had been for months. He, however, bade Bessie to watch over her, and above all things not to let her go out again.

But Geoffrey's thoughts were sent into a new channel in the course of the afternoon by a visit from Amos Pengelly, who came to him as he was walking up and down upon the cliff, thinking now of Rhoda, and whether the time had not come for him to leave Carnac; now of the mine, and whether, as a man, it was not his duty to try and find the new purchaser, and make known his knowledge.

"I might get a good post upon the strength of what I know," he said to himself; "and that would be just like me—to climb up and succeed upon another man's misfortunes. No: I'll keep to my old way. The ship may drift: she cannot come to worse wreck than she is in now. Hallo, Pengelly."

"How do, Master Trethick, sir?" said Amos; "I've brought you this."

"This?" said Geoffrey, taking a letter from the miner's hand, and turning it over to find that it was on old-fashioned paper, doubled in the old style, and sealed with a great patch of wax and a crest.

"Why, it's from old Mr Paul," he said, as he glanced at the crabbed characters.

"Yes, sir; he asked me to bring it down and wait."

Geoffrey opened the missive, and found it very short, but he read in it the effect that that day's meeting had had upon the old man. It was as follows:—

> Dear Sir,—Will you come up and see me this evening? I want to ask a favour of you once more. What I have seen to-day makes me hope that you can now meet me in a better spirit. Yours faithfully, Thomas Paul.
>
> PS. If you are in the spirit that I hope you feel, bring poor Madge.
>
> Geoffrey Trethick, Esq.

"Geoffrey Trethick, Esquire! Ha, ha, ha! Poor old fellow! Esquire! A broken-down mining adventurer in a smuggler's cottage. No, Master Paul, I am not in the spirit you mean, and it is of no use for us to meet and quarrel again."

"Will you write an answer, sir?" said Pengelly, after watching Trethick for some minutes, as he read and re-read the letter, and then walked up and down talking to himself.

"Yes—no—yes—no. Wait a few moments, Pengelly. I have not yet made up my mind. Tell him—tell Mr Paul—yes, tell him that I will come up and see him this evening. I will not write."

Pengelly nodded, and moved towards the cottage to get a sight of Bessie.

"Have you heard, sir, who has bought the mine?" he asked.

"No, Pengelly. I have been trying, but they keep it very quiet. You have heard nothing, I suppose?"

"Not a word, sir," said Pengelly, with a sigh; and he went on into the cottage.

"Papa-in-law elect does not seem to give him so much of his confidence as he does me. However, just as he likes. Now what am I to say to the old man?"

He walked up and down thinking for a few minutes, and then decided that the time had come for him to speak out frankly all that he knew, and to refer them to Madge for the rest.

"Poor lass! I'll speak up well for her sufferings. She has done wrong, but look at her. Poor lass! How a man can be such a scoundrel, and leave a poor weak girl to fight out her difficulties alone, is more than I can understand; and what Nature is about to allow it. Here's poor Madge dying of consumption, and scouted as an outcast for her wrong, and the scoundrel who shared her sin—bah, no! who made her sin—is in high feather, and about to be rewarded for his goodness with a beautiful and loving wife—

"Oh!" he ejaculated, grinding his teeth; "if I think about it, I shall go mad;" and he set off down to the rough shore, where, in a reckless way, he set about wrenching over great blocks of the granite, telling himself he was looking for curious sea-anemones and star-fish, when it was to weary himself out by his tremendous exertion, and dull the aching misery of his thoughts.

It was quite evening when he returned to the cottage, and sat and chatted with poor Mrs Prawle for a time, before following the old wrecker down to his den below the cliff, and stopping with him to smoke a pipe.

The old fellow was more sociable than usual, and chatted about the mine and the chance they had lost, but in quite a friendly spirit.

"It wur a bad job, my lad, but I'm not so sore now. I've got enough for me, I dare say, but I'd liked to have seen ye doing a bit better."

"Oh, I dare say my time will come, Master Prawle," said Geoffrey, lightly. "But I must go now."

"Go? Where are you going? It's a gashly dark night."

"Only as far as old Mr Paul's. Madge's uncle wants to see me."

"Oh, ay," said the old fellow, nodding. "Well, my lad, I hope good will come of it. Don't keep too stiff an upper lip."

Geoffrey looked at him sharply, and was about to speak, but he checked himself and started off.

"Why, where are you going?" said the old man.

"Down along by the shore," replied Geoffrey.

"You'll find it rough work."

"So much the better. Tame me down, so that I sha'n't fly out if I have such things said to me as you have just indulged in."

As he said this he went on down to the rough granite-strewn shore, and began to thread his way amongst the blocks towards Carnac; but at the end of half an hour, it had grown so much darker, the effort was so great, and the difficulty of getting along had become so much more apparent, that he gave up, and made his way towards the cliff, so as to reach the road at last by the pathway on the Carnac side of the old adit, faint and completely overcome by his exertions by the time he reached the familiar path down which he had run to save poor Madge.

If Geoffrey had stopped at the cottage he would have seen that instead of quietly taking to her work, Madge was dressing herself to go out. This she seemed to be doing secretly, listening from time to time to make out whether Bessie was noting her actions, which plainly indicated an attempt to steal away unseen.

She was deadly pale, and evidently greatly agitated, but she dressed herself with much care, bestowing unwonted pains upon her hair; and at last, quite ready, she stood there listening and waiting for her opportunity.

This did not come for some little time, but at last Bessie was busy helping her mother to bed, and the baby was lying there fast asleep in its cradle.

There was no one to see her now, and, gliding out, Madge softly raised the latch of the door, and left it ajar, before returning to the cradle, throwing herself upon her knees, and clasping her little one to her throbbing heart.

"My darling!" she moaned.

But Geoffrey saw nothing of this, or he might have compelled her to stay, and not tempt the danger of a walk along the cliff path on such a night. He was, however, playing no watcher's part, and there was no one to see the hurried figure that almost ran out of the cottage at Gwennas Cove, with a long cloak huddled round it, so as to cover the sleeping babe as well.

The night had grown darker, but the pathway was perfectly familiar to her, as it had been from childhood; and, thinking more of her mission than of the child she held so carefully wrapped, she hurried on, gazing straight before her, so as to avoid slip or fall over some awkward mass of rock.

So deeply intent was the girl upon her mission that she did not see the figure of a man standing against the cliff face, just by the opening by the ruined mine; and, as she reached the spot, she was so taken by surprise that the cry that rose to her lips was checked on the instant by a fold of her own cloak.

It was a matter of moments. There was a feeble struggle, a hoarse, smothered cry, a violent thrust, and in the darkness the cloaked figure was seen to stagger back—totter—and then her assailant seemed to throw himself upon his knees, and rest there, panting and listening, till from far below there came up a hollow, reverberating plash as of some heavy body falling into the depths of the deserted mine. Then twice over there was a hoarse cry, and then a curious sound of splashing which rose in a horribly distinct fashion upon the black night air.

Then all was still.

Chapter Fifty Four.

John Tregenna's Triumph.

The man rose softly then from his hands and knees, rubbing the former to get rid of the dirt that might be clinging there, and then taking out a white handkerchief to brush his knees—a needless operation, for the turf was short and dry, and left no marks.

Then, panting heavily, though his exertions had been slight, he stood listening again, not daring to go nearer to the edge of the shaft.

All was perfectly quiet, and, with a sigh of relief, he crept back to the pathway and listened.

All was still here too, but he could not flee yet without going back and searching about to see if there was any thing dropped—handkerchief, cloak, or the like.

But no; all was apparently as it should be, and he could find no trace; so once more going cautiously to the footpath, he listened, and, all being still, he walked swiftly in the direction of Carnac, till, reaching the path down to the shore, he turned down it quickly, and came in contact with Geoffrey Trethick.

"Hallo!" exclaimed the latter, sharply, "do you want to knock a man off the cliff? Oh, it's you, Mr Tregenna!"

Tregenna did not answer, but, trembling in every limb, pressed on to reach the shore; but before he had gone many yards a malicious spirit seemed to tempt Geoffrey, and he called after the retreating figure,—

"If you are going to see Miss Mullion, Mr Tregenna, you will find the upper path the better."

"Damn!" muttered Tregenna, as he almost staggered now down the cliff; "what cursed fate sent him here to-night?"

He was so completely unnerved by the encounter, that he paused for a few minutes to try and recover himself.

"If I could—if I could," he muttered; "but he is too strong. My God! what shall I do?"

The horror of discovery was so great that for a time he could not proceed, and in imagination he saw the body of his victim brought to the surface, and Geoffrey Trethick bearing witness of having seen him near the spot.

By degrees, though, he grew calmer, as he felt there was very little chance of poor Madge's body ever being found, the old shaft being many hundred feet deep. Besides, there was nothing to make people think she had been thrown down there. Even if she were found, was it not far more probable that she had committed suicide, especially as she had attempted it once before?

"I'll not go," he muttered. "Better to face it out. Bah! there is nothing to face."

He stopped and lit a cigar, the necessity for concealment having gone. Geoffrey had spoiled that portion of his plan, namely, to reach the other side of the town unseen. On the contrary, he felt now disposed to court observation, and walked on smoking along the rugged shore to the slope by the harbour, up which he passed, exchanging greetings with Tom Jennen and one or two men who were leaning over the rail that protected the edge of the cliff.

"It's gashly dark night, sir. Bad walking down there, bain't it?"

"Well, yes, it is rough," said Tregenna, "but it does for a change."

"Hah!" he ejaculated, taking a long breath, as he walked slowly up towards An Morlock; "it is hard work, but I dare say I can manage to keep cool."

But he could not, for once more a sensation as of panic seized upon him, and something seemed to urge him to fly for his life before it was too late. For he recalled Madge's visit to him, and Chynoweth's knowledge of that visit, and what she had said.

On all sides black threatening shadows of impending danger seemed to rise about him, and it was only by a savage wrench that he tore himself from the spot, and went on to his own house, where he washed, and carefully brushed his clothes, after taking a goodly glass of brandy.

This last gave him the nerve he had lost, and, feeling calmer, he went out once more into the cool night air.

Here he lit a fresh cigar, and at last, perfectly calm and unruffled, he went up the drive to the great house, gazing about him with a satisfied air, as if he claimed the place now as his own, and, nodding to the servant who admitted him, he took off hat and gloves, crossed the handsome hall, and stepped into the well-lit drawing-room.

Rhoda was speaking angrily as the door closed behind him, and she did not hear his entry. It was evidently her final remark after much that had gone before, and John Tregenna stood there paralysed, as the words fell from her lips.

"I'll not believe it," she cried. "Mr Trethick must have sent you here. What proof have you that Mr Tregenna is the wicked man you say?"

"His own looks," said Madge, as she stood there with flashing eyes and ashy face, seeming to the wretched man like some avenging spirit pointing at him with white and quivering hand. "Ask him, if you will, though you can read the truth there. Now, Miss Penwynn, can you marry such a man as this?"

Rhoda made no answer, for John Tregenna's brain had reeled. He had made two or three attempts to master, his craven dread, but in vain. Not an hour ago he had cast, as he believed, Madge Mullion down that hideous chasm in the earth, had heard her dying shrieks; and then, gloating over his release from one who would have blasted all his plans, he had come straight on to An Morlock, to find her standing pointing at him with denouncing finger, and telling Rhoda Penwynn of his guilt.

He had striven, fought like a drowning man, but in vain; and, after clutching at a table to save himself, he fell with a heavy crash upon the floor.

Chapter Fifty Five.

Sisters in the Flesh.

Madge kissed her child passionately again and again before replacing it in the cradle. Then she rose to steal to the door, but she could not go without running back to her helpless infant, which seemed somehow that night to draw her to its side.

It was as if she felt a presentiment that she was bidding it good-by forever, and, taking it to her breast once more, she rocked herself to and fro, sobbing over it silently, as she listened to the voices in the next room.

"He told Bessie not to let me go out again, I'm sure," she thought to herself; and, feeling that if she meant to go she must go at once, she unwillingly laid down the child after a passionate embrace, and went softly out into the dark night.

She was very weak, and panted with the exertion as she reached the top of the ascent, but here she felt the sea-breeze, and, glancing round for a few moments as she tried to regain her breath, she noted one or two things that pointed to the coming of a storm before many hours had passed. The lights on the point across the bay loomed up so that they were plainly to be seen, and her sea-side life made her read tokens of the tempest in the direction and sound of the wind.

She set off with the intention of going straight along the cliff path to the town, and then up to An Morlock, where she would see and tell Rhoda Penwynn all; but she had not gone far before a horrible feeling of dread began to oppress her. She recalled Tregenna's looks when he had heard her threat, and she felt now as certain as if she saw him before her that he would try and stop her.

"And if he does meet me?"

She stopped, shivering. Her blood seemed to run cold, and a nameless horror crept over her as she thought of what might be the consequences.

The chill of horror increased, for she dreaded that he would kill her, and now she felt that she would like to live.

Geoffrey Trethick had told her that she should live for the sake of her little one, and for its sake she would forget the world and its bitter ways. She had something indeed to live for now, and she blessed Geoffrey in her heart for awakening her to that fact.

Inspired by this idea, then, she went on cautiously, and with a step as light as that of some bird; but she saw nothing to cause her fear, and began to think that the darkness would befriend her, and hide her from the sight of any watcher who would stop her on her way.

She had already passed the rough path down to the shore, the one up which Geoffrey Trethick had carried her on that terrible night, at the recollection of which she shuddered, and still there was no sign of danger; when suddenly she stopped short, for ahead of her in the darkness there came, plainly heard, the impatient hiss that one might make by a hasty drawing-in of the breath.

She knew the sound. She had heard it more than once, when he had been waiting for her down by Wheal Carnac when it was in ruins, and now he was waiting for her again by this ruined pit—for what?

For a moment her heart beat wildly, and her imagination told her that, perhaps, after all, he had come in love to ask her forgiveness, and to take her once more to his breast.

Then the tumultuous beating gradually grew calmer and then nearly stopped, as a chill of horror seized upon her. It was not in love that he had come, but in hate; and trembling, and with her brow wet with terror, she crept softly back, reached the path, and descended its dangerous steep to the shore, crept cautiously along and by the mouth of the old adit, hardly daring to pass it, lest the sound of her step should go up to where Tregenna was watching for her a couple of hundred yards away, and ended by reaching the other path down which she had frantically run to cast herself into the sea, glided softly up it, reaching the regular cliff way again; and then, but always with the dread upon her that Tregenna was in pursuit, she hurried onwards towards Carnac churchtown.

The poor girl shivered as she passed the lane leading up to the cottage, and there was a longing, yearning look in her eyes as she turned them in that direction; but she kept steadily on till she reached the gate at An Morlock, where, after a little hesitation on the part of the servant, she was admitted, and at length shown into the drawing-room, where Rhoda stood, cold and stern, silently regarding her, and with her eyes seeming to do all the questioning part.

For a time they stood gazing at each other, till Rhoda, from her proud position of vantage, began to feel that there was strength in the standing-place of her erring sister—the strength that comes from being hedged round by weakness; and, after a few minutes' silence, there was that in Madge's large eyes and pallid face that quite disarmed her. The stern, harsh manner passed away, and she placed a chair for her visitor.

"Will you sit down?" she said softly.

Those few gently-uttered words affected Madge strangely. She took a couple of steps forward, and then in an instant she was at Rhoda's feet clinging to the skirt of her dress, and sobbing as if her heart would break. So violent was her agitation that Rhoda grew at length alarmed, and had serious thoughts of summoning assistance; but, on trying to move to the bell, she found Madge clinging to her tightly.

"No, no," sobbed Madge, "don't leave me—don't go away till you have heard all, and tried to forgive me. Oh, Miss Penwynn, why do you hate me? Why do you think such evil of me as you do?"

"I think evil of you?" said Rhoda, with a touch of scorn in her voice that she could not repress. "Madge Mullion, you had passed out of my thoughts."

"It is false," cried Madge, looking up sharply. "You think of me every day, and hate me because you think I came between you and your lover."

"Have you come here to insult me—to tell me this?" cried Rhoda, trying to release her skirt.

"To tell you, not to insult you," said Madge, clinging the more tightly as she felt Rhoda's efforts to get free. "It is I who ought to reproach you, who are blind and mistaken; it is you who have come between me and mine."

"Will you loose my dress?" panted Rhoda, growing excited now; "will you leave me?"

"Not till I have told you all," cried Madge. "Miss Penwynn, I don't think I have long to live. I could not tell you a lie."

"It was mad and foolish to let you be admitted," cried Rhoda, angrily. "You wicked girl, I thought you had come to me for help, and I would not send you empty away, but you insult me for my forbearance."

"No," said Madge, hoarsely. "I came to help you, not to ask for help. I feel free to speak now, and I tell you, Rhoda Penwynn, that you have cast away the truest man who ever saw the light."

"You wicked girl! Go: leave me," panted Rhoda. "I will not listen;" but she struggled less hard.

"You shall listen for his sake, if I die in saying it," panted Madge, as she twisted the stout silk more tightly in her hands, "Mr Trethick never said word of love to me. He never looked even lovingly in my eyes, though, in my pique, I tried to make him, for he loved you too well."

"It is false—he sends you here to insult me," panted Rhoda, "and to plead for him. I will have you turned from the house."

"It is true," cried Madge; "and you turn from this true, honest gentleman, whose clear, transparent heart you might read at a glance."

"This is unbearable," cried Rhoda, bending down and catching at Madge's hands, to try and tear them from her dress.

"You may beat me and fight as hard as you like," cried Madge. "I am weak and helpless; but I can cling to you till you have heard, and you shall hear all."

"I will not—I can not hear it; it is too late," cried Rhoda, ceasing to drag at Madge's hands, and once more trying to leave the room.

But, though she struggled hard, she found that she only drew Madge over upon her face, and that the poor creature clung to her more tightly than ever.

"It is too late; I can not—I will not hear you;" and she stood with her fingers thrust into her ears.

Madge turned her face up to her sidewise, and a sad smile trembled about her thin, pale lips as she said softly,—

"You must hear me—you cannot help hearing me; and it is not too late. I tell you that you threw aside that true-hearted gentleman, who is all that is manly and good, and now you have stepped into my place, to take to your heart my betrayer, the father of my poor, helpless babe."

Rhoda's hands dropped to her sides. She had heard every word, and, unable to resist the desire to know more, she went down upon her knees, caught Madge by the shoulders and gazed fiercely in her eyes.

"This is not true," she cried. "Wicked, false woman, you have come to blacken Mr Tregenna's character to me."

"Blacken his character!" cried Madge, half scornfully. "You have lived here all your life, and know all that I knew before I weakly listened to his lying words, thinking that I was so different from others who had gone before. Tell me, Rhoda Penwynn, would what I say make his character much blacker than it is?"

Rhoda groaned, and her hands left Madge's shoulders to clasp each other, while she raised herself once more erect, to stand with her broad forehead knotted and wrinkled by her thoughts.

"And yet you listen to him—you consent to be his wife," continued Madge. "Oh, Miss Penwynn, if not for my sake, for your own, don't let me leave you to-night feeling that my journey has been in vain."

"It is not true," cried Rhoda, rousing herself once more, and speaking with stubborn determination not to believe the words she heard, and fighting hard against her heart, which was appealing so hard for the man she really loved. "Get up. Leave this house."

Madge stood up now angrily, and faced her.

"Yes," she said, "I'll go, but you have heard the truth; and I'll come between you at the church, and claim him, for he swore that I, and I only, should be his wife."

"I'll not believe it," cried Rhoda, passionately. "Oh, would to God I could!" she moaned.

"You do believe it," continued Madge.

"No, no; I'll not believe it," cried Rhoda. "Mr Trethick must have sent you here."

The next minute she was gazing down at John Tregenna's ghastly face, as he lay where he had fallen, while Madge was looking at him cold, stern, and unmoved.

"Do you believe me now?" said Madge.

Rhoda did not answer, but stared in a horrified way from one to the other, as Mr Penwynn and a couple of the servants came hurrying in; and when they had succeeded in reviving the fallen man, Madge had quietly left the house.

"Let me go home," said Tregenna, hoarsely, as his eyes wandered round the room in a curiously wild manner. Mr Penwynn spoke to him, but he only shuddered and shook his head, repeating his request so earnestly that he was assisted home, and Dr Rumsey passed the rest of the night by his side.

Chapter Fifty Six.

Geoffrey's Boast.

"Well, Mr Paul," said Geoffrey, speaking in his bluff, frank way; "I said I would never come back to this house till you sent for me, and I have kept my word."

"Yes, yes," cried the old man, shaking his hand warmly. "I have sent few you—God bless you, boy. I am glad to see you here again."

"Good heavens!" ejaculated Geoffrey, for poor Mrs Mullion had thrown her arms round his neck, kissed him, and laid her head upon his shoulder, sobbing as if her heart would break. "Mrs Mullion," he continued, putting his arm round her and patting her shoulder, "come, come, come, be a woman, and let's talk and see if we can't put this unhappy affair all right."

"Yes, yes," she sobbed, raising her face and clinging to him still; "I always liked you, Geoffrey Trethick, and you will—you will try. You have been so good to my poor darling in other ways. We have known every thing, though we have kept away. Mr Paul here said it would be a lesson for you both, but I've gone down on my knees every night, Geoffrey, and prayed for you both, and that your heart might be softened; and now, my boy, have pity on her poor mother, who prays to you for justice to her weak, erring child—who prays to you on her bended knees."

"No, no, no, my poor soul," said Geoffrey, kindly, as he held her up. "There, there, don't kneel to me. Come, sit down," he cried, kissing her pleasant, motherly face; and the tears stood in his eyes as he spoke. "Come, Uncle Paul, let us try if we cannot see daylight out through this miserable fog."

"Yes, yes," said the old man, who was standing with his head bent. "Yes, yes," he continued, heartily; "sit down—sit down, my boy. We will have no more passion. It shall all be calm and quiet. Come, Geoffrey, you'll smoke one of the old cheroots with me again?"

He smiled in the young man's face as he took out his case.

"Indeed, I will," cried Geoffrey, catching the old man's hand and retaining it. "Why, Uncle Paul—old fellow, this is like the good old times."

They sat there hand clasped in hand for some moments, and then the elder shook Geoffrey's softly and let it go.

"Come," he said, "light up. I want to talk to you."

"Yes, let us light up," said Geoffrey. "Mrs Mullion, may we smoke before you? I don't want you to go away."

"Oh, no, I will not go," said the poor woman, tenderly, as she hastened to hand them each a light.

Then they smoked for a few minutes in silence, Mrs Mullion at a sign from the old man bringing out his handsome silver spirit-stand and glasses, with hot water and sugar.

"Come, Geoffrey, my boy," cried Uncle Paul; "mix for yourself, and let's drink to the happy future."

"Yes," said Geoffrey, "we will; but, Uncle Paul, Mrs Mullion, let me say a few words first. I had a father who gave me all my early education—all that was not given by my tender, gentle mother. My father in his lessons to me taught me what his true, sterling character had been through life. 'Jeff, my boy,' he has said to me a thousand times, 'when once you have put your hand to a task, keep to it till you have mastered it.'"

"Yes, yes, you learned your lesson well," said the old man, nodding his head approvingly, for Geoffrey had laid his cigar on the edge of the table, where it burned slowly beneath its pearly ash, and had paused, as if waiting for him to speak.

"Another thing my father said, too, as many times perhaps, Mr Paul, was this: 'Come rich, Jeff, come poor, strive to be a gentleman through life, and never let it be said of you that you told a lie.'"

"Good, yes—good advice, Geoffrey Trethick," said the old man, smiling. "If I had had a son, I would have said the same."

"Then, look here, Mr Paul," cried Geoffrey, excitedly, as he rose up and towered in his manly strength above the little old yellow nabob. "I tell you this: I never knowingly yet told a lie, and, God helping me, I never will!"

There was a strange silence in that room as the young man's distinct, loud voice ceased for a few moments, and mother and uncle sat eagerly waiting for his next utterances.

"Now that I have said that," continued Geoffrey, "let me look you both in the face, and tell you that you have done me a cruel wrong."

"A cruel wrong?" began the old man, hotly.

"Yes," continued Geoffrey, "a cruel wrong. Poor Madge has spoken out at last; and so will I."

"This is a cruel—"

"Wrong, Mr Paul," said Geoffrey, smiling, and laying his hand upon the old man's shoulder. "Uncle Paul, I like you,—I always have liked you; but you were unjust to me when you asked me to bear John Tregenna's sin."

The old man started back from him, his neck over the back of his chair, his withered throat stretched, and his lips parted, as he stared up in Geoffrey's face. Then, as the whole truth seemed to come home to him, he caught at Geoffrey's hand, and, trembling, and in broken accents, began to plead for pardon.

"My poor boy—my brave boy—my poor boy!" was all, though, that he could stammer; and, in his abject misery, he tried to struggle from his chair upon his knees: but, as soon as Geoffrey realised the truth, he smilingly held the old man in his place.

"No, no, Uncle Paul," he said. "Stand up, old fellow, and give me your hand, like the true, chivalrous old gentleman you are, and let us understand each other once and for all. Come, you forgive me now?"

"Forgive you?" faltered the old man. "My boy, can you forgive me?"

"Your hand too, Mrs Mullion. Do you doubt my word?"

"Oh, no, no!" sobbed the poor woman, sadly, for matters had not turned out as she wished, and her tears were falling fast, when Geoffrey exclaimed sharply, and held out his hand,—

"There is some one listening! Quick; there is something wrong."

He ran to the door, and as he flung it open there was a hasty step upon the gravel, and then a heavy fall.

The next moment he was raising the insensible form of poor Madge from the path, for she had been unable to resist the temptation to steal up and have one more glance at the old home before returning to Gwennas, but her strength was exhausted now; and when, after being carried into the house and laid upon the sofa, Mrs Mullion threw herself sobbing upon her knees beside her child, Geoffrey placed his hand upon the old man's shoulder, and pointed to the pair.

"Is she to stay, Uncle Paul?" he said, softly.

"God forgive her as I do, my boy," the old man replied, in a broken voice. "I need ask for pardon as well as she."

Geoffrey hesitated about leaving, but, on looking into the room again, he saw mother and child clasped in each other's arms, and he stole softly away to where Uncle Paul stood in the doorway.

"Come," said Geoffrey. "I must have another cheroot, Uncle Paul, and then for home."

"Home?" said the old man, gently; "will you not come here once more?"

"Yes—no—yes—no; I cannot say to-night, but whether I do or no, old fellow, the good old days shall come again for us. Why, Uncle Paul," he cried, puffing away at his fresh cheroot which he had lit from that in the old man's lips, and laying his hands upon his shoulders, "if it were not too late we'd go into the summer-house and have another row. Hallo! who's this?"

For hasty steps were heard coming up towards the gate, and a hoarse voice cried,—

"Trethick—Master Trethick! Pengelly said Master Trethick had come up here."

"Prawle," cried Geoffrey. "You here! Why, what's wrong?"

"Murder's what's wrong," cried the old man, hoarsely. "Quick, man, quick! You come along o' me."

Chapter Fifty Seven.

A Struggle for Life and Death.

Bessie was rather longer than usual with her mother that night, but at last the invalid was comfortably settled, and when she went back into the sitting-room the child was just beginning to be restless.

"Will you come and stay with him a minute, Madge?" she said. "I'll be back directly;" but there was no answer.

"Madge! Madge!"

Bessie felt frightened. She could not tell why, but, with a feeling that something was wrong, she ran to Madge's room, but only to find it empty, and her hat and cloak gone.

"And Mr Trethick told me not to let her go again!"

Bessie felt more troubled than she could express, and, recalling Madge's strange and excited ways, she felt now sure that there was something wrong.

"I might overtake her if she has gone along the cliff," she said to herself; and, without hesitation, she threw on her cloak and hat, and had gone to the door ready to run up to the cliff, when the little one began to remonstrate loudly about being left alone.

For the moment Bessie thought of calling up her father from his den down below, but as quickly she thought that if any desperate idea was in poor Madge's brain, the sight or touch of her child might act upon her more strongly than words; so, catching up the little one, she curled it up tightly in the cloak she wore, and started off, meeting John Tregenna, and in her surprise, and the suddenness of the attack, being hurled back helpless towards the brink of the old shaft, down which the next instant she was falling.

Even in the horror of those awful seconds, she clutched her burthen tightly, and, with her thoughts coming fast, and seeming to lengthen out the time, she felt herself falling—falling, as she had often dreamed of going down in some terrible nightmare.

Twice over she brushed against the side, and she knew that she had turned completely over in her descent. Then there was the shock of her plunge into the deep black water, and all seemed to be over.

She had some recollection of having shrieked, but it was faint. What she did realise the most distinctly was her plunge into the cold water, and then going down half stunned for some considerable time before she began to struggle wildly, and rose to the surface.

All was black around her, but she could for the moment breathe, and beat about with her hands, which touched the wall of rugged granite; and trying to cling to and thrust her fingers into its irregularities, she kept herself up for a few moments, during which the frantic feeling of fear which had mastered her seemed to die away; but the next minute her fingers had slipped from their frail hold, and she had again gone under.

She rose again directly, for Bessie was a stout swimmer and had been from a child; and as she struck out, panting and gasping, she swam now to the other side, and then, striking out with one hand, she kept beating the other against the wall of rock that formed the sides of the square shaft, and sent up a despairing cry for help.

Poor girl, she might have cried the night through and been unheard. She knew it, too, as she felt herself growing fainter, her clothes crippling her limbs as they clung to them, and in another few moments she knew that she would be exhausted.

"It is murder," she moaned. "Help, help!"

She had already swum along three sides of the shaft, when, as she reached the fourth, her hand and arm passed in, and she uttered a cry of joy, striking out vigorously, and finding herself swimming in an opening for a few strokes, when she struck again against the rock, and the chill of the horror of impending death once more came upon her. After a few more vain struggles, she clung to the slimy rocks, feeling herself sink, and that life, now dearer than she could have believed, was ebbing away. But as she felt this her limbs rested upon the bottom of the opening into which she had swum, and she knew now that she was in the adit or passage that carried off the water from the old pit, when it reached a certain height.

It was some minutes before she could subdue the trembling that shook her limbs, and summon courage enough to move, lest in that hideous darkness she should go the wrong way, and sink back into the deep water; but, as she grew more collected, she felt that if she crawled onward she would be right; and so it proved, for, dragging herself on to the rock, she was the next minute on the rough floor of the adit, kneeling in an inch or two of water; and here, sinking lower, she covered her face with her hands, thrust back her streaming hair, and burst into a passion of hysterical sobbing, as she prayed that she might be saved from this horrible death.

She was mad almost with terror for the time, but by degrees she grew calmer, and, putting out her hands, she touched the walls on either side, and just above her head.

"I know where I am," she said aloud, "only I'm frightened and confused, and—Oh, God of heaven, Madge's child!"

Her hands went down to her breast as if expecting to find it clinging there, and then, chilled once more with horror, she remained there in the horrible darkness, afraid to move, as she tried to realise whether the little thing had fallen with her.

She put her hands to her throat again.

The cloak was gone—it had broken away at the fastening in her frantic struggles for life.

She hesitated, but as she did so, she seemed to see the pale, white figure of Madge rising up before her, and saying to her, "Give me my child;" and, rousing herself to her terrible task, she slowly crept back into the water—in the shallow part within the adit—and waded step by step back three or four yards till, feeling cautiously with one foot before her, she found that she had reached the brink; another step, and she would be once more over the deep water, where it went down hundreds of feet into the bowels of the earth.

She dared not swim out, but, holding by the rugged wall of the adit, she thrust out her hand along the surface, feeling as far as she could reach again and again, here and there, but there was nothing; and she crossed to the other side, held on, and tried again, feeling giddy as she did so, and as if she dared do no more lest she should step back into that horrible pit.

Then her heart gave a wild throb, for her right hand touched something—her cloak, and she drew it softly towards her, backing more and more into the adit, as she gathered the cloth into her hands, and uttered a cry of joy.

The babe was there, twisted in the folds of the great cloak which had floated with it, holding within its saturated cloth plenty of air to keep the little thing upon the surface.

With the water streaming from her, Bessie crept on to the rocky floor of the adit, and, panting and sobbing hysterically, she hastened to unwind the clinging covering from the helpless babe; but, in the darkness and confusion, it was some minutes before she got it free and held it to her dripping breast, kissing it, holding it to her lips to feel whether it breathed, forgetting her own terrible position as her thoughts all went to her little charge, and calling it by the most endearing names.

There was no response, no fretful cry, no shriek of pain or suffering; the little thing lay inert in her arms, and in her agony, as a fresh horror burst upon her, Bessie spoke to it angrily, and shook it.

"Cry!" she exclaimed. "Oh, if it would only cry! Baby, baby! Oh, heaven help me! it is dead—it is dead!"

She held it tightly to her breast for a moment or two as she knelt there, rocking herself to and fro. Then a thought struck her, and, changing her attitude to a sitting position, she held the little thing in her lap, wrung out the cloak as well as she could, and wrapped the child in it once more to try and give some warmth to its little fast-chilling limbs. As she did so, Bessie felt how dearly she had grown to love the little helpless thing whose mother's illness had made it so dependent upon her.

"Oh, what shall I do—what shall I do?" she sobbed at last. "Will no one help me? Mr Trethick! Father! Help!"

"I might as well cry to the sea," she moaned at last, as she held the baby more tightly to her breast. "Now let me try and think, or I shall go mad."

She remained perfectly motionless, with her teeth set fast, for a few minutes, beating down the horror that threatened for the time to wreck her reason.

"I can think now," she said. "He threw me down the old shaft, and I got into the adit, where I'm kneeling. If I try, how can I get out?"

She thought again, but she was so confused by her fall that it was some time before she could realise the fact that she might creep through this old passage hewn in the rock, and, if not stopped by a fall from the roof, come out upon the shore.

"But the winzes!" she said, with a shudder. "The winzes!"

It was well for her that, as a miner's daughter, she called to mind the fact that, in all probability, the passage in which she knelt would have another parallel to it, some twenty or thirty feet below, and connected with it by one or two perpendicular well-like openings in the floor, openings which, like the passage below, would, of course, be filled with water.

Knowing that there were such dangers in her path, she at last started, creeping along on her knees, and, with one hand, feeling the way.

It was no such great distance, but, under the circumstances, it was painful in the extreme. Still her spirits rose as she went on, for at the end of five minutes there came to her the peculiar sound of the waves dashing upon the shore; and creeping onward, with her burthen clasped to her breast, and her head at times striking against the roof, she began to be hopeful that her worst troubles were to be the mud, and slime, and water through which she crept; when, all at once, the cautiously extended hand which guided her way, feeling ceiling, wall, and floor, went down into deep water, and she knew that she was on the brink of a pit, full to the brim, and this had to be crossed.

Bessie's knowledge came to her aid, and, laying the baby tenderly down, she brought both hands to bear, feeling cautiously about to determine the width of the winze.

If it were across the adit it would be narrow, and she hoped to be able to step over; if it were cut in the other direction there might be a rocky shelf at the side giving sufficient room for her to pass.

It was cut across the adit, for she could feel the square edge of the rock from wall to wall; and rising and feeling about over it for a prominence in the wall by which she could hold on, she grasped it tightly, placed her right foot close to the edge, and leaned forward, trying with her left to reach the other side.

Yes, she was successful. They are economical of labour in digging through solid rock, and she found that the winze was but a yard across, so, drawing herself back, she caught up her burthen, hesitating for a moment, as she felt that a false step would plunge them both into the well-like opening. Then, bending low, she made as bold a stride as she could, crossed in safety, and once more resumed her cautious progress, till the sea-breeze fanned her cheek as she crept out amongst the rocks, and, falling upon her knees, she once more sobbed and prayed aloud.

Rousing herself, though, to a sense of her responsibility, she rose and hurried along the rugged shore beneath the cliff to the sloping path down which Madge had come some time before; and, climbing to the cliff path, she gave one frightened, unnerved look in the direction of the opening leading to the old shaft, and then ran painfully towards the cottage.

But Bessie's strength was gone. Her run soon became a walk, her walk a tottering crawl, and it was with blanched face she at last staggered into the cottage, where her father was now seated, keeping up a blazing fire with wreck-wood to save the candle.

"Why, Bess, my lass!" he said.

"Oh, father, help!" she cried, in a hoarse, piteous voice, as she threw herself upon her knees by the fire to try and restore life to the little clay-clad form she held.

"Wet—drenched!" he cried. "In the sea?"

"No, father," she moaned. "Quick—the doctor. Mr Trethick. He threw me down the old pit-shaft."

"Trethick did?" roared the old man.

"No, John Tregenna; and he has killed his child."

"As I will him," roared the old wrecker, raising his fists to heaven. "So help me God?"

Chapter Fifty Eight.

A Strong Man's Weakness.

"Here, speak out," cried Geoffrey excitedly, as he hurried with old Prawle down towards the cliff. "What is it? What do you mean?" and as the old man hurriedly recited all he knew, Geoffrey felt his breath come thick and fast.

As they reached the cliff they came upon Dr Rumsey, who had been summoned by old Prawle before he had gone up to Mrs Mullion's to find Geoffrey; and, after a distant salutation, the doctor began to question Geoffrey, but without avail. Then they went on in silence to find Bessie, with her wet dishevelled hair and clinging garments, still kneeling before the fire with Madge's baby in her arms.

She looked up in a pitiful way towards Dr Rumsey as he entered, and rose stiffly and laid her little burthen upon the couch.

"A candle, quick!" cried the doctor; and Geoffrey lit one and placed it in the eager hands, to look on afterwards, in company with old Prawle, who stood there, with his hands deep in his pockets, scowling heavily at the scene.

Dr Rumsey's examination was short and decisive.

"I can do nothing," he said quietly. "Poor little thing, it has been dead some time."

Bessie burst into a low sobbing wail, and crouched, there upon the floor; but she raised her face again with a wild stare as she heard Geoffrey speak.

"But try, doctor; for heaven's sake try," he cried.

"I know my business, Mr Trethick," said the doctor coldly. "The child was not drowned. Place your hand here. Its head must have struck the rock. It was dead before it reached the water."

Geoffrey Trethick—strong, stern, trouble-hardened man—bent down as he heard these words, and placed his firm white hand upon the dead child's head, realising fully the doctor's words. Then, raising the little corpse tenderly in his arms, he stood looking down in the white, placid face, the doctor and old Prawle watching him with curious eyes.

"My poor little man," he said, in a hoarse whisper. "My poor little man! Oh, baby, baby, I couldn't have loved you better if you had been my own!"

As he spoke he raised the little thing higher and higher, and kissed its little lips and then its cold, white forehead, and the two men heard a sob start from his breast, and saw the great tears rolling softly down.

"Oh, Rumsey!" he groaned, "I'm afraid I'm a poor weak fool."

He laid the little thing reverently upon the couch, and the doctor looked at him curiously, till he was recalled to himself by old Prawle's hand laid upon his shoulder.

"See to her, doctor, she wants you badly;" and it was true, for Bessie had sunk back with her head against the couch.

"Where is Miss Mullion?" said the doctor. "I want some help."

"At home, doctor, as bad as your patient there. You must be nurse and doctor too."

Without a word old Prawle took a couple of strides across the room, and, lifting Bessie as if she had been a babe, he carried her into Madge's chamber and laid her upon the bed. The motion revived her, though, and, after a few words of advice, the doctor went off homeward, and Geoffrey and old Prawle walked up and down the cliff, the father going in at intervals to see that Bess was sleeping comfortably, and listening at her door.

"Not to-night," the old man muttered; "not to-night. I can't go and leave my poor lass there, perhaps to die. It'll keep a bit—it'll keep a bit;" and he rejoined Geoffrey.

The next morning at daybreak they took a lantern and explored the adit, the old man pointing out the traces of Bessie's trailing garments, and here and there a spot or two of blood upon the rock.

They crossed the winze, and Geoffrey wondered how a woman could have attempted it in the dark; and at last they stood in a stooping position at the end, looking at the black surface of the water in the old shaft, upon which was floating Bessie's hat and the child's hood.

They could not reach them, so they returned, old Prawle saying, in a curiously harsh voice,—

"She didn't tell a lie, Master Trethick, eh?"

"A lie?" exclaimed Geoffrey. "It is too horrible almost to believe."

"Horrible? Yes. Now let's go and look at the pit mouth."

Geoffrey followed him, feeling as if it were all part of some terrible dream, and wondering what effect it would have upon Madge.

"Why, Prawle," he exclaimed, stopping short, "that villain must have thought he was throwing in mother and child."

"Ay, I dessay," said the old man. "No doubt, but it makes no difference to me. He threw down my Bess, and that's enough for me. Come on."

There was little to see on the turf by the old shaft after they had climbed the cliff; but, as Geoffrey went close to the mouth and looked down into the black void, he turned away with a shudder, wondering how any one could have been hurled down there in the darkness of the night, and yet have lived to see another day.

"Come away, Prawle," he said hoarsely. "What have you got there?"

"Button off a man's coat," he said shortly. "Less than that's been enough to send any one to the gallows. But I don't want to send him."

"No," said Geoffrey; "the horror of what what he has done—the murder of his own child—will stay with him to his grave."

"If he ever has one," muttered Prawle.

Geoffrey looked at him searchingly, but the old man's face was as inscrutable as that of a sphinx; and, leading the way back, he went down into his favourite place by the boat below the face of the cliff, and as soon as Geoffrey had made a hasty breakfast, which he found Bessie had prepared, he went off to the cottage to see Mrs Mullion, and tell her of the events of the past night.

Chapter Fifty Nine.

Jonah.

The threatening storm was giving abundant promise that it would soon visit Carnac; and warned by its harbingers, the various red-sailed luggers were making fast for the little port. Several had made the shelter behind the arm of masonry which curved out from the shore, and one of the last to run in was the boat owned by Tom Jennen and three more.

They had just lowered the last sail, and, empty and disappointed, they were about to make a line fast to one of the posts, when John Tregenna ran quickly down to where Tom Jennen stood upon the stone pier, rope in hand.

"Stop," he cried.

"What's the matter?" growled Jennen.

"I want you to take me across to—"

He whispered the rest.

"Storm coming. There'll be a gashly sea on directly, master. Pay out more o' that line, will you?" he bellowed. "Don't you see she's foul o' the anchor?"

"Ten pounds if you'll put off directly, and take me," said Tregenna, glancing uneasily back.

"Wouldn't go for twenty," growled Jennen.

"Thirty, then, if you'll put off at once."

"Hear this, mates?" growled Jennen.

"No—er."

"Here's Master Tregenna says he'll give us thirty poun' if we'll take him across to—"

"Hush!" cried Tregenna. "Yes, I'll give you thirty pounds, my men."

"There'll be quite a big storm directly," said another of the men. "Thirty poun's a lot o' money, but life's more."

"Fifty, then. Here, fifty!" cried Tregenna, desperately. "Fifty pounds, if you start at once."

He took the crisp, rustling bank-notes from his pocket-book, and held them out, and it was too much for the men. They glanced at one another, and then their decision was made.

"Here, hand it over, and jump in," cried Tom Jennen; and, thrusting the notes into his pocket, he pointed to the boat, and no sooner had Tregenna leaped in than, shortening his hold of the line, he began to pull, while his mates handled their hitchers to set the lugger free.

Another minute, and Tom Jennen had leaped aboard, and they were hauling up one of the sails, which began to flap and fill. Then one of them ran to the tiller, the lugger gathered way, and rode round to the end of the pier, rising to the summit of a good-sized wave, and gliding down the other side, as a little mob of people came running down the pier, shouting to them to stop.

"Take no notice. Go on," cried Tregenna, excitedly.

"Why, what's the matter?" said Tom Jennen, who, like his companions, was in profound ignorance of the events that had taken place while they were away.

"Keep on, and get out to sea," cried Tregenna, fiercely. "I have paid you to take me, and you have the money."

"Stop that boat," roared old Prawle, who was now shouting and raving at the end of the pier. "Come back—come back."

"Don't listen to the old madman," cried Tregenna. "Haul up the other sail."

"We know how to manage our boat," said Jennen, sulkily; but he seized the rope, one of the others followed his example, and the second sail rose, caught the wind, and the lugger lay over and began to surge through the wares.

"Stop that boat! Murder!" shouted old Prawle, gesticulating furiously, while those who were with him waved their hands and shouted as well.

"Why, there's old Master Vorlea, the constable," said one of the men; "and he seems to have gone off his head, too. What's the matter ashore, Master Tregenna?"

"Matter? I don't know," cried Tregenna, hoarsely. "Keep on, and get me to Plymouth as quickly as you can."

"We'll try," said Tom Jennen; "but with this gashly storm a-coming on we'll never get out of the bay to-day."

"But you must," cried Tregenna, excitedly. "A man does not pay fifty pounds unless his business is urgent."

"Or he wants to get away," said Tom Jennen, surlily, as he looked back at the pier, now getting indistinct in the haze formed by the spray.

For the sea was rising fast, and as the fishers, who had made fast their boats within the harbour, joined the crowd staring after the lugger that had just put off, they shook their heads, and wondered what could have tempted Tom Jennen and his mates to go.

They were not long in learning that old Prawle had been after John Tregenna, charging him with the murder of the child, and the attempt to kill her he supposed to be its mother; but Tregenna seemed to have been seized by a horror of encountering Prawle, and he had fled as if for his life, while, with all the pertinacity of a bloodhound, the old man had tried to hunt him down, following him from place to place, where he sought for refuge, till, with the dread increasing in force, the guilty man had fled to the harbour, and, as the coach would not leave again till the next day, he had bribed the crew of the lugger to take him within reach of the railway.

As Prawle saw the boat get beyond his reach, he looked round for one to go in pursuit; and he turned to hurry back home, with the intent of putting off in his own, but as he did so his eyes swept the horizon, his life of experience told him what would follow, and he sat down upon one of the mooring posts with a low, hoarse laugh.

"Does Tom Jennen think he's going to get out of the bay to-day?" he said.

"He'll have hard work," shouted the man nearest to him.

"Hard work? He'll be running for home ere two hours are gone, if his boat don't sink, for they've got Jonah on board yonder, and the sea's a-rising fast."

Chapter Sixty.

The Lugger Ashore.

By this time half the town was out to watch the lugger in which John Tregenna was trying to make his escape, and, the story of his wrong-doing having passed from lip to lip, the crowd upon the harbour wall and the cliff began rapidly to increase.

Geoffrey heard of what had taken place, and hurried down to the cliff, and old Prawle was pointed out to him seated upon the pier, where the sea was already beginning to beat furiously as the wind rapidly gathered force.

"Why, Prawle," he cried, when he had hurried down to his side, "what have you been doing?"

"Doing, lad? Trying to do to him as he did to me and mine. He's got away," cried the old man, hoarsely; "but I'll have him yet."

"Yes, but you must leave him to the law," cried Geoffrey. "Come: walk home with me. You must not take this into your own hands."

"Come home!" said the old man, with a fierce look in his eye. "Yes, when I have seen him drown, for it will come to that before many hours are past."

Finding him immovable, Geoffrey stayed by the old man's side till they were driven back to the head of the harbour by the waves that now dashed right over the wall where they had been standing but a few minutes before; and from thence Prawle, after some three hours' watching, climbed to the cliff, where he leaned over the iron rail and gazed out to sea through his hands, held telescope fashion.

"She's labouring hard," he said, with a grim chuckle, "and they've taken in all sail they can. Look yonder, Trethick: see. There, I told you so. Tom Jennen's give it up, and he'll run for the harbour now."

Geoffrey strained his eyes to try and make out what the old man had described; but he could only dimly see the two-masted vessel far out in the hazy spray, and that she was tossing up and down, for the sea was rising still, and the wind rapidly increasing to almost hurricane force.

Old Prawle was right, as the excitement upon the cliff showed, for, after hours of brave effort, the crew of the lugger had proved the hopelessness of their task, and were now running for home.

What had been a long and weary fight in the teeth of the wind resolved itself into quite a short run, with scarcely any sail hoisted, and the great white-topped waves seeming to chase the buoyant lugger as she raced for shelter from the storm.

The fishermen stood watching her through the haze, and shook their heads as they glanced down at the harbour, where the rocks were now bare, now covered by the huge waves that thundered amidst them, tossing the great boulders over and over as if they had been pebbles, and leaving them to rumble back with a noise like thunder, but only to be cast up again. All the eastern side of the bay was now a sheet of white foam, which the wind caught up and sent flying inland like yeast; and so fierce was the wind now in its more furious gusts, that posts, corners, rocks, and the lee of boats were sought by the watchers as shelter from the cutting blast.

Old Prawle seemed to mind the furious gale no more than the softest breeze, and at length he descended the cliff slope towards where the waves came tumbling in a hundred yards or so beyond the end of the huge wall of masonry that formed the harbour; and as he saw the sturdy fishermen taking the same direction, with coils of rope over their shoulders, Geoffrey needed no telling that the lugger would come ashore there, for, if expected to make the harbour, the men would have made no such preparations as these.

As they went down along the rugged slope Geoffrey touched the old man on the shoulder, and pointed to the harbour.

"No," shouted old Prawle, in his ear; "she can't do it, nor yet with three times her crew."

The crowd had rapidly increased, for it was known now that Tom Jennen's "boot" must be wrecked, and quite a hundred men had gathered on the shore ready to lend a hand to save. No vessel could have lived in the chaos of foam between them and the lugger unless it were the lifeboat, and that was seven miles away, while the lugger was now not as many hundred yards.

Through the dim haze Geoffrey could make out the figures of the men on board when the lugger rose to the top of some wave, but for the most part they were hidden from his sight; and as he stood there, drenched with the spray, he shuddered as he thought of the fate of these, now so full of vigour, if their seamanship should really prove unavailing to guide them into a place of safety.

"Is there danger, Trethick?" said a voice at his ear; and, turning, there stood the Reverend Edward Lee, his white face bedewed with the spray, and his glasses in his hand, as he wiped off the thick film of salt water.

"I fear so. Poor fellows!" was the reply.

"Is it true that that unhappy man is on board?"

Geoffrey nodded, and their eyes met for a few moments.

"God forgive him!" said the vicar, softly. "Trethick, can we do any thing to save his life?"

As he spoke, Geoffrey for answer pointed to one of the huge green rollers that now came sweeping in, curled over, and broke with a roar like thunder upon the rocky beach.

"Nothing but stand ready with a rope," was the reply; and then the two young men stood watching the lugger till one of the fishermen came up with a great oilskin coat.

"Put it on, sir," he roared to the vicar. "It'll keep some of it off."

The vicar was about to refuse, but his good feeling prompted him to accept the offer, and a few minutes later another came up and offered one to Geoffrey, who shook his head, and, in place of taking it, stripped off his coat and moved farther down to meet the waves.

The vicar followed him quickly, for the crucial time had come. As far as those ashore could make out, the crew of the lugger had hoisted their fore-sail a few feet higher, and, as they raced in, there was just a chance that she might obey her rudder and swing round into shelter; but it was the faintest of chances, and so it proved.

On she came, light as a duck; and, as she neared the shore, she seemed almost to leap from wave to wave, till at last, when she came in, riding as it were upon one huge green wall of water, nearer and nearer, with the speed almost of a race-horse.

"Now—now—now, Tom!" rose in chorus, heard for a moment above the wind; and, as if in obedience to the call, the head of the lugger was seen to curve round, and in another minute she would have been in shelter, when, as if fearful of missing their prey, the waves leaped at her, deluging her with water; she was swept on and on towards where the crowd had gathered; and then there was a shriek as the lugger was seen to be lifted and dashed down upon the rocks—once, twice—and there was something dark, like broken timbers, churning about among the yeasty foam. The boat was in a hundred pieces tossing here and there.

For a few moments the fishermen ashore stood motionless, and then a man was seen to run out, rope in hand, into the white foam towards something dark, catch at it, and those ashore gave a steady haul, and one of the crew was brought in, amidst a roar of cheers, to where Geoffrey and the vicar stood.

Again there was a dark speck seen amongst the floating planks, and another man dashed in with a rope, and a second member of the little crew was dragged ashore.

Again another, who was stoutly swimming for his life, was fetched in; and almost at the same moment Geoffrey saw something that made his blood course fiercely through his veins.

"I can't help it," he muttered; "villain as he is, I cannot stand and see him drown."

There was no momentary hesitation; but, drawing a long breath, he dashed into the foam that seethed and rushed up the shore, for his quick eye had detected a hand thrust out from the surf for a moment, and his brave effort was successful, for he caught the sleeve of one of the drowning men. Then they were swept in for a time but sucked back; and but for the aid lent by one of the fishermen with a rope, it would have gone hard with them, though, in the excitement, Geoffrey hardly realised the fact till he found himself standing in the midst of a knot of fishermen and the vicar clinging to his hand, but only for the clergyman to be roughly thrust aside by Tom Jennen, for it was he whom Geoffrey had saved; and the rough fellow got hold of his hand and squeezed it as in a vice.

"Where's Mr Tregenna?" cried Geoffrey, hoarsely, as soon as he could get breath, for he had caught sight of the rough, dark figure of old Prawle running to and fro in the shallow white water where the waves broke up.

"Hasn't he come ashore?" said Tom Jennen, with his face close to Geoffrey's.

The latter shook his head and looked inquiringly at the rough fisherman; but Tom Jennen staggered away to sit down, utterly exhausted by his struggle.

Planks, a mast with the dark cinnamon sail twisted round it, the lugger's rudder, a cask or two, a heap of tangled net, a sweep broken in half, and some rope—bit by bit the fragments of the brave little fisher-vessel came ashore, or were dragged out by one or other of the men; but though a dozen stood ready, rope in hand, to dash in amongst the foam and try to rescue a struggling swimmer, John Tregenna's hand was never seen stretched out for help, nor his ghastly face looking wildly towards the shore. And at last, as the fragments of the lugger were gathered together in a heap, the crowd melted away, to follow where the half-drowned fishermen had been half-carried to their homes, and Geoffrey gladly accepted the hospitality offered to him by Edward Lee.

Tom Jennen had fared the worst, for he had been dashed once against a part of the lugger, and his ribs were crushed; but he seemed patient and ready to answer the questions of a visitor who came to him after he had seen the doctor leave.

"Were he aboard, Tom Jennen, when you tried to make the harbour?"

"Aboard? Who? Tregenna?"

"Ay."

"Of course."

"And he was with you when you struck?"

"Holding on by the side, and screeching for help like a frightened woman," said Jennen.

"And where do you think he'd be now?" said the other.

"Drowned and dead, for he hadn't the spirit to fight for his life," said Jennen, "and I wish I'd never seen his face."

"I'd like to have seen it once more," said Tom Jennen's visitor, grimly. "Just once more;" and he nodded and left the cottage.

"I don't feel as if I ought to face my Bess till I've seen him once again," he muttered, as he went on along the cliff path; "but I don't know—I don't know. He was too slippery for me at the last;" and old Prawle went slowly and thoughtfully homeward to the Cove.

Chapter Sixty One.

After Many Days.

"She's better, Trethick, much better," said Uncle Paul. "Poor child! I thought it was going to be a case of madness. But sit down, man, I've just got a fresh batch of the old cheroots."

Geoffrey seated himself in the summer-house opposite to the old gentleman, with the soft sea-breeze blowing in at the open window; and for a time they smoked in silence.

"Mrs Mullion is going away, Trethick," said the old man at last.

"Going away?"

"Yes; it will be better for Madge. Let them go somewhere to a distance. The poor girl wants change, and she'll never be happy here."

"No," said Geoffrey, "I suppose not. Then you go with them?"

"I? No, my lad, I seem to be so used to this house that I don't want to make a change. I can't live much longer, Trethick, and I thought, perhaps, you would come back to the old place. There'll be plenty of room for both of us, and we can smoke and quarrel in the old style."

Geoffrey shook his head.

"I should like it," he said; "but it won't do, Uncle Paul. My career's over here in Carnac, and I ought to have been off long enough ago, instead of idling away my time, and growing rusty."

"Only you feel that you can't leave the place, eh?"

Geoffrey frowned, and half turned away his head.

"Well," said the old man, "Rhoda Penwynn is a fine girl, and full of purpose and spirit. There, sit down, man, sit down," he cried, putting his cane across the door to prevent Geoffrey's exit. "Can't you bear to hear a few words of truth?"

Geoffrey looked at him angrily, but he resumed his place.

"I shouldn't have thought much of her if she hadn't thrown you over as she did, my lad."

"Where was her faith?" cried Geoffrey.

"Ah, that's sentiment, my lad, and not plain common-sense. Every thing looked black against you."

"Black? Yes; and whose lips ought to have whitened my character?"

"Ah! it was an unlucky affair, Geoffrey, my boy, and we all owe you an apology. But look here: go and see her, and make it up."

"I? Go to see Miss Penwynn, and beg her to take me on again—to be her lover, *vice* that scoun—Tchah! how hot-brained I am. *De mortuis!* Let him rest. But no, Uncle Paul. That's all over now."

"Don't see it, my boy. She never cared a snap of the fingers for Tregenna."

"But she accepted, and would have married him."

"After she believed you to be a scoundrel, Trethick."

"What right had she to consider me a scoundrel?" cried Geoffrey, hotly. "My character ought to have been her faith."

"Yes," said the old man, dryly; "but then she had the misfortune to be a woman of sense and not of sentiment. I think she did quite right."

"Then I don't," said Geoffrey, hotly.

"Ah, that's better," said the old man; "it's quite a treat to have a bit of a row, Trethick. It's like going back to old times. I like Rhoda Penwynn better every day; and the way in which she helps the old man is something to be admired, sir. But how he—a clever, sharp fellow—allowed that Tregenna to involve him as he did, I don't know."

"I suppose he is very poor now," said Geoffrey, who could not conceal his interest.

"Poor? I don't believe he has a penny. The girl's as good or as bad as destitute."

Geoffrey did not speak, but sat with his eyes fixed upon a white-sailed fishing-boat far out upon the blue waters of the bay.

"She would have sacrificed herself for the old man, and I dare say have married Tregenna to save him, if she had not found out all that about poor Madge. I say, Trethick, if you really care for the girl, I think I should see her and make it up."

"But I don't care for her," cried Geoffrey, hotly. "I detest—I hate her."

"Humph!" said Uncle Paul, taking a fresh cheroot, and passing over the case to Geoffrey; "and this is the fellow who boasted that he had never told a lie?"

Just then there was a step on the gravel path, and Geoffrey shrank back in his place, the old man looking at him mockingly.

"There she is," he said.

"You knew she was coming," cried Geoffrey, in a low voice.

"Not I, boy. I knew that, like the good angel she is, she comes to see poor Madge; and if you won't have her, I think I shall propose for her myself."

As he spoke the old man got up and went to meet the visitor, taking her hand, drawing it through his arm, and leading her into the summer-house, where she stood, pale as ashes, on seeing it occupied by Geoffrey Trethick.

"This is no doing of mine, Miss Penwynn," said Geoffrey, sternly, making a movement towards the door.

"Stop a minute, Trethick," said the old man. "I must go in first and find whether Madge can see Miss Penwynn."

They heard his step upon the gravel, and the stones flying; as he stamped down his cane, and then they stood in silence looking in each other's eyes.

Geoffrey was the first to speak, and it was in a bitter, angry voice that he exclaimed,—

"I never thought to have stood face to face with you again; but as we have met, Rhoda Penwynn, ask my pardon."

Rhoda's eyes flashed angrily, but the look was subdued on the instant by one that was full of emotion, and, with half-closed eyes, she joined her hands together, and was about to sink upon her knees, but Geoffrey caught her arms and stopped her.

"No," he said, sharply; "I do not ask you to degrade yourself. Ask my pardon."

"Forgive me, Geoffrey; my love for you had made me mad."

Anger, bitterness, determination, promises never to speak, all were gone like a flash of light as Geoffrey Trethick heard those words; and Rhoda Penwynn was clasped tightly to his breast.

The next moment—minute—hour—it might have been either for aught the occupants of the little look-out knew—they became aware of the presence of Mr Paul, who stood in the open doorway, leaning upon his cane.

"Well, Trethick," he said, mockingly, "when are you going away?"

"Heaven knows," cried Geoffrey. "When I have turned Cornwall upside down, I think."

"Hah!" ejaculated the old man, quietly, as he looked from one to the other. "It's a wonderful thing this love. It's all right, then, now?"

As he spoke he took Rhoda's hand, and patted it. "I'm very glad, my dear," he said, tenderly, "very glad, for he's a good, true fellow, though he has got a devil of a temper of his own. Now go in and see poor Madge, and I wish you could put some of the happiness I can read in those eyes into her poor dark breast."

He kissed her hand as he led her to the house with all the courtly delicacy of a gentleman of the old school; while, unable to believe in the change, Geoffrey walked up and down the little summer-house like a wild beast in a cage:

He was interrupted by the return of Uncle Paul, who took his seat and looked at the young man in a half-smiling, half-contemptuous fashion.

"Laugh away," cried Geoffrey. "I don't mind it a bit."

"I'm not laughing at you, boy. But there, light your cigar again, or take a fresh one. I want to talk to you."

Geoffrey obeyed. He would have done any thing the old man told him then, and they sat smoking in silence, Geoffrey's ears being strained to catch the murmurs of a voice he knew, as it came from an open window, for Rhoda was reading by the invalid's couch.

"There, never mind her now," said the old man. "Look here, do you know that she won't have a penny?"

"I sincerely hope not," said Geoffrey.

"And you've got none," said the old man. "How are you going to manage?"

"Set to work again now that I have something to work for," cried Geoffrey, jumping up and again beginning to pace the summer-house.

"Sit down, stupid, and do husband some of that vitality of yours. You'll drive me mad if you go on in that wild-beast way."

Geoffrey laughed.

"Ah, that's better," said the old man. "I haven't seen that grin upon your face for months. But now look here, boy, what are you thinking of doing?"

"I don't know," said Geoffrey. "A hundred things. First of all I shall try once more to hunt out the people who bought Wheal Carnac, and see if they will take me on."

"What, to lose their money?"

"No, sir, but to make money for them."

"Then you don't know who bought it?"

"No; I tried the agents in town, but they were close as could be."

"Of course," said the old man. "They were told to be. He did not want it known."

"How do you know?" said Geoffrey.

"Because I told them."

"Then you know who bought the mine?"

"Well, yes, of course. It was I."

Geoffrey's cigar dropped from his hand, and he sank back, staring.

"Do you know what you have done?" he cried.

"Yes, made a fool of myself, I suppose; but I thought I'd have it, and you shall realise all you can for me out of the place. I got it very cheaply. Perhaps I shall build a house there—if I live."

"Build! House!" cried Geoffrey. "Why, if old Prawle is right, the mine is rich in copper to a wonderful extent."

"And the water?"

"Can easily be led away."

"Then take it, my boy, and do with it the best you can," said the old man. "I bought it for the merest song, and money has ceased to have any charms for me."

"Mr Paul!"

"Geoffrey, my dear boy, I've never forgotten those words of yours. You said you were sure that I had a soft spot in my heart; and—God bless you, my lad!"—cried the old man fervently, "you were about the only one, with your frank, bluff way, who could touch it. I'd have given you something, Geoffrey, if you could have married Madge; but there, that's over, and I'm only an old fool after all."

Chapter Sixty Two.

Last Chronicles.

"I always did believe in her," cried Amos Pengelly proudly, as he saw, some six months later, the rich copper ore being brought up in a mighty yield from out of Wheal Carnac.

For old Prawle was right. There were rich veins of copper in the mine, which were easily obtained after an adit had been opened through the zorn to relieve it of the water.

The old man felt sore about it at the time, but on seeing what a lucrative position his son-in-law elect had taken in the mine, he soon got over his soreness, and was one of the first to congratulate Geoffrey upon his success, reaping, too, something for himself, while, by a private arrangement, Geoffrey was able to place Dr Rumsey's shares in a very different position, making that worthy, as he whipped the little streams, exclaim,—

"And only to think of it! I might have almost given those shares away."

Mrs Mullion and her daughter left Carnac, but not to go far—the old man objected, for he did not care for long journeys to visit them, and he did not seem happy unless he had paid a visit once a month, showing as he did a very genuine attachment to his niece.

The last chronicle to be recorded of the little Cornish town is that upon a certain morning Miss Pavey came blushing and simpering to Rhoda, while her father was down at his office, where, to Mr Chynoweth's great delight, there were business-matters to record once more upon the slate, and something of the old good times were beginning to return.

Miss Pavey kissed Rhoda affectionately, congratulated her upon the near approach of her marriage, and ended by simpering a good deal, and saying that she had a boon that she wanted her to grant.

"Do you mean a favour?" said Rhoda, smiling.

"Yes, dearest Rhoda; but you are so dreadfully matter-of-fact," simpered Miss Pavey; and then she laughed, and covered her face with her hands.

"I think I can tell you what you want to ask," said Rhoda, smiling.

"Oh, no, no, no! Don't say it. It seems so shocking," cried Miss Pavey from behind her hands.

"You want to be my bridesmaid," said Rhoda, "and I'm sure you shall, if it will make you happy."

"Oh, no," said Miss Pavey blankly, as she dropped her hands into her lap. "It wasn't that, dear."

"What was it, then?" said Rhoda wonderingly.

"I thought—I hoped—I fancied," faltered Miss Pavey, "that you would not mind my—oh dear! I can hardly tell you."

The hands went up over her face again.

"Why surely, Martha, you are not going to be married?" said Rhoda.

"Yes, dear. Isn't it shocking?" exclaimed Miss Pavey, more volubly now the murder was out. "I used to think that Mr Lee would have proposed to me, for no one knows what I have done for that man; and you know, dear, how much interest I have taken in the parish for his sake."

"Yes, you have taken a great deal of interest in the parish, I know," replied Rhoda.

"But I have long come to the conclusion, dear, that he is a man who will never marry. Oh dear no! I can read it in his countenance. Seriously though, to deal with the matter plainly, I do not think he would have done wrong; but, as I have said, dear, he is not a marrying man."

"But you have not told me the name of the gentleman to whom you are going to be married."

"Oh, my dear Rhoda, how droll you are. You are so wrapped up in your own affairs that you forget. Why, Mr Chynoweth, of course. Poor man, he has been so pressing of late, that I don't like to refuse him any longer, dear. It would be unkind; and I must own that we are very fond of each other, and I thought I should like for us to be married with you."

"I'm sure I congratulate you, Martha," said Rhoda, smiling; "and if it will afford you any gratification, by all means be married at the same time; but I must warn you that our wedding will be a very quiet, tame affair."

"Oh, yes, dear, and so will ours, for Mr Chynoweth says that we cannot afford to spend money upon ourselves. Oh, Rhoda, I am sure you envy me!"

"No," said Rhoda, smiling, as a strange sense of the happiness in her own possession thrilled her veins. "I only congratulate you."

"So strange, is it not?" said Miss Pavey. "You remember, my dear, my remark when I told you about the coming of the two gentlemen by the coach. Ah, Rhoda, dearest, that has not all come to pass, but what giddy things we were in those happy days."

Rhoda felt disposed to rescind her promise, but she did not, and Miss Pavey had her wish.

The last we have to record of Geoffrey Trethick is that, as a prosperous mine owner, his favourite practice is to get back to An Morlock and seat himself with his back to the rocks, and his knees up, the said knees nipping between them a portion of the garments of a sturdy baby, who nods and laughs at him, and makes catches at his face in the most absurd way; and somehow all this nonsense does not seem in any way to cause annoyance to the tall, handsome woman at his side. They both, perhaps, recall a similar scene that took place long back near Gwennas Cove; but there is never any allusion to that past; for whenever Geoffrey evinces any desire to speak of past troubles, somehow or another he finds that his lips are sealed.